The disappearing act

The disappearing act

The Impossible Case of MH370

FLORENCE DE CHANGY

MUDLARK

Mudlark
An imprint of HarperCollins*Publishers*
1 London Bridge Street
London SE1 9GF

www.harpercollins.co.uk

HarperCollins*Publishers*
1st Floor, Watermarque Building, Ringsend Road
Dublin 4, Ireland

First published in Great Britain by Mudlark in 2021

3 5 7 9 10 8 6 4 2

Photographs courtesy of the author with the following exceptions:
p.1 top: Laurent ERRERA from L'Union, France – Boeing 777-200ER
Malaysia AL (MAS) 9M-MRO – MSN 28420/404, CC BY-SA 2.0;
p.1 bottom left: © Photoshot; ; p.1 bottom right: Eyevine;
p.2 top: John Javellanna; p.4 top: REUTERS/Larry Downing;
p.4 bottom left: © Nicolas Kovarik/Pacific Press/Alamy Live News;
p.6 top right: MARK GRAHAM/AFP via Getty Images;
p.6 bottom: REUTERS/Zinfos974/Prisca Bigot.

Florence de Changy asserts the moral right
to be identified as the author of this work

A catalogue record of this book is
available from the British Library

HB ISBN 978-0-00-838153-0
TPB ISBN 978-0-00-838154-7

Printed and bound in Great Britain by
CPI Group (UK) Ltd, Croydon

MIX
Paper from
responsible sources
FSC™ C007454

This book is produced from independently certified FSC™ paper
to ensure responsible forest management.

Find out about HarperCollins and the environment at
www.harpercollins.co.uk/green

To the families and friends of the 239 people on board
Flight MH370 on 8 March 2014.

To all those, on whichever continent they live, who
have helped me in my investigation with their
testimony and explanations.

To all those who are persevering in good faith with
their research, so that one day we will know the full
story of what really happened to Flight MH370.

To all those who know something more, and who are
duty-bound to reveal their share of the truth and end
the terrible distress of the victims' loved ones.

To my family and friends, whose support and patience
have been essential to my work.

Contents

'It is a riddle, wrapped in a mystery, inside an
enigma; but perhaps there is a key.'
Winston Churchill, 1939

'We live in a world where the powerful deceive us.
We know they lie, they know we know they lie, they
don't care. We say we care, but we do nothing.'
Adam Curtis, *HyperNormalisation*,
BBC Documentary, 2016

'International affairs are very
much run like the mafia.'
Noam Chomsky, 2020

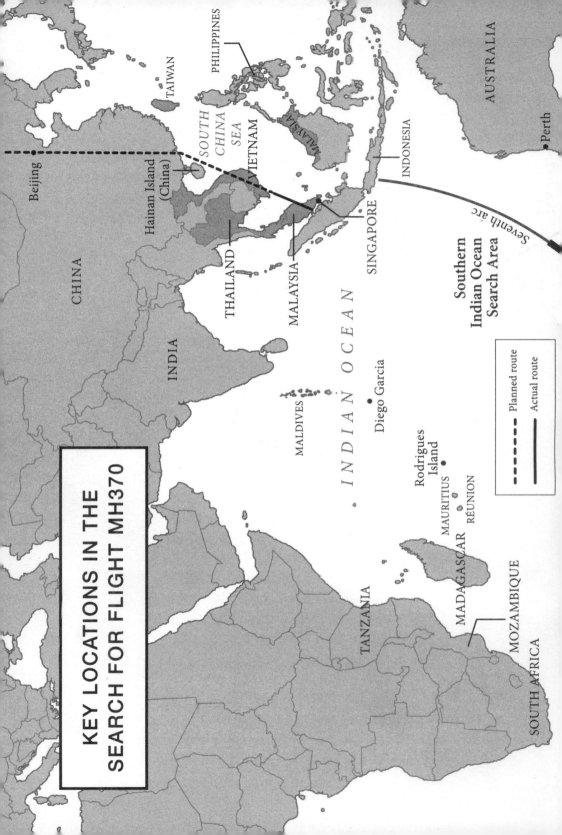

KEY LOCATIONS IN THE SEARCH FOR FLIGHT MH370

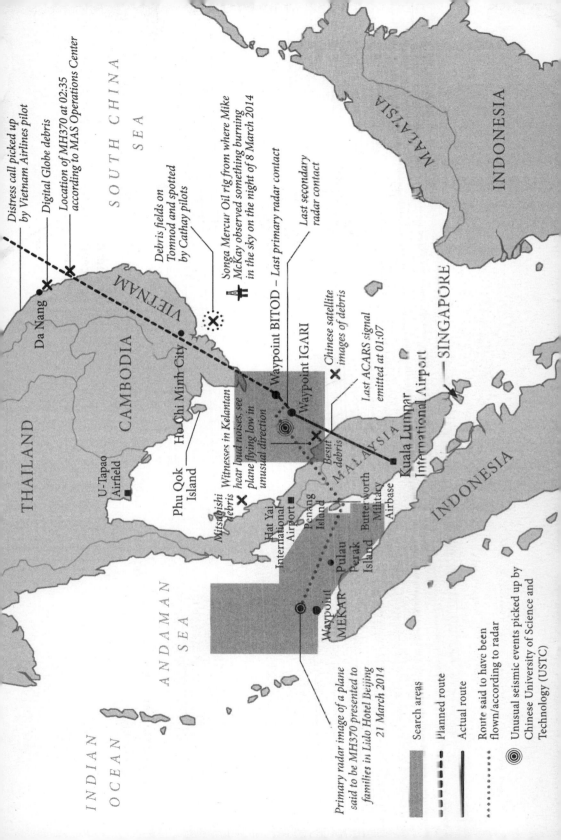

Distress call picked up by Vietnam Airlines pilot

Digital Globe debris

Location of MH370 at 02:35 according to MAS Operations Center

Debris fields on Tomnod and spotted by Cathay pilots

Songa Mercur Oil rig from where Mike McKay observed something burning in the sky on the night of 8 March 2014

Last secondary radar contact

Waypoint BITOD – Last primary radar contact

Chinese satellite images of debris

Last ACARS signal emitted at 01:07

SOUTH CHINA SEA

Da Nang

VIETNAM

Ho Chi Minh City

CAMBODIA

THAILAND

U-Tapao Airfield

Phu Qok Island

Witnesses in Kelantan hear loud noises, see plane flying low in unusual direction

Mitsubishi debris

Hat Yai International Airport

Penang Island

Pulau Perak Island

Waypoint IGARI

Besut debris

Butterworth Military Airbase

MALAYSIA

Kuala Lumpur International Airport

SINGAPORE

INDONESIA

INDONESIA

MALAYSIA

ANDAMAN SEA

Waypoint MEKAR

INDIAN OCEAN

Primary radar image of a plane said to be MH370 presented to families in Lido Hotel Beijing 21 March 2014

Search areas

Planned route

Actual route

Route said to have been flown/according to radar

Unusual seismic events picked up by Chinese University of Science and Technology (USTC)

Foreword

I first heard about the disappearance of a Malaysia Airlines jetliner as I was listening to the RAI news in the Fiat I had rented at Verona Airport. I was on a short visit to my childhood home. It was the morning of Saturday, 8 March 2014, and I pulled over so I could hear the details more closely.

As the days went by, RAI news kept talking about Malaysia Airlines and its wide-body jetliner, which had still not been located despite a massive search operation involving ships and aircraft. Seen from afar, the whole affair seemed decidedly weird. I really wanted to be on the spot. After several years in Kuala Lumpur a decade earlier, I still had a soft spot for Malaysia, a little-known country that, until recently, rarely rated a mention in the Western media.

When a week later Malaysian Prime Minister Najib Razak referred to a 'deliberate act', the affair assumed an even stranger dimension. Now we were no longer talking about a *simple* plane crash. So what were we talking about?

Just after I returned to Hong Kong, my home base for the previous seven years, French daily *Le Monde*, the newspaper I have been working for since the mid-nineties, asked me to go to Kuala Lumpur, where the disappearance had already become 'the greatest mystery in the history of aviation'.

While the whole affair was strange when seen from afar, seen close-up it was positively Kafkaesque. It was not possible in 2014 for a Boeing 777 carrying 239 people to have simply disappeared. Nothing 'mysterious' happened that night. The loss of the jetliner must have a cause, whether it was human, technical or political. What had really happened was simply not yet known to the general public, I told myself.

To me, claiming that Flight MH370 could have disappeared sounded like an insult to human intelligence. People and computers must necessarily know something; radar systems and satellites saw what happened. Whatever the nature of the event, traces must have been left behind, even if they were only slight. It seemed to me that it was my professional duty to find these traces, analyse the context, note down the inconsistencies, identify the red herrings and get any witnesses to say what they knew. Above all, to refuse to let the concept of 'mystery' be associated with the case.

1

Flight MH370

Friday, 7 March 2014. It is almost midnight. Kuala Lumpur International Airport (KLIA) is in night-time mode. Almost all the stores and cafés, including the shop that sells Malaysan pewter souvenirs, have pulled out their accordion shutters and switched off their window lights. The day's last passengers are left with just a few steel benches in large, empty corridors leading to the departure gate lounges.

In front of gates C1–C3, some 30 passengers for Flight MH370 to Beijing are waiting, standing in front of the information screen, at which they look up from time to time. At KLIA, passenger and hand-luggage security controls are carried out just before boarding. Seasoned air travellers are familiar with the procedure. Put your belongings on the scanner conveyor, take your computer out of its case, remove your belt and empty the contents of your pockets – coins, keys, glasses and mobile phone – into a plastic tray. Sometimes you even have to take off your shoes and socks. But security controls at KLIA are anything but zealous, and a certain slackness is visible in the security video of passengers filmed before they board Flight MH370.

As the passengers gather on the far side of the three electronic security archways, the security staff – half a dozen men and women in black-and-white uniforms – are talking to each other. Calm and relaxed, they await the instruction to start the control. The aircrew, meanwhile, have already gone through and are now on board, getting the aircraft ready. First through were six air hostesses and flight attendants, and then 10 minutes later the captain and his co-pilot. The two men put their peaked caps and luggage on the scanner. Neither takes anything out of his bag, not even his flight iPad. Nor do they take off their jackets. Both are given a quick body search. They do not speak to each other. The last time Captain Zaharie Ahmad Shah flew MH370 and its return Flight MH371 was on 22 February, just two weeks earlier. Other air hostesses arrive later. One at 23:33, and two more at 23:38. Passenger boarding begins at 23:46, just under one hour before take-off.

One of the first to pass through is a very stylish Chinese woman. She is wearing a frilly hat that she does not remove, with a matching pink-and-white outfit. She is followed by a young couple with a collapsible pushchair and a small girl who teeters around them. Although the passenger list notes that there are nationals of 14 different countries, the great majority of the passengers seem to be Chinese: Chinese from continental China, from Malaysia, Canada, Australia, the United States or Taiwan.

At this late hour, people's movements are a little clumsy. Faces are tired and drawn. This daily flight is usually one for regulars. It is sometimes called a 'red-eye flight', a night flight that is not long enough for you to sleep properly, as it takes less than six hours, including take-off and landing.* On weekdays, MH370 mainly carries businessmen, but the Friday night–Saturday morning flight is different. Its passengers are going home or spending the weekend in Beijing. Most are dressed for the cold weather of northern China rather than the equatorial heat they are leaving behind.

The families of the fated crew and passengers have kept on asking for this video without success, but I was able to view it through wholly unofficial channels. On the video, it is possible to

---

* According to *Factual Information: Safety Investigation for MH370* (8 March 2015), the planned flight duration was 5 hours and 34 minutes.

recognise some of the passengers referred to in subsequent press reports, such as the celebrated calligrapher with his magnificent white hair. The 20 engineers and researchers employed by the American electronics company Freescale Semiconductor, all of whom are Malaysian or Chinese, are harder to identify. You can spot a group of tourists returning from a trip to Nepal, and some 30 upper-middle-class Chinese who have gone to Kuala Lumpur for an investment trip at the invitation of a property developer, with a view to buying property in Malaysia. There is also a 32-year-old stuntman, who already has an impressive career under his belt. One month earlier he had moved to Kuala Lumpur to work on the new Netflix series *Marco Polo*. He is flying back to Beijing to spend the weekend with his wife and two small daughters. Two retired Australian couples stand out from the rest: Western in appearance, taller and more heavily built than the other passengers. One is holding an Akubra – a well-known Australian hat brand – in his hand. The four French passengers also stand out in this mainly Asian crowd – a mother, accompanied by three young people: her daughter, one of her two sons and his French-Chinese girlfriend. After a week's holiday in Malaysia, they too are returning to Beijing, where they live. At this very moment, the father is in Paris. He is set to board a flight to Beijing a few hours later, and when he does so all he knows is that his wife and children are on their way there too. The other Caucasian passengers are one middle-aged American, two young Iranians, a New Zealander, a Russian and two Ukrainians.

One year later, an American blogger was to suggest that the Ukrainians could be implicated in MH370's disappearance, as he suspects them – on the basis of a hypothetical scenario* – of having hijacked the plane to Kazakhstan. The two Ukrainians arrive together, in the last few minutes of boarding, and they look far

* In February 2015, Jeff Wise published *The Plane That Wasn't There* online at www.jeffwise.net.

more energetic than their fellow passengers. They have the physiques of US Marines and wear body-hugging black T-shirts. Each has a large carry-on bag, and they whisk them on to the conveyor belt with practised ease. I found out much later that their tickets were the only ones that were completely untraceable by the investigators. No idea where they were purchased, no travel agent, no method of payment, no place of issue. Highly abnormal apparently. The two men happened to be seated on row 27, right below the Satcom antenna. Of all the passengers who board the flight, if you had to pick out two as being hijackers, the Ukrainians are the ones who best look the part, in terms of age, physical condition, appearance and body language.*

Some passengers go through the security archways still wearing a coat, a belt or a hoodie. Looking unconcerned, they come through in small groups, and then go back again one by one. Wristwatches trigger the alarm too. The camera films this gently chaotic coming and going. One passenger opens a Thermos flask and turns it upside down to prove it is empty. Then another passenger takes a king-size bottle of Coca-Cola out of a bag that has just been scanned, and drinks it in full sight of everyone as he awaits his travelling companions.

An employee of Malaysia Airlines (MAS), in the turquoise jacket worn by ground staff, goes through the archway in the middle with a transparent plastic bag in his hand, seemingly containing rolls of fax paper. The light flashes red. No one reacts. He continues on his way without being checked. A little later, a wallet becomes lodged between the metal rollers after passing through the scanner; and then a female passenger gets her head stuck in her coat as she slips it back on, unintentionally creating a brief moment of comedy. In short, the boarding process is rather disorderly and lackadaisical. In

---

* There are some question marks over some other passengers, including the sole Russian. In fact, all the countries that had nationals on the flight cleared them of any possible links to terrorism, with the exception of Russia and Ukraine, who ignored the requests made by the Malaysian police.

less tragic circumstances, the legendary Malaysian happy-go-lucky approach would elicit a smile in anyone watching it back on video.

Obviously, air transport security regulations, although universal, vary from one airport to the next. But at Kuala Lumpur, it's difficult to find any information about regulations in the airport's official documentation. On its website, under the heading 'Airport Check-In Guidelines', the subsection 'Security Checks' consists of two lines of text: 'Security Regulation on Hand Luggage' and 'Hand Baggage Guidelines'.* The information stops there. No details whatsoever. Unbelievable – and highly unusual for an airport that serves more than 40 countries, and handles 30 million passengers each year.

Just when it seems that everyone has been through security, a young Chinese man, wearing a very tight-fitting white suit and sporting an Elvis-style quiff, leaves the waiting room and strides quickly through the security archways in the wrong direction. He heads back towards the terminal as though he has forgotten something. At the end of the video, at 10 minutes past midnight, with the security staff apparently shutting down their control station, the young man has not returned. Did he save his life by missing his flight, or did he rush back in time to board? More importantly, have some of the other passengers, who on this video can be seen heading towards the boarding gates, been able or allowed to step out at the last minute too?

Thirty minutes later, the Boeing 777-200, with the manufacturer serial number 28420 and the Malaysia Airlines registration 9M-MRO,† takes off as it does every night at the same time: 00:40, give or take one or two minutes. The aircraft's ascent, which takes 20 minutes, seems trouble-free.

---

* See www.klia.com.my.

† This aircraft also has the following Boeing references: block number WB-175 and line number 404. These identification numbers are referred to in the investigation.

At 01:01, the plane reaches 35,000 feet. Flight conditions are good, not to say ideal. The in-flight catering service can begin, but usually on this flight passengers take no notice as they try to get some sleep. At 01:07, the aircraft sends out its first ACARS message (the acronym stands for Aircraft Communications Addressing and Reporting System). The bulletin provides real-time data indicating the aircraft's technical performance levels, which are theoretically sent to the ground automatically, both to Boeing back in Chicago in the US, and to Malaysia Airlines. The system is activated at regular intervals, which depend on the subscription taken out by the airline. In the case of Malaysia Airlines, the interval is 30 minutes. For some airlines, the interval depends on the route.

Everything is normal. Malaysia Airlines enjoys an excellent reputation both for safety and service. Its fleet is very modern, and its aircraft are on average four years old, although the Boeing on Flight MH370 is 12 years old. The plane was delivered in 2002, and it has already flown for 53,465 hours, performing 7,525 cycles (i.e. flights) prior to this particular MH370 flight.

Its only recorded accident at the time was a ground collision with another plane at Shanghai Pudong Airport in August 2012. On 23 February 2014, 12 days before the night in question, the aircraft was in the hangars of Malaysia Airlines undergoing maintenance. One of the first announcements from the airline after the plane's disappearance states, 'There were no issues on the health of the aircraft.' The next maintenance control was scheduled for 19 June.

After flying for 40 minutes, the airliner is about to leave the airspace of Malaysia and enter Vietnamese airspace right next to it.* Less than five hours remain before the descent towards Beijing.

---

* The sky is virtually divided into different airspaces (called Flight Information Regions or FIR), where traffic control and flight assistance are provided by the designated ACC (Area Control Centre) or ATCC (Air Traffic Control Centre). In this case, MH370 is leaving the airspace controlled by Malaysia (KL ATCC) and is due to enter the airspace controlled by Vietnam (HCM ATCC).

Landing is scheduled for 06:30. At 01:19, the Boeing leaves the
Malaysian air traffic control zone with a routine message: 'Good
night, Malaysian three seven zero.' After the investigation, the
pilot's friends, family members and an expert were asked to identify the voices in the transmissions made between MH370 and air
traffic control. It was established that the initial speech segments
before take-off were those of the first officer, meaning that the
captain or pilot in command (PIC) was at the helm. The subsequent
voice recordings, including the last transmission, are of the captain,
meaning that it is the co-pilot who is flying the plane at the time it
disappears. The captain's voice is relaxed and does not sound
suspicious in any way. Normal procedure is that immediately after
leaving Malaysian airspace, the aircraft should declare its presence
to the Vietnamese authorities with a message such as 'Ho Chi
Minh control, Malaysia 370, flight level 350, good morning.' But
there is no call from MH370. In the ensuing minutes, the situation
veers dramatically into the abnormal, the unknown, the unheard
of.

At 01:20, five seconds after passing waypoint IGARI assigned to
Singapore,* and 90 seconds after its last radio transmission, the
transponder – the main means of communication between the
aircraft and air traffic control – is switched off. Or it switches itself
off. The button is located between the seats of the two pilots.
Switching the button is as easy as turning a car radio on or off,
requiring a quarter-turn in one direction or the other. But switching
the transponder off between two air traffic control zones is an
extraordinary thing to do – and highly suspicious. According to the
information provided by the Malaysian authorities one week later,
the aircraft first turns to starboard for a few seconds, and then
starts making a U-turn to the port side and heads west-south-west.
Then the ACARS system (which automatically controls the sending

---

* Flight paths pass through a series of virtual waypoints, which are given five-
letter names for ease of identification.

of technical information) is switched off as well. Or, again, it
switches itself off somehow. Pilots are not even taught the procedure for doing this, because there is no imaginable reason for
switching off the ACARS system, never any justification for doing
so, whatever the situation. Although often described later as
'complicated', the procedure is in fact not particularly complex.
With three clicks on the communications page of the trackpad, it
is possible to deactivate the three transmission modes. The two
actions – switching off the transponder and, a little later, the
ACARS system – at first sight rule out the most frequently encountered scenarios in any accident: technical failure, pilot suicide and
in-flight explosion. They suggest that someone has taken control of
the aircraft in a way that has never previously occurred in the
history of aviation.*

Deprived of its ACARS system, the aircraft does not transmit
even the slightest item of technical information, which, when
relayed by satellite, could have enabled it to be located. And so the
01:37 ACARS bulletin is not sent. Nor is the 02:07 bulletin. Is the
alarm raised immediately at Boeing, Rolls-Royce and Malaysia
Airlines? At first sight, yes, 'necessarily', assume all the experts
questioned just after the aircraft's disappearance. But not a single
comment, explanation or technical insight will be forthcoming
from the American plane maker Boeing or the British jet engine
manufacturer Rolls-Royce, these two cornerstones of the global
aircraft industry. When Air France Flight 447 went down between
Rio de Janeiro and Paris in 2009, the last ACARS bulletin made it

---

* Since the night in question, thousands of Boeing 777 pilots, of all ages and
nationalities, have tried to find out how this is done, and have succeeded. But why
is this procedure possible, if it can never be justified, whatever the in-flight situation? The best explanation I have heard, after consulting pilots, members of the
military and other experts on this intriguing question, is that an aircraft 'cannot
and should not be designed to fight its pilot'. This is indeed a very good argument.
The aircraft is a tool in the hands of the pilot, who is completely in charge of
everything on board.

possible to locate the crash site, as the indications gave the crash time to within five minutes.

So has a perfect hijacking, leaving no trace, just taken place? Or, more accurately, an almost perfect hijacking. For ever though it is no longer transmitting signals, the aircraft automatically receives a silent electromagnetic signal, called a 'handshake ping'. Only the echo of the ping indicates whether it has been received. Until this unique situation arose, these pings had never been used for the purpose of locating an aircraft. Mathematical extrapolations of the highest order of complexity will be needed in an effort to interpret these last indications of the aircraft's whereabouts, and thus deduce from them its final trajectory.

After the message 'Good night, Malaysian three seven zero', we know nothing more of what happened in the sky on board MH370. On the ground, however, it is the start of many hours of tragic blundering, during which time the Boeing vanished into thin air.

The register of messages logged between the control towers of Kuala Lumpur and Ho Chi Minh City reflects a remarkable string of failures. From 01:20 onwards, Vietnamese air traffic control knows that MH370 should be arriving in its zone. But it waits 19 minutes before alerting Kuala Lumpur about the strange silence of the Kuala Lumpur–Beijing flight. It should have reacted within three to four minutes at most. And meanwhile the Kuala Lumpur control tower does not receive any news either; MH370 has not returned to the local frequencies.

At around 01:30, on instruction from Vietnamese air traffic control, the pilot of a flight to Tokyo that was theoretically close to MH370 succeeds in contacting the aircraft on the emergency frequency (121.5 MHz), and asks if the flight has made its transfer to Vietnamese air traffic control.

'There were [sic] a lot of interference ... static ... but I heard mumbling from the other end,' said the captain. 'That was the last time we heard from them, as we lost the connection. If the plane was in trouble, we would have heard the pilot making the Mayday distress call. But I am sure that, like me, no one else up there heard it,' he told the Malaysian newspaper *The New Sunday Times* the following day.

The conversation is interrupted, which often happens. The pilot has to continue along his flight path to Japan; he does not try again. He has the job of flying the plane, after all. According to several investigators who have tried to find out which planes were close to MH370 in its final moments, it could be the pilot of Flight JAL750 or of Flight MH88. The conversation has not been made public by the authorities, even though, according to the pilot – who gave his testimony anonymously – all the other aircraft and ships in the zone at that time must also have heard it. However, the provisional report indicates that at around 01:54, Ho Chi Minh City also asks the pilots of Flight MH386, on its way from Shanghai to Kuala Lumpur, to try to contact MH370. No further details are given. The statement of the 'Duty Executive Despatch Operation' (*sic*) recorded by the Royal Malaysian Police mentions that Flight MH52 was also asked to try to contact MH370. The pilots of both MH52 and MH88 were interviewed by the police – according to their statements, both tried many times but failed to reach MH370.

At 01:46, Ho Chi Minh City tells Kuala Lumpur that the aircraft disappeared from the radar screens just after passing the next waypoint, BITOD, 37 nautical miles (approximately 68.5 kilo-metres) away.* At 02:03, after several fruitless exchanges between the controllers of the two neighbouring zones, the Kuala Lumpur control tower informs its Vietnamese counterpart that the operations centre of Malaysia Airlines has located the plane ... in Cambodia. This is good news, but also rather strange. Why would MH370 have left its flight path without warning the local air traf-fic controllers? And what is it doing in Cambodia? Ho Chi Minh

---

* Aviation uses nautical miles as a standard measurement of distances. One nauti-cal mile is equivalent to 1,852 metres.

asks the Malaysians for more details. Half an hour later, at 02:37 precisely, the operations centre of Malaysia Airlines sends the Vietnamese, who are somewhat dubious, the coordinates of the aircraft's alleged new position in the skies of Cambodia. A satellite call is attempted at 02:39 but without success. Once again, why do they wait so long? About one hour later, the operations centre of Malaysia Airlines corrects its earlier message; the position given in Cambodia was based on a 'projection' rather than the actual location of the aircraft. In other words, no one – not the airline, nor the air traffic controllers, nor anyone else – knows where MH370 has gone.

The airliner has, essentially, vanished for 2 hours and 10 minutes, somewhere between two hesitant and perplexed control towers, confused by a false indication supplied by the airline's own operations centre. The Vietnamese then try to contact Hong Kong and the Chinese island of Hainan, to see if by any chance they have seen the missing aircraft fly past.

It is discovered about two weeks later, thanks to a radar image from Thailand, that at 02:22 the aircraft is already north-east of Sumatra (Indonesia) on the other side of Malaysia. It has radically changed its route and clearly abandoned its initial destination. Why? Where is it going?

MAS does not raise the official alert until 05:30, an hour before its scheduled arrival time.

At Beijing Airport, the main display board in the airport concourse shows Flight MH370 as 'Delayed'. Both in Kuala Lumpur and Beijing, people are growing impatient; they have not received the customary 'arrived in Beijing' text, nor any reply from a mobile phone. When no one emerges from arrivals at the scheduled time, worry starts to set in. At 07:24, one hour after the scheduled landing time at Beijing, Malaysia Airlines issues an evasive news release, announcing that Subang Air Traffic Control lost contact with Flight MH370 at 2.40 am today (8 March). The waiting family and friends are terrified and panic-stricken. For all the families of the 239 people on board the flight, an interminable ordeal begins. What has been lost is not contact, but an airliner.

For many months, almost nothing would be known of the crucial details about the flight path actually taken by the plane, between its last point of contact with Malaysian air traffic control and the last indication of its presence at 02:22 on a Thai military radar. The details were reconstituted by trial and error, and assembled like a jigsaw puzzle over subsequent weeks, months and years, in the light of information that was released in dribs and drabs, for the most part diluted in an ocean of false or inaccurate data.

The first interim investigation report, dated 1 May 2014, provided very little information. 'Even if you have your wallet stolen, you get a longer report than that,' the brother of a female Chinese passenger said to me in disgust. Over the course of the following years, several reports, as well as various studies by the ATSB (Australian Transport Safety Bureau), tried to bring together in a coherent way most of the information known about the flight. But several independent investigations carried out since then by experts fascinated by the case, with whom I have been in regular contact, suggested that errors, inconsistencies and false information may have found their way even into the official reports on which this account of the aircraft's final hours was based.

It took me two years to first spot the many flaws and inconsistencies of the official narrative and another three years, approaching witnesses, searching for traces – as well the traces of erased traces – to put together a much more plausible version of what truly happened that night.

2

Where Is the Plane?

'It's best to stay at the Sama-Sama Hotel next to the airport. That's the journalists' headquarters and there are press briefings every day at 5.30 pm. But the investigation is going nowhere. It looks like a dead-end assignment, if you ask me.'

So said a friend and colleague from RFI (Radio France Internationale) even before I arrived in Kuala Lumpur a week and a half after the aircraft went missing. More than 160 media crews had been dispatched from around the world to cover the story in the immediate aftermath of the disappearance, and almost all of them had descended on the Sama-Sama Hotel. Camera tripods and assorted bags of equipment littered the corridors, while the huge but soulless, tasteless lobby of this luxury hotel hummed with activity. Some of the crews had set up their little company flags, surrounded by improvised groupings of tables and sofas. Others had laid claim to a column, stuck their corporate logos on it and set up camp nearby. The news-hungry throng was like an army of ants swarming over freshly fallen fruit.

Were it not for its slapdash organisation and the prickly tension that prevailed, this high-density media colony would have seemed much like the press gatherings at many international summit meetings and major sporting events. But there was a difference here. In the corridor leading to the auditorium used for press briefings, the press room was adjacent to the family room. When its door was ajar, wails of despair or bursts of anger sometimes escaped – a reminder of the human drama underlying this compelling mystery. The Chinese families, especially, were at the end of their tethers. Some family members had gathered at the Lido Hotel in Beijing, but many had made the trip to Kuala Lumpur, hoping to be on hand as soon as any new shred of information became available. A simple misunderstanding or awkward question by a journalist could trigger a fit of rage. Encounters with the authorities would frequently degenerate into shouting matches, walk-outs, bottles of water being hurled at spokespersons and so on. The anguish suffered by these men and women who had lost a loved one was mounting with each passing minute; they had been haunted ever since Huang Huikang, China's ambassador to Malaysia, came to see them a few days after the disappearance and said, probably at a loss for words, 'This is very complicated, you cannot understand.'

*How can he tell us it is 'complicated' when at the same time they are telling us they don't know anything?**

The celebrity news anchors of the major global networks were on hand as well. Notwithstanding Russia's annexation of Crimea and Putin's intentions for the rest of Ukraine, the disappearance of Flight MH370 was considered the most newsworthy story of the hour. The topic was ideally suited to the demands of live television, with 'breaking news' reports and updates running 24/7 in wall-to-wall coverage. In the early days following the plane's disappearance, coverage consisted of a series of statements, contradictions, denials, rumours, confirmations, retractions and clarifications … a vortex of information that gave rise to a nebula of hypotheses.

*　　*　　*

* Sometime in 2016 I met a young man who had lost his father in the flight. He recalled that during the third briefing (the first one he was able to attend), the Malaysian lieutenant told the families present, 'We know things we can't tell you.'

Within hours, China, Thailand, Indonesia, Singapore, Vietnam, Australia, the Philippines and the United States made search teams available to Malaysia. Backed by its experience with Flight AF447 from Rio de Janeiro to Paris, which went down in the Atlantic Ocean off the coast of Brazil on 1 June 2009, France dispatched a delegation from its air accident investigation bureau, the BEA. As required under Annex 13 of the Convention on International Civil Aviation, also known as the Chicago Convention, a joint investigation team was quickly formed. At its head was a former Malaysian director general of civil aviation. The team called on the expertise of specialist organisations in a number of countries in addition to the BEA (France): the NTSB* (US), the AAIB† (UK), the AAID‡ (China) and the ATSB§ (Australia), along with accredited representatives from Singapore and Indonesia. Boeing, Rolls-Royce and the British satellite company Inmarsat – of whom much more later – were also invited to take part. In accordance with the Chicago Convention, Hishammuddin Hussein, the Malaysian Minister of Defence and Transport, declared:

> The main purpose of the international investigation team is to evaluate, investigate and determine the actual cause of the accident so similar accidents could be avoided in the future. It is imperative for the government to appoint an independent team of investigators that is not only competent and transparent but also highly credible.

---

* National Transport Safety Board, United States.

† Air Accidents Investigation Branch, United Kingdom.

‡ Aircraft Accident Investigation Department, China.

§ Australian Transport Safety Bureau.

A person close to the investigation told me, 'Americans from the NTSB, the FBI and the FAA* were on the scene immediately. The British also sent two investigators. They went to see the people at Malaysia Airlines and requested access to all the data.'

As logic demanded, the starting point of the investigation was the last point of contact with the plane. This was in the South China Sea, midway between north-eastern Malaysia and the southern tip of Vietnam. At first, that was all anyone knew; contact with the plane had been lost over the Gulf of Thailand, along the interface between Malaysian and Vietnamese airspace, just after the plane had crossed waypoint BITOD. The Malaysians carefully refrained from saying that they knew the plane had executed a U-turn to the left. Instead, they ordered that search missions be confined to this single area.

On the first day of the search, a Singaporean plane was sent out to overfly the area. We were subsequently told that 9 planes and 24 ships had gone out for the search, although we never saw a detailed list of them, nor were we given the precise location of the search areas. From one day to the next, the numbers kept rising. It was hard to keep up. When the search area was expanded to include the other side of Malaysia, representing a total area of nearly 100,000 square kilometres, the media was told that 42 ships and 39 planes were deployed. At the peak of the search operation, 26 countries were involved.

In the dead of the night of the disappearance, a few witnesses reported the unusual presence of a plane overflying the Gulf of Thailand. They described noises out of the ordinary: white lights, a low-flying plane and even a plane on fire. These accounts bore no resemblance to the 'business as usual' ballet of long-haul jetliners between Kuala Lumpur and Tokyo, Seoul, Hong Kong, Taipei or Beijing that were barely visible because they flew at much higher altitudes.

* The FAA is the American Federal Aviation Administration, the regulator of civil aviation in the US.

Along the north-eastern coast, villagers in Panta Seberang Marang declared that they had heard a very loud noise coming from the direction of Pulau Kapas, a resort island. Under the headline 'Villagers heard explosion', the 12 March issue of *Free Malaysia Today* confirmed that the Terengganu police had taken statements from several villagers who reported hearing a loud explosion during the night of 7 to 8 March. Without consulting one another, the villagers gave the following independent accounts: at about 1.20 am, Alias Salleh,* 36, was sitting with friends a few hundred metres from the sea when they all heard a very loud noise, 'like the fan of a jet engine'. Another villager, Mohd Yusri Mohd Yusof, 34, stated that when he heard the strange noise, he thought a tsunami was about to hit. Other inhabitants of the area claimed to have seen weird lights above the ocean. In Kelantan State, 66-year-old fisherman Azid Ibrahim noticed a very low-flying plane 'below the clouds'† at around 1.30 am. The plane was in view for nearly five minutes. His fishing boat was about 10 miles off Kuala Besar. It would have been impossible to miss the plane, he said, as 'its lights were as big as coconuts'. Unfortunately, everyone else on the boat was fast asleep.

More or less at the same time, about 30 kilometres from Kota Bharu,‡ the young businessman Alif Fathi Abdul Hadi, 29, also noticed bright white lights. He insisted on reporting what he had seen to the MMEA (Malaysian Maritime Enforcement Agency)§ because the plane was flying 'opposite to the usual direction'. In the same area but much further out to sea, south-east of Vietnam,

* Quoted by Bernama, Malaysia's official press agency.

† Quoted by the *New Straits Times*, a pro-government English-language daily in Malaysia.

‡ Kota Bharu is the capital of Kelantan State.

§ This was the principal government agency tasked with maintaining law and order, and coordinating search and rescue operations in the Malaysian Maritime Zone and on the high seas.

a 57-year-old New Zealand oil rig worker named Michael J. McKay, who had gone outside to have a smoke in the middle of the night, insisted he saw an aircraft on fire at high altitude due west. 'I believe I saw the Malaysia Airlines plane come down. The timing is right,' he wrote in an email that he sent to his employers, after Malaysian and Vietnamese officials ignored his initial message.

Meanwhile the Vietnamese press was publishing some interesting information, but it went virtually unnoticed in the pandemonium of those first few days. As early as the morning of 8 March 2014, the daily newspaper *Tuoi Tre News* quoted a statement issued by the Vietnamese Navy, announcing that 'the plane went down 153 nautical miles [283 kilometres] from Tho Chu Island'. On Sunday, 9 March, a large oil slick stretching over a distance of 80 kilometres was spotted from the air about 150 kilometres south of Vietnam. 'This is the first and – for the moment – only potential sign of the missing plane,' reported the search plane's pilot, Lieutenant Colonel Hoang Van Phong.

Another highly surprising report was published by *China Times*, a pro-China news website based in Taiwan, as well as by the Chinese news website China.com. It told of 'an urgent distress signal from Flight MH370 picked up [by] the US Army unit based in U-Tapao, Thailand'. In his message, the pilot said the aircraft was about to disintegrate and he needed to make an emergency landing.* This information, if true, struck me as being extraordinarily important and intriguing, but at the time we learnt nothing further and it was generally ignored by the Western media.

There were other reports that corroborated the immediate and local crash scenario. Peter Chong, whom I met a year later during another assignment in Kuala Lumpur, was a friend of the missing pilot and had initially been told that the plane had crashed in the

---

* See www.chinatimes.com/realtimenews/20140308003502-260401 (a Chinese-language website).

Gulf of Thailand. Flying business class on Malaysia Airlines on his way back from Bangkok on the evening of Monday, 10 March, he asked the air hostesses to convey his condolences to the pilots of his own flight. 'I just wanted to express my solidarity in these trying circumstances,' he explained to me. To his very great surprise, a message scribbled on a paper napkin came back to him a few minutes later. In the note, which he tucked away for safekeeping, the captain thanked him and added, 'Wreckage to your left'. At the time, the plane was flying over the southern part of the Gulf of Thailand. Peter Chong peered out the window and saw a clearly lit area at sea where he said he was able to make out intensive search operations. Chong took this as evidence that, 'at that stage, Malaysia Airlines believed the plane to have gone down in that area and had informed its crews'.

Moreover, the day after the last contact with the plane, Chinese satellites detected three large floating objects believed to indicate 'a suspected crash sea area' for Flight MH370. The location of this debris – 105.63°E and 6.7°N – was compatible with the last point of contact with the jetliner. The images were supplied by Sastind* and dated Sunday, 9 March at 11 am. They showed the objects as small white spots against a background of grey sea. The dimensions of the three objects were given as 18 × 13 metres, 19 × 14 metres and 24 × 22 metres for the largest. It was not every day that one came across such large floating objects of a size comparable to that of a Boeing 777, which is 64 metres in length, with a wingspan of 61 metres. And three objects at once! Clearly, this was the first serious lead that had turned up since the searches began. Several news channels rushed to announce that the plane had been found. But Xinhua, China's official news agency, had waited three full days, until Wednesday, 12 March, to release these images. More surprising still, Minister Hishammuddin then asserted without

* Sastind is China's State Administration for Science, Technology and Industry for National Defence.

batting an eyelid that the images had been made public 'by mistake'. If this were indeed the case, it was undoubtedly the first time ever that the People's Republic of China had shared satellite images by mistake. The minister added that a Malaysian surveillance plane had patrolled the site and found nothing there.

The search effort in this area was dominated by two American warships equipped with helicopters, and one Singaporean P-3 Orion maritime surveillance aircraft. Numerous other vessels were supposedly patrolling these waters as well. This part of the sea is encircled by the Gulf of Thailand and the coast of Vietnam and China to the north, the Philippine archipelago to the north-east, the large island of Borneo along with Java and Sumatra to the south, and finally, Malaysia and Thailand to the west. Surely a jetliner – even one smashed to pieces – and dozens of bodies should have been noticed sooner or later.

The fact that the Chinese satellite images were released simultaneously with a new revelation that the plane had allegedly made a virtual U-turn to the west meant that the images did not attract as much attention as they otherwise might have. From that point, despite the mounting pile of clues, attention shifted completely away from the South China Sea.

Eyewitness accounts, reports by the Vietnamese Navy and Chinese satellite images, as telling as they may have seemed, quickly faded into oblivion, relegated to the large and increasingly crowded box of 'as-yet unexplained temporary clues' like pieces of a jigsaw puzzle that must be kept in a corner of the table until they can be made to fit into the overall picture.

Accordingly, from Tuesday, 11 March, scenarios other than a plane crash into the South China Sea began to take shape. In an apparently ill-advised burst of transparency, Rodzali Daud, the Royal Malaysian Air Force Chief, told the local newspaper *Berita Harian* (*Today's News*) that at 2.40 am that Saturday – one hour and 21 minutes after the last radio and radar contact with the plane – the aircraft had been detected by the Royal Malaysian Air

Force Base at Butterworth near Pulau Perak. This minuscule island at the northern end of the Strait of Malacca* was actually on the western side of Malaysia, the opposite side to the search area. That the Air Force had detected a plane was a fact. Or at least it would be confirmed as such later on. What it was at the time however, was a gaffe. The poor guy had spoken too soon and spent the following days attempting to deny his own claims. He released a statement saying that Butterworth had in fact received an unidentified signal at 2.15 am. The next day, the time was advanced to 2.30 am. Soon enough, no one had any idea what the Air Force had seen, or where, or at what time. If the Malaysian response was a mission to obfuscate, it was already well underway.

This did not stop Malaysia from secretly deploying two of its ships and a military aircraft to search along the country's western coast, even though the north-eastern coast was still the designated search area. *The New York Times*, citing American officials familiar with the investigation, reported that the missing plane had climbed to 45,000 feet, which is above the plane's service limit, then descended to 23,000 feet, well below a normal cruising altitude, as it approached Penang.† The newspaper later reported that a mobile phone tower had picked up a brief signal from the co-pilot's phone around this time. None of these elements were subsequently confirmed, but nor were they explicitly denied.

According to the first interim investigation report, which came out in May 2014, military experts viewed the radar recordings of the plane's inexplicable movements at 8.30 am on 8 March, or seven hours after the jetliner went missing. The data was sent to the minister of defence and transport at 10.30 am, who in turn informed the prime minister.

---

* The Strait of Malacca is the sea lane between the island of Sumatra (Indonesia) and the Malaysian peninsula.

† 'Radar Suggests Jet Shifted Path More Than Once', *The New York Times*, 15 March 2014.

Malaysia never explained how or why, having learnt that very first morning that the plane had radically changed its flight path by heading west, it nonetheless ordered a large-scale search operation to the east, in the South China Sea, calling on the assistance of China, Vietnam and Thailand in particular. These search missions were not officially called off until a week later. An Australian named Ethan Hunt, one of the organisers of the committee of families formed in June 2014 to raise funds for a private investigation, later said to me, 'If they had wanted to create a diversion to give them time to do whatever they were supposed to do with the plane, they couldn't have found any better way to do it!'

Meanwhile, a spontaneous army of volunteer detectives offered their services to the Tomnod web platform to help scrutinise millions of satellite images of the search areas. This site, a crowd-sourcing project originally launched at the University of California in 2010 and now 'retired', called on volunteers to study satellite images and detect forest fires or refugee settlements, map typhoon damage and the effects of other natural or man-made disasters. Prior to the search for Flight MH370, Tomnod had a few thousand contributors. After the search for MH370 began, Tomnod had to shut down on 11 and 12 March due to high traffic of up to 100,000 visits per minute. It reopened again with a more powerful algorithm. More than 8 million people have scrutinised Tomnod images a total of 98 million times and have identified 650,000 objects of interest. Even Courtney Love posted a satellite image from the Tomnod site on her Facebook page, with the following comment: 'I'm no expert but up close this does look like a plane and an oil slick.'

It looked as if the searches for the aircraft were continuing to target the wrong place, while distraction and diversion tactics took centre stage. The multinational search fleet kept chasing its own tail in the South China Sea, with no clear idea where or how to look for the plane. Meanwhile the families and the media stayed at the crisis centre established at the Sama-Sama Hotel, restless, champing at the bit, and wracking their brains to find meaning in the mass of incoherent and sometimes contradictory information served up at the daily press briefings.

With the release of the passenger manifest, the official accounts began to pussyfoot around in earnest. Malaysia Airlines issued four consecutive statements concerning the number of nationalities represented on board. The first gave a figure of 13, the second said 14, the third was up to 15 and the fourth back to 14. Admittedly, the Taiwanese were counted as Chinese, and the Italian and the Austrian listed on the manifest were in fact two Iranians travelling with stolen passports. Moreover, there were reports of four stolen passports for a while, but one of the press briefings revealed that 'in fact there were *only* two'. None of these details were of much interest to someone searching for a Boeing 777 and the 239 people on board, but they filled the airwaves. And it was a great way to sow confusion.

When the passenger manifest was first released at the end of Saturday, 8 March, a spokesman for the airline announced, 'This is the list of everyone on board. All the families have been informed.' Shortly thereafter, however, two 'survivors' came forward. Luigi Maraldi, an Italian on holiday in Asia at the time, heard his name among the list of missing persons. He immediately called his family to reassure them. Fortunately, his family had not been informed of his disappearance. Luigi's passport had been stolen six months earlier. As for Christian Kozel of Austria, he was at home when Flight MH370 went missing. He too had had his passport stolen in Thailand two years earlier.

It turned out that the stolen passports were being used by two young men from Iran, Pouria Nour Mohammed, 19, and Seyed Mohammed Rezar Delawar, 29, who had bought them in Thailand. Iran? At long last, the perfect terrorism lead that everyone had eagerly been awaiting seemed to be at hand. The two men had entered Malaysia with their Iranian passports, then changed their identities during their stay in Asia. Malaysia Airlines refused 'for security reasons' to explain how passengers holding forged passports had been able to buy their tickets. A flurry of contradictory information ensued. The Malaysian Department of Civil Aviation first claimed it was not sure that the two suspicious passengers had been picked up by the airport security cameras. Next, the Malaysian minister of home affairs declared that 'they had Asian features'. But then Azharuddin Abdul Rahman, the Director General of Civil Aviation, said that 'they did not look Asian'. When a journalist asked the director to describe the physical appearance of the two Iranians, he answered, 'Do you know the Italian football player Balotelli?'

That evening, the conference room full of journalists indulged in the only collective burst of laughter of the entire crisis, and confronted the Director General, who had just mispronounced the name of the famous Italian striker, born of Ghanaian parents. Was he trying to say one can *be* Italian without *looking* Italian? Or did he mean the Iranians had African features? In short, were they Asian or African? Football players or terrorists? Whom to believe? What were the facts?

Interpol then announced that the two men had no known terrorist connections. It appeared that they were hoping to join their families in Europe and trying to hide their nationality by travelling via Beijing. As a matter of fact, in the midst of all this confusion, the head of the international police agency Interpol said he did not believe the disappearance of MH370 was a terrorist incident. 'The more information we get, the more we are inclined to conclude it is not a terrorist incident,' said Interpol Secretary General Ronald Noble on Tuesday, 11 March 2014.

The story took yet another unexpected twist with the publication of the two men's photos, extracted from the security video of the boarding process. There was nothing 'African' about the men's appearance; they certainly looked Iranian. But the photos showed them as having the same lower bodies. Their torsos and faces were different, but they were both wearing identical jeans and trainers, triggering a new wave of scepticism. Had the photos been doctored? No, it was apparently 'just a photocopying error', for which the officials apologised. The Iranian terrorism lead fizzled out. After three days, no one believed it any more. Nonetheless, it had been the focus of the news coverage for at least 48 crucial hours.

Meanwhile, Bloomberg, BBC and many other news outlets quoted Director General Azharuddin as saying during one of the first press briefings, 'Before the flight took off, the airline removed the baggage of five passengers who didn't board after checking in [...] There are issues about the passengers that did not fly on the aircraft.' Five no-shows on the same flight is a lot, yet no further elaboration was given. Usually, removing the luggage of the no-show passengers in such situations would create a significant delay. But that did not occur here. Maybe these passengers only had carry-on luggage? That happens a lot with frequent flyers who want to avoid waiting to collect their luggage on arrival. But then, on 11 March, Malaysia Airlines denied the news articles that claimed five checked-in passengers had never actually boarded the aircraft. The airline did confirm, however, that four individuals who were booked onto the flight had never checked in. Their identities were not revealed, and because the individuals never came forward, this unresolved issue was merely added to the list, alongside the question mark hanging over another passenger, Zhao Qiwei, seated in 18D, whose name, according to the Chinese authorities, did not match the passport number provided.

The hours ticked by without a single clue being found by the search operation. Soon enough, however, the press would be able to feast on the latest media tidbit. On its programme *A Current Affair*, Australia's Channel 9 aired an interview with a young South African woman named Jonti Roos. Sharing some corroborating photographs, she recounted how two years earlier the co-pilot of Flight MH370, Fariq Abdul Hamid, had invited her into the cockpit on a flight from Phuket to Kuala Lumpur, along with one of her girlfriends. She explained that the captain of that flight (whom she did not name) and his young co-pilot Fariq, 25 at the time, had noticed the two young women queuing to board the aircraft as they walked past them.

Phuket is the tourist capital of Thailand, known as much for its beaches as for its hostess bars. As they entered the plane, the women were invited to join the two pilots in the cockpit, where they ended up staying for the entire hour-long flight, including the take-off and landing phases. In her televised interview, Roos described the two airline pilots as smoking a lot and constantly twisting around in their seats to face the young women, who were sitting on the folding seats at the back of the cockpit. Concerned about damaging the co-pilot's reputation, since his background was obviously coming under scrutiny with the investigation into the missing Flight MH370, Roos insisted that she never felt she was in danger at any time. She showed a few flirtatious photos in which it is hard to tell who was having the better time during this brief encounter, the pilots or the two young travellers sporting the pilots' caps on their lovely heads. Ms Roos was still a Facebook friend of the co-pilot, who had since settled down.

Fariq was 27 years old and had logged a total of 2,763 flight hours when he boarded the plane for Beijing for his last supervised flight* on a Boeing 777 on the night of 7 to 8 March 2014. Malaysia Airlines has a rule that a co-pilot trained on a new type of aircraft must be accompanied by a supervisor for their first five flights. The co-pilot was engaged to marry another pilot, Nadira Ramli, 26, whom he had met at the flying academy in Langkawi. Like Fariq, Nadira was from a good family, and she was employed by AirAsia, the low-cost rival of Malaysia Airlines. People had positive things to say about Fariq when asked to comment by the local press. They portrayed a conscientious and respectable young man who coached young people at five-a-side football in his spare

---

* The Captain was qualified to double-act as supervisor.

time. He had recently given the kids T-shirts for their team. A neighbour of the family reported that the co-pilot's father, a senior civil servant in Selangor State, was very proud of his son. His grandmother described the young man as 'a good son', 'obedient' and 'religious'. These comments concurred with the view of Fariq as 'a good Muslim, humble and quiet' voiced by people at his neighbourhood mosque. On 19 February, only a few weeks before the fated flight, Fariq Abdul Hamid had been a guest on CNN's *Business Travel* programme, where he came across very well. Although he had definitely flaunted safety rules on that Phuket–Kuala Lumpur flight under the responsibility of the flight's captain, all the other aspects of his life painted a rather reassuring portrait of him.

Actually, the unfortunate episode of the Phuket–Kuala Lumpur flight made the co-pilot simply appear as a high-spirited young man who was busy enjoying life. This was quite different from the terrorist, criminal or suicidal mindset that some would have preferred to find. Nonetheless, many in the media seized upon his one mistake to condemn what they termed a 'reckless attitude' and 'perhaps the first clue of guilt on the part of the crew'. There were 'intriguing personalities in the cockpit', 'the co-pilot was known to break aviation rules' and much more. The whole world was searching for an explanation and somewhere to place the blame.

On Tuesday, 11 March, Malaysia Airlines responded to this volley of criticism, saying that the company was 'shocked' by the claims about its employee, although it expressed doubts as to their veracity. If anything, the incident highlights the airline's lax attitude.

After the finger had been pointed at the co-pilot, all eyes turned to Captain Zaharie Ahmad Shah, 53, who became the target of an apparent smear campaign. One source said he was divorced. Another claimed that his wife and children had just moved out of the family home the day before the flight. Still others portrayed him as a political fanatic. The press quoted sources close to the investigation as saying that the pilot was allegedly distraught at the new five-year jail sentence for Anwar Ibrahim, the leader of the major opposition party, the Malaysia's People's Justice Party or Parti Keadilan Rakyat (PKR). The sentencing had taken place a few hours before the flight on 7 March 2014. Some sources reported that Zaharie had joined other supporters of Anwar to protest at the Court of Appeal in Putrajaya.* There were also reports that his diary was blank past the date of 8 March. He was even discovered to have 'distant relatives in Pakistan', as though this alone would make him, if not culpable, at least suspicious.

Like his co-pilot, Zaharie's home was searched, leading to the discovery of a flight simulator. At the press briefing on 19 March, it was revealed that data on this had recently been deleted. The FBI undertook the task of recovering the deleted files. According to the Malaysian news daily *Berita Harian*, of particular interest to the investigators were five of the landing strips found on the simulator, all of which were at least three kilometres long – the minimum required to land an aircraft the size of a Boeing 777. The runways were located in Malé, the capital of the Maldives and a regular destination of Malaysia Airlines; Diego Garcia, an overseas territory of the UK with a US military base where no civilian aircraft were supposed to land; and three other landing strips in India and Sri Lanka. Two weeks later, however, the American investigators declared that the simulator data contained 'nothing incriminating'.

A potentially compromising photo of the captain was soon published, first on the front page of the local newspaper *Utusan-Cosmo*. In the picture, he was sitting on a sofa with a pretty young Malaysian woman and two children. The wording of the photo

---

* Putrajaya is the administrative capital of Malaysia, 30 kilometres south of Kuala Lumpur. Anwar's five-year prison sentence for sodomy was upheld by the Federal Court, Malaysia's highest court, in February 2015.

caption was vague, but suggested that the pilot had a second family. In Malaysia, a Muslim man may have up to four wives, provided he can afford them and follows certain rules. The same picture was picked up by several British tabloids avid for anything that could pin blame onto the captain of the missing flight.

One of the most damning testimonies came from New Zealand. Lincoln Tan, Sino-Singaporean by birth, was serving as special correspondent for *The New Zealand Herald*. The journalist drew on testimony from a 'friend' of the captain to attempt to drive another nail into his coffin. In its 26 March 2014 issue, one of Tan's articles in *The Herald* cited but did not name a 'long-time associate of the pilot' who claimed that 'Captain Zaharie Ahmad Shah's world was falling apart. He had been facing serious family problems, separation from his wife and relationship problems with another woman he was seeing.' This anonymous informer told Tan that the pilot was 'terribly upset' by his wife's departure. He said he was convinced that Zaharie could well have decided to end it all 'by taking his plane to a part of the world he had never flown in'. The article went on to claim: 'The fellow pilot raised questions about the captain's state of mind. He guessed that Captain Zaharie may have considered the flight a "last joyride" – the chance to do things in a plane he had previously been able to do only on a simulator.'

Three months later, *The Sunday Times* reported that the Malaysian police had completed their investigation and cleared everyone on board the flight of any suspicions.* Everyone but the pilot.

I found these suspicions surrounding Zaharie somewhat incompatible with the portrayal coming from other sources, that of a smiling grandfather, a model-building and cookery enthusiast, a handyman, a man who always enjoyed a good joke and was well liked by his flying students. True, he readily talked politics and had

* *The Sunday Times*, 22 June 2014.

a sophisticated flight simulator at home. But even the 'long-time associate' quoted by *The New Zealand Herald* acknowledged that Zaharie lived for the '3 Fs: family, food and flying'. A year after the plane went missing, the interim report* had collected only mundane details about him: married with three children, fracture of the second lumbar vertebra in 2007, and good resilience to stress at home and on the job. 'No known history of apathy, anxiety or irritability', it stated. The report also said there were 'no significant changes in his lifestyle, interpersonal conflict or family stresses'. In fact, according to the interim report, there were 'no behavioural signs of social isolation, change in habits or interest, self-neglect, drug or alcohol abuse of the Captain, First Officer and the cabin crew'.

Once again, who to believe, what to believe? Everyone was well aware that the pilot was the master on board. Naturally, he bore primary responsibility in the event of failure, thereby making him a prime suspect. But as far as I was concerned, I knew I would need to make up my own mind about this essential member of the cast of characters.

When this all began, the media was being dragged from wrong track to dead end; very soon the various fleets of vessels taking part in the search were starting to question the way the operations were being coordinated and managed. A foreign emissary with access to the crisis management centre set up during the early weeks described to me a scene of 'unbelievable chaos', with 'Chinese and Korean officers standing around with their hands on their hips or scratching their heads, wondering what they were supposed to be doing or not doing'. On Wednesday, 12 March 2014, the exasperated Vietnamese government decided to scale back its involvement in the maritime search off its coast on the South China Sea, criticising 'the lack of detailed information coming out of Malaysia'. That same day, China's foreign minister echoed this sentiment: 'For

---

* Factual Information: *Safety Investigation for MH370*, 8 March 2015.

the moment there is too much confusion. It is very difficult for us to determine whether any given piece of information is accurate or not.' Coming from a Chinese diplomat, such direct criticism was vanishingly rare and attested to the prevailing din and discrder. Indeed, in the few short days since it began, the crisis, more than any military exercise to date, had trained an unforgiving spotlight on the lack of coordination and procedures for information-sharing in this part of the world.

Besides the criticisms from the Chinese anc Vietnamese authorities, Wednesday, 12 March marked another turning point. On that day, the cast of characters was joined by a new player who had been virtually unknown prior to that point: Inmarsat, a British satellite company that had been listed on the London Stock Exchange since 2005.

An executive at rival satellite telecommunications firm AsiaSat told me, 'Inmarsat has an excellent reputation. They are known for technical excellence across the industry.' He did point out, though, that their expertise lay in handling data transmission between commercial aircraft and the ground, rather than geolocating or tracking planes.

Despite this caveat, Inmarsat became *the* source of the final and official version of the jetliner's flight path after the loss of signal. For although the ACARS stopped transmitting technical data to Malaysia Airlines once it was disabled, we soon learnt that the plane continued to passively receive silent signals, those 'handshake pings' we met earlier, the final communication links with MH370 after it vanished from the radar screens. But determining the jetliner's location from these signals was a monumental task as the pings were not designed for that purpose, nor had they ever been used as such.

At Inmarsat, engineer Alan Schuster-Bruce, an alumnus of Queens' College, Cambridge, had already worked extensively on the case of Flight AF447. Pursuant to that accident, he made it possible to take some additional measurements of these passive pings, notably their duration and frequency. 'I was thinking we might need it one day [...] might be useful, might not be useful,' explained Schuster-Bruce in the only documentary that details Inmarsat's crucial role in this case.* So it was no surprise that upon hearing the BBC news report of a missing plane at 11 am on Saturday, 8 March 2014, he was the first to realise that Inmarsat quite possibly had data that would be of interest to the investigators. Inmarsat set off in a race against time. Although the handshake pings were but tiny electromagnetic signals, the scientific team felt it was worth trying to analyse them. Initially, knowing how long it took for the pings' echoes to bounce back would allow them to determine the plane's distance from the satellite.

I tried to picture these pings as tiny invisible dots that travelled eight times during the night of 7 to 8 March from the ground station in Perth (Western Australia) to geostationary satellite 3F-1 positioned 36,000 kilometres from earth above the equator, whence they were relayed automatically to the Boeing 777 of Flight MH370 before they turned around and travelled back through space to deliver their data to Perth, all at the speed of light. Incredible. And it was these tiny pings – the final ping more than the seven previous ones – that defined the story the world would be told about the fate of Flight MH370.

There is little point here in attempting to describe the complexity of the calculations required, especially given that satellite 3F-1, albeit 'geostationary', nevertheless moves constantly north and south over the equator. In other words, for each ping emitted there is a circle in the sky along which the distance between the plane and the satellite is constant. As it flew, the plane must have crossed these different circles, from the first to the seventh, each of which corresponds to the precise instant the ping was emitted. An eighth

* The BBC Two *Horizon* documentary *Where Is Flight MH370?* aired on 17 June 2014.

and final ping emitted at 8.19 am was different from the rest. Not only did it arrive much earlier than predicted – just a few minutes after the penultimate one timed at 8.11 am – but it contained a reboot instruction. Inmarsat's engineers surmised that once the plane engines had run out of fuel and shut down, the communication system automatically tried to restart. There were no more signals after that one. In conclusion, the plane continued to fly for seven hours after contact was lost. That was the first monumental discovery by Inmarsat.

In London a handful of scientists thus learnt that the plane had remained in the air until 8.19 am. But which way was it going? 'We suddenly realised that if you knew the initial position of the aircraft together with the likely speed of the plane, there was a good chance that maybe one could get a look at the track of the aircraft,' recalled Schuster-Bruce. A telephone meeting was then set up between Inmarsat in London and Malaysia Airlines in Kuala Lumpur during which, according to Schuster-Bruce, Inmarsat tried to convince the 'very reluctant' airline how crucial it was to hand over this additional data.

The Malaysian authorities had good reason for their reluctance. Answering Inmarsat's questions would be tantamount to admitting that they had been aware their plane had turned west and had been sighted north of Sumatra (off the western coast of Malaysia), even as an armada of 43 ships backed by 58 aircraft was acting on instructions to look for the plane in the South China Sea (off Malaysia's eastern coast). The task was complex. 'One of the concerns we had was that this could just be one big hoax that someone had played on Inmarsat [...] that the aircraft went down and someone at the same time pretended to be that aircraft,' said Schuster-Bruce.

But Inmarsat ultimately came up with a scenario compatible with the pings – its 'two-arc theory'. The plane must have flown along an arc heading either north (from Thailand to the border between Kazakhstan and Turkmenistan), or south (from Indonesia to the middle of the Indian Ocean). This was Inmarsat's second major discovery.

Inmarsat shared its two deductions with Malaysia on Wednesday, 12 March. There was no reaction from Kuala Lumpur. 'Clearly they've got all sorts of information coming in. They were also probably sent information that the plane was in the Pacific by other people,' said Schuster-Bruce. On Thursday, 13 March, *The Wall Street Journal* announced that the plane allegedly flew for several hours after radio contact was lost.* For two days, Defence and Transport Minister Hishammuddin Hussein denied the new information as vigorously as possible. This was his consistent attitude throughout the crisis, to the point where he could easily wear the moniker 'Mr No-No'.

The day *The Wall Street Journal* came up with their breaking news that the flight had continued to fly on for several hours, the Malaysian TV news station Astro Awani was pursuing a very different lead. An Astro Awani reporter asked Hishammuddin if there was still a possibility that passengers on MH370 had communicated with people on the ground around 2 am, 30 minutes after the plane had last been spotted. The TV station said they had seen a screenshot of some messages supposedly sent on the Kik messaging service by the only American adult on the flight, IBM employee Philip Wood, to a contact of his in Beijing, whose username on Instagram was Hun_l. Astro said they had verified the identity of Hun_l, and had talked to two people in Malaysia who knew him personally. In the SMS conversation, Wood mentioned to Hun_l that he was using his phone secretly, that the temperature in the cabin was 'warm' and that there seemed to be a problem with the aircraft's air-conditioning system. More worryingly, he also mentioned having 'difficulty to breathe', but he seemed to be in no panic because in his last message he said he'd be in contact once he

---

* 'Missing airplane flew on for hours. Engine data suggests Malaysia flight was airborne long after radar disappearance', *The Wall Street Journal*, 13 March 2014.

arrived in Beijing. Mr No-no completely dismissed this question. This troubling text message was soon to be replaced by another one, also supposedly sent by Wood, though it was much more headline-grabbing, as we'll see later on. The Kik app has now closed shop and I am not sure what to do with this other clue, whether it was genuine or not. Why would anyone make up such a message? I'd love to be in contact with Hun_1 for confirmation and to know the exact time and content of the messages he said he received from Philip Wood.

On Friday, 14 March, news broke from an unlikely source – a White House spokesman announced 'new information' and 'a new search area', referring to the southern Indian Ocean. In this manner, Washington forced Kuala Lumpur to emerge from its silence, but left it up to the Malaysians to disclose the details.

On Saturday, 15 March, Malaysia's Prime Minister Najib Razak finally made his first public statement since the start of a crisis that had thrust his country into the international limelight in a way that no other event had ever previously done. He stated that the situation was 'without precedent', corroborated the story that the plane had indeed changed course, as had been discussed over the preceding five days but denied until that moment, and confirmed that the data transmission systems of the Boeing 777 (ACARS and transponder) had been 'disabled' and that Inmarsat's theory that the plane flew until 8.19 am along a northerly or southerly corridor was correct. He also advanced the theory of 'a deliberate act by someone on the plane', with the proviso that whoever seized control of the aircraft would have to have had solid flying experience. After making his one and only statement to the press, Prime Minister Najib took no questions from journalists. The disappearance of Flight MH370 and its 239 passengers and crew had just entered a new phase. It had been planned – seemingly quite masterfully. So was it a hijacking, then, and if so, to what end?

After allowing its neighbours, allies and partners to search for the plane in the wrong place for a week, Malaysia had just waited two further days before officially confirming a major piece of information and setting in motion the appropriate response. Some people viewed this as sheer incompetence. Others suspected a deliberate tactic intended to hide an embarrassing truth. And as important as they were, the Inmarsat pings did not provide the definitive key to the mystery. On the other hand, they did increase the search area tenfold.

With no new information coming to light, the second week bore a strong resemblance to the first. The authorities used the press briefings above all to deny the information going around – the false as well as the true. No, the plane was not seen over the Maldives. No, the plane did not make a U-turn 12 minutes before the now infamous sign-off message by the captain: 'Good night, Malaysian three seven zero.' No, we do not yet have any intention of apologising to the families. No, we are not going to disclose the data received from the radars of neighbouring countries. No, we do not know what is contained in the pilot's flight simulator. No, we still do not know the plane's flight path.

Every evening at 5.30, Defence and Transport Minister Hishammuddin, the Executive Officer of Malaysia Airlines, the Inspector-General of Police and the Director General of Civil Aviation, arms by their sides, would line up to face the music in the press conference auditorium. With each passing day they looked a little bit more sheepish, a little bit more hemmed in by a room packed to the gills with cameras taking live footage, flashes snapping and journalists who were themselves becoming ever more frustrated as time dragged on. A tall, imposing Sikh acted as the MC, choosing which of the journalists got to ask their question.

On 19 March, a BBC journalist asked the Director General of Civil Aviation to confirm whether the Boeing had crossed this or that waypoint. The answer came back: 'We are still investigating.' Still investigating? This was the one piece of information that everyone had believed to be 'clearly established'! The Director General pointed out that it was no longer crucial to know 'which way' the plane had travelled, since attention was now focused exclusively on where it ended up. Eleven days after the plane went missing, the response from the media was a collective gasp of bewilderment.

At another evening briefing, a journalist with the *Financial Times* pointed out to Hishammuddin that Kazakhstan, mentioned a day earlier as being 'at the heart of the search mission along the northerly arc', did not seem to be aware of its own role in this operation. According to the journalist, this major Central Asian republic had not received a single request for assistance from Kuala Lumpur. But the press briefing was already coming to a close. The tall Sikh escorted the officials out the back door. They were rushed away from the conference room, leaving numerous raised hands and even more unanswered questions behind them.

The Malaysian authorities were regularly caught out by such blatant examples of incoherence or incompetence in this investigation. Journalists discovering Malaysia for the first time were dumbfounded, wondering in what kind of Kafkaescue country they had landed.

3

Malaysia Boleh!

When I arrived in Kuala Lumpur on 18 March 2014 and felt the stifling heat of Malaysia as I stepped out of the plane, the disappearance of Flight MH370 10 days earlier was still omnipresent. At the airport, large 'Pray for MH370' posters had been pasted on walls. In the metro and in the street there were makeshift shrines with bouquets of flowers, arrays of candles and messages: 'Please come back', 'Where are you? We are waiting for you.' Ever since Sunday, 9 March, the front pages of the Malaysian press had focused non-stop on the disappearance, adding small items of fresh information day by day, irrespective of whether anything new had come to light.

Malaysia was still in a state of shock. The Malaysians, usually easy-going and cheerful, looked saddened and concerned. The country's slogan over recent decades had been *Malaysia Boleh!* ('Malaysia can do it!'), the equivalent of 'Yes, we can!', although it pre-dated Obama's motto by some 30 years. Admittedly, over the last few years Malaysians had proclaimed the country's bold rallying cry, if at all, with more than a hint of sarcasm. With MH370, it was not just the scale of the disaster – with 239 lives snatched away, including several small children – but also the mysterious circumstances that people found hard to take. Not only was it terrifying, it was also incomprehensible.

Now that people knew there was a 'deliberate act', in the words of Prime Minister Najib Razak three days earlier, the only hope was a hostage scenario. The most optimistic observers thought that perhaps secret negotiations were underway, which would explain the confusion and the contradictory statements. In their view, a positive outcome was still possible. Given that there was no indication that the plane had crashed, it must have landed *somewhere*.

Every evening I would go to the Sama-Sama Hotel press briefings, travelling on the express train that hurtled through the thousands of hectares of palm plantations between Kuala Lumpur to the airport. My hotel was in the city centre, as my editors at *Le Monde* had told me that they did not want me to report on the press briefings – 'We have the AFP [Agence France-Presse] and Reuters to handle that' – and that my assignment was really to provide local background, explain the context and to take the country's pulse. What were people saying? What did Malaysians think about this inexplicable event? What were the possible lines of enquiry? In cases like this, who would be the usual suspects? If the cause is a *deliberate act*, in whose interest would it be – objectively speaking – to make a Boeing 777 with so many people on board disappear? Which cargo items or passengers on the plane were so special, precious or dangerous that they could not be allowed to arrive at their destination?

When I lived for several years in Malaysia in the early 2000s, I came to understand that truth was a rather vague concept in the country. On one occasion, when *Le Monde* had asked me to find out the impact of 9/11 on tourism in the region, I had to call someone back because what he had told me was completely at odds with the rest of my investigation. When he heard why I was contacting him again, my interviewee (the manager of a top hotel in KLCC,* not a chicken farmer from the depths of Sarawak) said

---

* Kuala Lumpur City Centre, the downtown area dominated by the Petronas Twin Towers.

naively, 'Ah, but I said that because I thought it was what you wanted me to tell you!' I could not believe my ears. It reminded me of Lenin's 'Tell them what they want to hear',* but in this case the hotel manager's words mainly demonstrated how far Malaysians would go to try to please others.

How can you dislike someone like that, when their heart is in the right place? Unfortunately, however, this was not always the case. The handful of free media outlets that took up the huge challenge of providing local news of good quality were running serious risks, and measures were regularly taken against them,† with websites and newspapers that were unable to set their operations up outside Malaysia risking having their licences withdrawn.‡

When I obtained my Malaysian press card, following a year of tiresome formalities, my talk with the official at Bernama, the national news agency, ended with a piece of friendly advice: 'Anyway, Miss Florence, there's no need to cover politics, is there?' When I expressed naïve surprise, and my determination that 'of course' I would be covering politics, Mr Azlan, after a series of pained sighs, contortions in his chair and saddened nods of his head, came out with it: 'Miss Florence, please understand, if you cover politics, very likely I'll be in trouble. If I am in trouble, very likely you'll be in trouble.'

Was that clear enough? It was expressed courteously, but the warning was explicit, particularly in a country that regularly made use of the ISA,§ a so-called emergency law enabling anyone to be

---

* Cited by Vladimir Volkoff in *Petite Histoire de la Désinformation* (Éditions du Rocher, 1999), although, ironically, this quote has never been clearly linked to any of Lenin's public statement or writings, according to my research.

† The whistleblower website Sarawak Report, based in London, was blocked in Malaysia in July 2015.

‡ The economic magazine *The Edge* had its licence withdrawn in July 2015.

§ The Internal Security Act was replaced in 2012 and in 2015 by a series of new laws that are even more repressive.

detained without charge or trial for a period of two years, which could later be extended indefinitely. Mr Azlan had in fact offered me a press card that was valid for two weeks ... We took leave of each other after agreeing on an arrangement; he would keep my card safely in his drawer, so it would be ready for me on the day I really needed it. I was slowly adjusting to a golden rule in Malaysia – truth is a relative concept, and it is often considered to be dangerous.

Let's focus now on the plane, flying in the colours of Malaysia Airlines System (MAS), to give the company its full if now discarded name. What about the airline? It was 70 per cent owned by the Malaysian government's sovereign wealth fund, Khazanah Nasional Bhd. Its air hostesses, in their flowery turquoise and pink sarongs, rivalled the elegance and charming manners of their counterparts at Singapore Airlines, the benchmark for this part of the world. When it came to service and safety, Malaysia Airlines had an excellent reputation, and its business-class travellers keenly anticipated the airline's charcoal-grilled chicken and beef kebabs with satay sauce. The airline's first commercial flight was in 1947, making it one of Asia's aviation pioneers. Until 8 March 2014, its last serious accident had been in 1977.* Malaysia Airlines was one of the top seven airlines worldwide, with five stars from the British airline-rating consultancy Skytrax, its fleet of 151 aircraft having an average age of four years, making it one of the most modern on the planet. Admittedly, the Boeing 777-200ER used for Flight MH370, purchased in 2002, was one of its oldest aircraft, but that was not considered to be an issue. In 2013, Malaysia Airlines joined the third-largest airline alliance, One World. So far, so reassuring.

* On 4 December 1977, Flight MH653, a Boeing 737 flying from Penang to Kuala Lumpur with 93 passengers and seven crew, crashed while attempting to land, after being hijacked in unclear circumstances.

But the airline's commercial results were not up to the same standard. Profitable for a time between 2007 and 2010, the airline made a loss in 2011; on sales of £2.6 billion (13.6 billion ringgits), Malaysia Airlines reported a net loss of £493 million. In 2014, the airline was losing close to £1 million each day. What was happening? The airline had raised its capacity by some 20 per cent in 2013 in a frenzy of jetliner-buying, while its total revenues, including the cargo business, increased by only 2 per cent. The airline also had too many employees and too many big earners.

And if the airline was losing shedloads of money, why did it buy so many new aircraft when the market was becoming increasingly competitive? Malaysia Airlines was facing competition from the arrival in Asia of European and Middle Eastern airlines offering long-haul flights, and from several low-cost operators, including AirAsia, offering regional flights. According to several media reports, the company was not well run. Yet Malaysia Airlines was buying the most expensive jetliners, and then had to make savings elsewhere. Unlike 75 per cent of Boeing 777 operators, MAS had not taken out a subscription to the Boeing Plane Health Management system, which remotely collects performance data from the plane in real time for the live tracking of possible problems and the optimisation of the maintenance programme. When I asked Jean-Paul Troadec, former head of the French air accident investigation bureau BEA, about this, he weighed his words carefully: 'I don't know to what extent not subscribing to this programme could lead to suspicions about maintenance failings or fraud, but you may well think it's not a good sign.'

As for operations, the airline's track record of incidents was normal – around 15 in both 2014 and 2015, according to the website aeroinside.com, which provides details for every case: tyres exploding on take-off, engine problems, a double generator failure, smoke in the cabin, a lightning strike, depressurisation and so on. At first sight, the list seems worrying, but clearly it was not enough to raise concerns at either the EASA (European Aviation Safety

Agency) or the FAA (Federal Aviation Agency), neither of whom had ever blacklisted MAS.

The fire that broke out at 4 pm on 26 March 2014 in the avionics workshop of Malaysia Airlines' maintenance facility caused something of a stir, however short-lived the blaze actually was. In this workshop in Subang, the town where Kuala Lumpur's former international airport was situated, MAS maintained and repaired all of its aircraft's electronic components (on the second floor of hangar number two), which meant it was crucially important. Malaysia Airlines did not report the fire until two days later, after it had been mentioned by former Malaysian MP and aviation specialist Wee Choo Keong in his blog. No explanation was ever given for this incident, one that was unprecedented in 30 years of activity in the same location. How did the fire start? What equipment and which documents were destroyed or damaged? Why did the fire protection system not work? It all remained shrouded in mystery.

When, four months later, Malaysia Airlines lost a second Boeing 777 over Ukraine, this time with 298 people on board, shot down – as established by the investigation report – by a Russian-made missile, the national airline's share price took an 18 per cent hit. The airline's ability to survive, after losing 85 per cent of its market capitalisation in five years, was now in question.

In July 2015, the new CEO of MAS, the German Christoph Mueller, who had joined the airline in May to lead restructuring efforts, said that, technically, the company was bankrupt; its strategy would now be to 'stop the bleeding in 2015, stabilise next year, and seek to start growing again by 2017'.* On 1 September 2015, Malaysia Airlines was reborn with a new legal identity. It did not change its name or logo, and even the pink and turquoise flowers of the air hostesses' sarongs remained identical. But Malaysia Airlines System (MAS) no longer existed – and neither did its debts.

---

* In 2015, 6,000 of around 20,000 employees were made redundant.

MAB (Malaysia Airlines Berhad) was starting again from scratch. In December 2015, Malaysia Airlines unveiled an alliance with Emirates to codeshare around 90 of the Dubai carrier's international routes, except for London, the only long-haul route that MAS* kept. MAS could now focus on Asia. February 2016 was the first break-even month for the company in a very long time. Still, in an interview with Associated Press in April 2016, the new CEO described the airline as a 'ship that has many leaks'. Less than two weeks later, the airline announced that due to 'his changing personal circumstances', Christoph Mueller was leaving MAS. That, in broad strokes, was the state of the company involved in the disaster.

Because everything is political in Malaysia, when I first arrived in Kuala Lumpur on 18 March I immediately went to the Malaysian parliament. The 'Parlimen' building is a large, 1960s-style white edifice, with several storeys that overlook the botanical gardens and the largely uncleared area of jungle around them, the whole sector being surrounded by a spaghetti junction of road flyovers. I went through the checkpoint in the car of a friend, Wong Chen, a former lawyer who was now an MP in the opposition People's Justice Party. A few words of greeting, the waving of a foreign passport with a wink to the security man, and the barrier was raised. Wong Chen had suggested I speak to one of his fellow MPs who held strong views on the events.

　　Dressed in his traditional costume, Mohamad Imran Abdul Ahmid was one of those Malaysian politicians who over the years have gradually mellowed. A former admiral in the Malaysian Royal Navy who exceeded military retirement age long ago, he remained firmly attached to his role as an MP. He told me that he was speaking only on his own behalf.

---

* Despite this official change, Malaysia Airlines has continued to be mostly referred to as MAS (and not MAB).

I have watched radar screens for decades. I can tell you that the only way a plane, or indeed a ship, can disappear from a radar screen is if it really vanishes – an in-flight explosion or a crash. I am going to ask Parliament to resume search operations at the point where the plane left the screens. I don't believe that we can lose sight of such a massive plane.

Moreover, the next day, the Malaysian economic magazine *The Edge* claimed that the Royal Malaysian Air Force was going to launch an investigation to find out why, after MH370 made almost a complete U-turn, it was able to cross Malaysian airspace from east to west without being picked up at all by the country's sophisticated British and French radars. Apparently, the team on radio surveillance watch was asleep in front of the screens. No one was at all surprised at this. It was 1 o'clock in the morning after all.

'There are so many mistakes and blunders that you don't know what to believe,' said the admiral, adding that, in the stolen passports affair, the country's immigration services had also been at fault. On this point too, he said, it was essential to find out who was responsible. And he was furious that there had been a wait of several days before the admission had been made that the jetliner had completely abandoned its scheduled flight path. Finally, to suggest that they had found a trace of the aircraft, only to discover that it was most likely Singapore Airlines Flight SQ68 on its way to Barcelona!* Well, he was not proud – to say the least – of his Air Force.

Opposition MPs were livid the day I visited Parliament; the previous day the government had held a secret briefing on MH370, inviting only MPs in the ruling coalition, Barisan Nasional. Even so, when I interviewed MPs from the majority party, there was not

---

* A tweet by @KeyserSquishy on 1 April 2014 suggested that, 'per radar plot, at 2:22 am, flight MH370 location coincided with UAE343 on N571 route not SIA68 on P268 route'.

the slightest sign of a more promising line of enquiry in the offing. All I heard was a litany of slow pronouncements, with the characteristic *lah* of Manglish, a word of no particular meaning in this locally spoken form of English, appended at fairly regular intervals to what they said. They express their 'great sadness *lah*', and pay tribute to the 'tremendous efforts made by the government *lah*' to cope with this 'unprecedented crisis *lah*'. 'We're just a developing country and this crisis is too big for us,' said Datuk Wira Ahmad Hamzaha, a coalition MP.*

Clearly, coordinating a search operation on this scale was no easy task. But the same views were stated repeatedly: 'You must understand, this has never happened before.' 'It's a situation that has never previously arisen in the history of aviation.' Malaysia was to hide behind this sort of excuse throughout the affair, claiming to be the hapless victim of an overwhelming event. In fact, it would be more accurate to say that no airline – or country – has previously managed to lose a Boeing 777, reputedly one of the safest aircraft in the world, on an easy and routine scheduled flight in very fair weather conditions. The coalition MP ended our interview by telling me that in his *kampung* (village), 'everyone is praying as hard as they can'. So clearly I could rest assured about the determination and commitment of the Malaysian political class.

Let's consider the jetliner again. It was on its way to Beijing. This is not just any destination – it's the political capital of the world's number two superpower. The majority of those on board were continental Chinese, and many others were Malaysian Chinese. What are Sino-Malaysian relations like? Are there any disputes between the two countries? The Secretary General of the Chinese Chamber of Commerce and Industry of Kuala Lumpur, Michael

---

* 'Datuk' or 'Dato' is a honorific title – like the 'Sir' of a British knighthood – conferred upon a man or woman in Malaysia by one of the nine sultans of Malaysia. The wife of a Dato or a Datuk is a 'Datin'.

Chai Woon Chew – like all the other members of his organisation – knew Flight MH370 well, and the corresponding return flight, Beijing–Kuala Lumpur, MH371. He told me that relations between Malaysia and China dated back five centuries, originating with the Chinese community in Malaysia, whose presence and role were essential. Everyone knew that it was the Malaysian Chinese – only a quarter of the population – who kept the country running. In fact, the three days of celebrations for the Chinese New Year effectively closed down business in Malaysia much more than the 30 days of Ramadan, in a country where Islam was the official religion and 60 per cent of the population were practising Muslims.

This did not mean there had never been any tensions or rivalries between the two countries, which could explain why there was a rather paranoid hypothesis doing the rounds in business circles, which were dominated by the Chinese community. The suggestion was that if the United States was involved in the missing jetliner affair, its motivation would be to sabotage relations between China and Malaysia. People told me that Malaysia tried to be friends with everyone. But if you were friends with everyone, you had no real friends. Malaysia, it was suggested, walked a tightrope on the international scene, particularly the one strung out between China and the United States.

In fact there was a spectacular rapprochement between Malaysia and the United States in the months following the jetliner's disappearance in March 2014. First of all, Barack Obama made an official visit in April 2014, the first by a US president since Lyndon Johnson in 1966. During his visit, Obama declared that 'the United States considers Malaysia to be essential for regional stability, security at sea and freedom of navigation'. Six months after this historic trip, Prime Minister Najib Razak was invited to Hawaii to play golf with the American president during the Obama family's Christmas vacation. What did Najib do to deserve such a privilege? If by any chance the two men had anything to say in confidence to each other, this was certainly the ideal setting. Less than a year later, Obama made another visit to Malaysia, for the US–ASEAN Summit held to coincide with the APEC meeting.* It seems that Obama and Najib had become quite the inseparable couple. Between Obama's two visits, Secretary of State John Kerry also visited Malaysia in August 2015, officially to pave the way for the signing of the Trans-Pacific Partnership Agreement (TPPA).

Although it was clearly in the US interest to counter China's burgeoning ambition in the region, particularly in the South China Sea, observers could not understand why Washington and Kuala Lumpur had suddenly become such close friends, particularly bearing in mind the increasingly serious challenges to Prime Minister Najib's reputation. Not only had the 1MDB national development fund, created by Najib and placed under his patronage in 2009, managed to accumulate debts of more than US$11 billion in five years – a scandal on this scale fully deserving a place in the highly popular *Malaysian Book of Records*† – it was also discovered in 2015 that the prime minister had 2.6 billion ringgit (US$700 million) credited to his personal account.‡ In his defence, Najib said that the money was a donation from a supporter in the Persian Gulf 'to support his anti-Israeli stance'. In another twist, however, it turned out that the generous benefactor, His Majesty Saud Abdulaziz Majid al-Saud, did not actually exist.§ With no plausible explanation, Najib's reputation became shadier than ever.

In January 2016, though, the newly appointed Attorney General Mohamed Apandi Ali entirely cleared the prime minister of any wrongdoing. After illicit payments on such a grand scale, would the political survival of the head of state have been possible

---

* The US–ASEAN (Association of Southeast Asian Nations) talks were held in Kuala Lumpur on 21 and 22 November 2015.

† Malaysians seem to be fascinated by records of all kinds, and launched their own *Book of Records* in 1995.

‡ *The Wall Street Journal*, 2 July 2015.

§ Article dated 6 October 2015 at www.sarawakreport.org.

anywhere else in the world? *Malaysia Boleh!* The surprising Kuala Lumpur–Washington love story continued uninterrupted, despite an extensive investigation announced in June 2017 by the US Justice Department into the 1MDB scandal. Three months later, despite jaw-dropping revelations produced by the website Sarawak Report, which continued to inform the world about the gargantuan greed of Prime Minister Najib, he was given a red-carpet welcome at the White House by President Trump, after which he committed to buying 25 Boeing 737s and eight 787 Dreamliners for Malaysia Airlines.* But the deal never saw the light. It was cancelled a year later.†

Until the 1MDB scandal took centre stage, another affair – in which France played an important role – was complicating the political life of Malaysia, and of its prime minister in particular. Since the first military contract between France and Malaysia (for French-made Exocet missiles in the mid-1980s), Malaysia's robust appetite for military equipment had turned it into a VVIP‡ client for France. An order for French *Scorpène*-class submarines, finalised in 2002, marked the beginning of an ever closer relationship between the two countries.

But then suspicions of illegal commissions began to emerge. In 2006, an attractive young interpreter from Mongolia, Altantuya Shaariibuu – who had made a trip to Paris with Abdul Razak Baginda, a key intermediary for the submarine negotiations – was shot dead. Her body, tied to a tree trunk in the jungle near Kuala Lumpur, was subsequently blown up using C-4 explosive. The

* Article at www.nytimes.com/2017/09/12/world/asia/trump-najib-razak-malaysia-white-house.html.

† Article at https://www.nst.com.my/business/2018/10/416622/exclusive-mascant-commit-boeing-deal. The group CEO said Malaysia Airlines' current aircraft fleet of 81 was sufficient for the airline to service its existing network of 38 destinations.

‡ In Malaysia, the concept of VVIP (very very important people) is widely used to describe the top level of powerful people.

gruesome murder, which had actually been carried out by police-
men under orders, seemingly to silence a potential witness to the
corruption case, shocked the country. Although these three shady
affairs – the French submarines scandal, 1MDB and MH370 –
have no direct links, they have one key person in common: defence
minister at the time, and later finance minister and prime minister,
a certain Najib Razak.

When I lived in Kuala Lumpur from 2000 to 2003, I gradually
built up a rather grim picture of the couple formed by Najib and
Rosmah Mansor. Rosmah Mansor, the self-styled First Lady of
Malaysia, was a controversial figure with a taste for opulence.
She was once described to me as 'an unfortunate mix of Cruella
de Vil and Imelda Marcos', with her collection of the most exclusive Hermès handbags and a particularly irresistible penchant for
the Birkin crocodile line. I did not meet a single Malaysian who
liked her, although many could recall the price (US$24 million)
of a diamond she allegedly bought in 2011 from Jacob & Co. in
New York. In her autobiography published in 2013, she denied
this claim, saying that the stone had been returned in 2012.
Rumour was also rife that she engaged in black magic. The mere
mention of her name usually triggered a clear scowl of disgust –
or fear – but despite her nationwide unpopularity, the country's
first couple maintained a tight grip on power. They knew how to
silence those who posed a threat. After promising to abolish the
brutal Internal Security Act (ISA), the prime minister went on to
have new repressive laws passed that were worthy of a country in
a state of emergency. When I returned to Malaysia in November
2015, one of my appointments was cancelled: the person I was to
meet had been arrested the previous week. It was, ironically, a
lawyer – Matthias Chang – who at the time could have spent
many years in prison without his case ever being examined by
a court.*

---

* Matthias Chang was released on bail on 18 November 2015.

It turned out that the man in the front line throughout the MH370 crisis, Defence and Transport Minister Hishammuddin Hussein – Mr No-No – was the first cousin of Prime Minister Najib. It was furthermore the first time ever that the Malaysian defence minister had at the same time been the transport minister.* With his two hats, the PM's cousin was in charge of both the army and civil aviation. If someone had been intending to completely control the information chain regarding a disappeared aircraft, it would be hard to imagine a more effective system.

The way the prime minister tried to survive a scandal on the scale of 1MDB was telling. When he became annoyed that Muhyiddin Yassin, his deputy, raised questions about it and that the court of the country would show so little understanding towards his case, the prime minister dismissed both Muhyiddin and the attorney general, Abdul Gani Patail, the latter for 'health reasons'.† Then in September 2015, shortly after he too had raised questions about the 1MDB scandal, Deputy Public Prosecutor Anthony Kevin Morais was kidnapped in his car on his way to work. His body was found 10 days later in a concrete-filled barrel, abandoned in marshland near the Klang River

With such methods in use, some understandably doubted that the April 2015 helicopter crash that killed the prime minister's personal secretary and one of his closest strategic advisors, Jamaluddin Jarjis, better known to his friends as 'Tan Sri J', was an accident.‡ The helicopter had been chartered to fly important

---

* The Transport portfolio is usually given to the leader of the MCA (Malaysian Chinese Association), the party representing the Chinese community in Malaysia that is part of Barisan Nasional, the coalition in government since independence. But due to poor results at the 2013 elections, the MCA declined the post temporarily and it was given to the defence minister, Hishammuddin.

† 'Gani Patail's Service as AG Terminated for Health Reasons', Bernama News, 28 July 2015.

‡ Tan Sri Jamaluddin Jarjis was Malaysia's ambassador to Washington from 2009 to 2012.

guests home following the wedding of Najib's daughter. None of the six passengers, including the pilot (who co-owned the helicopter company), survived the crash. I heard two, if not three, different views about this accident. The subsequent investigation's findings were never made public, despite the very high governmental level of at least two of the people involved.

Ugly and depressing stories continued to abound in the ensuing years in Malaysia. When in 2017 I attended the ceremony held by the families to mark the third anniversary of the loss of MH370, the talk of the town was all about another two scary incidents that had taken place only a few weeks earlier. On 13 February 2017, the North Korean leader's half-brother Kim Jung-nam was killed in broad daylight in full public view in the departure hall of Kuala Lumpur International Airport 2.* That very same day, a Christian pastor was abducted from his car in a highly professional operation involving several identical black SUVs. Over the following weeks, no fewer than five activists went missing in very unusual circumstances.

One thing is certain: if there is one man who knows more than anyone else in the country, about MH370 and everything else, it is obviously the now ex-Prime Minister Najib Razak.

So Malaysia not only boasted a long history of relations with China, a recent love-in with America, long and friendly mercantile–military relations with France, and a rapprochement with Singapore under Najib, it had also granted some favours to Australia, such as allowing a mining company, Lynas Corporation,† to build a huge rare-earth refining plant in Pahang, which happens to be Najib's home state. The environmental impact of this project was said by

---

* KLIA2, located close to KLIA, was opened in May 2014 as a second international airport.

† Lynas Corporation, based in Western Australia, has become the world's second-largest producer of rare-earth elements, essential in many industries. China controls more than 80 per cent of the world's rare-earth production.

its opponents to be disastrous. At the time of MH370, there were also strong suspicions of bribes paid to Malaysians in positions of influence in connection with contracts obtained by Securency International and Note Printing Australia, two subsidiaries of the Australian Reserve Bank* that made plastic banknotes † And, it must not be forgotten, Malaysia also had excellent relations with the Gulf States, for which it had become a popular tourist destination.‡ Each of these countries seemed to have come to their own specific cosy arrangements with Malaysia for their own reasons.

Astonishingly, this broadly strategic interpretation of the background to the disappearance was very much in vogue among the most educated people in Malaysia, who were themselves deeply disconcerted by the MH370 affair. No one seemed able to formulate the argument precisely, but the idea that Malaysia had no clearly established loyalties seemed to underlie the attempted explanations people gave me. I really had not been expecting any collective intuition of this type. I found it intriguing, but I did not see what I could immediately do with it to explain the disappearance of the Boeing 777. Because, objectively at first sight, there did not seem to be the shadow of any single dispute – be it economic, political or military – that was sufficiently serious for one to imagine any link with the loss of the jetliner.

A little later during my first MH370 assignment in March 2014, I had the opportunity to once again meet – and interview – Anwar Ibrahim, the charismatic leader of the opposition and former deputy prime minister. Taking advantage of a temporary spell of freedom between another guilty verdict on appeal, handed down

* The bank sold its 50 per cent stake in Securency in early 2013; see www.smh.com.au/business/securency-gone-but-risk-not-forgotten-20130212-2eb2e.html.

† Wikileaks revealed in July 2014 that Australia imposed a ban on publishing anything concerning this affair.

‡ In Malaysia, as in the Persian Gulf, the Sunni Muslim religion is practised.

the day before Flight MH370 disappeared, and the examination of his case by the Federal Court, set for February 2015, Anwar told me he was appalled that the government had tried to implicate him in the MH370 disaster by highlighting his distant family connections (which he does not deny) with the captain of the flight. He also reminded me that it was he, as finance minister, who placed the order for the state-of-the-art Anglo-Italian Marconi radar systems.

Since then, Malaysia had also acquired latest-generation radars, the Thales Raytheon GM400 system. Located at Kuantan and Kota Bharu (on Malaysia's east coast) and Butterworth (on the west coast), these radars could not have missed MH370 when it took the flight path described by the authorities. 'If they saw it,' Anwar asked me, 'why did they take no action? And if they did not see it, despite all the equipment we have, my country has a serious national security problem!' He accused the government of failing in its duty. As for the fact that the full manifest of cargo loaded on the jetliner had still not been made public, he found it simply outrageous. 'This lack of transparency ends up becoming a rumour factory,' he concluded. As he approached the age of 70, it seemed certain that his next period of imprisonment would – both legally and in practical terms – end any hope he may have had of leading the country. But he was one of those politicians who knew that you should never say never. Ironically, his political hopes were resurrected against all odds three years later, when his party won the 2018 general elections. He was then promised, within two years, the future position of prime minister of Malaysia.

Meanwhile, the Inmarsat scientists in London had refined their calculations. Although they had not previously used the ping frequency data, the two flight-path options, north or south, were so different that the frequency data could 'discriminate between those two routes', in the words of Chris Ashton, one of the Inmarsat researchers.* 'We had attempted this calculation two or three times

* In the BBC *Horizon* documentary referred to above.

and abandoned it. [...] We were [...] not getting a good match between the measured data and the predicted data.' But suddenly, one Friday evening, 'the graphs matched, the data worked, the calculation was solved'. Through their calculations, which had never previously been attempted, the scientists had reached their conclusion: the northern route was eliminated. Only the southern route remained. Inmarsat's evidence was sent straight to the Malaysian authorities. The scientists' sense of elation did not last long, as they realised immediately there was very little chance for the people on the aircraft'.

The worst-case scenario, a crash in the sea with no hope of any survivors, was finally announced on the evening of 24 March by Prime Minister Najib in a TV news flash: 'This evening I was briefed by representatives from the UK Air Accidents Investigation Branch [AAIB]. They informed me that Inmarsat [...] has been performing further calculations on the data.' Najib then solemnly continued, 'Inmarsat and the AAIB have concluded that MH370 flew along the southern corridor, and that its last position was in the middle of the Indian Ocean, west of Perth.' Although Najib did not speak of a crash or of deaths, he added, as if to eliminate all hope, 'This is a remote location, far from any possible landing sites. It is therefore with deep sadness and regret that I must inform you that [...] Flight MH370 ended in the southern Indian Ocean.'

The families were informed by text: 'Malaysia Airlines deeply regrets that we have to assume beyond any reasonable doubt that MH370 has been lost and that none of those on board survived.' Disregarding the fact that two-thirds of the passengers on board were Chinese nationals, the text message was only sent in English.

For the families this was another hammer blow. They were being asked to accept that their loved ones should be declared lost for ever simply on the basis of intricate mathematical calculations that were almost unverifiable, and without anything tangible – not a single piece of a seat or fuselage – as possible evidence for the theory. All of them were gripped by terror and consternation, while most were dubious and suspicious. 'We do not know how, we do not know why this tragedy took place,' said Ahmad Jauhari Yahya, CEO of Malaysia Airlines, completely at a loss.

On 25 March, the posters that had appeared spontaneously all over Kuala Lumpur, encouraging everyone to pray for the passengers of Flight MH370, were gradually replaced by messages expressing condolences. Many of the daily papers, whose front pages had been entirely devoted to Flight MH30 for the last 17 days, expressed their sorrow with black bands or shaded front pages. Recalling the final words transmitted by the flight's captain, the pro-governmental daily *The New Straits Times* ran the headline: 'Good night MH370'.

Even though the families did not want to hear it, and could not accept it, from 24 March 2014 onwards the 239 people who were on board Flight MH370 had effectively been consigned to the depths of the Indian Ocean for ever.

The truth is, at that point during the crisis, late March 2014, there was enormous confusion about the whole case. Malaysia had lost control of events to such an extent that the members of the international media gathered in their hundreds in Kuala Lumpur were on the verge of a collective nervous breakdown. It looked like anyone other than the Malaysian authorities could do a better job. Since Australia had already taken on the mantle of 'head of search and rescue operations' Down Under since 17 March, it somehow seemed natural – and certainly reassuring – that the country also took over the leadership of the overall search operation now that it was moving south.

Malaysia had been given a gentle tap on the shoulder, and had discreetly withdrawn from the search operations, while remaining officially in charge of the investigation. Invited on to the well-known television programme *Good Morning America*, Stephen Ganyard – a retired colonel in the US Marine Corps – first dismissed as irrelevant and worthless the interview by ABC's special correspondent with a fisherman on the East Coast of Malaysia, who said he saw a jet flying low over the water around the time the plane went missing. Instead, he said:

> The good news, here, is that we have the Australians with the NTSB* now in charge of this investigation. We've seen a lot of inconsistency out of the Malaysian authorities all week; their statements haven't matched up. But now we have the real pros on the scene, and really, we are now at day one in this investigation, because we have people who know how to do this.†

Above all, everyone could now hope that things would start to become a little bit clearer.

---

* National Transport Safety Board, the US equivalent of the French BEA or the British AAIB.

† Quoted in the independent report by Brock McEwen, *Time to Investigate the Investigators*, published in January 2015.

4

Australia Takes Charge

Following the announcement made on 24 March 2014 that it was now 'beyond reasonable doubt' that the final destination of MH370 was the southern Indian Ocean, the search operation – with ships and aircraft combing a vast area, from the warm waters of the Gulf of Thailand to the arid plains of Kazakhstan – was put on hold. The world's attention now turned solely to the 'southern corridor' in the south-eastern Indian Ocean, off the coast of Australia, in line with the Inmarsat engineers' indications. The newly defined search area was still huge. Initially, the searches of the ocean surface to find floating aircraft debris were to cover hundreds of thousands of square kilometres; they would be followed by underwater searches aimed at finding the wreck and the black boxes on the seabed.

On 31 March, Malaysia formally accepted the offer made by Australia – already in charge of air and sea operations in its official SAR (search and rescue) zone since 17 March – to head what was called 'the most extensive search and rescue operation ever'. Legally speaking, Australia was under no obligation to take charge of the operation, particularly at its own expense. In this region, its SAR responsibilities consisted of saving lives, not locating wrecks or debris. 'It's an act of good international citizenship by Australia,' was the explanation given by Australian Prime Minister Tony Abbott. He argued that such an act was only natural, given that the plane crashed in Australia's maritime zone, although, at 2,000 kilometres from its coast, it was a long way outside the zone.

This sudden act of philanthropy on the part of Australia, which lost six of its nationals on the flight, was quite surprising. When I was the South Pacific regional correspondent of *Le Monde*, based first in Sydney and then in Auckland, I reported on several spectacular sea rescues.* These stories of survival in extremely dangerous waters were some of the most remarkable human adventures I had ever covered. I also recalled that on each occasion the cost of the rescue operation had been controversial.† Yet these limited rescue operations were negligible in terms of cost and resources deployed, compared with MH370, an operation that initial estimates put at tens of millions of dollars.

And not everyone was convinced in any case that Australians were the 'real pros' as far as air accident investigations, let alone deep-sea searches, were concerned. That Australia had become involved with the coordination of the surface search was one – completely logical – thing. But that it then stayed in charge for the underwater phase puzzled many specialists. 'I was mystified by the selection of the Australians to lead the underwater search for the airplane,' said American aviation journalist and air safety investigator Christine Negroni.

At the time, the Australian Transport Safety Bureau (ATSB) was still tainted by the very shoddy investigation it had carried out into another air accident over water – the Pel-Air Westwing ditching off Norfolk Island on 18 November 2009. Once the ATSB investigation had been exposed by a TV documentary, it became a national

---

* During the Vendée Globe race in 1996–97, Thierry Dubois and Raphael Dinelli from France as well as, later, Tony Bullimore from the UK had narrow escapes. One was rescued by another competitor, Pete Goss, and the other by the Australian Navy.

† See www.nytimes.com/1997/01/11/world/australia-rescues-sailors-but-is-wincing-at-the-costs.html.

scandal.* Eventually the Canadian Transport Bureau was asked to review the ATSB's methodologies and processes, and a damning report on the ATSB was published on 1 December 2014. But by then the ATSB was well and truly committed to MH370, and it was too late to question their expertise or suitability for the task.

'It seemed to me that the Australians, including the ATSB's Martin Dolan, were eager to become the heroes in solving the world's most riveting air mystery. In an interview in June 2014, Dolan [the ATSB head] told me enthusiastically that coordinating the search was "the challenge of a career",' said Negroni. Beset by public humiliation, did the ATSB see the MH370 mission as an opportunity to redeem its reputation and bury past shame? Quite possibly.

Whatever the real motives behind its act of international citizenship, Australia thus took command of the search operations, with the blessing and encouragement of the USA. The Malaysians were relieved of their responsibility. But did they really have any choice in the matter?

The much-decorated Angus Houston, former Chief of the Australian Defence Force, with an exemplary record in the Air Force, was appointed to take charge of the mission and to head the search coordination centre, the JACC.† Houston had no previous experience of civil aviation accidents or underwater searches, but he had a strong background.

The zone of operations was hostile, remote and unforgiving. In winter, waves could easily reach heights of 10 to 12 metres. 'No

---

* After a TV documentary produced by Four Corners (a current affairs investigative programme) aired in September 2012 on the Australian TV channel ABC Television, the Australian senate launched its own investigation. The senate report released in May 2013 confirmed that the initial ATSB report into the Pel-Air incident was deeply flawed (it erroneously put all the blame on the pilot for the accident), and as a consequence the senate recommended that the accident report be withdrawn and redone.

† Joint Agency Coordination Centre.

one likes going down there. You're almost certainly in for a hard time,' a French naval officer told me. He was familiar with the immense seas of these southern waters, whose nicknames as their latitudes dropped ever southwards included the 'Roaring Forties', the 'Furious Fifties' and the 'Screaming Sixties'. And the weather was about to get much worse: the end of March was already autumn in the southern hemisphere. But with the 'real pros' at the helm, results should not be long in coming. The stated objective of the search was to locate and then recover the jetliner's two black boxes (which are in fact orange). One contained the final two hours of recordings from the CVR (cockpit voice recorder), and the other all the aircraft's technical data from the FDR (flight data recorder). Each was equipped with a cylindrical beacon, powered by a lithium battery (the size of a standard D battery). For one month after being triggered by contact with water, it transmitted an inaudible ultrasonic signal for a maximum range of 2,000 metres, indicating – like the Inmarsat ping – 'I am here'. The ping could be identified by its frequency of 37.5 kHz and its intermittence, a one-second interval between each signal.

After the Inmarsat handshake pings, which carried evidence of the final destination of MH370 through space (although this was not their intended purpose), the search was now on for the pings from the black boxes, which should tell us what had happened on the plane after the 'Good night, Malaysian three seven zero' message. These pings were being emitted from an abyss of pure and glacially cold water, at depths where there was virtually no under-water fauna, only total darkness and absolute silence.

Well before the location of the wreck and the revelations expected from the black boxes, what the families were waiting for – and the rest of the world, mystified by the disappearance – was some certainty about the fate of the lost plane and the 239 people on board. They wanted evidence, any evidence, as long as it was tangible, that the aircraft really did crash at the point indicated by the last Inmarsat ping.

China, Malaysia, Japan, the United Arab Emirates, the United Kingdom, the United States, South Korea and New Zealand sent around 15 ships and a similar number of aircraft to take part in the operation.

In the light of a possible crash at sea, especially after the confirmation of the Indian Ocean option, the experience of France's air accident investigation bureau (BEA) in locating and recovering the wreck of the Air France A330 that crashed off Brazil on the Rio de Janeiro–Paris Flight AF447 in 2009 became the model of excellence for the Malaysian authorities, with frequent mentions of 'the French experts' during their daily press briefings.

The success of the French accident investigation bureau in the AF447 operation was doubly useful to the Malaysians. It meant first of all that there was hope of one day finding the MH370 black boxes, in comparable geographic conditions – a long way from the coast and at a depth of several kilometres. People started to think: it's been done once already, so it's feasible. Second, the example of AF447 reminded those who were losing patience that it took the French almost two years to find the wreck,* so this would clearly be a long-term operation.

Seen as a symbol of France's outstanding expertise, Jean-Paul Troadec – former Director of the BEA and head of the delegation sent to Kuala Lumpur – was pursued by journalists both on leaving his hotel and then whenever and wherever he got out of his car, to his considerable irritation. Against all expectation, however, he agreed to my request for an interview for *Le Monde*, doubtless thanks to some judicious nudging from the French embassy.

He looked rather dour at first sight, and seemed suspicious. I got the feeling he was not very keen on journalists, particularly when they kept harassing him. A graduate of the prestigious École Polytechnique and the École nationale de l'aviation civile, a pilot

* The wreck of AF447 was found on 2 April 2011, 22 months after the crash.

and a parachutist, Troadec was also a seasoned sailor. With his knowledge of the sea and the sky, his insights would be most useful.

'It is unthinkable to begin underwater searches with such uncertainty about the plane's position. First of all, you must find pieces of debris and formally identify them as coming from the plane. The debris spotted up to now [by satellite or by aircraft] could very well have come from ships – the ocean is a dustbin – and from a long way out you arrive in the whirling currents of the Indian Ocean Gyre,' he told me straight off, without knowing that the Australians were about to make that very mistake over the coming days. 'Then the point of origin of the aircraft debris has to be determined by drift calculations based on winds and currents. And the margin of uncertainty rises very quickly as the days go by.'

According to Troadec, there was no doubt that 'it is only once reasonable limits have been drawn around this impact zone that the underwater search operations can begin'. In fact, even though finding AF447 seemed a difficult task, the circle of uncertainty was limited to five minutes of flight from the time that the last ACARS signal was transmitted.* 'At least, in our case, we knew it was there,' he said. 'In the MH370 situation, we do not have the last point of communication. Just a probable flight path.' So the search operations were to be concentrated along an immense area described by an arc 60 to 80 kilometres wide, and some 4,000 kilometres long, from 16°S to 38°S.

During the search to find the wreck of AF447, while ships were trying to recover debris and some 50 bodies that were floating on the surface, two towed ping locators (TPLs) were used to detect signals transmitted by the beacons of the black boxes, also referred to as 'pingers'. A TPL is designed rather like an underwater mini-glider, and resembles a small, bright yellow stingray. It has to be towed slowly at a depth of around 2,000 metres, a very tricky operation indeed. The ship then makes very long passes across the

---

* This meant that the circle had a radius of 75 kilometres.

demarcated zone. Those familiar with the system call it 'mowing the lawn', but it is worth remembering that the cable pulling the TPL is six to nine kilometres long. 'Just turning round while pulling a cable some 6,000 metres long takes several hours,' said Troadec.

'When the pingers stop transmitting after one month, give or take a few days, towed sonars will explore flat or slightly sloping seabed areas, while on uneven subsea terrain sonars mounted on Autonomous Underwater Vehicles [AUVs] have to be used, or probably both at once,' he continued 'After 20 hours, the AUV resurfaces and informs the ship of its GPS position. You go and recover it, download the data [sonar images that can only be interpreted by an experienced eye], and then send it off again. If something unusual shows up, the AUV is sent back to the same location, and this time it takes real photos.'

The Malaysians clearly had great confidence in the expertise of the French, but very surprisingly Angus Houston, the Australian search operation chief, often made mistakes when alluding to the AF447 case. Referring to the AF447 wreck, he said it was at a depth of 3,000 metres instead of 3,900 metres. He also stated that the first pieces of debris from AF447 were located within 24 hours, when in fact it took six days.* Australia's deputy prime minister meanwhile was wrong when he stated that the recovery of surface debris from AF447 was completed in fewer days than it took for the MH370 debris search to begin.† Why do these people in positions of authority make so many mistakes? As in the case of Malaysia, were we talking about incompetence – or a deliberate attempt to misinform?

Everyone forgot to mention, however, that during the AF447 search the towed ping locators twice passed close to the wreck, on

---

* Press briefing, 1 April 2014.

† Press briefing, 5 May 2014. In the case of AF447, the first pieces of debris were not found until 6 June 2009, five days after the crash, and surface searches lasted until 26 June, 25 days after the crash. In the case of MH370, the Australian air searches began on 16 March 2014, eight days after the loss of the aircraft.

22 and 23 June 2009, without picking anything up. This cast serious doubt on the effectiveness of the beacons. The technique was certainly not infallible.

For the moment, the general public had high hopes that all this technology would produce results. But no time was to be lost. The race against the clock to detect the pings had already started on 8 March, as the guaranteed lifespan of the battery powering the beacons of the two black boxes was only 30 days from the crash date.* In fact, as soon as the southern option was given priority on 15 March, many countries adjusted the positions of their satellites to cover this part of the world, without even announcing the fact. On several occasions, objects that seemed compatible with debris from a Boeing 777 were spotted.

After the first images supplied by Australia on 16 March, one showing an object 24 metres long (43°S, 90°E), bigger than the largest shipping container, and another 5 metres long (44°S, 91°E), 2,300 kilometres south-west of the Australian coast, the Chinese satellite Gaofen-1 saw an object 22 metres long about 60 kilometres away (44°S, 90°E). On 20 March, France also provided images, taken by the Pléiades 1-A and 1-B satellites and Airbus's Terra SAR-X. Unlike the geostationary satellites of Inmarsat, these observation satellites had polar orbits and their altitude was 600 to 700 kilometres, with a revolution period of about 90 minutes. They therefore had a minimum revisit period of 24 hours.

Some of the images provided by Airbus and by France were interpreted by the Malaysian authorities,† while others were supplied together with their analyses. These also showed a field of

---

* The AF447 investigation report made recommendations that the lifespan of black-box batteries should be extended to 90 days and that the black boxes should float.

† The images from the Airbus satellite, TerraSAR-X, were analysed by the MRSA (Malaysian Remote Sensing Agency).

debris that was relatively concentrated in the same zone. 'With the time required for a satellite to be sent to the zone, for it to take pictures, and for analysts to interpret them, a wait of a few days is understandable,' I was told by a contact who took part in the French operation. Finally, on 24 March, images from the Thai authorities showed roughly 300 floating objects about 100 kilometres from those spotted by the French satellites. Simon Gunson, a New Zealander with a keen interest in the MH370 disappearance, brought all the available satellite images linked to the search together on a Google site.* He also kept a screen capture of a CCTV announcement made on 24 March, which showed a reverse-drift study† for the three objects seen by the Chinese satellite and then deduced the probable impact zone.

In Gunson's view, the fact that two objects of a size comparable to a Boeing 777 wing – and hundreds of pieces of debris nearby – were spotted should have made this sector an absolute priority for exploration, even if it was a few degrees of latitude further south than the edge of the arc indicated by the Inmarsat calculations.

But quite the opposite happened. According to Gunson, 'The Malaysian authorities responded to the Chinese study by publishing a new flight-path estimate [...] making a point of impact so far south impossible (between 43°S and 45°S and 89°E).' The effect of this was to undermine the credibility of the Chinese images. As a result, no ship was ever sent to this zone, even though it contained the highest concentration of debris spotted by the satellites of three different countries. Gunson has always refuted the suggestion that the debris did not exist. He said there were pieces of debris, but – for reasons he could not fathom – the surface searches made every effort to avoid them.

*   *   *

* See sites.google.com/site/mh370debris/home/debris-images/.

† The study was made by the China National Marine Environmental Forecasting Centre.

It was not easy for the media, let alone the general public, to keep tabs on the searches. The zone was huge and in a sense virtual, as it was defined only by longitude–latitude coordinates. This was rather abstract, even if as a child you used to play battleships ('A4–B5, hit; A4–B6, missed'). The pictures showed that nothing looked more like a day's search in the Indian Ocean … than another day's search in the Indian Ocean, 1,000 kilometres north or south of the previous one. It was always the same blue-grey sea, sometimes undulating with low, smooth waves, at other times raging with towering breakers. So the changing courses of the ships and the switches of search zones went largely unnoticed, and the announcements are what people remember. And when it came to announcements, Australia was in a class of its own.

On 19 March 2014, Australian Prime Minister Tony Abbott spoke of 'new and credible information' after a number of large objects were spotted by satellite. He even held a briefing for MPs in which he described some obscure objects – one of which was grey or green and round, and another orange and rectangular – assuring the MPs that this was 'probably the best lead we have right now'.*

Three aircraft – a US Navy Poseidon, a second Australian Orion and a Japanese Orion – were sent to the zone, but they all returned to base after finding nothing. We are still waiting to find out why these unidentified floating objects, with none of the specific characteristics of aircraft debris, constituted 'new and credible information' or were considered worthy of an announcement in parliament by the prime minister. But this was just the first in a long string of flops.

Three days later, on 22 March, an aircraft spotted a wooden pallet with straps of different colours around it, but did not take a photograph. An Orion from New Zealand went to check and

---

* See www.smh.com.au/federal-politics/political-news/missing-malaysia-airlines-flight-mh370-pm-tony-abbott-says-satellite-images-could-be-wreckage-of-crashed-plane-20140320-354ij.html#ixzz40tSEKo5O.

returned without finding anything.* False alarm followed false alarm. The ocean was, just as Troadec said, a huge dustbin. But still there was nothing that seemed in any way associated with MH370, its cargo or its passengers.

On 31 March, Tony Abbott visited the air search headquarters at the Pearce Air Base, north of Perth. He thanked the 550 pilots and flight crew working on the mission. The flights usually lasted from 10 to 12 hours, with more than half that time being spent reaching the zone and returning. Meanwhile, more than a thousand sailors were involved in the sea search. The prime minister was asked how confident he was that the mission would be successful. 'The best brains in the world are applying themselves to this task,' he replied. 'All of the technological mastery that we have is being applied and brought to bear here, so if this mystery is solvable, we will solve it.' Warren Truss, the Australian Minister for Infrastructure and Regional Development, took the opportunity to remind the audience that the black box was an Australian invention and that the ATSB had unique expertise to exploit the data contained in the recorders, in due time.†

On 3 April, Malaysian Prime Minister Najib Razak in turn paid tribute to the multi-national operation under the leadership of Australia. The flotilla was expanding daily, with the arrival of six Chinese ships, including a polar exploration vessel, just having been announced. The United Kingdom was sending a nuclear submarine, HMS *Tireless*, while in addition to ADV *Ocean Shield*, the Australian Navy sent three ships: HMAS *Success*, HMAS *Perth* and HMAS *Toowoomba*.

But despite the hundreds of air patrols and the many ships searching the zone, not the slightest trace of MH370 was found on the ocean's surface.

---

* Statement by Mike Barton, Rescue Coordination Chief at the Australian Maritime Safety Authority (AMSA).

† David Warren invented the black box, initially a single unit, in 1953.

When the imposing Australian Border Force *Ocean Shield* cast off from Perth at the end of March, with its 110-metre-long gleaming red hull, its crane, its helicopter landing pad and all the equipment needed for underwater searches, there were only 11 days left before the beacons stopped transmitting. With four days at sea to reach the zone, that left seven days to search. Seven days. If only the ship knew where to search. But the sector for the seven-day search covered tens of thousands of square kilometres of ocean. Objectively, with such a vague estimate of the point of impact in the ocean and no debris yet found, the probability of picking up a ping was tiny, at best. But no one pointed this out. Everyone seemed happy to pretend that this mission impossible was feasible.

And so, despite the absence of the slightest tangible indication to confirm that the search was in the right place, the best thing to do was to take a chance and lower the towed ping locator into the water from the *Ocean Shield* and begin the underwater acoustic search for the pings. Even with zero chance of success, some action was desperately needed and it made for great television.

Adopting the same lucky-break strategy, aircraft on search patrols had already dropped dozens of small buoys equipped with sonar at various points in the search zone. Each buoy's sonar device sent a signal down to a depth of just over 300 metres to pick up the ping frequency of the black boxes, transmitting what it detected back to an overflying plane. After a few days, the buoys sank. Of the hundreds of small buoys put into the water in this way, only one detected anything – the sound of a cargo ship passing through the area.

But the TPL towed by the *Ocean Shield* sprang a surprise. Just after being lowered into the water by the specialist US Navy team, it detected some pings. And it was not the only one. The Chinese ship also detected pings, even though it was hundreds of kilometres from the *Ocean Shield*. The news was so good that it justified a press release on the night of 5–6 April. The Joint Agency Coordination Centre thus confirmed that both the Chinese ship,

Haixun 01, and the Australian ship, *Ocean Shield*, had picked up 'signals consistent with those emitted by aircraft black boxes',* although it did not specify the frequency or period of the pings.

Despite its optimism, the message from Angus Houston was cautious, and he also advised the media to be circumspect. He announced, however, that the British frigate HMS *Echo*, better equipped to analyse the pings than the Chinese ship, was heading for the zone where the Chinese pings were detected, while *Ocean Shield* explored its own 'acoustic events'. He went on to say that he had received confirmation of a series of white floating objects some 90 kilometres from the (Chinese) ping location. Houston also said that a correction made to the satellite calculations by the investigation team suggested that the search should be focused more on the southern part of the search zone. Even though the different indications were incompatible and contradictory, the excitement continued over the following days. 'Call it a triumph of science, or incredible luck, but on the very first path, the *Ocean Shield* detected a steady series of pings,' was the comment from CNN on 8 April.

On 9 April, Houston announced that *Ocean Shield*, which had already identified two signals that could be black box pings on 5 April, had picked up two further pings on 8 April, at 16:27 and 22:17. So now there were four pings. But we were almost out of time, as the black boxes would stop transmitting on or around 8 April.

On 11 April, Tony Abbott said on a trip to China that he was 'very confident the signals we're detecting are from the black box from MH370'. Speaking from Shanghai, the Australian prime minister added: 'We are confident that we know the position of the black box flight recorder to within some kilometres.'† This was a

* jacc.gov.au/media/interviews/2014/april/t-007.aspx. [Please check.]

† www.smh.com.au/national/tony-abbott-very-confident-signals-are-from-mh370-black-boxes-20140411-36hi4.html#ixzz40txE8tpD.

real shock for the families. Abbott also said that a 'series of detections' from the towed ping locator aboard *Ocean Shield* had enabled the authorities to narrow down the search area significantly. Angus Houston, asked to corroborate the prime minister's remarks, had some difficulty in confirming that any significant progress had been made over the last few days. But his background in the military had taught him not to contradict his superiors, so he said: 'I'm now optimistic that we will find the aircraft, or what is left of the aircraft, in the not too distant future.' The BBC reported that 'the mood of the Australian search team has never been more positive'.

On 14 April, Houston announced a new development: '*Ocean Shield* detected an oil slick yesterday evening in her current search area […] approximately 5,500 metres down-wind and down-sea from the vicinity of the detections picked up by the towed pinger locator on *Ocean Shield*.' Was this an indication of the MH370 crash site? But if MH370 had crashed in the search area, it was because it had run out of fuel. And even if it had crashed with some fuel in the tank, did this experienced military officer really think that a slick could be found on the surface 38 days later? So why pass on such information, as useless as it was misleading, even if it did come with the rider that the liquid collected still had to be analysed?

On the same day, Houston made the important announcement that following the detection of the four pings by *Ocean Shield* a week earlier, the search would move into its second phase involving underwater operations, with the launching of the autonomous submarine *Bluefin-21*. It was essential to go and look more closely at the source of the pings, he told a Chinese journalist from Xinhua News Agency.*

---

* Press conference for the Chinese media on 14 April 2014.

There was one signal which has been analysed very closely, which was a very strong signal. Very strong, and it had all the characteristics of being from a man-made device and the characteristics of the transmission were very, very similar to those […] from an emergency locator beacon. So we have the four signals; our experts have had a look […] and […] they have established a datum on the ocean floor – probably the most likely place where you might find wreckage of the aircraft or a black box.

During the same press briefing, Houston added: 'I am very hopeful that we will find something.'

As euphoria spread via the international media, the small number of scientists worldwide who were really familiar with underwater searches became increasingly alarmed. 'I went on CNN about 15 times to try and make people understand there was absolutely no chance that the pings were from MH370,' says Paul-Henri Nargeolet, one of the world's most respected wreck searchers. A former naval officer, and qualified as a clearance diver, among his countless underwater assignments were leading six expeditions to the wreck of the *Titanic* from 1986 onwards* and heading part of the search for AF447 in 2010. In 1979, he recovered the wreck of the DHC-5 Buffalo that missed the runway at Dakar with the Mauritanian prime minister on board, and in the Mediterranean he raised parts of the DC9 brought down near Ustica in 1980, allegedly by an unidentified missile. His assessment of the search to date was scathing, to say the least:

I know the US Navy people who were on board [*Ocean Shield*], and they would never have made such elementary mistakes. But the announcements were made by spokesmen. A 33 kHz ping, or

---

* The wreck of the *Titanic* was located in 1985 by a Franco-American expedition (WHOI–Ifremer). Nargeolet joined Ifremer in 1986, mainly to take charge of expeditions to the *Titanic*.

a 35 kHz ping, cannot become a 37.5 kHz ping, either because of the pressure or because of failing batteries as I heard it explained. That's nonsense. The frequency of a pinger can vary by 1 kHz on construction, but after that it does not vary, and it is certainly not affected by the depth of immersion. And thank goodness the pingers transmit the same frequency at the surface as at a depth of 6,000 metres, because if not our task would be impossible.*

As for the Chinese, to judge from the images I have seen, what they put in the water from their Zodiac [inflatable boat] are Edgerton devices, made by Benthos, a technology that is made for use by divers. This type of detector has a horizontal range of a few hundred metres, and the range is even lower at depth! There was no chance whatsoever of these devices hearing black box pings from depths of several thousand metres.

Nowadays there are all sorts of pings in the marine environment. Fishermen put pingers on their nets to scare off seals and dolphins, and marine biologists often used them to track large creatures such as turtles, whales, sharks and penguins. There were several major problems with the pings detected by *Ocean Shield*. As Nargeolet pointed out, they were not at the right frequency. Instead of 37.5 kHz (which may possibly vary by 1 kHz), the pings picked up by the little yellow stingray of *Ocean Shield* were at 27 kHz and 33.3 kHz. Frequency is the most essential characteristic of a ping: wrong frequency, wrong ping. This fact on its own should have been enough to eliminate all the pings picked up by *Ocean Shield* before the information was even sent back to HQ and then immediately passed on to the whole planet.

Another elementary mistake was that the first ping was heard at a depth of 300 metres below the surface. According to US Navy

---

* At depths over 6,000 metres, the pingers no longer transmit because they are destroyed by the pressure.

Captain Mark Matthews, on board *Ocean Shield* to handle TPL operations, the detector must be less than 2,000 metres from the black box to pick up the ping. With a seabed depth of some 4,500 metres in this area, there was no way a ping picked up at 300 metres could have come from the seabed. That ping should therefore have been eliminated straight away for two reasons: wrong frequency and wrong depth.

Bearing in mind that the range of the black box transmitter beacons was limited to around 2,000 metres and could often be much less, what should we have made of another ping that the moving ship managed to pick up for two hours and 20 minutes? Had the black boxes suddenly sprung to life and started chasing the little yellow stingray? We weren't talking here about a Walt Disney fairy tale but about the largest search operation of all time, led by the world's 'top experts'. At least when a ping was picked up over a long period by the frigate HMS *Echo*, someone finally realised that it was an echo from the ship towing the device.

And then how could one have explained the distance of 10 to 14 kilometres between the four pings picked up? Perhaps there were four black boxes, instead of two that sank 10 kilometres away from each other? In the AF447 crash, most of the pieces of debris had been spread over a zone of 600 metres by 200 metres, at a depth of 3,900 metres. The heaviest objects had sunk vertically and the others had been only slightly deflected as they sank. Many of them were, moreover, easily identifiable and relatively well preserved. A hundred or so bodies also remained in the wreck. Quite clearly, there was very little likelihood that the two black boxes of MH370 were several kilometres away from each other on the ocean bed. In short, Nargeolet reached the conclusion that the whole business was 'a complete and utter shambles'.

And yet CNN, perhaps intoxicated by the rapture of the deep, kept serving up its Australian pings 24/7, ignoring the messages of warning and caution it was receiving from the few people who really knew what they were talking about. But don't ever let the truth get in the way of a good story.

William Meacham, a former archaeology professor who was close to the Institute of Marine Science at Hong Kong University, was taking a close interest in the search. He also tried to warn CNN that the channel was making a big mistake in suggesting that the Australian pings could come from the MH370 black boxes. He drew up a list of the marine creatures carrying pingers that could well be inside the search zone: he found a total of 86 loggerhead sea turtles, 30 flat-backed sea turtles, 30 hawksbill sea turtles, 14 green sea turtles, 7 humpbacked whales and 5 dugongs. At the time, one of William Meacham's university colleagues also mentioned a 36 kHz pinger on a great white shark that had crossed the whole Indian Ocean from South Africa to Australia's west coast. Had the Australians confused the ping of a great white shark with the ping of a black box? What a headline that would have made!

But the doubting Thomases, however professional they may have been, were overruled by the so-called experts and specialists wheeled out in quick succession by the TV channels. It is worth remembering that competition is tough in the small and extremely specialised sector of underwater operations. Everyone knew that sooner or later highly lucrative contracts were going to be signed for the next stage of the MH370 search. Even one of the leading experts in the sector, who admitted privately he had 'not met a single scientist who believes in the validity of the pings for one instant', let himself get carried away by the enthusiasm about the Australian pings when he found himself in the CNN studio. After all, stating categorically that the pings were nothing to do with the jetliner would not have been the best way to win a contract with the Australians as a consultant or operator.

The official Australian position, however, remained unshaken by all the detractors. The key message was hammered home. In a sense, the operation was just too big to fail. 'These pings are the best lead, and the only lead, we have. We must keep following it,' went the party line. So on 15 April, the autonomous submarine *Bluefin-21* was lowered into the water as planned, but the operation was quickly called off. The submarine could not go deep enough at the location where it was launched and the images it brought back were therefore useless. Never mind. It would be relaunched a little further on, in the hope that the ocean bed was not so deep close to the next ping. The show had to go on. By now, we had lost count of the number of flops.

On 19 April, Defence and Transport Minister Hishammuddin Hussein helped to keep the ping myth alive by saying in Kuala Lumpur that the next 48 hours were going to be 'crucial'. What did he mean? Crucial in what sense? But then finally, no, no, nothing more; no more pings. That meant no black boxes and no MH370 wreck.

Despite all the bluffing from the highest authorities of Australia and Malaysia, doubt was beginning to creep in. As the weeks passed by, the awe-inspiring Australian mission was threatening to become a washout after its string of flops. The search sectors kept on changing, but no clear explanation for this was given. Only a few determined and watchful observers – of whose existence I was only to become aware much later – realised what was happening and expressed their alarm.

On 24 April, the British submarine HMS *Tireless* bade farewell to Australia. Its crew were exhausted, said Commander R. Hywel Griffiths, adding: 'Overcoming some of the most inhospitable sea conditions ever experienced by my crew, we searched 7,000 square nautical miles in a 16-day period. […] I am also very proud of the professionalism and enthusiasm of my ship's company.'*

On 28 April, three weeks after the last pings were picked up, Australian Prime Minister Tony Abbott threw in the towel and brought the ping hunt to an end. He regretted the fact that nothing

* BBC News, 25 April 2014.

had been found, but called the sea search 'the most difficult in human history'. It had already been the largest search operation ever, and now it was also the most difficult. And that was official, because the prime minister said so himself. 'We focused on the best leads we had,' he assured us. (I can just picture the great white shark triggering the alarm as it passed underneath the little yellow stingray.)

He now thought it was 'highly improbable that we will find the slightest debris on the surface [...] 52 days after the crash, most of the debris would have become waterlogged and sunk'. And so Abbott announced that a new kind of search was going to begin, subcontracted out to specialised companies. The call for tenders would be issued shortly. The arrival of winter meant that the search must be put on hold. He ended with a heartfelt admission regarding the whole affair, couched in dramatic terms: 'We owe it to the troubled citizens of the wider world to do everything we can to solve this extraordinary mystery.'

The following day, Hishammuddin rammed the point home: 'The fact that we still have not found MH370 illustrates the complexity and difficulty of this search operation.' After all, it was common knowledge that when a result was not achieved, it was because the task was difficult. In just the same way, if you succeeded, it showed that the task was easy. Just another fine example of Malaysian Newspeak. When at the end of May 2014, Michael Dean, the US Navy's Deputy Director of Ocean Engineering, said on CNN that everyone now agreed that the pings did not come from the black boxes, a US Navy spokesman appeared on the same channel a few hours later to dismiss Dean's comments as 'premature and speculative'. It was as though confusion about the true nature of all these pings was supposed to last a little bit longer.

In fact, promising news still kept arriving, but at a slower pace, and it was just as misleading as ever. In mid-September 2014, the JACC announced that it had found '58 hard objects' in the course of the search. The new Malaysian Transport Minister, Liow Tiong

Lai, said that it would now be necessary 'to deploy our equipment on the ocean floor to see if these objects belong to the MH370 wreck, other wrecks or are just rocks'. Once again it was meant to 'raise hopes' of solving the now-six month-old aviation mystery.

During his trip to Perth in late October 2014, Hishammuddin echoed the surreal optimism that prevailed around the deep-sea search. He confidently asserted that, 'Based on the technology we are using and whether we are looking in the right place, then we are talking about 99.9 per cent optimistic.' Most experts would have actually agreed with the minister about this assessment, given his caveat as to 'whether we are looking in the right place'. But did the authorities for a moment consider the disastrous impact the invariably misleading announcements made since 8 March must have been having on the victims' families?

Every time I met with any of the next of kin – in Hong Kong, Kuala Lumpur, Beijing, Paris, London or Melbourne – their suffering seemed to be aggravated both by their lack of closure, given the absence of any satisfactory explanation, and – possibly even more so – by the feeling that the authorities were messing them around.

At the end of the first search phase (March–April 2014), it was time to take stock. At the start of May, a trilateral meeting was held between Australia, Malaysia and China in Canberra. Australia reported that 334 air patrols had been carried out, with a total of 3,137 hours of air reconnaissance. Ten civilian aircraft, 19 military aircraft and 14 ships had been used in the operation. The Chinese emissary said that 21 satellites had been used, 18 ships (including 8 equipped with helicopters) and 5 aircraft, which had covered a total area of 1.5 million square kilometres. China had also asked 88 Chinese-registered vessels inside the zone (68 merchant ships and 20 fishing vessels) to help with the effort. But despite everything, there was not the slightest sign of MH370 on the surface. Had something gone wrong?

Warren Truss, the Australian Minister for Infrastructure and Regional Development, then announced two simultaneous initiatives for the next phase. First, a priority search zone would be established. This task was to be completed by the end of June, after calculations had been refined or revised in the light of the Inmarsat data. Second, contracts would be awarded to private operators for underwater searches in the zone identified. He mentioned that only a handful of machines capable of this task were available worldwide, the machines being basically the same ones as previously described to me by Jean-Paul Troadec: TPL that could search strips of seabed, and autonomous submarines to explore zones where the seabed was more uneven.

Before the start of the second search phase, scheduled for August, a Chinese ship, the *Zhu Kezhen*, and a ship chartered by Australia, the *Fugro Equator*, would carry out bathymetric cartographic reconnaissance over an initial zone of 60,000 square kilometres, which was considered to be a priority by the Australian Transport Safety Bureau (ATSB). 'There is no way you can tow a high-definition sonar at the end of a cable measuring up to 9,000 metres long if you don't know the relief of the seabed,' explained Paul-Henri Nargeolet. The Dutch company Fugro was awarded the search contract. A second ship, the *Fugro Discovery*, thus joined the *Fugro Equator* in the Indian Ocean. On 21 September 2014, the Malaysian national oil company Petronas sent out its ship *Go Phoenix* (generally used for oil exploration) to join the small specialist flotilla that was scanning the seabed in search of MH370.

In the end, and to judge from the first phase of the Indian Ocean search, Australia ran Malaysia pretty close when it came to the art of bungling a search operation and providing deliberate or accidental misinformation. Whether or not the aircraft's path ended somewhere around there, the decision to ignore several fields of debris seen by satellites, the total fiasco surrounding the pings, the sudden and unexplained changes in search zones, the opportunistic switches in the official line, along with a string of totally

unfounded declarations, were not what we were expecting from
the 'real pros'.

For the few people who knew enough to analyse the episode
properly, it did not look like a scientific search worthy of the name,
conducted with the aim of finding the wreck of MH370 – much
more like a show to impress the TV audience with the incredible
efforts being made out in the ocean.

When 'the best brains in the world', using their 'technological
mastery' – in the words of the Australian prime minister at the
outset – confused pings from fishing nets or even possibly a great
white shark with pings from black boxes, the credibility of the
Australian operation was severely undermined. But with the southern winter approaching and time running out, the Australian search
operation continued unquestioned.

The relocation of the search coordination centre, the JACC, was
symbolically important. In early May, it was moved from Perth to
Canberra, 6,000 kilometres from the theatre of operations but
right next to the seat of political power. In July 2014, Angus
Houston was appointed as Australia's special envoy to Ukraine for
the investigation into the MH17 disaster. And in January 2015 he
was given a knighthood,* partly thanks to what was claimed to be
his outstanding contribution to the MH370 search operation.

From then on, in Australia as in Malaysia, it was essentially
ministers or prime ministers, and not civil aviation experts, who
expressed their views about the affair. This clearly broke the established rules in this field, which recommended that in civil aviation,
the accident investigation authority should 'have independence in
the conduct of the investigation'.† I then discovered that in
Malaysia, too, the Department of Civil Aviation had been taken off

---

* On 26 January 2015, Angus Houston was made a Knight of the Order of
Australia (AK).

† Annex 13 to the Convention on International Civil Aviation (Chicago
Convention).

the MH370 case, much to its dissatisfaction, with ministers taking over. 'When the politicians start getting involved, conflicting agendas are inevitable,' I was told by someone with considerable experience of aircraft accident investigations.

Why was the MH370 search being controlled by governments at the highest political level? Hadn't the aircraft been on a commercial flight with civilians on board? Without any official explanation being given, the case was everywhere being classified as 'sensitive'. If MH370 had just been a civil aviation accident, the experts from all the relevant organisations and companies – including Boeing and Rolls-Royce – would have been in charge. The politicians would only have been briefed on the progress of the operation and issued a statement once in a while. But with MH370, the case was in the hands of the politicians and the military. Why? Was it a different type of accident?

It was at about this time that a handful of scientists, fascinated by the remarkable scientific and mathematical enigma of the Inmarsat calculations, refused to accept the official conclusions without first having understood and then verified them. This group of volunteer experts were passionate about their subject, and they tried to make the data talk, even though it was harder to interpret than ancient hieroglyphics. Their motivation was to mitigate the suffering of the victims' families, and also to solve 'the greatest mystery in the history of aviation'.

The Inmarsat pings could only produce an end location on the basis of very substantial assumptions, mainly about the speed and altitude of MH370, for which there was no proof and barely any clues. If just one parameter was tweaked, the suggested flight path of the aircraft changed radically. And in any case, it was going to be impossible for 99.99 per cent of the general public to understand the calculations and their logic, not to mention the theorems and in some cases the statistical laws upon which they were based. But for this small group of mathematicians, astrophysicists, nuclear physicists and information technology specialists, who in many cases had some experience of piloting planes, the challenge was tremendous. They began to discuss among themselves the calculations and the search locations based on them. Initially they exchanged views on the blog of Wellington-based British astrophysicist Duncan Steel, a consultant for NASA who had written several books and dozens of articles, often with rather abstruse titles. Steel had discovered some 'secondary' stars, and one planet even bore his name. This impromptu group, consisting of 17 mostly British and American scientists, quickly became a real brains trust of the highest level. Theories were constructed, tested and debated.

American blogger and TV commentator Jeff Wise recalls that it all started with a flurry of emails. One of the contributors, who wanted to publish something on the subject, suggested the name 'Independent Group' (IG). The principle of the group was to work collectively while sharing different tasks between the members. Wise told me that some of the group's members were mind-bogglingly good when it came to crunching numbers and solving equations, while others could track down hyper-specialised data in little-known databases. Someone found a performance table from a flight manual for the Boeing 777-200ER, the same aircraft used for Flight MH370, but the forum decided not to use it as the engines were made by General Electric and not by Rolls-Royce.

I first contacted Duncan Steel at the end of 2014 to put some questions to him about the civilian and military radar map in the flight-path zone. I also wanted to tell him how unsettled I was about the reliability of Inmarsat's stunningly complicated calculations. This despotic set of pings had, I felt, imposed its version of truth on the whole world. Instead of reassuring me, Duncan Steel explained that the calculations were in fact much more complex than I had originally thought. First, because the inclination of the Inmarsat 3F-1 satellite, which oscillates around the equator, had been greater than normal for some time because the satellite was nearing the end of its lifespan and was thus beginning to run out of the fuel used to stabilise it.*†

The second reason for the mathematical complexity was because Inmarsat, which began its activities with ground bases only in the northern hemisphere, had never taken the trouble to update the satellite's software, which was not designed to calculate the position of the ground base in Perth at negative latitude (32°S). But, Steel added, he was satisfied that 'everything was taken into account with a sufficient degree of precision'.

Linked to this group, without being a member, was the Canadian Brock McEwen, who highlighted the flawed logic of the Australian operations. He relentlessly challenged the Australian Transport Safety Bureau about the lack of consistency in their explanations when the search zones were changed, as for example on 28 March, when the search was suddenly moved 1,100 kilometres north-east of the zone previously being explored. In January 2015, he published his analysis, *MH370: Time to Investigate the Investigators*, with its telling subtitle, *An unflinching, scientific critique of key search decisions, April–November 2014*,‡ in which he focused on all the illogical and inconsistent decisions taken during the Australian search operation.

Together, the scientists made a powerful counter-appraisal of the analyses set out by the official experts. They demanded all the raw Inmarsat data, which to date they had not obtained. They noted errors and suggested corrective actions to the official team. And in the end, people started listening to what they had to say. After a

---

* In addition to its two wings covered with solar panels, the satellite had small motors for stabilisation purposes; when the satellite initially deployed, it was provided with reserves of fuel and combustive gas.

† Combustive gas is a chemical substance used in the fuel combustion process. For space missions, rocket engines are supplied with fuel and combustive gas.

‡ See the whole document at drive.google.com/file/d/0B-r3yuaF2p72L W04dlJnQXQ4cTQ/view.

few months, the underwater search zone was moved – under Australian command – to bring it into line with their recommendations. But yet again, nothing was found.

'The absence of proof is not proof of absence,' Duncan Steel told me. What he meant was that just because no debris – and no plane – had been found, did not mean there was no debris or that the wreck was not on the ocean bed. But Jeff Wise took the opposite view: if, after a year of searching, the aircraft had not been found, it was possibly because the aircraft simply was not there. Wise published a book online entitled *The Plane That Wasn't There.** Based on the principle that some of the Inmarsat data was simply misleading, he suggested a scenario involving the hijacking of the plane by the two Ukrainian passengers to Kazakhstan, where he identified, using satellite images, an underground hangar in which the plane could have been hidden. Following the publication of his theory, Wise was excluded from the Independent Group, given their rule of sticking strictly to the available scientific data, but despite this the main blog for those fascinated by the disappearance was now Wise's website. This followed Duncan Steel's decision to close his own blog, after losing patience with the extreme and sometimes crazy theories of some contributors.

As scientists know, nature abhors a vacuum. With no tangible evidence or debris to support the idea that the MH370 crashed in the southern Indian Ocean, many theories emerged – from the most intriguing to the most unlikely – both on the web and in everyday conversations.

---

* Jeff Wise, *The Plane That Wasn't There: Why We Haven't Found MH370*, Kindle ebook, February 2015. See also www.jeffwise.net.

5

Alternative Scenarios

In the absence of any coherent explanation of what might have happened aboard Flight MH370 after it went missing, it did not take long for a host of theories to emerge.

Thousands of people all over the world – let's call them 'MHists' – became literally obsessed with this mystery. Naturally, they fell into several categories: the savants, the amateurs, the moderates ... not to mention the cranks, the radicals and the monomaniacs. I even heard of one American lawyer who had spent years hunting for the Lost Ark but then redirected all his energy, determination and, I suspect, some of his savings to the search for Flight MH370.

Other MHists were convinced the plane had been captured by aliens from outer space; one of this group informed me that the plane would be back 'in six months'. A website specialising in the astrological analysis of crimes (astrologyincrime.com) posted the astrological chart of Flight MH370. Here we saw: 'Natal Uranus/ Neptune = transiting Mercury (yellow) at 20° Aquarius – *mind playing tricks; common sense required*'. Little did the stars know how close they were to the truth! Numerologists, too, had their go. Some noted that the name of the flight consisted of the 13th (M) and 8th (H) letters of the alphabet. This gave 13 + 8 = 21. As the plane model was a 'triple 7' or 3 × 7 = 21, like 370, the writing was clearly on the wall.

The MHist movement knew no rules or borders, and the motivations of its members differed. For some, such as the scientists of the Independent Group, solving the fuzzy maths of the Inmarsat data proved to be one of the greatest intellectual challenges they had ever faced. For others, an accident that had so far eluded rational explanation was a prime target for projecting convictions, pointing fingers and blaming the usual scapegoats.

But for many people, myself included, the motivation was merely to reject the absurdity of the official version, which was not only utterly anachronistic given the high-tech era in which we live, but also contrary to common sense and inconsistent with the lessons learnt from past aircraft accidents. In short, the point was to reject what I viewed as an insult to human intelligence.

Among those who had dared challenge the official narrative concerning the disappearance, by far the most authoritative, the most qualified and the least political was Sir Tim Clark, President of Emirates Airline, the company with the world's largest fleet of Boeing 777s. He expressed his frustration in a lengthy interview conducted by the German journalist Andreas Spaeth in October 2014 and published in *Der Spiegel.* 'There hasn't been one overwater incident in the history of civil aviation, apart from Amelia Earhart in 1939,* that has not been at least five or ten per cent trackable,' said Clark. 'This one has disappeared. So for me that raises a degree of suspicion, and I'm totally dissatisfied with what has been coming out of all of this.' He noted further, 'When you press questions on this, I sense a degree of belligerence; the more belligerent people become, the more worried I become.'

According to the official narrative, the flight was diverted from its route as a result of 'deliberate action by someone on the plane'. Was the aim simply to prevent it from reaching Beijing? Or was the

---

* Amelia Earhart was an aviation pioneer. She disappeared, along with navigator Fred Noonan, when their plane – a Lockheed Model 10E Electra – crashed between Papua New Guinea and Howard Island during an attempt to circumnavigate the globe in 1937.

goal actually to make MH370 vanish? If the point was to ensure the flight would not land in Beijing, was it because of someone on board? Or something in the cargo hold?

In the course of my investigation over the ensuing months and years, I came across various strange pieces of information that supported both of these possibilities – that is, persons of interest on board and unusual items carried in cargo.

A rather elaborate rumour concerning possible persons of interest among the passengers gained traction in Kuala Lumpur and on the internet. It was such a juicy story – so ready to become a tremendous blockbuster – that it caught my attention. All a screenwriter would need to do would be to transform its murky and tragic *dénouement* into a happy ending of his or her choosing, and bingo! The film would be an instant hit …

Freescale Semiconductor: the James Bond scenario

The aircraft's 227 passengers included a group of 20 people (12 Malaysians and 8 Chinese) all employed by the same company. It was not just any company. This was Freescale Semiconductor (now called NXP). Although little known to the general public, Freescale was a huge US multinational electronics corporation in the vanguard of the semiconductor industry, whose operations spanned some 20 countries, including China, Malaysia and France. Freescale Semiconductor was relatively well known in Malaysia, where its logo was displayed on motorway billboards on the road to the airport. Since 1972, it occupied an eight-hectare site in a suburb of Kuala Lumpur, home to a semiconductor manufacturing plant and a test laboratory.

Freescale Semiconductor was the world's leading manufacturer of microprocessors for several sectors of industry, including defence and aerospace. The company made chips for radars and microcontrollers for missiles, and it boasted expertise in radiofrequency power products and battlefield communications. According to information from its website, the company's products were designed for applications in aeronautics, radar, electronic warfare, missile guidance systems and identification friend or foe systems. An executive with ST (STMicroelectronics), a Freescale competitor, told me, 'For most major manufacturers of these systems, Freescale is the go-to supplier.' In 2006, Freescale Semiconductor was bought out for nearly US$18 billion by a financial consortium led by the Blackstone Group and the Carlyle Group. The purchase was the largest private buyout of a technology company at the time.*

Blackstone and Carlyle were tentacular empires with interests across the globe. It would be difficult to imagine being any closer to the heart of the American military–industrial complex. The Carlyle Group was widely known to be chummy with the Bush clan and to have clients such as the Saudi Binladin Group, the business owned by the prominent Saudi Arabian family of the same name. The Blackstone Group was founded in 1985 by two former Lehman Brothers executives and emerged as one of today's leading private equity firms, headquartered on Park Avenue in Manhattan. At the end of 2015, Blackstone Group had a portfolio of US$334 billion in assets under management. Thus, Freescale Semiconductor placed us at the nexus of Wall Street (New York), the Pentagon (Washington, DC) and Austin (Texas), the birthplace of the company. This was money, political power and strategic technology all rolled into one, at the very highest level.

As it happened, Freescale Semiconductor filed a patent for a new manufacturing technology on 11 March 2014, three days after the plane went missing. The invention can be found online under the patent reference U.S. 8671381.

Shortly after the plane's disappearance, Mitch Haws, Vice President, Global Communications and Investor Relations at

---

* Then in March 2015, NXP, market leader in secure microcontrollers, acquired Freescale Semiconductor for US$11.8 billion.

Freescale Semiconductor, told the press that the 20 Freescale employees on Flight MH370, 'were people with a lot of experience and technical background and they were very important people. [...] It's definitely a loss for the company.' He further noted that they were 'mostly engineers and other experts working to make the company's chip facilities in Tianjin, China, and Kuala Lumpur more efficient'.* All were travelling in economy class. In January 2015, I met with Yuen Ying, the wife of one of the Malaysian engineers employed by Freescale. He had decided to leave on the evening of 7 March 'to have time to visit Beijing'. The Chinese co-workers had come to Freescale's facility in Malaysia the week before, and now it was the Malaysians' turn to spend a few days at the Freescale plant in Tianjin, China.

These were the facts. They were easily verifiable and within the realm of reality. The incredible rumour going viral on the internet, however, tipped the balance sharply towards a blockbuster scenario.

From the internet, I discovered that the group of 20 Freescale employees on board supposedly included four co-owners of a patent of great strategic and technological importance that was due to be filed any day. If anything were to have happened to the four co-owners (each of whom held a 20 per cent share), the full ownership of the patent would fall to the remaining co-owner, namely Freescale Semiconductor. The internet and its discussion forums were rife with claims that the plane had been spirited away and annihilated to secure American control of a patent of utmost strategic importance. The theory was even picked up by Russia's government-funded broadcasting network, Russia Today. Of course, there were undoubtedly better yardsticks of credibility, but what did it matter? It was a terrific story.

It did, nevertheless, suffer three major weaknesses. First, employees who introduce a patentable invention never obtain co-ownership of the patent. And so at Freescale Semiconductor, as

* Reuters, 9 March 2014.

at every other major corporation, all patented inventions systematically become the full property of the company that developed them. As such, before even examining any of the other details, the very basis for this scenario lacked plausibility. Second, none of the inventors' names shown on the patent matched the names of any of the Chinese passengers listed on the manifest of Flight MH370. Finally, there was really nothing revolutionary about patent U.S. 8671381; it concerned the optimisation of the number of dies that could be fabricated on a wafer.* This invention might cut overall manufacturing costs by 3 to 4 per cent, at most. That was certainly not enough to justify getting rid of 239 people.

So it was back to square one. Whatever happened had never been intended to give Freescale Semiconductor full control of a revolutionary patent. The whole story was a scam. Yet to dismiss the ludicrous patent theory should not also entail the dismissal of the 20 people on board from Freescale.

The cargo: rotten fruit

Might the reason for the plane's disappearance have been hidden in the cargo holds of MH370? The plane's load could be roughly broken down as follows: the passengers and crew weighed approximately 17 tonnes and their luggage 3 tonnes. The cargo stored in the holds weighed 10 tonnes and the fuel for the flight 50 tonnes.† When I met with Malaysia's political opposition leader Anwar Ibrahim about 10 days after the loss of all contact with the plane, he felt it was 'quite simply outrageous' that the plane's cargo mani-

---

* Wafers are round slices of silicon that serve as the substrate for the fabrication of dies, which are square, explaining why optimisation would be useful.

† Page 102 of the report entitled *Factual Information: Safety Investigation for MH370*, by the Malaysian ICAO, Annex 13, Safety Investigation Team for MH370, updated 15 April 2015.

fest had yet to be made public, something about which everyone in the airline industry agreed. The document could have been made public within minutes of the plane going missing. 'I wonder what kind of cargo could be so secret that the cargo manifest of a commercial flight is treated like a classified document,' said Anwar. When Flight MH17 went down four months later, Malaysia Airlines supplied the cargo manifest two days after the crash. But for MH370, it took the airline nearly two months to produce it.

When the document was finally published on 1 May 2014, it was obviously incomplete. The official website dedicated to Flight MH370 (mh370.gov.my) showed eight PDF files numbered 1 to 9, untitled and in no apparent order. Not only was 'doc3' missing, but 'doc7' and 'doc8' were identical. The documents on the website were a series of poor-quality scans: air waybills, of course, invoices and lots of scanned blank pages.

What immediately struck the Malaysians was the enormous quantity of mangosteens listed on the cargo manifest. This fruit, consisting of a thick purple rind that stains more than blood, which protects a juicy, slightly tangy and somewhat fibrous white pulp, is widely considered to be one of the most delicious tropical fruits in the world. The fruit allegedly came from Muar in Johor State south of Kuala Lumpur. Flight MH370 was carrying 4,566 kilograms of them. Four and a half tonnes, equivalent to the world's largest hippopotamus carrying its offspring on its back! This quantity seems even more staggering given that it was not even mangosteen season. It is well known in Malaysia that the fruit ripens between June and August, something confirmed by botany reference books. There is in fact a brief second fruiting season for mangosteens between November and January. However, fruit to be exported must always be picked before it is ripe. In other words, March is well past the harvest date for mangosteens. Moreover, when word of this cargo got out, the Federal Agricultural Marketing Authority (FAMA) declared that there were no mangosteen trees in Johor State likely to bear fruit in that season. The local media added to the confusion by pointing out that Muar, the town listed on the manifest as the place of origin, did not even have any mangosteen orchards.

In response to mounting questions and suspicions, Tan Sri Khalid Abu Bakar Tan, Malaysia's Inspector-General of Police, clarified that the fruit had not *come* from Muar but had merely been *packaged* there. But in that case, where could such an industrial quantity of off-season mangosteens have possibly originated, and why send it to the small town of Muar, 100 kilometres from Kuala Lumpur, if the crop was intended for China? In fact, the fruit is so endemic to Asia's tropical regions that, according to legend, Queen Victoria promised to give a hundred pounds sterling or bestow a knighthood upon anyone who could bring her a few perfect specimens. Fruit growers explained that even at the peak of the season, mangosteen yields had declined in recent years; the trees were not responding well to climate change. Further, FAMA maintained that China imported 'mainly durians' from Malaysia. As for the Muar-based company mentioned on the Malaysia Airlines air waybill, it did not even appear on the official list of mangosteen exporters. One final sticking point: to import this fruit, China required 'a five-page form, the same as the one needed for durians'. This phytosanitary certificate was not mentioned anywhere on the air waybills for the goods carried in the hold.

The cargo of mangosteens therefore seemed about as probable as a monsoon rain in the dry season. Logic notwithstanding, the investigation report published a year after the plane's disappearance ignored this anomaly and stated: 'The mangosteen fruit on board MH370 [...] originated from Poh Seng Kian [...] Muar, Johor, Malaysia. About 2,500 kilograms of the fruit was harvested from Muar and the rest from Sumatra, Indonesia.'* In other words, the press, the police and the agriculture authorities concurred in March 2014 that the mangosteens could not possibly have come

* Ibid., p. 107.

from Muar. But in March 2015, the official report claimed that 2.5 of the 4.5 tonnes of this cargo had in fact originated in Muar. *Malaysia Boleh!*

Each new page of the investigation report added more weirdness to the mystery. It was revealed that between 3 March and 17 April 2014, Malaysia Airlines transported not one isolated cargo of off-season 'fresh mangosteens' to Beijing without a permit and from a dubious originating source, but around 50 additional cargos of mangosteens.* I eventually reached the conclusion that, like the fake passports of the Iranian passengers, there may indeed have been something shady going on but it was not out of the ordinary; dozens of other Malaysia Airlines flights were carrying 'off-season mangosteens' as well, yet nothing prevented those flights from reaching their destination. In December 2015, I attended a press conference at Hong Kong University on the trafficking of ivory and wild animals in Asia. One of the slides showed the region's various hubs for this illegal trade, and Kuala Lumpur International Airport was by far the biggest circle on the whole map. Could it have been that the 'fresh mangosteens' were merely a cover for cargos of pangolin scales, elephant tusks or rhinoceros horns? This interpretation would explain away most of the anomalies relating to that part of the cargo, at least. Years later, the 'final report'† reiterated that MH370 was carrying mangosteens to China. Contrary to speculations that the fruits were out of season, it was found to be in season in Muar, Johore and neighbouring countries. And the report even said that 'at the time of writing of this report the fruits are still being exported by the same company to Beijing, China'. I also had access to the statement of the owner of Poh Seng Kian Company in Muar recorded by the Malaysian police. In it, the

---

* Ibid., Appendix 1.18J, p. 580.

† *Safety Investigation Report MH370*: Malaysia Airlines Boeing 777-200 ER (9M-MRO), 8 March 2014, by The Malaysian ICAO Annex 13 Safety Investigation Team for MH370, issued on 2 July 2018.

man, described as a 'fruit seller since 1985', insisted that the exported fruits were from his own orchard and also from other suppliers around Muar, Tanah Merah, Raub and Taiping. With so many contradicting clues, I see no other option but to let the mangosteens mystery endure and blame some very muddled cargo documents as well as climate change for the confusion.

The other cargo: 2.5 tonnes of electronics, including 221 kg of lithium-ion batteries

In addition to the 4.5 tonnes of 'mangosteens' that probably originated in Africa, Flight MH370 was carrying a consolidated consignment of more than 2,453 kilograms of 'lithium-ion batteries, walkie-talkie accessories & chargers [sic]'. The shipper was Motorola, with NNR Global Logistics as the forwarding agent. The air waybill stipulated explicitly that the items in this parcel had to be handled with care due to their flammability hazard, particularly in the case of damaged packaging. After asserting on 17 March 2014 that the aircraft was not carrying any dangerous goods, Malaysia Airlines CEO Ahmad Jauhari Yahya acknowledged a week later that the plane was in fact carrying 'about 200 kilograms of lithium batteries', although he did stress that they were 'properly packaged'.

Lithium batteries had been known to cause fires in planes, electric cars and even inside computers. In at least two cargo flights, the fires resulted in the loss of the crew and the aircraft.* In fact, in the case of MH370, the scenarios involving a crash triggered by a technical fault almost always started with a fire in the hold or a serious short-circuit. The main stages envisaged were as follows: a fire cut out all means of communication; a decision was made to make an emergency landing, which explained the U-turn to the

---

* See the UPS6 case in the Addendum, p. 406.

nearest or the most appropriate airport; depressurisation of the plane occurred; the pilots and all others on board suffered hypoxia – a condition in which the body or part of the body is deprived of adequate oxygen supply – quickly followed by hypothermia; then the phantom flight continued on autopilot until it crashed because of lack of fuel.

'For me, it all starts with a fire in the E/E bay [electrical and electronic compartment] that destroyed critical computers and affected the systems including the communications. A lot of smoke filters in the cabins, through the trapdoor located on the floor between the cockpit and the business class or first-class cabin,' explained Kim Stuart, a Boeing pilot for the last 35 years whom I often consulted about the case. Because the E/E bay was the vault for all the aircraft computers, the consequences of a fire in there could not be overstated. This would have led to multiple messages and warnings to deal with for the pilots, which, according to Kim, could mean them missing the warning regarding the slow depressurisation going on at the same time. 'Messages are not prioritised,' Kim told me. But sooner or later, the cabin crew would have notified the pilots of the smoke in the cabin. 'Their response, as would be my immediate response, would be to press the "heading select" button that disengages the navigation from the auto-pilot, and aim for the nearest landing strip, unless they thought they could get back to Kuala Lumpur.' Every pilot knew the correct sequence to be followed, contained in the rule 'Aviate, navigate, communicate'. But such a crisis would unfold in a matter of minutes and very quickly reach the point of no-return. 'The longest survival from detection to write-off is only 18 minutes in the air. A fire on-board is the most gut-wrenching experience I can think of,' Kim said

To my surprise, Kim told me there was no alarm for smoke in either the cockpit or the cabin. 'There are fire alarms for certain things: there is a heat detector on the engines and there are smoke detectors in the hold, but in the case that smoke appears in the cabin or the cockpit, there are only two ways to detect it: smell or vision.' What about at night and what if you had a cold? I asked. He assured me that pilots and crew would notice. 'At night, smoke would interfere with the lights. And, for many reasons, pilots are not supposed to be flying with a cold, including the fact that in a depressurisation system it would rip your sinuses apart.' In any case, due to the airflow in a plane – from front to back – the cockpit was usually the last place to be engulfed with smoke.

In MH370's case, according to Kim's scenario, a fire in the E/E bay would have destroyed multiple computers, leaving the pilots to deal with multiple system-failure messages while remaining unaware that the outflow pressurisation valves had opened. Although the induced absence of oxygen as well as the outside temperature at 35,000 feet (around –40°C) would most likely have smothered the fire, the real danger would be the depressurisation. The cabin's pressure, normally maintained at a level of around 4,500 feet, could rise at a rate of around 11,500 feet per minute, meaning that in just over two minutes it may already have reached a pressure equivalent to the summit of Mount Everest, where breathing is very difficult without supplementary oxygen, even for altitude-acclimatised mountaineers.

Of course, providing the system worked, when the cabin pressure reached the equivalent of 13,500 feet, oxygen masks would fall automatically for passengers and cabin crew, although the flow of oxygen only lasted for 20 to 30 minutes. In the cockpit, however, nothing would trigger the pilots' masks. The pilots would have to decide if and when they needed oxygen, and grab their masks manually. That's why, for the passengers and crew's survival, as soon as a depressurisation was identified it was crucial for the plane to rapidly descend to an altitude where the air was 'comfortably' breathable (generally around 14,000 feet) and the temperature less extreme.

As this manoeuvre of immediate descent had apparently not been executed by MH370, the supporters of this scenario concluded that the pilots did not understand the situation and lost consciousness shortly after setting the plane on its new course with the U-turn. 'You only get a few seconds to realise you lack oxygen. A depressurisation sucks the air out of the plane and out of your body faster than you realise. It is very quickly too late,' Kim said. He then told me of a friend of his, a senior steward with Philippine Airlines, who once had his own children on board when a rapid depressurisation happened. Instinctively – and quite ignoring the rules – he turned around to attend to his children. He could not even make one step in their direction before he collapsed. 'When they tell you during the safety briefing, "In case of depressurisation put your mask on before attending to the child next to you," it's because if you do the child first, you most likely won't be able to do your own.'

Depressurised and set on autopilot to return to Kuala Lumpur or another nearby airport, MH370 would have quite simply continued to fly in the same direction beyond its destination, as in the tragic case of Helios Airways Flight 522 (see p. 405), until its engines flamed out because of fuel starvation. In the cabin, some passengers would have guessed the seriousness of the situation and put their oxygen masks on. Those who were fast asleep would have missed the smoke in the cabin and the masks' fall and swiftly gone from sleep to hypoxia. Besides the lack of oxygen, the extreme cold would have quickly placed everyone on board in hypothermia. At –40 degrees Celsius, whether you're wearing a coat or not is basically irrelevant.

Almost six years after MH370's disappearance, Kim believed that the absence of any field of debris with significant parts of the wreckage, bags, clothes, seats and other detritus indicated that the plane ended up gliding down and ditched in an almost flat patch of the southern Indian Ocean. On contact, the hull would have lost some appendages (the wings, tail and other parts) and slowly taken on water. Eventually, the plane would have sunk, more or less in one piece, burying both the 239 people on board and the mystery of its fate 20,000 feet under the sea.

As several cases of fires on board aircraft have shown, a fire in the hold could cause a breach in the fuselage, which would depressurise the cabin even faster. If, as with the fatal UPS Airlines Flight 6 (see Addendum, p. 406), a lithium-battery fire broke out in the hold (in MH370's case caused by one of the batteries in the 221 kg batch), the fire would have been very violent indeed and extremely difficult to put out. Conventional extinguishers are not very effective against such fires. The authorities recommend using water if possible to put out a fire caused by a lithium-ion type battery, but if the fire comes from a lithium-metal battery, the contact of water with the lithium-metal will make the fire worse.

In the months and years after MH370's disappearance, I noticed an increase in articles and scientific papers about how dangerous it actually was to transport lithium batteries by air, and, more specifically, in the hold of a passenger aircraft. In its 15 December 2015 newsletter, the Air Line Pilots Association (ALPA) explained the hazards involved:

> These batteries are particularly dangerous because of their unique characteristics. One flawed battery in a box can start a chain reaction that will ignite the entire load. In addition to burning incredibly hot, FAA testing has found that these batteries generate thick smoke than can fill an entire plane, including the cockpit, in less than 8 minutes after ignition. The gases released during a lithium battery fire are also flammable and can result in explosions.

This association was astounded by the number of airlines that had recently decided to ban the transport of hoverboards, a new type of skateboard with a motor powered by a lithium battery, but continued to allow lithium batteries in the holds of their aircraft. ALPA has launched an appeal for measures to be taken to ban lithium batteries on all aircraft. 'Passenger airlines have recognised the grave dangers posed by just one lithium battery,' it warned.

'Imagine the incredible threat a pallet-full or an entire cargo compartment of these batteries can pose.'

The issue of transporting lithium batteries was included on the agenda at the September 2015 conference of the International Civil Aviation Organization (ICAO) in Bangkok. Some MHists read this as a sign that international civil aviation authorities knew perhaps more than they were letting on about the real cause of the loss of MH370. If the authorities were indeed aware that a fire caused by lithium batteries was behind the aircraft's catastrophic loss, then it's easy to understand the urgency with which they tried to impose measures so that such a scenario would not be repeated.

Boarding a Los Angeles to Hong Kong flight in January 2016, I was asked for the first time ever by ground staff – in this case from Cathay Pacific – how many lithium batteries were in my luggage (camera, telephone, laptop, toothbrush, remote controls and so on), and they reminded me that a certain number of gadgets with large lithium batteries were now totally banned in both hand and checked-in luggage. This kind of screening has now become common practice.

What was especially amazing in the MH370 case was that the batteries were part of a much larger Motorola cargo, of which very few details were given. 'All the freight carriers use this trick,' a Hong Kong forwarder told me. 'They make a consolidated consignment with a general description, especially at the last minute.' For the sake of comparison, another parcel in the hold weighing only six kilograms was accompanied by half a dozen documents, including the invoice.* This parcel was known to have contained 2,000 microchips with a unit price of US$5.04. In a similar vein, documents accompanying a shipment of children's books showed every single title: *Who Stole Mona Lisa?*, *The Secret of Whale Island* and others. When compared with the level of detail provided for some of the other parcels, it seemed all the more aberrant that virtually

---

* Sent by Freescale Malaysia to Freescale China.

no information was given about the large Motorola shipment – the only consignment containing potentially dangerous goods. What could possibly be deemed as gross negligence on the part of Malaysia Airlines became the basis for the theory of a fire on board the aircraft.

Compared with the four and a half tonnes of out of season mangosteens, the two and a half tonnes of very vaguely documented Motorola electronic equipment, including 221 kilos of lithium batteries, were equally, if not more problematic. For some MHists, the vagueness surrounding the two largest cargo consignments was proof that the aircraft was carrying 'something else'. Something that was not supposed to reach China.

Some believed the mysterious cargo was the remains of an American drone downed in Pakistan. Others claimed it to be military equipment captured by the Taliban during a particularly deadly ambush that was known to have taken place in late February 2014 in eastern Afghanistan. Some smugglers would have sold it to China. Each new theory latched on to a few verifiable details gleaned from the news, and these serve to anchor the whole scenario in reality.

Another alternative theory linked the disappearance of Flight MH370 with the suspicious death of two former US Navy SEALs serving as ship's guards on the container ship *Maersk Alabama** when it docked at Port Victoria in the Seychelles† on 18 February 2014. This element of fact – a very peculiar incident that raised questions of its own – inspired one MHist to imagine that the two men had in fact been drugged by local prostitutes to enable Somali pirates to get their hands on an entire set of American drones

---

* The *Maersk Alabama* is the ship that had been hijacked in 2009, an episode later turned into the Oscar-nominated movie *Captain Phillips*, starring Tom Hanks.

† 'Hired to fight pirates but doomed by boredom', *The New York Times*, 23 February 2015.

from the ship's hold. The Somali pirates then transported their loot to Kuala Lumpur, where the Chinese embassy acquired it and stepped in to deliver the goods to Malaysia Airlines. And here we had yet another well-crafted scenario, partly based on documented facts.

Actually, there were many variations on the theme of China's voracious appetite for any kind of classified American surveillance or stealth technology swirling around the internet. And whatever the exact nature of the Western secrets so coveted by China and covertly transported to Beijing in a civilian airplane, the Americans learnt about the plots too late to stop the precious cargo from being loaded onto MH370, forcing them to hijack or destroy the plane to prevent the flight from reaching its destination.

The most seductive aspect of this line of imagined scenarios was that it explained why both China and the United States would have an interest in keeping quiet and covering up the incident: the United States because its actions were utterly despicable (sacrificing 239 lives for the sake of military secrets), and China because it was caught red-handed in a blatant attempt at spying or stealing US technology, which would be nothing to brag about either. The silence of both countries in this whole unsavoury business was one of its few recognised facts.

Enter 'Diego Garcia'

To me, pronounced as you heard it said around town, with six syllables, a rolled 'r' and a hint of a Spanish accent – *Di-e-go-Gar-ci-a* – the name of this 16th-century explorer was more evocative of *Pirates of the Caribbean* than of the vanished Boeing jet. I eventually figured out that, although it was formally a British territory, the name referred to a vast top-secret American military base located mid-way between Africa and Indonesia, due south of India, just below the equator. The base had been used as a launch pad and rear operating base for the major US military operations of recent years. Since 2001, there were suspicions that it was also being used as a military interrogation site and secret prison.* Like Freescale Semiconductor and Inmarsat, until Flight MH370 went missing, few people had ever heard of the existence or purpose of Diego Garcia. Yet according to the strategic analyst John E. Pike, director of the research consultancy GlobalSecurity.org, Diego Garcia was nothing short of 'one of the United States' most important military facilities'. Separately, I was told by a French intelligence source that nuclear warheads were stored there. It was the headquarters of US Central Command (CentCom), which was responsible for the entire central area of the globe spanning Europe, the Middle East, Afghanistan and Pakistan. 'We can no longer do without it,' added Tim Brown, a senior fellow at GlobalSecurity.org. Pike went on to confirm, 'It is from here that all the strikes have been launched [by drone] in the region.'

Since the Diego Garcia base became part of the backdrop to the disappearance of Flight MH370, it had been given several different roles, from victim of an attempted terrorist attack and perpetrator of the capture of civilian hostages, to theft and concealment of a Boeing 777.

Some people considered that Diego Garcia was the target for the hijackers who allegedly took control of MH370. In this scenario, the aircraft was believed to have been shot down by the US Air Force to defend the military base. This, moreover, became the version that some intelligence agencies leaked to people investigating the case. Others presented Diego Garcia as an accomplice to the diversion of the plane arranged by the United States to prevent it from reaching Beijing. In this scenario, the base served as a hiding place for the aircraft. For those convinced that Diego Garcia was part of the story, accounts of a low-flying plane on the morning of 8 March by Maldives islanders offered further 'evidence' that this

---

* 'U.S. used UK isle for interrogations', *Time* magazine, 31 July 2008.

was the angle to explore. One more reason to keep Diego Garcia in mind was provided with the compliments of the FBI, who helped analyse 'recently deleted data' from the pilot's confiscated home flight simulator. According to leaks by the Malaysian police, Captain Zaharie Ahmad Shah allegedly practised landing a plane on five runways on islands in the Indian Ocean – including the three-kilometre-long landing strip on the Diego Garcia atoll. This aroused further suspicion as to his intentions.

In the prevailing confusion of the early weeks, one rumour spread like wildfire among the most credulous of the MHists. It told of a call for help sent via text message by Philip Wood, the only adult American passenger on board.

> I have been held hostage by unknown military personal [*sic*] after my flight was hijacked (blindfolded). I work for IBM and I have managed to hide my cellphone in my ass during the hijack. I have been separated from the rest of the passengers and I am in a cell. My name is Philip Wood. I think I have been drugged as well and cannot think clearly.

Websites that disseminated this hoax added that the text message metadata 'confirm 100 per cent' that the message had been sent from a building located in the southern part of the Diego Garcia atoll. Yet my 17-year-old nephew Nathan, who studied computer science, told me, 'Changing the metadata of a photo is a cinch for anybody who knows how to do it. Let's say it may take five minutes the first time you do it.'

Nevertheless, the story of the text message had been read and commented upon by millions of people. And although this fake text message topped the list of the most far-fetched and widely believed tales spawned by the disappearance of Flight MH370, it could be credited with drawing attention to an island that was deliberately shrouded in secrecy and was anything but innocuous.

Approaching Diego Garcia without a permit was strictly prohibited. Permission had to be requested from London, because the island belonged to Britain and was leased to the United States. During my investigation in the Maldives, the inhabited archipelago located closest to Diego Garcia, a senior Maldivian civil servant with whom I discussed his discreet southern neighbours commented, 'Even though they are only 350 nautical miles south of the Maldives, we have no contact with them. No air service. They often fly over us. But we are not allowed to overfly them. They don't even call on us for supplies. I think they get everything from Singapore or the Middle East.'

Actually, if this base had been involved either actively or in some defensive role in the foul play suspected in the disappearance of MH370, it would have easily fitted into the shameful tradition that had haunted the island since the mid-1960s. *Stealing a Nation*, a 2004 documentary by John Pilger, covered the sordid dealings over the island between the British and American governments. Their scheme led to the expulsion of the 2,000 indigenous residents of an island paradise, the Chagos archipelago, inhabited since the late 18th century. Among their other disgraceful acts, these two governments told the United Nations that the island had no indigenous peoples, 'just imported labour'. Between 1967 and 1973, all native Chagossians were deported like livestock, *manu militari*, and dumped on Mauritius, where they had been trying to survive ever since, living in utter poverty, despairing and homesick for their confiscated island. As for the Americans, to circumvent the need for Congressional approval of the £5 million agreed as payment for the use of Diego Garcia for 50 years,* the debt was disguised as a discount on an invoice for a missile delivery. The money trail between Washington and London remained totally invisible.

---

* The initial agreement remained in force until 2016, with the possibility of extending the lease for an additional 20 years.

Half a century after the Chagossians were forced into exile, their miserable fate enjoyed a brief day in the sun when human rights lawyer Amal Clooney helped to defend their cause before the UK Supreme Court. Then in May 2019, the UK suffered a stunning rebuke when the United Nations General Assembly adopted a resolution affirming that the Chagos archipelago 'forms an integral part of the territory of Mauritius'. It requested that the UK 'withdraw its colonial administration … unconditionally within a period of no more than six months'. During the debate, the Mauritian prime minister described the expulsion of the Chagossians as 'akin to a crime against humanity'. Yet even with the best lawyers in the world, what were the chances of this small island community that had been forcibly pushed into exile, and reduced to poverty and despair, ever recovering its confiscated lands, now that their island had become a huge American military base? Despite the historic judgement, the UK government ignored the UN deadline of November 2019, as if it had never existed. 'This resolution will not change the situation overnight, but it will surely allow the Chagossians to be able to return home, one day,' commented human rights lawyer and war crimes specialist Philippe Sands, QC, who acted as counsel for Mauritius on the case.

Since 1987, the base had also been home to a space surveillance station. The GEODSS* system possessed the capability to 'track or observe objects in space that are the size of a basketball at a distance between 5,500 and 37,000 kilometres from Earth'. A Boeing 777 therefore flew much too close to the ground to be detected by the GEODSS telescopes. One might be forgiven for thinking, however, that on a military base where telescopes had the capability to see a basketball 37,000 kilometres above the earth's surface, other equipment – radar, satellites, surveillance planes – should certainly be able to pick up a large Boeing 777 stuffed with electronics, the size of two blue whales placed end

---

* Ground-based Electro-Optical Deep Space Surveillance.

to end, which flew just 2,500 kilometres away at a presumed altitude of 35,000 feet, especially given that Diego Garcia was initially designed as a US Naval Communication Station and became a Naval Computer and Telecommunication Station (NCTS) in 1991. The base was also equipped with a very long-range over-the-horizon radar. Yet Diego Garcia saw nothing, heard nothing, said nothing. Nor did any of the other major US military bases in the region, such as Okinawa (Japan) and Guam – not to mention Singapore, considered by some to be an annex of the US Army.

MHists who were convinced that the plane had been diverted to Diego Garcia went so far as to explain that some of the vessels searching for the wreckage in the Indian Ocean stopped at Diego Garcia to pick up parts of the MH370 plane, which they were then to ditch into the ocean in the search area in order for them to be 'found' later on. And sure enough, various ship-tracking websites (analogous to sites that tracked planes, such as Flightradar24) told us that the British frigate HMS *Echo* had indeed called at Diego Garcia on its way to Perth. But, in fact, it was just a routine bunkering stop for HMS *Echo*, just as for any other US or UK military vessel sailing in the region.

Another theory suggested that MH370, under US military control, made only a *technical* stop at Diego Garcia. During this stop, the US Army had allegedly removed any valuable or strategic items that were not to reach Beijing. Then the aircraft and its passengers were made to vanish in the middle of the Indian Ocean, to be found someday, thereby validating the theory about the Inmarsat pings. A crash in the vicinity of Diego Garcia gained popularity when in June 2014 Australian scientists from the Centre for Marine Science and Technology at Curtin University in Perth reported that some of their sensitive underwater microphones had detected a distinctive signal at 01:30 (UTC) on 8 March. But a few months later, new data from an additional sensor suggested that the sound probably originated from the geologically active

Carlsberg Ridge halfway between the Horn of Africa and India. 'The sound signal also had a low amplitude tail, and taken together these two findings suggest that the event was geological – caused, for example, by an earthquake, underwater landslide or volcanic eruption,' said Alec Duncan from Curtin University.

Unfortunately, no matter how compelling a place like Diego Garcia may have seemed in this sorry affair, along with its military might and its colossal surveillance capabilities, none of the scenarios that involved it were supported by the slightest shred of tangible evidence, apart from the following slightly odd occurrence. On 8 March, a notice came up on the official Facebook page of the Diego Garcia Passenger Terminal, the one used for personnel moving in and out of the base. It said: 'No scheduled flights in and out of Diego Garcia for the following 72 hours.' Apart from during extreme weather conditions, which were not occurring at the time, such a ban would have only been implemented in a case of very intense military activity involving constant take-offs and landings. Some people questioned whether the fact that the US Department of Defense officially launched its new Laser Weapon Systems (LaWS) on 6 March 2014* was in some way related to this drastic measure. Another plausible explanation would be that US military were contributing much more than claimed to the search and rescue operation of MH370 and therefore needed 'all hands on deck' to assist. If so, why keep it secret? In any case, no official explanation was ever given for this exceptional measure.

* The promotional video was uploaded on 6 March 2014 at www.youtube.com/watch?v=Px87SP01eKw.

A twin plane in an Israeli hangar

By posting an article online revealing that a Boeing plane matching the fated MH370 aircraft was being stored in a hangar in Tel Aviv, the American investigative journalist Chris Bollyn paved the way for theories of even greater complexity, such as the idea that a squadron of Boeing 777 aircraft was being created with plans to perpetrate another 9/11. This news of a twin of MH370 being stored in Tel Aviv was certainly intriguing, and photos posted on Planespotters.net appeared to confirm it. The twin plane was a Boeing 777-200ER, registered as 9M-MRI. The plane used for Flight MH370 was registered as 9M-MRO. The manufacturer serial number of the twin plane was 28416; that of the plane registered as 9M-MRO is 28420. Boeing delivered the twin to Malaysia Airlines in 1998; the plane used for Flight MH370 was delivered in 2002. Both aircraft were equipped with the same engine, the Rolls-Royce Trent 892. 'Same same but different!' as they say in Asian markets. Everything pointed to the two planes being twins. One had been reported missing since the night of 7 to 8 March; the other was inexplicably in storage in Israel. In a statement released on 4 October 2013, the Florida-based company GA Telesis, a major player in the aviation sector, had announced that it had bought the twin Boeing 777 from Malaysia Airlines, re-registered it as N105GT, and commissioned the Israeli contractor IAI, based in Tel Aviv, to disassemble it.

Planespotters.net is a website that publishes inventories of planes worldwide. At the end of 2015, the plane stored in the Tel Aviv hangar (registered as 9M-MRI) finally showed up on the Planespotters.net inventory as 'scrapped', meaning that the aircraft had been removed from the lists of Boeing 777s still in operation. At first sight, there was no reason whatsoever to scrap a Boeing 777 that had been flying for only 15 years with no major accident. Yet this was not the only one. Of the 17 Boeing 777-200s bought by Malaysia Airlines from 1997 to 2004, only six of the company's fleet were still in active service. Six out of seventeen! This was plane wastage on a massive scale. Besides the two lost planes (those flown for flights MH370 and MH17), the remainder had either been stored, sold or scrapped* (in fact, dismantled). These numbers did not at all fit my idea of the just-in-time management of an aviation fleet. I had always heard that planes that spent too long on the tarmac between flights were money-losers for the airline. For the sake of comparison, Air France bought 12 Boeing 777-200 planes between 1998 and 2004 (same aircraft model, similar period as MAS). All of them were still in service in 2014.

In other words, the plane flown for Flight MH370 had not just one twin stored in Tel Aviv, but half a dozen clones sitting idle in aircraft hangars.† Was this the harbinger of an imminent 9/11-type attack, or merely another sign of lax fleet management on the part of Malaysia Airlines? As with the mangosteens, there was obviously a problem here, with implications more far-reaching than we had initially suspected, yet nothing pointed clearly to a causal link with the disappearance of Flight MH370.

'Someone is hiding something,' says Dr M

In the United States, the disappearance of MH370 bred fascination and monopolised the major television networks. The eminent retired US Air Force Lieutenant General Thomas McInerney suggested that Pakistan was the place to hunt for MH370. Admittedly, Lt Gen. McInerney appeared regularly as an analyst on

---

* According to Planespotters.net, this was notably the case of the MAS B777s with manufacturer serial numbers 28415 ('Withdrawn from use in August 2015'), 28416 and 28418.

† According to Planespotters.net, in December 2015, B777s with construction numbers 28409, 28417, 28419, 28410, 28413 and 28414.

Fox News, an American television network that was a close rival of Russia Today in terms of objectivity. However, he claimed to base his theory on 'highly reliable sources which he cannot name', as well as on an analysis posted on Lignet, a website reportedly close to the American intelligence community. He pointed out that Pakistan had several airstrips long enough to land a Boeing 777, and that the plane could be hidden in a hangar. 'My fear is that this plane could be used as a weapon of mass destruction to attack one of our aircraft carriers, Israel, or our allies,' he said. 'We must remain on alert until the plane is found.'

According to the Lignet analysis quoted by McInerney, a source at Boeing said its company believed the plane did land in Pakistan. This was especially surprising given that Boeing had said virtually nothing whatsoever since Flight MH370 went missing. Fox News also quoted *The Times of Israel* as saying: 'Consequently, Israel is mobilising its air defence and scrutinizing approaching civilian aircraft.' On Fox News, Lt Gen. McInerney added, 'It is possible that the United States knows much more than it is saying.' Let's pause for a minute to commend Fox News for airing this under-statement bearing the hallmark of McInerney's common sense: 'It is *possible* that the United States knows much more than it is saying.'

That was probably one of the few times in his life when Mahathir Mohamad, the formidable and cunning former Malaysian Prime Minister, might have agreed with an American military officer. 'Dr M' had stepped down as prime minister in 2003 after governing the country with an iron fist for 22 years. While he actively promoted Malaysia's modernisation, Mahathir remained a contro-versial figure, partly on account of his introduction of positive discrimination in favour of the Malays, which disadvantaged the Chinese and Indian communities of the country. Most likely unaware that he would return to the prime ministerial office some years later (which he did in 2018 at the venerable age of 93), Mahathir clearly expressed his misgivings concerning the case of

MH370. 'Someone is hiding something,' he wrote in his blog in May 2014. He voiced explicit suspicions that the CIA was behind this 'disappearance'. But his innuendo came as no great surprise, given that his mistrust towards the West had long earned him a reputation of being essentially anti-American.*

Between 'Cobra Gold' and 'Cope Tiger'

One former political adviser to Mahathir also refused to believe that the United States knew nothing. According to lawyer Matthias Chang, 'Even though Malaysia has radars, we've never claimed to be a global power ... Who on earth has the means to see everything and hear everything, down to the private conversations of heads of state? Not us!' he insisted, referring to the revelations made by Edward Snowden about several global surveillance programmes, often run by the US National Security Agency, and the 'Five Eyes' intelligence alliance.† He was amazed at how badly the media had treated Malaysia: 'It is all fine and well to depict Malaysia as ignorant, incompetent and incapable of coordinating the searches. But we are a mere Third World country. We need the technology of our allies in this kind of situation!' He repeatedly made the same point on his website and in the interviews he gave a few weeks after MH370 vanished.

Mr Chang also pointed out to me that two major military training exercises – 'Cobra Gold' and 'Cope Tiger' – were taking place in the area where MH370 went missing, right about the same time. The Cobra Gold exercise had been organised jointly by Thailand

---

* When Mahathir returned to power in 2018 after 15 years in retirement, he expressed no further interest in the matter. He resigned in February 2020 but said he had no intention of retiring from politics.

† The 'Five Eyes' intelligence alliance is an intelligence gathering and sharing alliance between the US, UK, Australia, Canada and New Zealand.

and the United States every year since 1982, and involved several thousand American military personnel (4,300 in 2014). These war games included drills on land and at sea, mock beach landings, live-fire exercises (Calfex, or Combined Arms Live Fire Exercise), search and rescue missions, and humanitarian aid drills for natural disaster scenarios. Life in the jungle was part of the show – here was an opportunity for military personnel to have their pictures taken with snakes wrapped around their necks or their mouths stuffed full with disgusting live insects. Over the past 10 years or so, what began as a Thai–American exercise had widened to include Indonesia, Malaysia, Singapore, South Korea and Japan. Twenty additional countries participated with observer status. The Seventh Fleet had been sending an increasing number of ships from its regional bases in South Korea, Japan and Guam to participate in the exercise.*

'It is critical to building our multinational coordination, our interoperability with all our partners in the region; and allows us to collectively be able to respond to crises,' said Admiral Samuel J. Locklear III, Commander of the US Pacific Command (PaCom) at the opening ceremony for the Cobra Gold exercise in 2013, the year before the disappearance of MH370. Why then had there been no immediate demonstration of such regional coordination when Flight MH370 went missing in the area, with 239 people on board? Was this not precisely the type of situation that would have required the sort of coordination mentioned by Admiral Locklear?

Furthermore, on 8 March 2014, Thailand was preparing to host another large-scale military exercise – Cope Tiger – which focused on aerial defence. The United States, Thailand and Singapore all took part in this exercise, with the latter two countries having the best-equipped armies in the region. 'Ironically, the theme of the 2014 Cope Tiger exercise was search and rescue,' said Chang. 'Did

---

* The US Seventh Fleet's area of responsibility covered the West and South Pacific, as well as most of the Indian Ocean. Its base is in Yokosuka in Tokyo Bay, Japan.

all this military muscle help with the searches, as they were all on location? If so, why have we not been told of it? And if not, why not?'

I confessed my surprise to Chang. I was not aware of these large-scale military exercises having taken place or being about to take place in the Gulf of Thailand and the South China Sea. No one was. In dozens of press briefings, there had not been a single mention of them. The fact that so many. American, Thai and Singaporean vessels and aircraft were pre-positioned in the area of the disappearance should have been hailed as a godsend. But with so much maritime and aerial military activity going on in the region, the silence of the radar screens was all the more astonishing – not only all the local radars, but also all the American radars aboard the American ships deployed in the area for these exercises. What rational explanation could there be for the fact that this high density of military resources did not contribute so much as a single radar echo to pin down the erratic movements of MH370 over the Gulf of Thailand during the night of 7 to 8 March 2014?

How could the plane have been diverted?

Whether MH370 was lying on the floor of the Indian Ocean, as claimed in the official investigation report, concealed on Diego Garcia as thousands of web surfers reckoned, or had been confiscated by Pakistan's secret services in preparation for an attack against Israel as Fox News would have had us believe, we still needed some answers about the actual manner in which the plane might have been diverted.

According to Emirates Airline President Tim Clark, the plane was 'under control, probably until the very end'. If this was indeed the case, how so? The most straightforward hypothesis, of course, was that the flight's captain or co-pilot simply flipped. Although as yet unproven, this theory had been widely promoted, including in leaks from the authorities. As such, it was hard to rule it out completely and I will return to it later. Meanwhile, two other revelations of a technical character had surfaced, suggesting new possibilities for how someone might have seized control of the plane.

As frightening as it may seem, the electrical and electronics bay (E/E bay) of a Boeing 777 – nothing short of the aircraft's brain – was easy to access for anyone who knew where to find it. An eight-minute video had been posted anonymously online on 18 March 2014 showing a Varig Airlines pilot pointing the way to the central controls of a Boeing 777. The video sowed fear among pilots because it demonstrated how to access this vital area of the aircraft – one merely had to lift up the carpet and open the hatch located in the floor of the front left section of the first-class cabin. Any plane could be controlled from the E/E bay. If a hostile crew managed to gain access to the controls, the cockpit would automatically be deactivated, leaving the legitimate crew powerless to act. They could not even send out an alert, as the transponder would be switched off from below.

One Boeing 777 pilot told me that until that video appeared online, neither he nor any of his colleagues had realised the danger of having an unsecured hatch. 'We ourselves are theoretically not authorised to go down there, except to get the emergency oxygen tanks for the pilots,' he said. It took some time for the video to gain traction, but when it did it had a powerful impact on pilots of Boeing 777s, as well as on MHists hungry for new theories. In his online book *The Plane That Wasn't There*, Jim Wise suggested that the two Ukrainian passengers took control of the aircraft from the E/E bay and diverted it to an underground hangar in Kazakhstan.

The other possibility regarding MH370's 'diversion' discussed in the immediate aftermath of the plane's disappearance was a remote hijacking. It is true that in 2006 Boeing patented the technology that would enable this. This was former Malaysian Prime Minister Mahathir Mohamad's favourite theory at the time. On 18 May 2014, he made a direct challenge to Boeing in his blog. Mahathir quoted an article* that detailed the possibility of someone remotely seizing control of a civilian aircraft and setting it in the 'uninterruptible autopilot' mode to bring it down at a designated landing location, with the pilots in the cockpit helpless to do anything about it. However, no one knew which planes, if any, had been equipped with the technology or who would use it. Boeing? The airline? A government? And above all, to what end?

Another mind-boggling explanation came three and a half years after the disappearance of MH370, in September 2017. Fugitive Chinese billionaire Guo Wengui, who was staying in Washington, DC, said publicly that the real reason behind the plane's loss was to get rid of people who were privy to an organ-harvesting operation in a Nanjing hospital that involved Jiang Mianheng, the son of former Communist Party General Secretary Jiang Zemin. But as much as there was mounting evidence of illegal organ harvesting and transplants going on in China – and Guo didn't spare us the details about these frightening operations – it seemed to me utterly disproportionate to bring down an entire civilian plane if you're just aiming at a few targeted people. It would be much easier to eliminate them in a considerably more discreet manner in other circumstances.

The range of possibilities opened up by the research, knowledge and imagination of MHists was as immense as the Indian Ocean. There seemed to be as many leads to pursue as there were fireflies in the famous wetlands of Sungai Lebam.† But once I'd immersed myself in the job of sifting through the mass of information relating to MH370, from the true to the plausible, the possible to the

* John Croft's article on flightglobal.com, 1 December 2006. See www.flightglobal.com/diagrams-boeing-patents-anti-terrorism-auto-land-system-for-hijacked-airliners/70886.article.

† The Sungai Lebam Wetland Preservation Area in southern Malaysia is famous for its mangroves populated by millions of fireflies.

far-fetched ... all the way to the lunatic fringe of sheer invention, things started to look a lot clearer.

The hoax about Philip Wood, who allegedly used his mobile phone to text a distress call from the US military base at Diego Garcia, could readily be rejected, along with the fanciful theory based on Freescale Semiconductor's 'crucially important' technology patent. The investigation of these leads nonetheless uncovered some peculiar and disturbing information about the cargo and the passenger list, which both remained highly problematic. It also brought to light the existence and impressive capabilities of the Diego Garcia facility, the unlikely story of the squadron of Boeing 777s owned by MAS but prematurely withdrawn from service, Boeing's patented technology for remote control of commercial aircraft, and the extensive deployment of military muscle of which no one had been aware in the area where MH370 went missing.

As early as autumn 2014, a persistent rumour was reaching me to the point that I even mentioned it to some colleagues at *Le Monde*. This rumour was supporting one of the first theories that had circulated on the web involving the US base on Diego Garcia, but now it was coming from more reliable sources than just wild internet forums: diplomats from different regions, and highly placed and well-connected businessmen. The same rumour was even being circulated within the Elysée Palace, the official residence of the French president. According to what was being whispered, Flight MH370 had been shot down by the US Air Force because its flight path was set to crash on Diego Garcia. I could find no satisfying answer as to why a mad terrorist would go all the way to a military base in the middle of nowhere to crash a plane and kill its passengers, when he might do so with much more swagger and immediate impact by targeting the Petronas Towers, to choose one possible example.

Despite being full of holes and sounding not in the least bit convincing, this theory nonetheless continued to gain traction, and was repeated in circles of power and influence. Many people who refused to believe the official narrative were happily settling for it. In this scenario, the attack on the US base would explain the defensive shooting by US forces, and the shooting would explain the cover-up.

Back in Paris in the summer of 2015, I was having lunch at the Waknine, a smart bistro near the Pont de l'Alma, with a colonel in the French Army Reserve who had worked for 15 years on strategy for the French government, a mission closely associated with intelligence gathering and the secret services. When our coffees arrived, I asked her – the colonel is a woman – what she thought about this rumour. In her view, if the rumour had become as widespread and persistent as I was contending, then the United States was necessarily aware of it; they may even have orchestrated it. 'If they don't shut it down, then that's probably because it suits them that way. Because it creates a diversion from the truth, which is likely to be far less palatable.' A decoy rumour. It made so much sense _.

In the case of MH370, as we just saw, we had heard decoy rumours and false leads by the dozen. The media actually carried a heavy responsibility for promoting anything and everything related to MH370, although they would give the sorry excuse that the story has been selling so well. 'When a rumour gets too close to the truth that you don't want known, you can either nip it in the bud, drown in it a lot of other rumours, or simply feed the doubt,' explained my expert in disinformation over our coffees.

From then on, I became increasingly aware that in this complicated story we were not only dealing with false rumours but also with fabricated rumours. That something catastrophic happened to Flight MH370 in the night of 7 to 8 March 2014 was nevertheless a concrete reality. Finding any remaining shreds of that reality was the task ahead.

6

The Families' Committee Launches
a Private Investigation

Time went by, and there was still no trace of the jetliner in the Indian Ocean. Summer 2014 was behind us, and media interest had gradually declined after the announcement on 24 March that it was 'beyond reasonable doubt' that MH370 had ended up in the southern Indian Ocean. The searches were destined to go on, however, with no end in sight. In the case of Flight AF447, it had taken two years to locate the wreck, even though the crash location was established to within 70 kilometres and hundreds of pieces of debris had been recovered. How much time would it now take to find MH370, with the crash site still unknown and, six months later, not a single piece of debris having been identified?

When, on 18 July 2014, Malaysia Airlines lost another Boeing 777-200ER, this time over eastern Ukraine with 289 people on board, the story was of course covered from Europe. But *Le Monde* asked me for a local angle: the MH17 crash as seen from Malaysia. 'A tragic day in what has already been a tragic year,' said Malaysian Prime Minister Najib Razak, adding: 'We must – and we will – find out precisely what happened to this flight. No stone can be left unturned. If it transpires that the plane was indeed shot down, we insist that the perpetrators must be swiftly brought to justice.' In my article, I pointed out that these promises left 'a bitter taste as they have been heard before [...], even if the situation this time seems more clear-cut than in the MH370 disappearance, which remains a mystery'.

For some Chinese Malaysian friends, the latest tragedy provided further evidence that the country lay under a curse and was being punished for the government's corruption. In Chinese history, ever since the Zhou Dynasty roughly 3,000 years ago, whenever the country was hit by numerous disasters, it was because the emperor had lost the 'mandate of heaven'. It was time for him to be overthrown.

So I kept thinking about MH370, whose disappearance had still not been explained. With summer over, I made my customary visit to *Le Monde* in Paris. Béatrice Gurrey, head of the investigation section, agreed when I offered to write an update on the affair that I should highlight its bizarre aspects. But she didn't want an article that simply said that nothing new had emerged. I returned to Hong Kong with her commission.

Over the previous couple of months some new angles had emerged about MH370, but never anything important enough to justify an article. On 20 August 2014, the Malaysian newspaper *The Star* revealed that 30 computers linked to the investigation (belonging to staff at the Civil Aviation Department, the Council of National Security and Malaysia Airlines) had been targeted by a high-level cyberattack on 9 March, the day after the jetliner disappeared. It also said that the IP address of the computer receiving all the data was in China. Dr Amirudin Abdul Wahab, Malaysia's cybersecurity chief, said in *The Star* article that the data stolen from the targeted computers included 'confidential data, in particular minutes of meetings and confidential documents some of which relate to the MH370 investigation'.

There was also the news, taken up by media outlets worldwide from 15 September onwards, that General Sutarman, Indonesia's Chief of Police, 'knows what really happened to MH370'. The scoop was first reported on 12 September on the Indonesian online news website Kompas.com. The police chief was quoted as saying:

'I spoke to the Malaysian police chief, Tun Mohammed Hanif Omar, I actually know what had actually [*sic*] happened with MH370.' On 13 September, the Tempo.co website also quoted Sutarman: 'Malaysia police and I truly know the cause but I can't say it here.' Other media outlets relayed the quotations worldwide, but few of them took the trouble to find out that the man he described as the 'Malaysian Police Chief', Hanif Omar, had in fact left the police force way back in 1994, which partly undermined the story's credibility. In any case, the report was denied by both Indonesia and Malaysia. The statements were nevertheless a wake-up call, and bore out the general impression that there might be another version of the truth out there that did not match the official one.

During this period I often heard tell of a Frenchman, or rather 'the Frenchman', who – after losing his wife and two of his three children on MH370 – was battling to uncover the truth. I was told that he often appeared on television back home, and was raising money to fund a private investigation. A senior executive of the French cement group Lafarge, just before the plane's disappearance he had been transferred from his job in Beijing to a new position in Paris, while his wife stayed in China with their two youngest children so they could complete the school year. His friends said he was a thoroughly good person, upright and determined. I meant to contact him at some point, even though I didn't really see what the families could contribute to the investigation itself. I saw the next of kin as tragic collateral victims, engulfed by a tragedy whose mysterious nature kept on torturing them day after day. In the end I obtained the Frenchman's email address through friends of friends in Beijing, and asked if we could talk by phone. I explained that my newspaper would shortly be publishing an update on the investigation, and in my message I repeated the instructions given to me: 'Do not say that nothing else has emerged.'

Without bothering to greet me with a 'Hello' or a 'Thank you for your message', 'the Frenchman' answered in his email:

Unfortunately the media are all the same!

Nothing more has come to light, so they're not interested!

This should be a story in itself, I think it's really outrageous.

We know that 239 people disappeared two hundred days ago, on the safest plane in the world, flying with one of the safest airlines in the world, in one of the most closely monitored zones on the planet.

We also know that from the outset we have been lied to, but the media don't talk about that and have let themselves be taken for a ride from the start.

At any rate, in this affair, it is about time you reacted.

But you're going to have to work hard because t's extremely complicated. If you are ready to really get involved, and not to relay the misinformation, which today is Australian, I will be happy to talk to you, but I am in Paris now. We can Skype, and Saturday would be ideal for me (would that be possible for you, it would be Saturday afternoon).

Best regards,
Ghyslain Wattrelos

That's what you call speaking your mind. From the outset. And he sounded determined. I could see why the TV channels liked him; from a journalist's viewpoint, he was a straight talker who came over well on television. We made a date to Skype on Saturday, 27 September. But the date and time of our first live contact proved ill-fated.

I spend part of that Saturday near the Hong Kong parliament building, where a large gathering of students and high school pupils had formed. Tension was unusually high. The previous night, dozens of students had stormed Civic Square, a small area just in front of the new Hong Kong government buildings, and Joshua Wong, their remarkable young leader,* was arrested by the police. No one knew what had happened to him. Following Beijing's announcement of the method to be used to elect the Hong Kong chief executive, the Hong Kong Federation of Students planned a week-long strike, which began on Monday, 22 September. But instead of ending on Friday evening, as scheduled, the protest had escalated and took on a completely new dimension. Caught up in the action of local events, and then stuck in a bus in the Saturday traffic jam, I contacted Wattrelos to say I would be slightly late in reaching my computer. But that didn't suit him, so we put it off until later. On the following night, the organisers of another demonstration, 'Occupy Central', initially scheduled to start three days later and last for 48 hours, called on their supporters to immediately join in with the student protest. On Sunday, the police used tear gas against the protesters, which had never happened before in Hong Kong. Umbrellas were opened to form a defensive shield. This was the birth – in the midst of tears and clouds of white smoke – of the Umbrella Movement, which ended up lasting 79 days.

With this sudden whirlwind of events in my local area, all further attempts to Skype fell by the wayside. Finally, I had to put the MH370 investigation on hold for the time being. Wattrelos replied, saying that he understood.

One and a half months later, on 8 November, when the movement briefly quietened down, Skype contact was finally established. I sensed that this was someone who was angry, impatient and determined to obtain 'the whole truth'.

His message was unwavering: 'It's all untrue, we have been lied to from the outset.' I had already heard him say as much in the

---

* Joshua Wong, when only 15, had led a huge protest about education and social issues in 2012.

YouTube clips of interviews in the studios of various TV channels. He quite rightly emphasised that the Malaysians 'had a search carried out in the South China Sea for a week before admitting they knew the plane had turned in a right angle to the west. Just to create a diversion and win time ...'

He was furious that 'of the 300 pieces of debris apparently identified by satellite, not a single one has been recovered'. He did not believe a single word of the official version and was convinced that the Inmarsat pings 'had been invented'.

I asked him about the families' committee, set up in June in connection with the 'Reward MH370' crowdfunding project. The founding principle of the committee was that the truth about the affair was being hidden, and that somewhere, certain people knew what had happened. The initial objective was to raise US$5 million as a reward for anyone providing information enabling the investigation to advance. The committee had been set up with five members, Wattrelos told me. Although he would have liked the Malaysians and the Chinese families to have been involved, the scheme was finally launched very quickly, probably too quickly, via the specialist crowdfunding website Indiegogo. Alongside two Indians and himself, the project was mainly run by the American Sarah Bajc (pronounced 'Bay-jack'), a teacher of economics and business studies (then in Beijing and now based in Kuala Lumpur), and the Australian Ethan Hunt, a businessman who worked in Shenzhen and Hong Kong. The crowdfunding campaign had now ended, after raising only US$100,516. This was a disappointment. The money would be used to fund a private investigation, although the US$5 million reward was still posted online.

As our discussion continued, Wattrelos told me that he had been warned, both directly and indirectly, about 'the American woman' – Sarah Bajc. Various rumours about her were circulating on the internet. For two years she had been the partner, indeed fiancée, of the American Philip Wood, whose mobile phone reportedly sent what seemed to be a fake distress message from Diego Garcia before Flight MH370 went off the radar. Wattrelos said that Bajc was just too much. She was ubiquitous, running and controlling everything: interviews, Facebook pages, crowdfunding and the private investigation.

Although the two main communities hit by the tragedy were Chinese and Malaysian, it was the American Bajc who monopolised the media whenever the subject of MH370 raised its head. She became, within a few hours of the plane's disappearance and in the following months, the voice and face of the MH370 families and friends on all the major international TV networks.

Wattrelos did not contest the fact that Bajc was a professional when it came to communication. She clearly was, and she knew how to break into tears at just the right moment. Some MHists had even raised questions about her 'TV performances', and dismissed her as a 'crisis actress' taking centre stage in a 'false flag' story. It was amazing what you could find on the internet.

Yet, at any rate, Bajc's LinkedIn profile was flawless, even though she had almost never stayed in the same job for more than two years. She held senior executive positions in Tel Aviv with Tescom, an Israeli software quality assurance and testing company, which also had an armaments division. She spoke Chinese, and in Beijing she was Business Director of the Strategic Partnership Group of Microsoft China Research and Development. Each job in her profile came with several references. According to her former colleagues, she was passionate, strict on detail, and a good leader who left nothing to chance and held the reins firmly. Reading between the lines, she may have been inflexible with those around her, but above all she seemed to be extremely professional. 'My mom left when I was seven; my dad was an alcoholic. I've been independent since I was 16. I put myself through college. We had to pull ourselves up by our bootstraps,' she told the *Guardian*.*

* Jon Ronson, 'Nobody cares any more', *Guardian*, 28 February 2015.

Was it slightly unusual, then, that after having been such a high flyer with companies as sensitive as Tescom in Israel and Microsoft in China, she suddenly decided to become a teacher because of 'her love of children', as she stated on the website of the British International School of Kuala Lumpur, where she had been working since 2014? Should questions be asked about her move from Beijing to Kuala Lumpur, a few months after the disappearance of her fiancé Philip Wood on MH370, when her only reason for going to Malaysia was to join him there? 'It's very surprising she got a visa with no good reason to come here, particularly if she once worked for an Israeli company.* That means she has unusually good connections or support from the US embassy,' I was told later by a member of the Malaysian families' group.

Paradoxically, while the Western media kept on contacting her long after 8 March 2014, Bajc had never managed to win over the other next of kin. As they saw it, she was only representing herself. Furthermore, she did not attend the ceremonies organised by the families to mark the first anniversary of the disappearance, in March 2015.

In one of her many TV interviews on CBS News, she said that her apartment in Beijing had twice been broken in to, but without anything being stolen. She hinted that the Chinese secret service were not very good. Yet why would they be so interested in her that they entered her apartment twice? She also said she had received 'death threats' in the weeks following the MH370 disappearance.

Perhaps, then, she was not a 'crisis actress' at all but rather a 'sleeper agent' of the kind described in John le Carré's novels, held in reserve by the CIA or other secret services, and activated when the time came, if necessary. But why? To keep the families under control? To steer communication about the whole affair?

* Malaysian passport holders are prohibited from travelling to Israel, and Israelis are not allowed into Malaysia without special permission from the Interior Ministry.

At a birthday party one evening in an elegant Hong Kong apartment containing the beginnings of a collection of contemporary Chinese art, I met an American journalist who used to be based in Beijing. We began talking, as journalists frequently do, about the people and work we had in common, about colleagues, postings and assignments. She too had covered MH370, but from Beijing. Her name was Shannon Van Sant, a journalist with the NBC News TV network, and she was the one who first called Sarah Bajc.

'It was both easy and difficult,' she said, 'because we were good friends.' I dipped my nose into the large wine glass I was holding in an attempt to conceal my surprise. Shannon was in fact very close to Bajc, the woman previously described to me as a potential Mossad or CIA agent. So this friendship was part of the reason why Bajc had given so many interviews. Shannon explained that, well before 8 March 2014, Bajc had reached out and linked up with a group of her own friends, who like her were American journalists. They frequented the same places. Clearly, this could be interpreted in two ways. Was it a strategy on Bajc's part, building up a useful network in case she needed one? Or just a coincidence?

My meeting with Bajc in February 2015 at a bar in Taman Tun Dr Ismail (aka TTDI), the suburb of Kuala Lumpur where she lived, was somewhat inconclusive. I could not decide whether or not she was sincere. She mentioned 'close to two dozen scenarios that we have not been able to rule out', though she had suggested just before that one of the best explanations she could think of was a 'systematic failure caused by incompetence and corruption that is so pervasive in Malaysia'. She also mentioned a possible 'intentional cover-up' and went as far as declaring that 'the UK or the United States were very likely involved'. Was she testing me, deliberately misleading me, or was she genuinely confused? A new John le Carré-esque twist was added to her story in April 2016 when she informed her fellow members of the families' group that she was going to leave Malaysia after her two-year stay. As of July, she was going to be based in Panama City, of all places. 'Exactly as I always predicted: she finished her two-year mission!' commented Ghyslain Wattrelos, who had always suspected her of playing a two-faced role in this drama.

As for her fiancé, Philip Wood, the only adult American on the flight,* Wattrelos found him just as problematic. Employed by IBM, whose links with the American government were well known, his profile on LinkedIn was as short as Sarah Bajc's was long. It began in 2011, with IBM, as though he had at that point been suddenly invented. But up to the age of 47, what did he do? And who in fact was Philip Wood? There was almost nothing about him on the internet. No participation in a conference, in a sports event, in an organised trip. His family, his children, his ex-wife and his parents never contacted the other families nor did they reply when contacted themselves. Only one of Wood's LinkedIn contacts responded to the message I sent, but he did not want to talk to me about Philip Wood.

On the internet, the many photos of Bajc and her fiancé looked slightly too good to be true. The two lovebirds in their fifties, often pressed closely together, with a light tan from the sun of Thailand or Bali, posing in front of idyllic warm seas or setting suns. By contrast, the Asian families – whether Chinese, Malaysian or Indian – and the two French families, initially put very few pictures online. Perhaps it was just a question of cultural differences.

Ghyslain Wattrelos took a more neutral stance about 'the Australian [who had become] fascinated by the investigation'. Ethan Hunt did not have the slightest connection with MH370. He knew no one on the flight. And he had no connection whatsoever with Tom Cruise, other than sharing the same name as the main character in the film *Mission: Impossible*. On the crowdfunding website

---

* Among the passengers, there were also two children (aged two and four) who had Chinese parents but were US passport holders.

Indiegogo, Ethan Hunt presented himself as the CEO of Rapide 3D Limited (a 3D printer company based in China), a former pilot, an experienced private investigator and a highly successful Indiegogo crowdfunder. 'With him, the phone calls go well,' Ghyslain Wattrelos told me.

Wattrelos also said that the private investigation had been launched and a private detective agency in Singapore selected. Sarah Bajc apparently explained the choice – which she made alone – to the other members of the committee by saying, 'Very good people, close to the CIA.' The private detectives were supposed to provide regular investigation reports, although Wattrelos was never sent any, as his email was supposedly not secure. Bajc received the reports, combed through the information, removed any sensitive names and then passed them on to the other committee members.

I found what he was saying to be completely out of order. How could the MH370 Families Committee effectively be run by the partner of the only American adult on the flight and by an Australian with no connection to any of the passengers? This obviously raised issues of legitimacy and credibility. The Malaysian and Chinese families who represented three-quarters of the jetliner's passengers had their own organisations, and had not really become involved in the 'Reward MH370' initiative. In fact, each group was guided by its own mindset and influenced by its own context. I came to realise this gradually through my subsequent meetings with the different groups.

As Wattrelos was not yet able to come to the region to see all this for himself, I suggested to him that I should meet the Australian. Like me, Ethan Hunt was based in Hong Kong.

On 21 November 2014, I sent the following message to Wattrelos:

Dear Sir,

The person whose particulars you gave me did not turn up for the appointment. I would like to give you some details by Skype or FaceTime when you are available.

Thank you in advance.

My attempted meeting with Hunt was indeed very strange. On the day in question, I was right in the middle of filming for a TV report. I had left my cameraman to his own devices after an interview with a political scientist, and rushed off to the appointment arranged by email with Hunt, at the FCC – the Foreign Correspondents' Club – in Hong Kong Central. This pre-war brick building is redolent of Hong Kong's colonial past, with high ceilings, whirling fans, period tiles and an impressive bar in dark wood. It was the unofficial headquarters of foreign correspondents during both the Vietnam War and the Boat People crisis, and a meeting-place for China watchers before China was opened up to the rest of the world.

On the way there, I called Hunt several times, but there was no reply. He finally answered when I tried his Chinese number. Clearly surprised, he said he was on his way. After waiting at the FCC for 45 minutes, I called the Chinese number again, to no avail. Ethan Hunt had disappeared. Two hours later and after one final text ('Hello Ethan, It's getting late and I have more interviews. Are you still on your way?'), I returned to my filming session, rather perplexed by what has just happened. We were in Hong Kong, after all, not India. Missed appointments hardly ever happened in a city where there were no strikes, no power cuts, few traffic jams and rarely any surprises. I followed up with a message expressing my concern: 'I waited till 6 o'clock. Are you OK?'

The answer arrived two and a half days later, and seemed like a tall story:

Hi Florence

I am so sorry about Friday. I was on my way to meet you when I fell over in the street, breaking my phone and doing a little damage to myself. As my phone was broken, I did not have your contact details and I was taken to the hospital for a check-up. I am OK but needed to get a new phone. I have just got back to China but will come over and speak with you early next week if you let me know a suitable time to come over to see you.

I couldn't imagine how you fall in a way that smashes your mobile phone. In any case, you could buy a phone as easily as a pack of cigarettes in Hong Kong, at any time of day or night. And why should he have had to return to China to find my email address? But he then sent me a two-page email, trying very hard to sound sensible and convincing, setting out his position at length. Intrigued by this odd character, I decided to give him a second chance. We agreed on a new meeting, this time in the little Café Corridor in Causeway Bay, hidden – as its name suggested – at the end of a narrow hallway. Understated, on the trendy side, it was completely atypical of this district of Hong Kong, said to be the most expensive place on the planet in terms of key money to rent a commercial property.

He began by showing me his passport, to remove any doubts about his name. I barely looked at it, making a joke as I did so. I wanted to get him on my side. After all, what were the odds of someone having the same name as the character in a blockbuster film? Well, he did! We talked for three hours, and I filled 13 pages of my notebook. He seemed to know all the ins and outs of the MH370 affair. Leaning low with his elbows spread wide across the table, he filled my ears with information as though he were passing on secrets.

There had been manipulation, misinformation and bungling from day one, he told me. They did everything they could to win time, so as to keep secret what they had to keep secret. He too did not believe the official 'southern corridor' explanation, which he found far too convenient. That said, it seemed certain that the plane would not be recovered, if it really was there. So this was the ideal scenario if you had things to hide. Furthermore, if the plane did run out of fuel when flying, sooner or later it would have gone into a spin when the engines stopped working, exploding when it hit the sea. That would have created a huge field of debris. He referred to the case of a small aircraft with two passengers that had crashed near Cuba two months earlier; pieces of debris had been found more than five kilometres away in every direction. And the aircraft in question was barely a twentieth of the length of a Boeing 777. He said that on the night of the disappearance, villagers in the Maldives had seen an aircraft flying very low. West of Thailand, in the Andaman Sea, three unidentified bodies had been recovered from the sea. Why not search over there?

He talked quickly, almost without stopping: 'Hard to believe' that the Australian Prime Minister Tony Abbott was spending such large amounts to explore the abyssal depths for something that was probably not even there. 'Absurd', the excuse that the ultra-powerful Australian over-the-horizon radar (JORN*) had been 'switched off on the day in question' and thus did not detect the huge jetliner that flew for around two hours off the Australian coast. 'Inconsistent and incomplete', the cargo manifest. 'Suspicious', the fact that passengers were placed at the front and rear of the plane, suggesting that the jet was carrying very heavy cargo that was not listed on the manifest. He also mentioned the call, referred to by some media outlets but never confirmed, that the co-pilot had apparently made over Penang when the jetliner was about to head west, away from the Malaysian coast.

Next came the MH17 crash in Ukraine: '800 planes used the same route and once again it is Malaysia Airlines that is hit. Do

* Jindalee Operational Radar Network, an over-the-horizon radar (OTHR) network.

you think that is a coincidence: two identical jetliners from the same airline in four months? Statistically, that is impossible!' And what about the mobile phones? Anyone who takes a plane in the region has seen the Chinese when they are on board; all of them have several mobile phones, and most never bother to switch them off. All the mobiles start beeping when the aircraft starts its descent before landing. Why hasn't anyone geolocated these hundreds of mobile phones? Apparently they can be located even when switched off. Apple could have said something. He suspected that blockers were placed in the aircraft. These small devices cost a few dollars in China, and were increasingly widely used, often to ensure no external calls came in during meetings. Hunt also had questions about CNN, which had given the affair such copious coverage but had been made to look ridiculous by the inconsistencies and contradictions of its reports. There were lots of new pieces in the jigsaw puzzle to be examined and sorted out.

Hunt was a great admirer of Sarah Bajc. 'A very clever woman, with her head firmly on her shoulders.' It was partly because of her that he had taken up the challenge. 'I have time, money, I have no family ties, I am the boss of my company, and I have the perspective that the families lack,' he said.

In short, Hunt looked like the right man in the right place. I found out later that all the money raised by the Indiegogo campaign passed through his bank account in Hong Kong. I looked for flaws in what he was saying, but I couldn't find many. I still noticed that he mentioned the figure of '5 million dollars' three times in three different contexts. Was that his lucky number? He also said during the conversation that he never went out 'without at least one or two phones, an iPad and a computer'. I resisted the temptation of saying: 'Never? Except last Friday!' A few weeks later I read a portrait of Hunt in the *Guardian* that seemed less than enthusiastic and a little hesitant about him.* 'It took him eight weeks to find

---

* 'Nobody cares any more', *Guardian*, op. cit.

Sarah, even though he calls himself, in his online CV, an "experienced private investigator",' the journalist wryly noted. His profile was complex – time in the military, private investigator, businessman, manager of fitness centres and now maker of 3D printers in China – and in the article he seemed to boast about how he sometimes used Chinese mafia-style methods to get what he wanted. It definitely made you wonder what kind of person he really was.

During our meeting, he confirmed that the committee had given the detective agency in Singapore a few leads to follow up as a matter of priority. But to protect the secrecy of their investigation, they had decided not to say which agency had been chosen. And they wouldn't share the results either. At least not for the time being.

When I left the Café Corridor, feeling slightly dizzy after this rambling yet intense encounter, night had already fallen. But it never really got dark in this part of Hong Kong, bathed in light by shop windows, gigantic screens showing commercials and the headlights of red taxis queuing for their next customer. '*Som wan doh!*' These three syllables – my address in Cantonese – were all any Hong Kong taxi driver needed to drive me home.

It so happened that a long-time friend of mine, also engaged in private investigation work in the region, was very familiar with the detective agency hired by the families' committee. He did not share Sarah Bajc's enthusiasm. It was one of the longest established agencies in Singapore, run by a former military man. According to my friend, an expat in Asia for 30 years or more, the people who ran it were 'decent people', but their results were often 'quite poor'. I realised, of course, that he was talking about a competitor. But once I read some of their 'secret and confidential' reports that I'd got access to, I couldn't help thinking that he might just have been right.

The codename of the MH370 private investigation assignment was 'Melon'. The first item in the report dated 14 October 2014 had three parts: 'Objective', 'Tasks' and 'Findings to date'. Nothing surprising there. It read:

Objective: Verify the cell phone pings when it flew over Penang. Is it accuate [*sic*] that only the first officer's phone was pinged?

Tasks: Establish sources in the Malaysian telco [*sic*] industry, obtain information on the mobile phone signals from the MH370, obtain technical information on mobile cell phone pings when the phone is in flight mode.

Findings to date: Conversations with sources in Telcon [*sic*] industry have provided conflicting information. One source says it is impossible for the phones to give our [*sic*] ping signals once turned off as, they should be, when passengers are on board a flight. Another says that the phone can give out signals when it is off.

I was stunned by the mediocrity of what I was reading. It reminded me of the press briefings of the first few weeks: 'Yes, no, perhaps, we'll tell you later …'.

In the 'Indonesia' section of the same report, the 'objective' was to 'verify the story of General Sutaraman [his name is actually Sutarman] that he knows what happened to MH370'. The 'task' will consist of locating the address of 'Gen Suman [his name is still Sutarman] and his movement patterns when we can get to speak to him alone'. It was starting to sound like a case for Sherlock Holmes. Unfortunately, my mounting excitement was nipped in the bud. Findings to date: 'We have located the General and monitored his movement to note that he will have his aide and security with him.' It seemed that they were unable to meet the general for the time being.

The report for November – under the title 'Maldives' – covered less than a page and contained zero information: 'Our field agent has not been able to get confirmation from sources that can give us the private jet landing information on 8 March 2014. While initially, it was promising that he can get sources to provide information, it appears that no one is talking. We will continue to follow up.'

But the report of 6 December 2014 did contain a potential scoop. The investigators' source, reportedly a member of the police or army, was said to belong to the official team investigating the flight's disappearance. The source revealed two important things. First, the pilot had requested two hours of additional fuel before taking off without being questioned about his request. Second, the pilot asked specifically to be on the flight. These two pieces of information were dynamite. If they were true, they almost certainly pointed to the guilt of the pilot, Zaharie Ahmad Shah.

I put this information to three friends – Tom, Wolf and Jason – all of whom were Boeing 777 pilots for one of the world's top airlines. Their verdicts were unanimous. There could be no justification on a flight of less than six hours, such as Kuala Lumpur–Beijing, for requesting two hours of extra fuel. Why? Because each hour of flight represents around 7 tonnes of kerosene for a B777, and there was no reason to carry an extra 14 tonnes. Even if a pilot had made such a request, it would be bound to be followed by a call from his or her superior to check the situation, and normally the request would be rejected. Furthermore, the perfect weather conditions that night meant that no complications were expected on Flight MH370.

In fact, we knew precisely how much fuel was in the tank before take-off, thanks to two matching sources: the ACARS report transmitted before take-off and the technical data sheet of Malaysia Airlines. Aircraft 9M-MRO was carrying 49.1 tonnes of fuel, give or take 0.1 tonnes. 'Basically all those figures seem about right to me,' I was told by Tom, who broke down the calculation. 'KL to Beijing is about 6 hours' fly time. We work on an average of 7 tonnes per hour, so that's 42 tonnes plus enough for an alternative airport [30 minutes from Beijing] and an extra 30 minutes reserve fuel [...] giving another approximately 7 tonnes, so 49 tonnes seems reasonable, if not spot on! [...] Take-off and climb thrust to cruising at level flight burns a lot more fuel than the cruise.'

In other words, the pilot did not take off with fuel to fly for two hours more than scheduled. And in view of his reputation and experience, it was highly unlikely that he would have made this request and made himself look foolish.

But objectively, it was also just as unthinkable that the private investigators' source – the police or army officer on the official team – would have made a mistake on a point like this. Unless of course it had been intentional, with the aim of misinforming the private investigators, and thus the families. This would point to a deliberate attempt by the investigators' source to discredit the pilot.

As for the suggestion that Captain Zaharie specifically asked to be on this flight, it too surprised the pilots I contacted. They said that as a pilot you just didn't do that in normal circumstances.

People were not happy if you asked for a change in the service roster, so everyone avoided doing it. For safety reasons, pilots were not allowed to choose their co-pilot either. When in the first few days after the disappearance there was a rumour to this effect, Malaysia Airlines stated that the pilot had not asked to be on the flight; rather, he had been designated. I passed these doubts on to Ethan Hunt, suggesting to him that he should seriously challenge the private investigators to up their game. They replied that they were sure of their source and confirmed their version of the events.

Although it was unlikely – and frowned upon – for a pilot to request a last-minute change in his flight schedule, a change of pilots could be initiated by the airline. More than two years after the loss, someone close to the case in Malaysia told me a very unsettling story that I was unable to double-check with other sources. According to this source, a different co-pilot was initially supposed to have been on the flight – a young Sikh pilot. But to his great surprise he was told he would not be flying on the plane when he turned up for the job. The story, as it was related to me, went that the first officer was actually kept at the airport after the plane took off and his phone was even taken from him, so his family were initially extremely worried about him when they heard the news that the plane had been lost. He finally got his phone back and called them to say that he was not on the plane. If this was true, it would require solid explanations from MAS as to why such a change was imposed at the last minute. Considering the fate of the flight, it would be highly suspicious.

For the time being, I had not been able to identify nor talk to this pilot, if indeed he existed. But according to the official 'individual crew roster' of the co-pilot that I got access to, Fariq Abdul Hamid was marked for Flight MH370 leaving that night. He was supposed to fly the returning Flight MH371 the following day – Sunday, 9 March – after a day's rest in Beijing. So either the document I saw had been fabricated, or the last-minute-replacement story was just another rumour to haunt this case. A rumour that fitted quite well, by the way, with the suspicions between races that are rampant in Malaysia.

In another document from the 'Melon project', the private investigators state that the plane flew 'under radar deliberately'. But this does not square with the speeds shown in the Australian reports. In fact, there is a near-direct correlation between the altitude of a jetliner and its speed.

Very oddly, the private report also indicates that the captain, who had shut himself inside the cockpit, flew the jetliner to an altitude that was beyond the aircraft's limits in order to 'lose everyone'. 'Pilot is safe. Not sure who else could have lived. Search was deliberately late because they needed credible excuse. Chinese government was also aware.' It is unclear how they arrived at this astounding conclusion. The private investigation also established that a package had arrived from Pakistan a few days before 8 March. 'Cargo personnel remember because the packages were collected by a Chinese technician from China (which is out of the ordinary). These packages were loaded on Flight MH370. After the incident the cargo guys came up with the theory in their small talk that these packages contain images for drone system technology stolen from U.S. Base in Afghanistan when Al Qaeda raided the base.' So the American drones reappeared on the scene, but this time they arrived by aircraft from Islamabad or Karachi, and not by cargo ship from Africa via the Seychelles. If this part of the private investigation was accurate, it showed a new flaw in the cargo manifest because nowhere did it mention any such packages. Unless mangosteens grow in Pakistan ...

The report also referred to two American servicemen who had laid claim to the 5 million reward, stating that they were in possession of a video showing the last moments of the jetliner but with no further details as to whether the scene was over land or water, or how it ended. The investigators said that they checked the identity of the two men, only identified by their initials: one was a pilot and racing driver from Arizona, the other in the Signal Corps and stationed at a US base in Germany.

After going through these documents, I didn't know what to think. First, I found it hard to believe that a 'private investigation' that cost some US$100,000 consisted only of these few pages of often self-contradictory and half-baked information.

There were only two possible conclusions in my view (besides the fact that I had picked the wrong job).

Either the detective agency set out to manipulate the families by making them believe one scenario (the guilt of the pilot) rather than another. Or the investigators themselves were manipulated, at least on certain issues such as the pilot's responsibility. This would confirm the rather negative view of the detective agency that I had previously obtained.

In either case, the initiative had turned out to be a fiasco for all those who funded it, as well as for the families' committee that commissioned it. I could see why Sarah Bajc decided that the information should never be made public but be restricted to the committee. Interestingly, in laying out the 'objectives of the second phase investigation', which, to my knowledge, never took place, the firm indicates: 'The first phase of investigations have focused on work in Asia Pacific region but our findings strongly suggest that the answers could lie with the USA.'

Chun-jie Song lost his sister on MH370. She was returning from a package tour to Nepal and was on her way to Canton. At the last minute, she gave up her seat on a direct flight to Canton to an elderly traveller, sparing that person the trouble of a long and tiring detour via Beijing. As a result, she never arrived home. When I met Chun-jie for the first time, some eight months after the loss of the jetliner, he was depressed, desperate and exhausted. He remained in almost constant contact with the other Chinese families via the WeChat forum, the most popular messaging platform in continental China. He had built up a rough overview of the Chinese passengers: in addition to the 23 people on the package tour to Nepal that included his sister, there were about 30 calligraphers who were returning from an exhibition, around 40 building labourers working in Singapore, some 50 junior and senior investors (whose trip had been paid for by a property developer), the eight Freescale Semiconductor engineers (among the 20 Freescale employees in total) and a handful of people travelling alone.

Chun-jie told me that those members of the families' group who were retired went every day to the information centre opened and run by the government in Beijing. The centre was in the middle of nowhere and could not be reached by public transport. Determined not to be discouraged, they had organised themselves and took it in turns to go every day to ask for the latest news about the investigation. 'It's just to show that they have to continue to look for the plane, otherwise they'll close the centre,' he said. On one occasion the Chinese families got together and drew up a letter, which they handed over during a demonstration in front of the Malaysian embassy in Beijing, but they were forbidden to speak to foreign media outlets, while being openly encouraged to take legal action against Malaysia Airlines.

International lawyers had even been placed at their disposal free of charge for this purpose. It was not clear to them what their best course of action was, and receiving compensation was the least of their concerns at that point.

In the Chinese families' group, no one understood why China did not start up its own independent investigation. With over 130 Chinese passengers on board and Beijing as the destination of the flight, China surely had plenty of ground to open an investigation. 'With all the Boeings they buy, they should only have to say, "Tell us the truth or we'll stop buying!"' the Chinese next of kin told themselves. But since there was no Chinese investigation, the Chinese families pinned most of their hopes on the French judicial inquiry. When an interview with Ghyslain Wattrelos was published in France, together with a photo of him, the whole forum expressed its delight with the article. 'He's our hero. At least he is really fighting for the truth,' Chun-jie told me, scrolling through the list of enthusiastic comments about the Frenchman on his mobile phone.

February 2015, Kuala Lumpur. The first anniversary of the disappearance was drawing near. The three young women who arranged to meet me in a Mexican restaurant in Bangsar Village, a residential quarter of the Malaysian capital, had known each other for almost a year. Together they had lived through a nightmarish experience. They greeted one another like good friends, gently rubbing each other's backs and attempting a slight grin. But they were unable to properly smile. Life would never have brought them together if MH370 had not vanished into thin air. Grace Subathirai Nathan, a young Malaysian lawyer, lost her mother, who was travelling to join her husband, Grace's father, a worker who had been posted to Beijing. Yuen Ying, meanwhile, had encouraged her husband – a Freescale Semiconductor engineer – to take the weekend off to visit Beijing. As for Kelly Wen Yan, her Chinese husband was prospecting for real estate in Malaysia; he was returning for the weekend, as usual, to join her and their three-year-old daughter.

Kelly had moved to Kuala Lumpur for a few months to sort out her husband's business affairs. She was constantly on the verge of tears, and was outraged by Malaysia Airlines' latest gaffe

A few minutes before the press briefing of 29 January 2015, the airline advised all the families on its contact list to 'switch on the TV and watch CNN'. Is it possible to imagine the state of people's hearts and minds, when they are holding on despite everything to the hope of a miraculous outcome, and are then told to watch CNN as a matter of urgency? It awakens the wildest hopes and triggers the most terrifying anxiety. When they did watch CNN, it was to find out that the disappearance of MH370 had now been classified as an 'accident'. But Malaysia Airlines compounded its insensitivity: 'When they saw that the families were going to attend the press briefing, they cancelled everything. And yet, we were the ones who should have been notified first!' the young women protested angrily. 'The worst is that they stated that the disappearance was an "accident" without providing a shred of new supporting evidence. They have just one thing in mind: close the file as soon as possible,' added Grace Subathirai Nathan.

In China too, the announcement stirred up the anger of the families and friends once again. Twenty or so relatives of MH370 passengers therefore resolved to come to Kuala Lumpur to give Malaysia Airlines some idea of the immense frustration they were experiencing. They all still held on to the hope that they would learn something about what happened. The Chinese group finally decided to camp out on the pavement in front of the Malaysian airline's offices on the night of their arrival. A brief meeting was held on 13 February with MAS, who had nothing new to say.

Two weeks earlier, on Friday, 30 January, Kelly Wen Yan had managed to obtain an appointment with Malaysia's newly instated Minister of Transport, Liow Tiong Lai. At the meeting he promised to provide her with all the raw data supplied by Inmarsat on the following Monday. The families wanted an independent expert appraisal of this data, on which the whole explanation of the crash in the middle of the southern seas was based. After asking the minister's office repeatedly for the documents, Kelly Wen Yan was finally informed in mid-February that the documents in question would not be handed over to her. There was no point in her insisting.

So what sensitive information lay buried in the satellite data, and why were the data supplied at the end of May 2014 following pressure from the media not complete? While the Inmarsat table glimpsed on TV had 28 columns of figures, the table finally made public by Malaysia had only nine. 'If there was nothing interesting in the other columns, why not just show them?' wondered Duncan Steel, the British astrophysicist and a member of the Independent Group.

The families were asking for the complete Inmarsat data, just as they were asking for the unedited tape of the 52 minutes of verbal exchanges between the MH370 cockpit and Malaysian air traffic control. Because, according to two forensic sound recording experts called in by the NBC News television network, the recording made public by Malaysia Airlines in May 2014 was quite clearly cut and edited, or, in other words, doctored. 'When evidence or valuable recorded information is claimed to be "edited to remove the silent places where no dialogue took place" and I can clearly hear the edits, then in my professional opinion, I would much prefer that they give us the entire cockpit communication with the towers and we will fast forward through the silent places,' said Ed Primeau, one of the two experts, confirming the suspicion of creative editing. Since then, I was told by a different source, in Malaysia, that there may have been far more information on the original tape than on the version that had been made public. It was even hinted there were odd noises in the cockpit, and voices possibly speaking in Arabic or some other Middle Eastern language shortly before what was felt to be the end.

What may have been said – and what may have happened – in the cockpit up to the loss of contact that cannot be disclosed? If the recording of the exchanges between the ground and the pilot were corroborating the official narrative of the accident, it would not have been doctored. The very fact that the recording had been tampered with suggested that there was something – a phrase, a word, or noises – in the cockpit during the final minutes or seconds of communication that would have given crucial indications about this instant of crisis, when the final outcome was played out. It was essential for the families to be given access to an original version of the recording, providing it still existed.

The publication of the first provisional investigation report, entitled *Factual Information: Safety Information for MH370*, exactly one year after the loss of the jetliner, was basically a non-event. Apart from a few hardened MHists whose motivation was still intact, among them the members of the Independent Group, almost no one paid any attention to the 586 pages of technical information. There, were, however some new revelations, particularly that the recommended limit date (December 2012) of the battery powering the FDR black box transmitter beacon had expired.[*] Malaysia and Australia had failed to indicate this 'detail' when the whole world's attention was focused on detecting pings in the Indian Ocean. If they had done so, they would have had to admit that they were not hunting two pings in the vast expanse of ocean, but just one, effectively halving the already tiny probability of success. 'Before starting their search, the Australians necessarily asked MAS for a few technical details about the black boxes, such as their brands and date of manufacture. They couldn't not be aware that one of the two beacons no longer had any chance of working,' I was told by a well-informed MHist.

As for the passenger list, the report published one year after the event contained only a link to the Transport Ministry website, which did not even work. The fact remained that no full official list

---

[*] *Factual Information: Safety Investigation for MH370* dated 8 March 2015, op cit., p. 60.

had ever been made public. The only list available, even two years later, still contained 'the Italian' and 'the Austrian' among the passengers, rather than the two young Iranians. How bad was that? The families were therefore also calling for a full official and updated list of all the passengers on board.

It was around this time that I heard talk of the passenger-embarkation video. The Malaysian police had shown some clips from the video to members of certain Malaysian families at the start of the investigation, to help with passenger identification. But few people had seen the video in its entirety. The families had asked for this too, in vain. However, it turned out that someone had a pirate copy.

Making contact with the person who had it in his possession was a tricky process. I went off one day on a trip, with no mobile phone or computer, bearing only the address of a meeting point in a city several hours by air from Hong Kong. I met the contact at the appointed place, overcoming an initial misunderstanding about the name of the building that almost blew the whole thing. The contact led me to his home with very few introductions. He drew the curtains across the window of the room, in which there was a large flat screen, and then took a small memory card out of a Ziploc bag and inserted it into his DVD player. After showing me briefly how the remote control worked, he went off to do something else. I didn't know what I was expecting from the video, but I thought it was important to see it, just in case. I described what it showed in Chapter 1 of this book. It was just one of the thousands of videos produced each day by all the modern airports on the planet. The only difference was that this video showed the last moments of the 239 people who boarded MH370 in all their everyday normality. Later, another person who had been told of my visit joined me, and helped me in the laborious process of counting the passengers and crew. As the surveillance camera was not directly opposite the scanner archways, it was sometimes hard to see the archway through which a particular person had passed. We zoomed in on each zone, and proceeded to describe every passenger by noting a few distinctive characteristics, in most cases his or her racial type, body size, age group and colour of clothes, filling several pages of an Excel file. What was the point? I didn't really know. But I had travelled a long way to view the recording, and when faced with this moving procession of unknown people, set to suddenly disappear, I didn't know what else to do.

Alongside the enigmatic Sarah Bajc and the unfathomable Ethan Hunt, Ghyslain Wattrelos turned out to be a far more dependable contact in the course of my investigation. But that did not necessarily mean that he was any less complex.

From our very first exchanges he seemed hard to pin down. When I met him, in Hong Kong or Paris, it was easy. He was a strong figure, dignified and concentrated, and his suffering, which had fossilised into anger, inspired respect. Most of the journalists who met him felt a desire to help him – a desire to help him understand what might have happened. But I felt that, when he was on his own, he was once again plunged into the nightmare. He could not bring himself to mourn his triple loss, even though time was passing. He tried, he said, to protect his elder son, who was also deeply troubled by the lack of evidence, the general impression of orchestrated confusion and the rule of silence.

But if he was obsessed by the affair, why did he leave so many messages unanswered, why did he not keep the appointments made for phone conversations?

Perhaps he had moments when he would have liked to forget, whereas I was examining the cause of his unfathomable distress from every angle, with clinical detachment and a compulsiveness driven by my deadline. By uncovering the many inconsistencies in the case, I was unintentionally blowing on the embers that were consuming the surviving members of these broken families.

'We don't have the same agenda at all!' he said to me one day. But we did have the same objective: to understand what had happened and to overcome the pseudo-mystery that surrounded the affair.

One morning, when he sent me a piece of information, I responded with a laconic comment: 'Thanks, very interesting.' I was mightily surprised when an answer arrived straight away: 'So now you're getting up early?' I was taken aback. A joke! I was delighted, and replied: 'So now you're making jokes?' He replied once again: 'Maybe we'll end up getting along fine.' A welcome light-hearted moment that brought some relief in such a sombre and tragic case.

I found out through our exchanges that he had an entourage of people with a wide range of backgrounds who regularly supplied him with information, some confidential, some wholly sourced from the internet. So many things had been said to him that he no longer knew which piece of information came from which source.

In July 2015, he asked me to meet him at the Saint James Club, a classic Napoleon III mansion at Porte Dauphine in Paris, where he met most of the journalists who asked to see him. His office was 50 metres away, and the establishment's fat black cat insisted on keeping me company as I awaited his arrival. The meeting was simply to review the latest news, the recent studies published by the Australian bureau or the Independent Group, and the new rumours.

He seemed rather worried when he arrived. He had to go to the United States the following week, but several people had told him not to. Furthermore, someone had stolen his name (spelling it with one 't' instead of two) and his photo to create a false Facebook account, which the impostor then used to send inappropriate messages to many of his female friends. Wattrelos, of course, had been entirely unaware of the fact until it was brought to his attention. 'I had been warned that when I became a problem, they would try to discredit me in all kinds of ways,' he told me. He was starting to think that more and more strange figures were making their unwelcome presence felt in the investigation. His postal mail did not seem to be arriving normally and he wondered if his phone was being bugged. On the other hand, the company he worked for was giving him strong support, but he was unsure how long it would last.

On the morning in question, his interest had understandably been aroused by a new lead. An Australian by the name of Paul Power had been hinting for weeks that he knew where the aircraft was – and the passengers. Power was ready to pass on the information if, and only if, they could find a secure means of communication. I had already run a quick search on this informer, and had immediately told Ghyslain Wattrelos about my doubts. Power's website looked like one of those false sites that can be conjured up in a few moments, and there was no answer when I rang the hotline number indicated. His Facebook photo looked rather sinister – you could only see the lower part of a bearded face, as the rest was in the dark. There was nothing there that inspired any confidence at all. But the prospect was tremendously tempting, and I fully understood that Ghyslain Wattrelos wanted to know more. The man was based in Melbourne. This was still a good time to call him, allowing for the time difference. We went out into the walled garden. Ghyslain Wattrelos put his mobile on a small table, with the speaker switched on. Power picked up after a few rings. I recorded the conversation.

Power said that the jetliner was in 'hostile territory' and that the passengers were alive. He stressed that it was essential that the information he provided was not made public, as the only way to achieve a satisfactory outcome to the crisis was to offer an amnesty to the hijackers. After 40 minutes, he promised to send an encrypted document containing all the information, and the programme needed to decrypt it. I didn't believe a word of it, but I couldn't manage to convince Wattrelos that Power was a nutcase or an imposter. At one point, Ghyslain Wattrelos said to the Australian: 'Do you realise the implications for me of what you are insinuating?' He replied: 'Yes, of course. I'm not doing this for me. My greatest reward will be to see all these people come home.'

I was appalled to see that such a crackpot could appear out of the blue and cause so much trouble. The more hope, the more despair afterwards. But now we'd gone this far in our dealings with Power, we should go all the way. Once the document had been received and decrypted, it stated, after 14 pages of trigonometric calculations, that the jetliner was in Somalia. I asked Brock McEwen, a Canadian mathematician and MHist I'd been keeping in touch with, to take a look. He quickly reached his verdict: 'Regarding the document sent, I can see no other way of putting it: "garbage in, garbage out".' A complete waste of time, in other words. McEwen pointed out that the author of the study confused milliseconds with microseconds* ... I passed his message on to Ghyslain Wattrelos, for whom this was just one more bitter disappointment.

How many false leads would have to be eliminated before the truth came to light and the families could finally find closure?

---

* 1 millisecond = 1,000 microseconds.

7

Counter-investigation
in the Maldives

Sunday, 3 May 2015. I set off for the Maldives, very curious about what I was to learn there.

When the plane disappeared, several islanders on the southern Maldives island of Kuda Huvadhoo claimed they had seen a 'big plane' fly over early in the morning at low altitude and that it was making an 'incredibly loud noise'. The time of day seemed to correspond, as the plane had been seen at dawn (MH370 had been scheduled to land in Beijing at 6.30 am). As the geographic location of the Maldives put the islands easily within reach of Flight MH370 (3,200 kilometres from Kuala Lumpur to Malé, compared with 5,500 to Beijing), the scenario seemed credible. Accessible distance, time match – both seemed to coincide. Moreover, when this information came to light in mid-March 2014, the entire world was still hoping to find the lost jet. For the families, this information came as a sort of relief. They could imagine what had potentially happened, and many believed the story.

But hardly had this information been published by the Maldivian newspaper *Haveeru Online*, and picked up by several major media outlets, than Hishammuddin Hussein, the Malaysian Minister for Defence and Transport, declared it to be false. 'The Head of Malaysian Defence contacted his counterpart in the Maldives, who has confirmed that these testimonials were unfounded,' he declared at the 19 March 2014 press briefing. In fact, given the climate of mistrust that had developed between the authorities on the one hand, and the press and families on the other, the authorities' denial probably added to the credibility of this scenario. The Maldivian hypothesis continued to intrigue.

Quite early on, I telephoned the *Haveeru Online* journalists who had published the information. 'When they called us, the Kuda residents were very insistent. But we didn't believe them. You know, the people living on these small islands say they see a lot of things ...' Shan Anees said to me on the phone. I was surprised by this young journalist's reaction, because if experience has taught me one thing, it is to take the opinions, intuition and judgement of locals seriously. They know the context, which they then use to help interpret an event, although not necessarily with precision. But their judgement is often more informed than it might at first appear. For a long time, therefore, I put this story to one side, while noting that many MHists continued to believe in it. I was probably counting on other journalists to go there to clarify the situation and get a definitive answer to the question of what these people had seen fly over their island at daybreak on the day of the plane's disappearance. Was it, yes or no, the plane we were all looking for?

Fifteen months after the event, only two international media outlets, the French weekly *Paris Match* and the Australian daily *The Australian*, had taken the step of sending someone to the Maldives to verify these eyewitness accounts.

The report by the well-known French novelist Marc Dugain in *Paris Match*, published in the 18–23 December 2014 issue, was eagerly taken up by the English-speaking media. I was surprised and frustrated by this article in equal measure. The author got the date of the flight's disappearance wrong in the very first sentence about his investigation in the Maldives.* No witness was named or quoted directly, and there were no descriptions of the sites he visited or of the people he met. But the article mentioned a turn

---

* He referred to 'the morning of 9 March' instead of 8 March.

that the low-flying plane was seen to have made, consistent with it heading towards the Diego Garcia base. The novelist had long defended the thesis of a shoot-down of MH370 on its approach to the US military base and he seemed to me a bit desperate to prove it. Flying so low, so far away from the target, however, made the whole scenario a non-starter.

The report published on 4 April 2015 on the front page of the Sunday edition of *The Australian* was far more detailed. It was this article that put the discussion back on the table and once again raised people's hopes. Because if MH370 really had been sighted in the Maldives at dawn on 8 March, the underwater search led by Australia, 5,000 kilometres away on the bed of the Indian Ocean, was way off. In Australia, the subject was being followed all the more closely as the search area had just been doubled in April 2015, the first 60,000 square kilometres in the priority search area having yielded absolutely nothing.

This new article annoyed Ibrahim Faizal, the Chairman of the Maldives Civil Aviation Authority, with whom I had been in relatively frequent contact over the past few months. I was impressed by his intellectual honesty right from our first discussions. In the course of our email exchange, Faizal told me that he intended to speak to the locals and 'see for himself' on site. I offered to accompany him

'*Tuan Tuan, Puan Puan, Assalamualaikum ...*' ('Ladies and gentlemen, may peace be upon you ...'). The crew was particularly relaxed and upbeat on board Flight MH073 to Mae. The chief flight attendant was addressing the passengers with the term of endearment 'darling', unusual for Malaysia Airlines. At around 10 pm, according to my in-flight entertainment screen, we were 5,542 kilometres from Mecca and 2,378 kilometres from the Nicobar Islands. Our flight path was virtually horizontal on the map: 3,150 kilometres from east to west, parallel to the equator.

The following morning, despite a blue sky and turquoise water just like in the tourist brochures, the atmosphere on board the ferry connecting with the island that was home to the capital Malé bore no resemblance to the relaxed and smiling faces of the South Pacific islands that I was familiar with. Here, the women all covered up with veils. Many even wearing black stockings and long gloves, despite it being 35°C in the shade. The Maldives, the smallest country in Asia, was not the friendliest at first encounter.

'Turn right as you leave the ferry, then left after the Bank of Maldives,' were the instructions that Ibrahim Faizal had given me. Malé was a mushroom city of just over 150,000 people built atop an island measuring slightly under two square kilometres, making it one of the most densely populated places on earth. At the ferry terminal, you were immediately thrown into a cacophony of scooters, delivery carts and taxis, mostly in a pitiable state; a mixture of India, Africa and the Middle East, with its very strange language, Dhivehi, which rang, sang and pinged all at once. But the tourists in the dream resorts, where they swam with turtles directly from their bungalows built over the water, saw none of this chaos.

The offices of the Civil Aviation Authority were on the 11th floor of the Government Building. With its 12 floors, it was the second-tallest building in the capital. Faizal was waiting for me behind the glass doors of its seemingly empty offices, and greeted me with a firm and reassuring handshake. He seemed somewhat amused by my visit, and despite being an imposing figure, his broad smile fitted well with his relaxed manner.

The Maldives Civil Aviation Authority (CAA) was an independent entity managed by a board of directors chaired by Faizal. This board still reported to a government minister appointed by the president of the Maldives – in March 2014, this was the charismatic Minister of Defence, Mohamed Nazim, although Nazim had been in prison since January 2015.* 'Political life in the Maldives is somewhat turbulent' was a phrase I would hear repeatedly

---

* Mohamed Nazim was released in November 2018, after the September 2018 elections.

during my stay. Since the arrest of Nazim, the Civil Aviation Authority had been placed under the authority of the minister of tourism.

Faizal wasted no time in telling me that he no longer had time to go to Kuda Huvadhoo as planned. His job involved a lot of travelling and he had to leave the Maldives in a few days' time. He nonetheless talked to me about his frustration with regard to the disappearance of Flight MH370. 'People like me [that is, his counterparts in other countries' civil aviation authorities] have a serious problem with the fact that Boeing has remained almost totally silent about this affair since the beginning.' He had known his Malaysian opposite number, who has been at the centre of the affair right from the start, for years. And not without reason. Placed between Malawi and Mali in the alphabetical order of countries, Malaysia and the Maldives always found themselves seated next to each other at major international civil aviation meetings.

As far as the local aspect of the matter was concerned, if indeed there was one, Faizal said he would like to see it settled once and for all. Claims that MH370 might have travelled through *his* airspace clearly annoyed him, especially since it was the police, and not the CAA, that had written the report that was sent to Malaysia. Despite repeated requests from his office, the police had never provided the CAA with a copy. 'I have no doubt as to the complete reliability of the report. All I ask is to see it,' he said. As soon as word got out that people had seen a plane flying at low altitude over the south of the archipelago, the police and the MNDF* dispatched investigators from Malé to Kuda Huvadhoo to question several witnesses.

Faizal's right-hand man, Ibrahim Rasheed, the Director of Flight Operations, joined us in his boss's office overlooking the small but

---

* The Maldives National Defence Force is the combined security organisation responsible for defending the country and acting as its coastguard.

bustling capital. He was a former MNDF pilot, whom Faizal called 'Captain Rasheed'. He recounted how he had made a few phone calls to people who had seen the much-talked-about plane. 'Right from the first accounts,' Rasheed recalled, 'the plane seemed to be flying in a more or less north-west–south-east direction, and not east to west as logic would dictate if it were coming from Asia.' In his opinion it was just one of the many flights between the Middle East and Australia. He had constructed a tentative explanation that he wanted to share with me. Each day, around 20 scheduled international flights passed over the Maldives along two main flight paths that formed an X over the archipelago: Middle East–Australia and India–Africa. On 8 March 2014, 18 international flights passed over the archipelago.* Early morning flights from the Gulf flew over the Maldives at dawn, local time.

'When they arrive in our airspace, because of the weight of the fuel still on board, they are still flying at a relatively low altitude of between 31,000 and 33,000 feet, but often as they leave Maldivian airspace they request our permission to climb to 39,000–40,000 feet, where the air is rarer and flight conditions far better,' said the former pilot. But I objected that, by the sound of the reported descriptions, what the Kuda Huvadhoo islanders had seen was flying much lower than 30,000 feet. As a matter of fact, the Director of Flight Operations was not totally satisfied with his own explanation either.

On the other hand, he was far more sure of himself concerning the extinguisher found on 24 March on the island of Baarah in the northern part of the archipelago. Although this spherical object looked like a sea mine, its shape corresponded to a certain type of extinguisher found in aircraft holds. It was identified by a Maldivian aeronautical engineer, who was quoted by *Haveruu Online* as saying it was 'very probably an aircraft extinguisher', although the engineer said he could only confirm his impression if he had a

---

* Notably eight Emirates Airline flights, two Cathay Pacific flights, two Qatar Airways flights and one Qantas flight, among others.

chance to see the actual object. *Paris Match* ramped up the discussion when it claimed to have sent the photos taken by the Mayor of Baarah 'before the object was confiscated by the military [...] to a maintenance manager of a major airline and a specialist based in Los Angeles. [...] Both concluded there was a strong similarity with a Boeing extinguisher. A member of the Maldivian military, not wanting to be named, also confirmed to us that it was definitely an extinguisher.'

According to the people I spoke to, everything about this story was false. Not only was this object far from being a Boeing part (because, as I was told, Boeing or its sub-contractors numbered everything, even bolts in some cases, and the numbers here were not Boeing ones), but it was the CAA and not the military that produced the report on this object. Rasheed placed the 12 photos included in the technical report sent to Malaysia on the table in front of us. His own experts had confirmed that none of the serial numbers on the parts corresponded to Boeing parts. For him, that was the end of the matter and there was nothing further to be gained from discussing it.

However, while the matter of the extinguisher was closed, we still had doubts after an hour and a half's discussion as to the nature of the unidentified flying object that a handful of islanders saw 150 miles south of the capital. So just what were the conclusions in the official police report sent to Malaysia?

Three days later, back in Malé from my trip to Kuda Huvadhoo, I too tried to get this report – or at least to see it – by taking a letter to the police HQ with the *Le Monde* letterhead and signed by the newspaper's director, Jérôme Fenoglio. Despite being shunted from one office to another, I only managed to get a brief meeting and a laconic response from the young spokesman for the Maldives Police Force, who went by the name of Firax: 'The eyewitness accounts were very incoherent. That's all I can tell you.' And his boss was out of the office …

* * *

After my first meeting with the CAA, my next priority was to find a way of getting to the much-discussed island. As Faizal could no longer find the time to go, I would not be able to simply tag along with him.

On the map, the Maldives looks like a string of islands hanging down from the south-west tip of Sri Lanka. Some 1,200 coral islands, of which around 200 are inhabited, are distributed between 26 atolls and form a long, vertical loop, with a few isolated islands scattered in the south. 'Small islands', 'small atolls' and even a 'small archipelago' the Maldives might be, but each island is still separated from the others by tens if not hundreds of miles.

My single contact on Kuda Huvadhoo was not answering. The only way I had to get in touch with him was a local Maldives number on Viber, the free communication app that everyone there seemed to use. I started to put together some options about how to get to the island. Everything was expensive and complicated. There was a resort on the north of Dhaalu Atoll, from where I could rent an outboard to cross the atoll to Kuda. There was also another hotel – seven stars, this one – geographically closer to the village, but the 45-minute seaplane flight cost three times the price of my ticket from Hong Kong to the Maldives. I could not see myself putting 'Maldives seaplane flight' on my report expense account. I scanned the list of domestic flights at the airport to see if something would get me close to my destination. There was a small airport on the neighbouring atoll. A one-way flight to Thimarafushi cost 1,444 rufiyaas (£72), but the somewhat perplexed sales assistant implied that it would not be easy to get from there to Kuda by sea.

During the evening of my first and very long day in Malé, my belief in the low-flying aircraft story started to flag; the local journalists never really believed it, the Civil Aviation authorities did not believe it either (even if they had trouble explaining precisely what had been seen), and the reports coming out of the village might have attempted to lend credence to the MH370 theory but were not convincing. What more would I find? This island was too far away, I had already cost the newspaper too much for too little in return, and, to make matters worse, the lukewarm curry served to me by the humourless and bespectacled owner of the tiny hotel on the airport island where I was staying was virtually inedible. However, sitting under the restaurant's garish neon lights and holding a somewhat forced conversation with this man, I learnt by chance that his nephew, who sometimes ran the hotel reception, was an air traffic controller in Malé. I suddenly found the grumpy owner quite pleasant.

When I turned my phone on again the following morning, I finally had news from my local contact, Shamsul Falaah. He used to be a legal advisor to the former president of the Maldives and was currently holed up in New Zealand, under the pretext of studying there. Political life in the Maldives was indeed 'turbulent'. The time difference explained his lack of response all afternoon and evening the previous day. His help would be crucial. His cousin Hussain Shakir was the vice president of Kuda Huvadhoo Council, and Hussain would find transport for me. One of Hussain's best friends had seen the plane.

Suddenly, after a few hours of Viber phone calls and emails, my visit to the island was practically arranged. I had a new network of friends – Shamsul, Ahmed, Shawad and Siam – all of whom had been made aware of my impending arrival in Kuda, where Hussain would act as my guide. It was Hussain who convinced me to take the night ferry. 'Very comfortable,' he said, with an air-conditioned salon and 'power outlets to plug in your computer'. I could even go out on the deck to admire the almost full moon if I felt like it. And to make sure everything went smoothly, Hussain's brother was going to accompany me. This ferry crossing in the Maldives archipelago was starting to feel like an idyllic summer-night cruise. Anyway, there was only one ferry a week, and it was leaving tonight.

Night had already fallen several hours prior to my arrival at the port in North Malé. The air was filled with the smell of the sea, diesel fuel and grilled fish. Along the poorly lit wharf, fishing boats and bulk carriers were moored tightly together. Their myriad hull shapes, in heavy steel plate eroded by the sea, had been visibly painted many times over. Nets were being folded. Boats loaded and unloaded – passengers, chicken cages, scooters, sacks of rice and onions, the occasional TV or fan.

I finally located the *Nabura Express*. It was no different to the other boats, in no worse or better shape, and with no obvious clues as to the '*Express*' part of its name. The headroom in the dormitory, accessed via a short ladder, was too low to allow people to walk upright. In fact, you had to crawl on all fours, which proved quite tricky when wearing a dress. Narrow mats were laid out edge to edge and a tiny vinyl-covered pillow indicated at which end to place your head. I had only just settled myself in when an employee started signalling wildly to me through the openings in the portside gangway. I understood from his concerned gesturing that he was saying 'Get out of there!'. It turned out that my place was in the upper dormitory, where you could stand up straight and where, as Hussain had told me over the phone, there were separate male and female WCs. Quite a step up, actually.

When Hussain's brother – in fact a distant cousin – found me several minutes before we set sail, he greeted me with a degree of unease. To accompany a foreign woman such as myself was quite evidently a chore he would have happily avoided. The ferry was full, and I realised I would not have made it without Hussain's help. When it cast off at 10 pm, the passengers all unpacked the things they would need for the night: torch, food and sleeping sheet. Above all, I envied them their sleeping sheets, as that would have avoided my having constantly to worry about the position of my skirt. The two square neon lights cast a dull light along the central aisle but it was not enough to read by.

The night of my idyllic cruise turned out to be almost as turbulent as political life in the Maldives. At one stage, the storm tossed the boat about to such an extent that the passengers, sleeping packed against each other, were thrown slightly up in the air with each wave before thudding back on the floor. The little blue bags hanging on the posts now came in handy. At the start of the trip, the women had taken a few of them to stow their shoes in But at the height of the storm, their intended purpose became quite clear. That's how rough the crossing was. Mobile phones rang incessantly – Arabic dances, Bollywood hits and even a rather comforting 'Hotel California' around four in the morning. At exactly 5 am, the Muslim call to prayer rang out throughout the dormitory – from a phone.

As day broke, the *Nabura Express* made her first stop. In the pale dawn light, an enormous Hitachi refrigerator was being unloaded onto a waiting cart. The storm had put us significantly behind schedule and the small green patch that was Kuda Huvadhoo only appeared on the horizon at around 8 am. From this distance, it really did look like confetti sprinkled on the sea. The island's population had suddenly jumped from around 2,300 to some 3,000 in 2004, after all the survivors from two neighbouring islands were transferred here following the destruction of their homes by the Boxing Day tsunami. But until the spate of articles recounting the story of an unidentified plane sighted here on the morning of 8 March 2014, this small island had once again disappeared from the world's consciousness. Everything and everyone had gone back to their old routine, punctuated by the reassuring and regular calls to prayer.

There was no mistaking Hussain Shakir on the dock. He was wearing a mauve shirt and a tie. He had cancelled all his meetings to be free to help me, he said, while at the same time apologising for not having a car available despite the passing showers. I would find out later that there were only four private cars on the island. In fact, the island's statistics are pretty simple: five mosques, four cars, two schools ... I'd like to add 'and one tie'.

The roll call of the eyewitnesses to the sighting of the unidentified plane could now begin. There was a lot to get through.

Zuhuriyya Ali was 50. She was a homemaker and welcomed us in the internal courtyard of her raw breeze-block home, handing out glasses of rose-flavoured milk and bowls of freshly sliced mango. Her daughter was there too, along with two young children curious to see the strange white woman who wanted to talk to their grandmother. Her husband watched the scene unfold from the comfort of his rocking chair. Leaning against a homemade dresser piled high with pots from previous meals, Zuhuriyya scrunched up her eyes as she searched her memory for the most precise description possible of what she had seen that morning.

'I was standing here and I heard this huge noise. I looked up and I saw a big plane coming from almost the same direction as usual, but a lot lower.' She pointed to part of her corrugated iron roof and traced an arc in the sky. She was sure of the time: 6.15 am, give or take a minute or two, because prayers were at 5 am, when the men went to the mosque and the women prayed together or at home, then at 6 she had started sweeping the courtyard while her husband had gone back to bed.

A military plane? Impossible. Her husband, who had worked for the MNDF,* had already asked her this question. It was not that fast. She had spoken to two strangers prior to this visit, but the police had not interviewed her and she did not know who broke the story to *Haveeru Online* in Malé a week later.

Five minutes away by scooter, a young high-school student told us his version of the events. Humaam Dhonmonik, 16, wearing a football shirt with the number 13 on the back, had gone to fetch something off the clothes line. Like every Saturday, he was getting ready for his religious instruction class that started at 7 am. He also pointed to a point in the sky where he had first seen the plane, between two big trees. He talked about it in class and another student told him that her father had seen the plane too. Holding up the compass on his mobile phone, the direction that the plane had

---

* Maldives National Defence Force.

come from was the same as that indicated by Zuhuriyya Ali: west-north-west. That's also what the Director of Flight Operations had understood. When I pointed out that MH370 should logically have come from the opposite direction (due east), his eyes opened wide with astonishment and he decided to check the position of Malaysia on Google Maps. He was disturbed by this piece of information. He saw blue and red paint around the cockpit, but 'no [Malaysia Airlines] logo'. 'I don't know if it was MH370,' he added, a little put out by the issue of the plane's direction.

I was keen to meet a certain Abdu Rasheed Ibrahim, because the article in *The Australian* presented him as a key witness. A full-length photo of him had been used on the front page of the news-paper's 4 April 2015 issue, and it was probably to him that the article in *Paris Match* was referring when it said, without giving a name, 'a fisherman aged around 50 standing in the water up to his waist'.

Abdu Rasheed Ibrahim was 46 years old. Erroneously referred to by *The Australian* as an 'Officer of the Magistrates Court', he was actually the court's handyman. On the morning of 8 March, when he heard the plane, he had been standing in the water fishing, at the spot where he could be found most mornings at the same time before heading off to work at 7 am. But as a strong wind was blowing from the north-east, he said he only really saw the plane just as it was passing overhead. As he had been standing at the water's edge, he was the only witness to have seen the plane change heading, bearing off more to the south-east. It was at the precise moment when the plane banked to turn that he saw 'red under the windows and red around the door'. The plane was flying low, but not so low that it looked as though it were about to land or crash. In any case, it did not frighten him. In fact, the incident did not concern him at all really. Nonetheless, Abdu Rasheed did tell his daughter Zynia about it when he got home. Zynia, who went to the same Saturday-morning religious instruction class as Dhonmonik, was therefore able to tell her friend that her father had seen the same plane as him when Dhonmonik spoke in class about what he had seen. The Kuda Huvadhoo villagers only heard about the disappearance of the Malaysian plane in the evening news on national TV. Some people then wondered: 'What if …?'

Once the story of this strange plane had been published, first in the local press, then in the international media, Abdu Rasheed Ibrahim remembers that investigators, the police and MNDF teams came to the island. They asked him to go back exactly to where he was when he saw the plane. Readings were taken. He spread his big hands in front of him to around 90 centimetres to show how big the plane had been in his field of vision. Since this report, I have travelled by plane many times and have often tried, including when approaching an airport by train or by taxi, to work out at what distance and at what altitude a plane would have to be to measure 90 centimetres in my field of vision. The police said that air traffic control had not observed any plane flying around here. But before I had set off for Kuda, the air traffic controller nephew of the restaurant manager had told me that the Malé radars were not strong enough to track that far. So either the police or the ATC were bluffing to cover their lack of evidence.

'There has to be some truth behind all this, but what?' said a perplexed Hussain Shakir, opening his betel nut kit at the end of our brief lunch. In his view, if Flight MH370 had crashed in their sea, the *dhonis*, the 100-foot boats that go to sea for two to three weeks to fish yellowfin tuna, would necessarily have seen floating debris. They all have radios and mobiles, and would call in an alert immediately if they saw something out of the ordinary. It happens. In November 2014, US military planes from the Diego Garcia base, 300 miles due south of the last of the Maldivian atolls, performed an unauthorised fly-over of the central part of the Maldives, exactly at the spot where we were. Fishermen caught in their nets a fairly sophisticated object comprising a box filled with electronic gadgetry and a metallic part with two sensors attached to an orange ball float. A photo of the object that had been handed to the Maldives coastguard was published by *Haveeru*. The minister for defence issued a statement saying that the Americans had apologised – an 'administrative error' had caused this misunderstanding.

My vice president friend and I continued our round of meetings, slaloming on his scooter between the puddles left in the middle of the rutted earth road by the torrential rain.

There were two obvious facts we could not ignore. First, this plane came from virtually the opposite direction to that from which MH370 was supposed to have come. Second, it was sighted after 6 am and well before 7 am local time in the Maldives, which was between 9 and 10 am local time in Beijing.

The aircraft that the Kuda residents saw therefore could not have been MH370, quite simply because at 6.15 am it was already 9.15 am in Beijing and Kuala Lumpur. MH370 would not have had enough fuel to fly for such an extended period of time. And the amount of fuel the plane carried was one of the few things we knew for sure.

According to the technical information provided by Malaysia Airlines and the first ACARS message issued on take-off, the plane had 49.1 or 49.2 tonnes of fuel. With this amount, the plane could have flown until 8 or 8.30 am, local time in Malaysia or China, that is, 5 or 5.30 am local time in the Maldives. Certainly not an hour more. Furthermore, according to the Inmarsat data, the plane had reached fuel exhaustion at 8.19 am local time in Perth, Australia, on 8 March (5.19 am local time in the Maldives).

Had the plane changed course and headed for the Maldives from its last known position, at 2.22 am north of Sumatra, it would have easily reached the Maldives, 2,400 kilometres from this last point. However, it would have got there much earlier, at around 5.30 am local time in Malaysia or 2.30 am local time in the Maldives.

What's more, I'm convinced that had a Boeing 777 flown over this village at low altitude, most of the islanders would at least have heard it. The trees and houses would have shaken as this huge

350-tonne flying machine – bigger and heavier than a whole fleet of *dhonis* – passed overhead.

That the 'big plane' seen that morning could not have been MH370 was now self-evident. Even so, these people still saw something that was neither a long-haul plane from the Gulf flying at 30,000 feet, nor a giant albatross. It made me think of the question that *The Australian*'s journalist, Hedley Thomas, signed off with at the end of his video report: 'If it wasn't MH370, then what was it?' Finally, it was Adam Saeed, a teacher of Dhivehi, the Maldivian language, at the Dhaalu Atoll Education Centre, who set me thinking.

'I was playing football with my son in the courtyard, when he pointed to the sky and said, "Look, Dad! A plane!" I immediately thought it was a plane coming in to land at the nearby airport. I was just annoyed that it was flying so low and disturbing us like that on a Saturday morning,' he said to me. A plane landing at the nearby airport? He too had given his testimony to the police. The flight to Thimarafushi costing 1,444 rufiyaas came to mind. The neighbouring atoll, its brand new airport, the strong north-east wind – rare at the equator – the sudden change of heading to the south-east … Everything was starting to fall into place. I was impatient to get back to Malé and find out about this airport and its domestic flights.

Ibrahim Faizal, leaning on one elbow, listened to what I had to say but looked dubious. 'We totally agree that it wasn't MH370. But from what you say, they did still see a plane?' I knew he had the means to check my hypothesis, but was it in his interest to do so? He would see what information he could find, he told me as he accompanied me back. On my way to the ferry back to the airport island, I passed in front of the office of Maldivian (the national airlines in the Maldives) on the chaotic Malé waterfront. In the window, there were several advertising posters for the best-known local destinations. The planes were painted white and had the company name written in red in a sort of handwritten script around the windows, and the splash of a blue wave on the tail. I also noted 'red around the door', echoing what the magistrates' court handy-man had said. And there was no red around the doors of Malaysia Airlines Boeing 777s. I returned to my little hotel on the airport island, wondering whether a simple Maldivian comestic flight, off its normal course, might not finally be the solution to this enigma that had been the subject of so many column inches around the world. The air controller nephew was unfortunately not behind the reception desk. I would have liked to have sounded him out.

In the meantime, I discovered that the airport in question had been inaugurated in September 2013, although it was not yet in service at the time. The President of the Maldives, Mohammed Waheed, said as much in his inaugural address, meaning that in March 2014 it was brand spanking new. Because it did not have a control tower, approaches had to be made by sight. For such routes, Maldivian (the airline company) was using twin-engine, 50-seater Bombardier DHC-8s. Various technical reports for this aircraft stated that it was 'renowned for being noisy'. Hardly a Boeing 777, but it must be said that Kuda residents had never said they had seen a Boeing 777 or even a wide-bodied, long-haul jet. They only ever talked about a big plane flying low and making a lot of noise. Anything else was mere extrapolation.

On Sunday, I at last received a message from Faizal, titled 'Flight movements Thimarafushi airport 8 & 9 March 2014', containing a complete table of all the arrival and departure flights for this airport on 8 and 9 March. There were five arrivals and five depar-tures on both days. On the morning of 8 March, Maldivian domes-tic Flight DQA149 landed at 06:33. A perfect fit!

So was that the noisy plane, considerably bigger than a seaplane, with a white body and red detailing (around the windows and doors) and blue on the tail, that had flown over Kuda Huvadhoo that morning at dawn? Was it the stronger than usual north-east wind mentioned by the fisherman that had forced the pilot to adopt a different approach? Without any local air control, the pilot had to make all the decisions. He could – and indeed had to – change his flight plan to suit the conditions. The only thing he needed to do was announce his intentions over a general frequency used by all other aircraft in the vicinity. Or did the pilot make an approach error and mistake one atoll for another? It was clear from looking at a map of the archipelago that Thimarafushi Airport was located at the bottom of one atoll, just as Kuda village was at the bottom of the other. An Air France pilot thought that this hypothesis was credible. He mentioned other instances where pilots have confused two airports – Eilat in Israel with Aqaba in Jordan – or have had to make a sharp climb after having made an approach to Oujda Airport in Morocco instead of Tlemcen in Algeria. In the 1980s, these airfields had a control tower but no radar. Thimarafushi had neither.

Whatever the reason the pilot of flight DQA149 took certain liberties with his flight plan on 8 March 2014, no one knew or saw what happened. No one, that is, except a handful of Kuda Huvadhoo villagers.

I was aware to what extent many MHists, including the families, clung to the idea that MH370 had ended up there. When I sent a brief message to Grace Subathirai Nathan (the young lawyer whose mother was on the flight) to say that the plane seen in the Maldives was not Flight MH370, she simply sent me back a sad-face emoticon. This exercise only brought us closer to the truth by default. It at least eliminated one of the many rumours that had been circulating around this affair from the outset. It was one less avenue of inquiry to explore.

Following my article's publication, *Media Watch*, a reputable current affairs programme broadcast on the Australian Broadcasting Corporation's national TV network since 1989, criticised the validity of the report featured in *The Australian*.* Before the programme

* See www.abc.net.au/mediawatch/episodes/mh370-maldives-theory-debunked/9973218.

went on air, *The Australian* published a new article in its 20–21 June 2015 weekend edition titled 'MH370 Maldives theory dismissed'. *Paris-Match*, by contrast, never acknowledged the flaws in their story.

And yet, the Maldivian lead kept cropping up. In August 2015, a spokesman for the president of the Maldives told a major press agency that debris that 'may have been part of the MH370 plane' found in the Maldives had been sent to the Malaysian authorities. He also asserted that no plane had ever flown over Kuda Huvadhoo on the morning of 8 March 2014. But I knew, thanks to the air controller nephew of the restaurant owner, that, just like the police, the president's office actually had no idea, as the civil aviation radars in Malé cannot track that far. How many times does a lie have to be repeated for it to become the truth?

8

Will the Réunion Flaperon Solve the Enigma of Flight MH370?

On Wednesday, 29 July 2015, a new chapter in the investigation opened. All the indications were that debris from the plane that had *disappeared without a trace* had just been found washed up on a beach on the island of Réunion.

Was this finally something concrete, a physical piece of the drama? If so, it would be the first tangible proof that the plane had indeed come down somewhere in the immense expanses of the Indian Ocean. The missing debris. Up until this point, the complete absence of debris was the major flaw in this whole affair, making it seem highly suspicious.

The absence of any debris – compounded by the confused and opaque explanations linked to the mathematical extrapolations from a few pings recorded by Inmarsat, and by the repeated blunders of the Malaysian authorities – makes it easy to understand why the official theory had lost all credibility with the families. Most had not even started to grieve, although it was now more than 500 days since contact with the plane had been lost. When they heard about this latest discovery, their dismay was obvious. Better than anyone, they understood its significance; if this part turned out to be a piece of Flight MH370, then all hope would indeed be lost. Up until now, some had been hoping against hope to see their loved ones again, contrary to all rational logic. 'These overwhelming emotions and the sense of a violent shock that had become so familiar came flooding back. But it was worse this time. I had to convince my heart to abandon the hope I had kept alive over the past 16 months,' explained Jennifer Chong on the families' Facebook page. Her husband, Chong Ling Tan, had been on the flight.

On the morning of Wednesday, 29 July 2015, on the north-eastern coast of Réunion island, Johnny Bègue, team leader of the 3E association responsible for keeping the coast clean, took advantage of a break for his men at Bois-Rouge Pond in the township of Saint-André, to go to the beach and look for a *kalou*, a large stone used as a pestle for grinding spices. It was 8.45 am. That day, two days before the full moon, the sun rose at 6.51 am, with the promise of a fine southern winter day.

'That's when I saw this big thing, half on the sand and half in the water,' he explained in his sing-song French over the following days on the many TV networks that asked him to tell his story. In all the excitement of this first find, he forgot to mention the badly damaged suitcase he also saw on the beach, level with the flaperon, and which he finally mentioned the next day. In the meantime, he called his men to come and help. Together, they dragged the large piece of debris higher up on the shore to prevent it from floating away, as the tide was coming in.*

Interestingly, when Bègue made his formal report to the French police on the afternoon of his finding, he said that he thought the piece was 'not too wet [for something] that had stayed in water'. 'I think it must have landed during night time and had time to dry on the sand before we arrived.' Then, despite the fact that Bègue clears up litter from beaches for a living, his interviewer asked him if he had any aeronautical expertise. 'No, I am no plane expert, but I saw at once that this was a plane part,' replied Bègue. He would

---

* On 29 July 2015 in Reunion, the first high tide was at 0.35 am, followed by a low tide at 7.05 am, with the next high tide at 1 pm. The tide's coefficient was high (81) and on its way up.

repeat to the media that he was never in any doubt that it was aircraft debris: its large size, rounded corners and the fact that the rivets had not rusted.

The group's first intention was to turn their find into a small memorial on the beach and plant flowers around it. They had no idea of the object's importance. Bègue called Radio Liberté, the island's most popular station. 'It's our local newswire,' explained Julien Delarue from the *Journal de l'île de La Réunion*, who immediately took himself off to see the debris. 'Here, when people see something, they call the radio first – and then the emergency services.'

The police and press arrived shortly after. The first reports referred to an object three metres long that was initially believed to be the end of an aircraft wing. But from which aircraft? 'We took a heap of photos, including a part model number, 657-BB. The editorial team made the link with MH370 fairly quickly. At first jokingly!' recalled Delarue. The object seemed to be in relatively good condition. It was handed over to the BGTA, the French gendarmerie's air transport brigade, before the BEA, France's air accident investigation agency, was alerted.

In a few hours, the mystery of Flight MH370 was back in the world's headlines. The word 'flaperon' was being pronounced in every conceivable accent: a flaperon, *un flaperon, uno flaperon, jinfùyì* (襟副翼) in China, *serpihan flaperon* in Malaysia. This portmanteau word, combining 'flap' and 'aileron', refers to a part located on the rear section of the wings of certain aircraft, including the Boeing 777. The one found on Réunion was a right flaperon.

Thanks to the many photos, often of good quality, that rapidly found their way around social networks, a French MHist, Xavier Tytelman, a regular media consultant on aviation matters, identified and confirmed with the assistance of a group of experts that a part numbered 657-BB was most certainly a flaperon belonging to a Boeing 777. Boeing concurred two days later. Still, it remained to be proven that it was debris from the Boeing 777-200ER used for

Flight MH370 on 8 March 2014. As mentioned earlier, the plane was numbered 28420, or WB-275 by Boeing, and registered as 9M-MRO by Malaysia Airlines. Not only was it the first and last Boeing 777 to have disappeared, but, as we were constantly being told, Boeing numbered all its parts, as did Airbus for that matter, so the matter should be quickly settled.

In all this naïve, early excitement, the solution to the enigma, the end of the mystery, was already being announced. Malaysia declared: 'We are close to solving the mystery.'* Without waiting for the results of any technical investigation, Australia echoed the same sentiment. Martin Dolan, Director of the ATSB,† asserted that he was 'increasingly confident that the debris came from MH370'.

The French were already congratulating themselves for the transparency and professionalism that their services would undoubtedly provide. Malaysia had disappointed. Australia had disappointed. China and the United States had kept a low profile since the start of the affair. But France would deliver a precise and comprehensive report on everything there was to know about this object, and within the shortest technically feasible timeframe. And so began another new episode, full of hope.

The appearance of this object in French territory caused some unease in Australia and Malaysia, both of which would have liked to have got their hands on the flaperon. I was told that they exercised a degree of rather undiplomatic pressure on France. 'Nothing better to get a witness to say what you want to hear than to subject him to your own interrogation methods,' said an old Breton forensic pathologist when I explained the situation to him.

* Comment by Abdul Aziz Kaprawi, Deputy Minister in the Malaysian Transport Ministry, reported by AFP on 31 July 2015.

† The Australian Air Transport Safety Bureau, in charge of the search operation in the Indian Ocean since 17 March 2014.

Although we were confronted with the unprecedented situation of two competing investigations – the official Malaysian investigation and the French 'anti-terrorist' judicial inquiry – France cited its own ongoing investigation into MH370 to justify keeping control over the object found in French territory, and over the analyses that would be performed in France. It was totally within its rights and it would have been wrong to have done otherwise.

The MH370 affair had been referred to French judicial authorities in the days following the plane's disappearance, then put under the authority of the anti-terrorist bureau in 2015, which was supposed to grant the judges improved access to foreign authorities. But apart from changing its name and being passed from one court office to another, the French investigation had made little or no progress up until this unexpected and welcome discovery 500 days after the event. Indeed, more than a year had gone by since the disappearance before letters rogatory were sent to Malaysia, the first response to which was basically a non-event.

So if it turned out that this flaperon, washed up on French territory after having floated thousands of miles in the planet's most unforgiving ocean, was indeed a piece of MH370, it would be a godsend for the French investigation. The magistrate could then use it as a quid pro quo to finally get certain information, particularly from Malaysia. The former head of the BEA, the very logically minded Jean-Paul Troadec, with whom I had remained in contact since we met in Malaysia at the very beginning of the crisis, even described it as a 'miracle' for France.

Despite now having the upper hand, France nonetheless played fair. It invited all parties involved in Malaysia's official investigation to participate in the analyses that would be performed in the Balma laboratory of the DGA-TA (France's Directorate-General of Armaments – Aeronautical Techniques) in Toulouse. It is France's most sophisticated laboratory for aeronautical analyses, and had performed all the analyses of parts recovered from the Rio de

Janeiro–Paris Flight AF447, which crashed in 2009.[*] The flaperon arrived under seal in Balma from Réunion during the weekend of 1 August 2015.

On the afternoon of Wednesday, 5 August 2015, François Grangier, the aeronautical accident investigation expert appointed to this affair, accompanied by several members of the BEA, together with Malaysian, Chinese, American, British, Australian and even Singaporean experts, as well as two Boeing representatives, met in Balma under the authority of the examining magistrate, to open up the sealed wooden crate and observe the much-discussed flaperon. No list of the meeting's participants was published. The 'happy few' were seen on TV entering and then leaving the centre after the preliminary analyses had been completed, at around 7 pm. But the parties in the civil action were left out in the cold. They were not allowed to attend.

'The provisions of the [French] Code of Criminal Procedure state that the parties in a civil action are entitled to be in attendance when expert analyses are performed. We requested to be allowed to attend, but were refused,' explained lawyer Pascale Beheray Derrien, whose sister, Laurence Wattrelos, was on Flight MH370. She went on to say, 'It's only by being present during the experts' analyses that we would really have been able to understand what this object represents.'

At the end of the day, the public prosecutor in Paris announced a press conference for that very evening at 8 pm at the Palais de Justice (the Paris law courts). As chance would have it, I was in Paris that day, taking part in a programme about Singapore on France Inter, the main national radio station. When I called by to say hello at France Info's Foreign Service, for which I have worked for many years, a colleague mentioned the press conference and gave me the details. It was a magnificent summer evening and a cluster of tourists were still milling around in the courtyard of the

---

[*] The aircraft's parts are still stored at this laboratory.

Sainte-Chapelle, right next to the Palais de Justice. It was somewhat daunting to think that French justice has been dispensed from this very place since medieval times. I followed close behind a handful of journalists and cameramen, who seemed to know the way. They bounded four-by-four up the steps of an old service staircase in the Palais de Justice, Stair I, to the fourth and final floor. A maze of corridors led to a room that was too small for the event, with too few chairs and stools to seat everyone. It was the public prosecutor's meeting room.

Before the deputy public prosecutor, Serge Mackowiak, arrived, a clerk announced that he would not be answering any questions. Really? In China or Malaysia, when a press briefing is held without any questions from the floor, it is described as a flagrant violation of the freedom of the press. But here, in the middle of the Palais de Justice in Paris, in a proceeding concerning an affair that fascinated the whole world, it did not seem to arouse any particular reaction. I questioned my colleagues. They answered with a shrug of their shoulders, saying, 'It happens.' Since the assistant public prosecutor simply read out a statement, I asked for a copy of the 'press dictation' at the end. 'We never give out copies of press releases,' said the same clerk imperiously. I could not believe it: no questions, no press release. I asked her if it was to make sure journalists would make mistakes. She said that people could call to check. I'd left France 25 years earlier; at that very moment, I was suddenly hit by what could only be described as a deep sense of disillusionment with my own country.

Whatever. The main information provided that evening was that the flaperon found on the island of Réunion 'very probably' belonged to the Malaysia Airlines' lost Boeing. There was an audible critical sigh in the room. Couldn't they provide a definitive answer? In my view, this 'almost yes' suggested that the experts were not in a position to state unequivocally that it was indeed a piece of the lost plane.

And yet, one hour before the deputy public prosecutor

announced the official result of the preliminary analysis of the flaperon, Malaysia had beaten France to declaring that it was actually
part of the MH370 Boeing. It was all arranged well in advance, the
international press agencies in Kuala Lumpur having been tipped
off the previous Monday that Prime Minister Najib Razak would
be making an important announcement late on Wednesday evening.
Finally, at 1.30 am local time in Malaysia, sweeping aside the
protocol that should have had France, in charge of this part of the
investigation, be the official spokesperson, and flouting the agreement between all the participants in the analyses that any
announcement would come with a proviso, the prime minister in
person declared explicitly that 'all the experts have confirmed that
the part was off MH370'. He added, 'We now have physical proof
that, as I announced on 24 March last year [2014], Flight MH370
clearly ended up in the Indian Ocean.' Ludicrous!

This followed a classic rule of disinformation. The first piece of
information is unconsciously treated as the best, the strongest. Not
only is the brain more open to the first piece of information it
receives, but it latches onto it. There's nothing more annoying than
to be given information contradicting something you have already
heard or understood relating to the same event. Even if the second
piece of information is better sourced, more reliable or more logical than the first, the brain will naturally doubt the second, preferring to accept the first. So the world first heard, from Malaysia,
that it was 'unquestionably' a piece of the plane, and then, later
and from France, that it was 'very probably' a piece of the plane.
Advantage to 'unquestionably'.

Totally without scruple, Malaysia Airlines followed the
Malaysian prime minister's lead and released its own equally false
media statement:

Malaysia Airlines would like to sincerely convey our deepest
sorrow to the families and friends of the passengers on board
Flight MH370 on the news that the flaperon found on Réunion

Island on 29 July was indeed from Flight MH370. This has been confirmed jointly today by the French Authorities, Bureau d'enquête et d'analyses pour la Securité de l'Aviation civile (BEA), the Malaysian Investigation Team, Technical Representative from the People's Republic of China and Australian Transport Safety Bureau (ATSB), in Toulouse, France, and subsequently announced by the Prime Minister of Malaysia, Dato' Seri Najib Tun Razak.

In France, no one reacted to the erroneous declarations coming out of Malaysia. No one …

For the families, it was hard to swallow. The fact that the statements issued by France and Malaysia failed to concur reawakened their pain and plunged them again into a state of agonising uncertainty. 'We are appalled by the premature announcement [by Najib Razak],' Jennifer Chong said. 'This declaration has created confusion and anger for the families. It leaves more questions than answers, confusion instead of assurance.'

In order to clear away all doubt in the families' minds, the flaperon had to be unequivocally proven to be part of Boeing number 28420, registered as 9M-MRO by Malaysia Airlines, the Boeing plane used for Flight MH370 on 8 March 2014. The families trusted France's word and opted to wait for the French verdict. With the exception of the families and people who were following the affair closely, the rest of the world had more or less already accepted that the flaperon found on Réunion came from MH370.

The day after the Paris press conference, the appointed expert François Grangier explained to the two French families why the analyses could not yet conclude for certain that it was a piece of the missing plane. This time, the meeting was held in the Galerie Saint-Éloi, that section of the Palais de Justice under high-security surveillance, day and night, because it houses the Anti-Terrorist Division. The first and highly problematical defect was that the flaperon no longer had its ID plate, the only thing that would have made it possible to identify it for certain.* This was clearly reported in the initial confidential eight-page report that I had access to, many months later. A photo of the side panel where the plate should have been found was included, with the caption: 'We observe the absence of the identification plate of this element.' The report made no other comment about this major anomaly.

According to an expert consulted about this point, it would have been virtually impossible for water or oxidation to dislodge this plate from its backing. However, it may have only been glued on, as is sometimes the case. But 16 months floating in the sea would not dissolve mastic designed to withstand innumerable changes in pressure, temperature and humidity. This question of the missing glued or riveted ID plate would be the subject of discussion for many long weeks among people with a keen interest in the affair. And rightly so, because without its ID plate, the flaperon's authenticity could, and should, be called into doubt.

The second problem was that Malaysia Airlines stated that repairs had been carried out on this flaperon in September 2013. However, the information provided about these repairs, notably certain technical drawings, did not correspond exactly to what the experts saw during the first laboratory examination. *The New York Times* then wrote that neither Boeing nor the American National Transport Safety Board which saw the flaperon, were convinced it belonged to Malaysia Airlines Boeing 28420. The experts requested further analyses. 'Their doubts were based on a modification to the flaperon part that did not appear to exactly match what they would expect from airline maintenance records,' claimed the American newspaper, quoting a source from inside the investigation, who was not authorised to discuss the matter publicly. Many months later, when I got to see some of the confi-

---

* The ID plate would always mention the number of the model of the allocated plane, the manufacturer identification code as well as the reference number, the serial number and the name of the inspector of the piece.

dential documents relating to this initial session, a seemingly matching repair was mentioned: 'In order to verify the existence and the trace of a repair that took place on the left side of the part, a piece of rail and joint are pulled off.' The next pictures were captioned: 'The repair is real. Three layers of metal are present.' 'Sometimes, there are mistakes in maintenance logs,' said Jean-Paul Troadec, the former director of the BEA.

I called the expert, François Grangier, to try to get more details about these points. He was very annoyed by my call. He wanted to know how I'd got his number; it wasn't very hard to find – on his website it was listed as 'fax'. He told me it was a criminal investigation and that he was under strict instruction not to release any information. I simply explained that I wanted to write a piece with the information he gave to the families that I had gathered from several sources present at the meeting and that there was an obvious risk of inaccuracy. Not his problem. Not his job to help me. He hung up.

Still, the two most reliable ways to identify this flaperon – the ID plate and the match with the maintenance log – had now been eliminated. Contrary to what was initially thought, the part's paintwork was not going to help either, as these parts of the aircraft were not personalised by airlines. Although the paint here was the same as on dozens if not hundreds of planes of the same generation, this did not stop the Malaysian minister of transport from declaring on CNN that 'the precise colour of the paint on the flaperon is exactly the same as that used on MH370'.

I finally learnt that having been unable to identify the flaperon as a single part, the experts were going to try to identify its components; next step, back to the sub-contractor. After several interviews with contacts, each of whom had some information and who, at times, grudgingly passed on to me what little they did know, I understood that the sub-contractor was Spanish, that a dozen numbers had been found on the components inside the flaperon, and that these numbers had been sent to Seville in the hope of finding a link between them and the Boeing numbered 28420 delivered to Malaysia Airlines in 2002. The problem was further compounded by the fact that Malaysia Airlines did not take out the Boeing maintenance service contract, which would have provided much more precise and scrupulous tracking. When I tried to reach the Spanish sub-contractor, I was told they were on holiday and we would have to wait for them to resume work at the end of summer. *Le Monde* published this information, prompting several sarcastic reactions in the English-speaking press. Rightly so! This excuse presented to the families by the expert was indeed weak. It looked like everyone on the investigation side was trying to buy time.

Few people in the sector thought that an international high-tech company, even a Spanish one and even in the middle of August, would be incapable of finding someone who, in a few hours at most, could carry out the necessary search in order to say whether or not the company had any records for these parts. And if so, when, to whom, and for what aircraft they had been sold. Moreover, the brochure published by Airbus Defence and Space, which took over the Casa company in Seville, referred to 'round-the-clock availability'. Pending information from the sub-contractor, the experts took an even closer look at the flaperon: they floated it and sampled the barnacles that had colonised it. The crustaceans were subjected to bio-marine analyses to determine their age, health and, if possible, their origin and history. Barnacle larvae, omnipresent in all of the world's oceans, attach themselves very quickly to any piece of floating debris that passes by. If only these barnacles could tell us exactly at what latitude and longitude they had attached themselves, for better or for worse, to the flaperon, then finding the plane would only take a matter of weeks.

At the same time as this analysis was being undertaken in France, the beaches on Réunion were being scoured. Volunteers and media scrums joined the clean-up teams and law-enforcement officials assigned to the task. On Mauritius and Réunion, the hunt for aircraft wreckage was declared open. *Paris Match* offered to pay for Ghyslain Wattrelos to travel to Réunion. The man who had lost his wife, daughter and one of his two sons could join in the search on the island's beaches for other bits of suitcases or fuselage, and all the magazine was asking for was a few pictures and an exclusive interview. He declined the offer. Was he still capable of being shocked by the lack of decency of some media outlets?

Even tiny Rodrigues Island, over 500 kilometres east of Mauritius, joined in the regional effort. Two water bottles, bearing 'Asian lettering', one of which was the Malaysian Cactus brand, were picked up there during a patrol of the Anse-Bouteille and Trou-d'Argent area. According to French news channel BFMTV's special correspondents in Réunion, 'shoes made in Vietnam and bottles manufactured in Malaysia'* were also found. Police stations in Réunion, bombarded with the abundant bounty from this vast treasure hunt, became worried that they would soon turn into temporary repositories for all the waste that had fetched up on the island's beaches.

After a week of this, the prefect of Réunion announced that over 80 objects had been recovered: a crushed teapot, rattles, a piece of a sailing boat, flip flops 'made in China', a plastic doll of Korean singer Psy … Tongue in cheek, Clicanoo.re, the island's online news site, published a photo of a car wreck under the title: 'This is not debris from MH370.' The number of clues was banking up.

Air searches had also begun. A Réunion Casa, a long-range patrol aircraft often used for reconnaissance or maritime rescue operations, systematically covered a vast area of ocean. If its crew spotted anything, a helicopter and boat would take over. Mauritius also sent out air patrols off its coast. But no one found anything credible.

No one, that is, except the Malaysian team dispatched to Réunion to take part in the search. No sooner had they arrived than they found 'numerous pieces of aircraft debris'. *Malaysia*

---

* Report broadcast on 11 August 2015.

Boleh! The information was immediately released by Liow Tiong Lai, the exceedingly affirmative Malaysian Minister of Transport. Unlike his predecessor, Hishammuddin Hussein, this minister was so affirmative that he seemed capable of making positive statements based on nothing at all. On Thursday, 6 August, after giving a press conference to announce the much-vaunted discovery of 'numerous pieces of aircraft debris' by the 'Malaysian experts', an announcement relayed by the press worldwide, Liow repeated on CNN that his teams had found bits of aircraft windows and seats. He was unable to confirm that they were bits of MH370, but one thing was definite: they were pieces of an aircraft. The CNN journalist Andrew Stevens, clearly dubious, asked him how he could be so sure. Minister Liow simply replied that his men on the ground were 'experts from the technical side trained in this field'. If they said it was a bit of an aircraft, then it must be, because they would know. The minister added, 'Once we collected [the bits], immediately we handed [them] over to the [French] military police.'*

The French gendarmerie, in response to questions from Agence France-Presse and Associated Press, replied that they were unaware of any aircraft parts handed in by the Malaysian team. Of the entire collection of waste recovered throughout this exercise, the only part that could, ever so briefly and on a moonless night, have possibly been mistaken for a plane window was in fact the yellowed plastic base of a sewing machine. As for 'aircraft seat cushions', perhaps it was just coconut coir.† Appearances can be deceptive. So much for Malaysian aeronautical expertise!

Arnaud Andrieu is a photo-reporter in Réunion. On 8 August, ten days after the flaperon's discovery, he went to Saint-André Beach, now deserted as the excitement had quickly died down. 'As always,

* cnn.com, 'Transport Minister: 100 percent certain flaperon from MH370', 8 July 2015.

† Coir is the thick fibrous coating of a coconut.

it was covered in rubbish, stuff dropped there by the locals or washed up by the ocean,' he said. Tyres, a car seat, car wrecks, an old bicycle, toys … but among it all, he did see and photograph a large dark orange foam object, a little under a metre wide by around two metres long, with burn marks on the foam side. On the other side was a sort of black linoleum that looked like floor covering. A piece of aircraft aisle? It was not very heavy, and he was easily able to turn it over. A gendarmerie helicopter was flying over the area, and soon a police patrol arrived in their Land Rover Defender. Seeing the item for the first time themselves, the police explained that they had been briefed to sort through any objects found. They were looking for large items liable to float. And the white attachments with black hooks on the sides of this part gave it a technical character that, according to their recent information, meant it could be an aircraft part. They took it away with them.

Two days later, *Le Quotidien de la Réunion* announced that on 8 August a police patrol may have discovered 'a new element that was being taken seriously', which had been sent to Toulouse for analysis. On 10 August, when Andrieu called Captain Fouquet of the BGTA,* who was in charge of the search operations, he was told that the captain was 'on holiday'. The reporter was left with a strange feeling from everything that had happened since he found the piece of foam: neither the police, nor the gendarmerie, nor the Air Force were releasing the slightest bit of information to the press. At the same time, the resources deployed to carry out a search worthy of the name seemed insufficient. On 10 August, he tweeted: 'Shit day. No one on the coast. No transparency from the authorities. Censored?' In fact, this second piece of debris would never be officially mentioned. And, as for the flaperon, several months later, no results from the analysis, nor indeed any information at all, had been made public.

* * *

* France's Air Transport Gendarmerie Brigade.

Australia was visibly caught off guard by the flaperon appearing in Réunion. The fact that the 'most extensive search operation ever' carried out under its authority had not managed to locate any floating debris, let alone the wreckage on the ocean floor, had already seriously undermined the credibility of its operation. Added to which, the debris drift and dispersal studies made by Australian scientists following the plane's disappearance had never included Réunion. Australian Prime Minister Tony Abbott had long closed the case for any further debris when he stated on 28 April 2014: 'I am now required to say to you that it is highly unlikely at this stage that we will find any aircraft debris on the ocean surface. By this stage, 52 days into the search, most material would have become waterlogged and sunk.'

So in the hours following the appearance of the flaperon, Australia began furiously backpedalling. Without even waiting to know if what had landed in Réunion was in fact a piece of MH370, Tony Abbott declared that the find 'does seem to confirm that the plane went down in the Indian Ocean, it does seem very consistent with the search pattern that we've been using for the last few months'. In other words, the location of the Australian search operation had been correct from the start. Really? Not only had most of the drift models published so far failed to include Réunion, but eight months earlier, at the end of November 2014, the Australian Transport Safety Bureau crash investigator Peter Foley* had said, 'Something is going to wash up somewhere on beaches, probably in Sumatra'. Yet Sumatra is a very long way, 5,000 kilometres to be precise, from Réunion ...

*   *   *

* See 'Debris from missing jet will soon start washing up in Indonesia', *Mirror*, 23 November 2014. www.mirror.co.uk/news/world-news/flight-mh370-debris-missing-jet-4679689.

In the weeks following the loss of the aircraft back in March 2014, I had called the office of the French Southern and Antarctic Lands based in Réunion – just on the off-chance. Had an observation alert been issued to Saint Paul and Amsterdam islands?* Was France getting ready to help with the search operation? 'Our designated SAR zone is limited to the south-west of the Indian Ocean,' I was told over the telephone by the district commander's deputy.

'Moreover, if the plane fell further south and so closer to our southern lands, the dominant current in these southern latitudes will drive the debris eastwards. It might even pass under Australia and end up in South America. So, it's relatively unlikely to see anything at all come near us,' was my contact's final prediction. Based on this logic, it would be even less likely for anything to wash up on Réunion.

On 24 August 2015, Metron Scientific Solutions, a leading American consulting company, issued a memo to the scientific community following the case. Its calculations and method were explained in 16 pages of equations riddled with mathematical symbols that brought back memories of some of the worst hours of my schooling: functions, square roots, logarithms, integrals, deltas, cosines† I turned straight to the conclusion, in which the authors asserted that the plane's crash zone was '10 times more likely' to be much further north than the current search area. Australia was not going to be happy …

Several days later, Germany's highly respected GEOMAR Helmholtz Centre for Ocean Research Kiel stuck its oar in. GEOMAR also suggested, but using its own arguments, that the plane had probably fallen several thousand kilometres north-east

---

* Saint Paul and Amsterdam Islands lie about 2,500 kilometres south-west of Perth.

† The empirical debris transport model used was that of the oceanographer Erik van Sebille, from the Grantham Institute, Imperial College London.

of the current search area.* Jonathan Durgadoo, one of the study's authors, explained their scientific approach to me over the phone. 'I launched 2 million virtual debris samples where the flaperon washed ashore and looked to see where they could have come from.' Not only did barely a quarter of the virtual debris arrive from the east of the Indian Ocean, but, more importantly, only an extremely small amount of debris arrived from the seventh arc, the flight path consistent with Inmarsat's signals in which the plane would have come down. Worse, not one of the samples arrived from that section of the seventh arc where the current search was based. This constituted two serious challenges to the search area on which Australia was doggedly focused. However, I heard that the science of oceanographic drift studies was still somewhat approximate. Not as approximate as a *bomoh* prediction,† but to be viewed with a degree of caution all the same.

While Australia had up until then been intimating that nothing might ever be found on the ocean surface, another scientific institute, Australia's very own CSIRO (Commonwealth Scientific and Industrial Research Organisation), published a study on 4 August 2015 proving that there was normally debris after a plane crash at sea, an apparent scoop if ever there was one. This study quoted four of the best-known cases of crashes at sea: SilkAir Flight 185 (19 December 1997),‡ Adam Air Flight 574 (1 January 2007),§ Air

---

* GEOMAR used the drift model of Mercator-Océan, based in Toulouse.

† A *bomoh* is a Malaysian shaman.

‡ Pieces of the tail of the Boeing 737 fell off as it spiralled earthwards. The rest of the plane plunged into the Musi River in Sumatra, western Indonesia. No part of the plane ever resurfaced.

§ The Boeing 737 crashed off Sulawesi in eastern Indonesia. In the space of one month, 200 objects (bits of seats, meal trays, suitcases, bits of plane tyre, life jackets, headrests, etc.) were found.

France Flight 447 (1 June 2009)* and Air Asia Flight 8501 (28 December 2014).† However, the demonstration was not entirely convincing, as all the examples showed that such a large piece of debris as the flaperon had never been found as long after a crash or as far from the estimated point of impact with the sea. Indeed, these examples highlighted the singular nature of the Réunion case.

Réunion is around 4,000 kilometres (2,160 miles) from the seventh arc. For the debris to have landed on Saint-André Beach on 29 July 2015, it must have travelled over seven kilometres a day in a straight line from the assumed crash area. The vagaries of sea currents and winds, the impact of the waves and, at times, crashing swell aside, it would have had to survive numerous storms. 'The surprising thing is that such a part could float for as long after the crash. It is truly astounding,' said Jean-Paul Troadec on the set of the *C dans l'air* programme‡ So, here we were, back in the realm of the 'never-before-seen'.

I had a meeting with Troadec at the Port du Château, in Brest, Brittany, a few hours after the triumphant arrival of the replica of the *L'Hermione*§ from New York in the summer of 2015. I had not seen him since his first MH370 assignment in Malaysia in March 2014. He was intrigued by this case, like many other air transport experts, and he had been keeping abreast of the developments reported by the more credible groups, albeit from a distance. He was among those who, right at the start of the flap-

---

* It took five days to find the first debris from the A330 that crashed into the sea off the Brazilian coast. Over the following fortnight, more than 700 objects and around 50 bodies were recovered from the surface, then nothing further after 20 June. The plane's fuselage was found in April 2011, at a depth of 4,000 metres.

† The A320 crashed into the Java Sea. A number of pieces of debris were found two weeks later, up to 100 miles (185 kilometres) away.

‡ The *C dans l'air* programme's 'The First Response' report aired on 6 August 2015.

§ *L'Hermione* was the frigate that ferried General Lafayette across the Atlantic to bring support to the American insurgents in 1780.

eron episode, said that it was unlikely to solve the case, although it could put it to rest. At best, it might provide a precise idea of the flight's final moments, the type of final impact: kiss landing,* nose-dive or explosion. He was also aware that during the search for Flight AF447, the reverse-drift calculations had led the investigators far from the crash site, wasting several months and a lot of money.

The size and excellent condition of the flaperon could in fact be used to support two virtually opposing scenarios, the first one much more realistic than the second. If the plane had nosedived at very high speed (around 900 km/h), its appendages might have snapped off in the fall and hit the water with far less force than if they'd remained attached to the fuselage at the time of impact. The Independent Group (IG) considered this the most probable explanation. The shear mark along the flaperon's edge was moreover consistent with those on certain appendages thought to have been ripped off in more or less vertical nosedives, which IG team member Mike Exner had been able reproduce in a simulator.

The second scenario was that the plane made a successful splash-down in a similar manner to the Hudson River case.† But none of the people familiar with the Indian Ocean and aviation believed that this would have been at all feasible. 'It is simply impossible to imagine how the pilot could have chosen a wave like a surfer to splash-down in the same direction as the swell and over a sufficient distance for a Boeing 777 to alight on the sea,' explained a fighter pilot familiar with deck landings on aircraft carriers. For any large object, let alone one the size of a B777, water is as hard as concrete, and the aircraft would have certainly exploded on impact.

---

* Smooth landing or splash-down.

† On 15 January 2009, both engines of an A320 failed after multiple bird strikes, and the pilot ditched the plane into the Hudson River in New York. There were no fatalities, with only a relatively small number of passengers and flight crew injured.

The Malaysian authorities nonetheless attempted to put forward the unrealistic scenario of a soft splash-down through the intermediary of a 'satellite communications expert' called Zaaim Redha Abdul Rahman. 'I believe that when the aircraft went out of fuel, it glided downwards and landed on the water with a soft impact', he told Bernama, the Malaysian news agency. 'That's why I believe the plane is still largely intact.' In his view, the discovery of the aircraft's flaperon on Réunion supported his theory that the aircraft could have ditched smoothly into the water and floated before sinking, rather than crashing into it. Another half-baked theory promoted by someone with no understanding or expertise whatsoever in the field he was commenting about, this time openly put forward by Malaysia.

Despite nothing filtering through from the analyses underway in Toulouse throughout August 2015, things suddenly started to hot up in September. The events came one after the other, as swiftly as a troop of monkeys descending on a rubbish bin depot in suburban Kuala Lumpur.

Monday, 31 August and Tuesday, 1 September 2015. Jean-Yves Le Drian, the French Defence Minister, was in Malaysia to 'present France's complete proposal for 18 Rafale aircraft'. He met with his Malaysian counterpart Hishammuddin Hussein, whose ministerial duties for a little over a year had been reduced to the defence portfolio alone. Le Drian explained that the Rafale had been one of several topics of discussion as part of a 'broad cooperative arrangement' with Malaysia, a 'strategic partner' for France in South East Asia. The French minister referred to 'submarines, frigates, aircraft …'. Neither of the two politicians mentioned Flight MH370 once, the four French citizens declared missing or the flaperon being analysed in France, nor for that matter the fact that France and Malaysia were still not singing from the same hymn sheet about whether or not the flaperon belonged to the lost plane. Wasn't it about time for France to at last confirm what Malaysia had been saying for almost a month now?

Wednesday, 2 September 2015. The French families had a further meeting with the case expert in the magistrate's office in Paris. They were told that the bio-marine analyses had been completed, that the barnacles were 'at least a year old', and the fact that these little animals could only survive in water of 18°C or above meant that the date and place of the supposed crash fitted with the evidence. The magistrate also explained that he intended to go to Seville the following day, to meet with ADS-SAU, the Spanish sub-contractor more commonly known in the industry by its former name Casa.

Thursday, 3 September 2015. The magistrate and his expert set off for Seville on the only flight of the morning, scheduled to arrive at 11.55. ADS-SAU's facilities were located within the city's San Pablo Airport zone – a happy coincidence, because it seemed that the two Frenchmen were in a hurry. The ADS-SAU technician interviewed by them had the minimum amount of information they wanted. He was able to confirm that one of the 12 numbers found on the inside of the flaperon, forwarded to ADS-SAU beforehand, was a definite match with the serial number of the flaperon on Boeing WB-175, otherwise known as Boeing 28420, the one that Boeing sold to Malaysia Airlines in 2002 and that was registered as 9M-MRO.

If one of the 12 numbers provided could be linked to this plane, then what about the 11 others? But under these circumstances, who cared about the 11 others? The important thing was that there was a link. A tenuous one, but a link all the same. The magistrate was satisfied. He required nothing further.

Immediately after his meeting, and without waiting till he got back to Paris, the magistrate informed the public prosecutor in Paris, who quickly put together a media statement, published that same day in the middle of the afternoon. The magistrate and the expert were still in Spain when the AFP's urgent message pinged in all the major editorial offices around the world.

'It is possible today to confirm with certainty that the flaperon found on Réunion Island on 29 July 2015 corresponds to the plane used for Flight MH370,' stated the Paris public prosecutor in his media release, partially quoted by AFP. The media latched on to just two words from this dispatch: 'with certainty'.

The public prosecutor's media release had, however, taken certain liberties with the actual information. It stated that the endoscope analyses revealed three numbers inside the flaperon.* Yet, the expert had clearly indicated to the families at the beginning of the investigation that 12 component numbers identified inside the flaperon had been sent to the subcontractor. And another key source within the investigation confirmed to me that Spain had been advised of 12 and not three serial numbers.

If the fact that only one out of 12 numbers 'identified by endoscopy inside the flaperon' corresponded to MH370, then this precious 'certainty' would have seemed less, well, certain. For sure, 'one out of three' certainly gave better odds than 'one out of 12'. But what the hell. Twelve could easily become three, once the Réunion flaperon was said to clearly belong to MH370.

Later on, I got to see the confidential documents that the French magistrate used to confirm 'with certainty' that the flaperon found on Réunion was that of MH370. We won't quibble over the fact that the flaperon was found on 29 July 2015 and not 31 July 2015, as stated in this very official document. What surprised me most was that on the only document that seemed to link the serial number of the only identified component (3FZG81) to the flaperon RH405 (used on Boeing MSN 404), the clinching number was one among six similar numbers hand-written, and therefore easily forged, on a rather messy document ... The proof was already weak. It suddenly seemed wobbly as well. There were other

---

* The media release stated: 'The immediate communication of the data concerning the orders and manufacture of the aircraft's parts, explained in an interview with an ADS-SAU technician, makes it possible to formally link one of the *three* [my italics] numbers found inside the flaperon with the serial number of the flaperon of the Boeing 777 used for Flight MH370.'

mistakes in these important documents that puzzled me.[*]

Was it conceivable, even for the most respectable companies, that a small favour be paid to a large client or country, in the form of little mix-up on an order line or with a serial number to achieve a desired outcome without compromising safety or the company's reputation? The answer to this question varied considerably depending on whom you asked. From one extreme: 'Never! It's out of the question! We have very strict procedures,' to the other: 'Of course! What? Do you think that people in the aeronautical industry are saints or something?' But I don't think anything in particular. I'm just asking questions.

Eventually, I discovered that the only occasion when an ID plate would be taken off any plane part was when the plane was being dismantled. Under international rules of civil aviation, the procedures to 'mutilate unsalvageable aircraft parts' clearly include the destruction of the identification plate. In other words, if you saw a plane part without an identification plate on it, you could fairly assume that it came from a dismantled plane. Once I knew this, I lost all confidence that the flaperon found in Réunion was a part of MH370.

Friday, 4 September 2015. Everything was in place for a meeting between the families and French President François Hollande at midday at the presidential Élysée Palace. The president had a thorough knowledge of the case. At the meeting, Hollande listened carefully to everyone and impressed his visitors with his humanity. Then he asked the head of the BEA, Rémi Jouty, who had taken over from Jean-Paul Troadec (also at the meeting), to provide the families with a copy of the BEA report from the March 2014

[*] Another document referred to 'flaperon number 404', which was the aircraft serial number but not the flaperon number. According to the table in the file listing the matches, the right flaperon 404 was to be mounted on Boeing MSN 400 and not Boeing MSN 404. Basically, the flaperon number had been mixed up with the Boeing aircraft number.

mission, if there was one. In addition, he agreed to arrange a meeting for them with Bernard Bajolet, the head of the DGSE (France's external intelligence agency, equivalent to the UK's MI6 or the American CIA). Finally, he announced that he was intending to go to Malaysia in 2016, triggering a moment of panic among his staff, who were apparently taken by surprise. This would be the first ever visit by a French president to the country. It finally took place in March 2017, a few weeks before the French presidential elections, but all we heard was that the Rafale deal was progressing.

True to the president's word, the family members met with Bajolet on Friday, 9 October 2015. But this meeting would be just one more in a long line of disappointing encounters for the families. He, who was supposed to see and hear everything, knew 'nothing'. 'No, truly nothing ...' That is, with the exception of a couple of terrorist claims that the families had never even heard of, but which were in any case not taken seriously by the French secret service. One had been made by an Indonesian group, although, according to the DGSE, it did not have the resources to carry out such an operation and had only made the claim on its website. The other came from an unknown Uyghur group.* In short, the head of the secret service had no new leads since the search had first begun. Nothing was standing out among the passengers. Impossible to take remote control of a plane. Unthinkable that a DGSE agent spoke to Ghyslain Wattrelos about American involvement in this matter. When pressed, Bajolet answered, 'Don't believe what you are told. People here don't talk.' In these kinds of situations, the Malaysians might cite a proverb of theirs: 'When you don't want to dance, you say the ground is wet.'

As we saw earlier, France was treating Malaysia with kid gloves. Was this because of the ongoing tender for the 18 Rafale aircraft? Or was it for other very good reasons about which the public had no idea? In any event, this case was considered *sensitive*. Why?

---

* The Uyghurs are a Sunni Muslim Chinese minority.

From the beginning, the loss of MH370 should have been a civil aviation case, dealt with by engineers, technicians and scientists, not military personnel, ministers and governments.

The group of families, who had not been expecting any revelations anyway, left the Paris spies' headquarters more convinced than ever that the French state had no intention of helping them in their search for the truth. And if there was a cover-up of some kind about what truly happened, France surely seemed to be acting its part.

While the absence of any semblance of transparency had been the most negative aspect of the case since the beginning, the French episode did nothing to improve matters. France, which could have demonstrated the efficiency of its technical expertise by openly presenting even just part of the results of its analyses, preferred to hide behind a wall of secrecy. That France was not obliged to release anything given the judicial and anti-terrorist status of its investigation did not mean that it was forbidden from doing so, or that it was not in its interest. But who knows what France's interest really was in this affair?

It was easy to understand Malaysia's interest in, at last, possessing its missing debris; it would confirm the official version of the plane coming down in the Indian Ocean and enable the families to gain a sense of closure. But in all of human history, has there never before been a case when proof was fabricated to hasten the conclusion to an investigation?

The inherent inconsistencies in the flaperon story nevertheless provided work and sleepless nights for months and even years to many dogged MHists, who went on to explore at great length its impossible buoyancy, the problematic distribution of the smooth gooseneck barnacles (*Lepas anatifera*) on its two sides, and all the vagaries of the currents of the very wild southern Indian Ocean. Once I realised that the flaperon was most likely not from the wreck of MH370 – otherwise it would have had its identification plate – I was all the more keen to find out where it actually did come from. Basically, if this flaperon had not floated all the way from the supposed MH370 crash site, thousands of miles away, how did it turn up that morning on a beach on Réunion?

As soon as the flaperon appeared, we all witnessed the following line of reasoning: it's a Boeing 777 flaperon; there's only one Boeing 777 missing (the one that flew Flight MH370); therefore it must be the flaperon of the Boeing 777 used for Flight MH370. But the logic of this argument was flawed. Aircraft and their spare parts were not as perfectly inventoried and tracked as we liked to think.

As a 2008 article in *Le Monde* had already explained, 'for the past decade or so, Boeing and Airbus had been "deconstructing" rather than "destroying" their aircraft at their end-of-life'.* Recycling 'is becoming a specialist industry in itself', wrote the CEO of Boeing France, Yves Galland, in *Révolution aéronautique, le défi de l'environnement (Aeronautical Revolution: The Environmental Challenge)*, published in 2008 and quoted in the *Le Monde* piece. 'According to Airbus, no fewer than 6,000 aircraft will reach end-of-life in the coming 20 years,' *Le Monde* wrote. 'Boeing's forecast for the same period is higher: 7,000 to 8,500 aircraft will be withdrawn from service.' Both aircraft manufacturers were keen to prevent the growth of a black market for spare parts, according to the newspaper.

Airbus and Boeing pulled their planes apart and recycled a substantial proportion of the materials. Each year, several hundred Boeings, including several Boeing 777s, reached their end-of-life and were therefore deconstructed rather than destroyed. It would therefore not have been impossible to get hold of a stand-in flaperon. All the more so for MAS Boeing 777s, since many had been retired early, stored or even scrapped, as we discovered earlier (see Chapter 3, p. 108).

---

* 'Ces avions que l'on désosse' ('These planes we hack up'), *Le Monde*, 8 October 2008.

Some MHists had even come up with the theory that the flaperon might have more simply been recovered from the debris of Flight MH17, shot down over Ukraine four months after MH370. The picture of a similar part, identified in the considerable wreckage of MH17, was circulated on the internet among suspicious MHists. If this really was an MH17 part, the ID plate would have been taken away so that the link with 9M-MRD, the MH17 plane, could not be established. And considering that the two planes were basically twins, it should not have been too difficult to find some kind of match with the sub-parts. The flaperon was then clumsily transformed into a seemingly nomadic flaperon by being soaked in seawater for a few weeks or months until a convincing colony of barnacles established itself all over it. Surely it's a coincidence, but I noticed that the French marine biologists commissioned to study the barnacles found on the flaperon had said in their report that the creatures were about a year old. It so happens that MH17 was shot down in mid-July 2014 and the flaperon was found in late July 2015. It also so happens that the French scientists who took meticulous swabs on the flaperon 'in order to detect traces of explosives' along with samples of the molluscs, were instructed 'not to collect anything from the *intrados* (bottom side)' of the flaperon, according to an internal memo that was leaked on the internet. Because a missile is more likely to hit a plane from below than from above, the likelihood of finding explosive traces is obviously higher on the lower side of the part. Yet the expert in charge of the investigation ordered the technicians not to check the lower side. What a strange, not to say suspicious, instruction which fits only too well with the MH17 piece option.

If this rather pathetic operation ever took place, I can't help but feel a bit sorry for the supposed secret service agents who may have had to do it. The broken flaperon, once nicely covered in real-life barnacles, would be casually dropped, preferably at night, on the beach of a country able to deal with it in a credible manner. That would be a complete fabrication of evidence. But whoever could disappear a plane could, by the same token, make a flaperon appear ...

Another blatant example that parts and even complete planes were not that closely monitored appeared in December 2015, when Kuala Lumpur Airport placed an advertisement in *The Star*, the Malaysian daily, asking that the owner of the three Boeing 747s that had been abandoned for several years on the airport's tarmac come and collect them, otherwise they would be disposed of. This item triggered several ironic responses, such as 'Anyone lost three Boeing 747s?' and 'Boeing 747s left unattended will be destroyed!'

Despite the months and years that have gone by, the French experts have not published a single detail on the results of their analyses. We still do not even know the flaperon's precise size and weight, which many MHists would have liked to know so they could include these details in their own reverse-drift models. France has not held a single press conference about the flaperon. The experts involved have never been named or made available to answer all the intriguing questions that everyone is justifiably asking about this fascinating piece of plane debris, almost as mysterious as the plane it was said to come from.

It all left one wondering, because, ultimately, the flaperon served no useful purpose. It did not even fulfil its prime purpose of persuading public opinion that MH370 really did plummet into the Indian Ocean, and by no means all the families were convinced. When, in early 2018, Australia announced its intention to build a memorial in Perth for the MH370 passengers, the families vehemently opposed it. In a communiqué to the Australian government, the Chinese next of kin in particular stated that they wanted their loved ones to be considered 'missing' rather than dead. The flaperon episode merely sowed further confusion in people's minds by raising more questions than it answered.

9

Some Debris Surfaces in the Gulf of Thailand

On 23 January 2016, almost two years after the very short-lived search in the South China Sea based around waypoint IGARI – and seven months after the the flaperon washed up in Reunion, another large piece of what seemed like aircraft debris was found. It had washed up, against all expectation, on a beach in Nakhon Si Thammarat province, southern Thailand, almost opposite the island where the Vietnamese authorities had reported the MH370 crash back in March 2014.

The object measured two metres by three metres, and had a clearly visible serial number and large bolts, also numbered. Judging by the barnacles attached to this piece of debris, Thai fishermen estimated that it had been in the water for at least a year. Quoting Pongsak Semachai, the Royal Thai Air Force spokesman, Agence France-Presse declared, 'Thai army aviation experts have already inspected the debris and agreed it was likely to be from an aircraft [...] A specialist Thai team [...] will go to Pak Phanang district Monday to collect the panel.' The French press agency also quoted the Pak Phanang District Chief Officer, who thought the piece of wreckage could be part of an aircraft nose 'because there were electric wires and insulators'. 'Numbers on the panel should help identification,' he added. On 24 January, CNN quoted a Royal Thai Air Force spokesman saying that he believed the debris was 'from a commercial jet'. 'From seeing the pictures in local news, this is definitely not a piece from [a] military aircraft, but it looks like a section from a big commercial aircraft in my personal opinion,' Air Marshal Pongsak Semachai added. He reiterated to CNN that the Thai Air Force was planning to dispatch a team to collect the debris and bring it to Bangkok on the following Monday.

For its part, the *Bangkok Post* claimed on 25 January 2016 that 'Thai aviation experts who had inspected the plane wreckage confirmed [on] Sunday [that] serial numbers found on its bolt parts belong to the Boeing 777 model.'* I called the journalist who wrote the story, and he confirmed the information but wanted to protect his source in the Royal Thai Air Force, who, I was told, gave his opinion on condition of anonymity. If real, this piece of debris could be the smoking gun for the theory that the plane had crashed in the South China Sea and not thousands of miles away. The news had only just started to circulate when Jon Ostrower, an American journalist from *The Wall Street Journal*, claimed on his Twitter account that the information was false and that in fact the debris was more likely from a Japanese rocket. He also tweeted a photo that at first glance seemed to support his statement, given the resemblance between the fairing (the protective cone on the upper stage of a rocket that separates a few minutes after lift-off) and the piece discovered in Thailand.

Then Gerry Soejatman, a hardcore MHist, provided more pictures and arguments on his blog in favour of another model of Japanese rocket that seemed even more similar to the piece found. 'Although we cannot yet be absolutely certain, we think that it is *likely* that this object is a piece of the H-IIA or H-IIB rocket,' said Sayo Suwashita, the spokesperson for the rocket manufacturer Mitsubishi Heavy Industries, to AFP. *Likely* became 'highly likely' in *USA Today* and many other media outlets, and, in no time, the debris found in Thailand had been somehow 'confirmed' as a piece

* www.bangkokpost.com/news/general/837316/air-force-to-examine-jet-debris-amidst-mh370-conjecture.

of rocket made by Mitsubishi Heavy Industries. I followed this episode with a degree of bemusement, but did not look into it any further at the time.

A few days later, on the same stretch of coastline but just a little further south, a young man called Zakaria Muhammad was taking a stroll with his daughter on Benting Lintang Beach near the town of Besut and found a very large piece of debris. 'After closer inspection of the two-metre object, it crossed my mind that it may belong to the missing aircraft. When I pulled it out of the water, I realised that it was a stainless aluminium metal,' Zakaria told the Malaysian news agency Bernama. The discovery was confirmed by District Police Chief Khaled Che Lah. On 29 January, Bernama published an article entitled 'Public advised against speculating on object found in kampung [village] Benting Lintang'. 'Let them investigate first. We hope the public will not make any speculation until an official statement on the matter is issued,' the Terengganu Police Chief Datuk Rosli Ab Rahman was quoted as saying.

It was interesting to contrast this attitude of 'no speculation, please' with the full-blown speculation campaign that the same government had indulged in just seven months earlier, when the flaperon found on Réunion was claimed *ex cathedra* by Kuala Lumpur to undoubtedly be from MH370 before any scientific analysis or even close inspection had taken place. The Bernama article also stated that 'a team from the Department of Civil Aviation and Malaysia Airlines were at the site for about an hour to inspect the object'. The next day, Malaysian Transport Minister Liow Tiong Lai declared: 'The assessment found that the debris does not match those [*sic*] of a Boeing 777, thus confirming that the debris is not from MH370.' But if it was a piece of plane debris, as the minister's statement seemed to imply, then to which lost plane did it belong?

The beaching of these two very large metallic pieces of debris a few days and a few kilometres apart on the same coastline kept on bothering me. It seemed too big a coincidence. I found the speed with which a close-up of a Japanese rocket was produced – one that showed striking similarities with the part found – to be quite remarkable, almost magical. I also considered the fact that the Malaysian authorities tried to dissociate the piece of debris found near Besut from MH370 to be somewhat suspicious, although they did not say that it belonged to a Japanese rocket. So if the Besut part was from an aircraft, why not make the numbers marked on it publicly known so that its precise identity could be revealed?

Of course, if plane debris appeared in this part of the world, the first plane that would come to mind was Indonesia AirAsia 8501, because it crashed in the Java Sea in late December 2014, about 800 miles south of Besut. But the A320 was painted red, pretty much all over, with some parts dark grey, whereas this latest piece was almost white. More importantly, the main sea currents in this part of the world flow in a southerly direction as it's a spillway from the North Pacific into the Indian Ocean. And the north-east monsoon season that takes place between November and March would reinforce the southbound movement of most floating debris. For these two reasons alone, it was almost impossible that this piece of plane could have been from the Indonesia AirAsia A320.

It was only in March 2017 – more than a year after these pieces of debris were found – that I got a chance to travel to where Zakaria lived, on the east coast of Malaysia, and ask him directly about his find. A Malaysian friend volunteered to accompany me and help out on this trip when I mentioned it to her over a breakfast of nasi lemak a few days earlier in Kuala Lumpur. Finding Zakaria in his kampung required the help of two MPs, to whom I am very grateful, a travel agent based in Kuala Terengganu, a driver called Zaki, who met us in his battered Proton at the airport, and a middleman who was supposed to escort us to Zakaria's house once we reached our meeting place, a recently built Shell petrol station along the coast road in the State of Terengganu.

Zakaria and his wife Sabrinah lived with their seven-year-old daughter Tasha and a cousin of theirs in a simple wooden house on stilts by the side of a dirt road. A few goats ran freely inside the little compound and birds were kept in cages hanging outside, safe from the two big cats that roamed around as the real masters of the place. We were invited to sit in front of the single-room house, around a colourful plastic mat that covered the landing's uneven planks. Zakaria started by saying that he was very surprised by our visit, because after the two days of excitement created by his discovery more than a year earlier, no one ever came to follow up.

'It was about 6 pm when I saw something big floating in the water. It was about this deep,' he said, holding his hand horizontally at hip height. His daughter Tasha interrupted to say that she was actually the one who first spotted the floating object, something that he conceded with a wide grin. He estimated the weight of the piece, vaguely shaped like a kite and with only one straight side, to be around 30 kilos. There were shells on parts of it, he recalled. To him, there was no doubt it was part of a plane because of the aluminium material, the rivets and other details (although he earned a living as a builder nowadays, he had spent some time in the Royal Malaysian Air Force when he was younger). He pulled the piece out of the water so that it did not float away and left it there on the beach. But once home, he grew a little concerned that his find would be stolen – everyone knew the value of aluminium. At the current rate of 85 cents a pound, 30 kilos of aluminium would have been worth over US$50, quite a booty by the low standard of living that prevailed in this remote community. His comment made me realise the possibility that other pieces of debris that had landed here or elsewhere in the world might never have been reported but instead simply sold to the nearest scrap dealer.

When I looked a bit further into this possibility, which might go some way to explaining why there had been no MH370 debris, I came across the case of PMTair Flight 241 from Siem Reap International Airport to Sihanoukville's Kang Keng Airport, which had come down in the densely forested mountains of Kampot province in Cambodia on 25 June 2007, killing 22. A few weeks later, Kampot Deputy Provincial Governor Khoy Khun Hua was quoted in the local press as saying that villagers had taken most of the wreckage to sell as scrap metal.* Sar Sareth, the President of PMTair, said that he was pleased the villagers had collected the scattered debris because it saved his company from having to do so themselves – 'We allowed the villagers to take the scrap because we would have spent a lot of money to transport the debris.'

As far as Zakaria was concerned, he did not consider for even one moment selling what he had found. He had a strong feeling that the piece had some sort of importance and should be further investigated. His intuition was confirmed when officers from the Royal Malaysian Air Force from the nearby base of Gong Kedak, one of Malaysia's thirteen military airbases, came round to take a look. They agreed with him that it was obviously a piece of an aircraft.

Zakaria told me about another large piece found at the same time, possibly the same day, by a shopkeeper on another nearby beach. It was also big, of the same colour and material, and it too had a curved shape. To his eye, these two pieces were parts of the same object before they broke apart.

Once the police got involved and took the debris away, things changed completely. When Zakaria went to enquire about their findings a few days later, he was told to let the matter drop and stop asking questions. He was also told that the piece he'd found was actually part of a ship. I asked him how he felt about this explanation. He gave us a vague smile, leaning his head back against the wall of his house. He then thought for a very long time – awkwardly long. He finally adjusted his seating position by changing his crossed legs over and said: 'This is very wrong. We know it is not part of a ship. Why do they say that?'

---

* 'Airplane crash wreckage scavenged by villagers', *Cambodia Daily*, 4 August 2007.

When, later on, we all went to have a meal together in a roadside restaurant, we were told many stories about people seeing and hearing things on the night of the loss of MH370. It had been the talk of the town for a while. 'Some fishermen said they saw many things on fire falling from the sky,' said Zakaria. But most of these witnesses were from further north, on the coast of Kelantan. I was advised to go and find them to hear the stories directly from their lips.

Leaving the east coast of Malaysia, the friend who had escorted me was convinced there was something fishy in the way the authorities had handled this debris. Of course, this was Malaysia, where confusion was the norm. But still.

If Zakaria's piece of debris were ever proved to be a piece of MH370, it would completely expose the duplicity of the official narrative. But the only way to identify it as such was to have access to some serial numbers. Unfortunately, the only one that was ever pictured was not clearly readable.

By contrast, the debris that had been found in Thailand just a few days earlier and a few miles further north offered up many more clues. Having been unable to check the numbers on the Besut debris, I decided to have a second look at the Thai debris, the piece that had been called 'Mitsubishi rocket debris' in the tweet by an American journalist and endorsed as such by the world's media.

After the discovery of the 'Mitsubishi' debris, whenever I came across someone who knew anything about rockets, I casually tried to get a better understanding of how accurately fairings fell, whether they are recovered from the ocean and recycled for further use, how well tracked their pieces are and so on. The bits and pieces of information I gathered (such as the fact that rockets are always fired towards the east) did not fit very well with the debris found in Nakhon Si Thammarat province in Thailand. But until my trip to Besut in March 2017, I let my doubts linger, unexamined.

The good news about the Thai debris was that it was very well documented, unlike its potential cousin found near Besut. The local

Thai journalists had done rather a good job of taking detailed, close-up pictures and interviewing the officials on site during the first few hours. The discovery created quite a stir in the neighbouring communities, and people came from the surrounding villages to have a look. I also found an excellent video of the debris, which I watched many times.*

A closer look at the piece of debris showed that it was a very heavy part that was unevenly broken at one end. According to press reports, the object was about 2 metres by 3 metres (6.6 by 9.8 feet) and 3 inches deep (7.6 cm), which tallied with the relative size of people standing next to it in the video. It weighed about 100 kilos and was obviously part of a round object but not a perfectly cylindrical one, as it seemed slightly cone shaped. The large pivoting bar inside indicated that it was meant to move from its support, which was confirmed by the fact that one straight side was covered with hinges. A red wire that seemed loosely attached to the inside part of the unidentified item was covered with barnacles and its clamp carried a serial number. Actually, there were many numbers that could be identified on the item: SG5773-103 on one fastener, SG5773-1 on another, NAS6204-31 on many bolts, and then much larger numbers painted on the outside of the piece: 307, 308, 315, 316, 323, as well as a II in Roman numerals, implying there might be a I of the same. There was also a longer series of numbers with the logo of KHI stamped next to it. KHI stands for Kawasaki Heavy Industries. When the Mitsubishi theory came up, one observant MHist noticed the KHI logo and made the link 'Kawasaki–Mitsubishi: it's all Japanese.' In his view, the Kawasaki logo seemed to corroborate the Mitsubishi rocket hypothesis.

While it was accurate to say that Kawasaki built some parts of the rockets that Mitsubishi launched (specifically the H-IIA and H-IIB), it was equally true and relevant to know that Kawasaki (alongside Mitsubishi and Fuji) had been closely involved in joint

---

* See www.youtube.com/watch?v=Gc-gslfnjuE#action=share.

development and production with Boeing for several decades, and in particular with the B777.* In other words, the KHI stamp could have led you to Boeing just as easily as to Mitsubishi.

With the help of a young Japanese journalist called Mayumi, we managed to get some answers from Mitsubishi and Kawasaki. Interestingly, the same spokesperson who gave the original statement to AFP in January 2016, Sayo Suwashita, told Mayumi in April 2017 that what they had said at the time was 'just an assumption based on some pictures'. Then she added that 'if there are any mistakes it would cause trouble, so we haven't yet identified [the piece] and publicised which type of model or which launch'. Another contact at Mitsubishi said that the company had no intention of investigating the matter any further, or even collecting the piece from Thailand. 'The debris is in the control of the government of Thailand, so we just leave it with them.'

In her research, Mayumi had found out that after separation, and once it had fallen in the ocean, the rocket fairing would transmit a signal indicating its location so that a waiting ship could collect the debris without fail. She therefore asked Mitsubishi how it was that, despite this system, there might be parts that weren't picked up. 'The possibility [of there being a pieces of uncollected fairing] is close to zero,' replied the Mitsubishi spokesperson, 'but it is not zero.'

So we were, at best, in a highly unusual situation. Unusual because Mitsubishi loses almost none of its fairings, more unusual because this debris has been found 4,000 kilometres from where fairings normally fell, and then still more unusual because Mitsubishi showed no interest in claiming this fairing back.

I shared the detailed video of the Thai debris with several contacts: B777 pilots, an engineer friend who happened to produce

---

* In the mid-nineties, in order to produce the new plane that was deemed necessary to revolutionize the market and the industry, Boeing worked out a partnership with three major Japanese manufacturers: Fuji, Mitsubishi and Kawasaki.

small rockets in composite material in the US, and an aeronautics engineer who had worked for Boeing for many years in Seattle and Oklahoma City and who knew the B777 'pretty well'. They pointed to several features that made this debris a most unlikely rocket part, especially a Japanese one. 'Way too much weight everywhere,' one said. 'When assembling a rocket, saving weight is an obsession, because every gram translates into extra fuel to carry.' Nor did the shape seem to match a Mitsubishi rocket fairing. If it were the nose, it would have been much more cone shaped, and if it were the body, it should have been cylindrical, which this debris was not. Then there was the red dangling wire very loosely attached by a single clamp, which would never have sustained the acceleration to Mach 6.

In one of the close-ups in the video there was also what seemed like a rather cheap repair to the hinges that bordered one side of the debris. Fairings are brand new when launched and are only used once; they could be damaged by the crash into water but they would never carry the slightest trace of a botched repair. All of the serial numbers surprised my contacts too. Precisely because a rocket was used only once, the issue of traceability did not apply in the same way as for an airplane that travelled round the world and was dismantled endless times. If all this alone was not enough to prove that this piece of debris was not a rocket fairing, there was then the question of the bolts.

Thai aviation experts quoted in several press reports had originally declared that the debris was covered with bolts used by Boeing. But these comments were quickly dismissed or ignored. Once again, a case had been closed before it was really heard, to the point where I, like the rest of the world, simply accepted the rocket story. Who would take the *Bangkok Post* and much lesser known local media seriously once all the big international media outlets had agreed on the Mitsubishi story? So I finally tried to double-check by myself, and it turned out to be not that difficult at all.

On some macro pictures of the bolts, the number NAS6204-31 was clearly readable. 'NAS' stood for National Aerospace Standards, an American standard that was used by Boeing among others.* So these were super-common bolts, made of stainless steel, which suggested that they came from either a commercial, a military or a private plane, but certainly not a spacecraft or a rocket that would require a high-performance aluminium alloy with titanium or magnesium. So, despite the almost universal consensus that this debris was a piece of a rocket, the presence of these bolts completely undermined the statement by Mitsubishi that it was 'likely' one of its parts. Of course, the fact that this piece of debris was fairly small-scale might explain why Mitsubishi which claimed to collect almost 100 per cent of its discarded fairings, had not identified which launch or which rocket this part belonged to and had no plans to collect the piece. After all, the company didn't want to 'cause trouble', as its spokesperson had said ...

But if this debris was *not* part of a Mitsubishi rocket, what on earth was it? And more specifically, since it was manufactured by KHI, a company that provided Boeing with several parts for the B777, could it be a piece of MH370?

The B777 pilots I contacted said that they had never noticed either such big bolts protruding nor the large panel numbers around the fuselage when they went around the plane on their pre-flight inspection tour. The former Boeing employee said that the skin of the debris was too thin to be part of the cabin's fuselage. The fuselage on a B777 is about 5.25 inches thick, but this part was only 3 inches thick. He also agreed that such protruding bolts would certainly not be from an external part of a rocket – or even a plane – that was exposed to wind flow. His best bet was that we were looking at one of the inside cowlings of an engine, the Rolls-Royce Trent 892, which happened to be the largest engine ever

---

* Japanese bolts by contrast are normally marked 'JIS', for Japanese Industrial Standard.

nicians that the plane skin in the designated area was not strong enough to be stepped upon. The Mozambique find made headline news around the world. For the vast majority of people who only followed the MH370 story with passing interest, it lent a bit more credence to the general story that the plane crashed 'somewhere down there'. But among close observers of the mystery, questions were raised about the piece itself – its clean condition, and the circumstances and the timing of the discovery.

The man who found the first piece of 'new wave' debris was Blaine Gibson, the American adventurer mentioned earlier. He dedicated most of his time searching for MH370 around the globe, having given up on both his search for the Lost Ark of the Covenant in Ethiopia's desert and elsewhere, and solving the riddle of the ending of the Mayan civilisation. Clearly, the cowboy-hat-wearing sleuth liked the big issues.

His father, Phil Gibson, was a highly respected judge with liberal views, someone who was remarkably ahead of his time. As Chief Justice of the Supreme Court of California, he was credited with 'revamping the state's court system during his 25 years on the bench, making it into one of the nation's most efficient and best administered'.* But when Gibson senior retired in 1964, Blaine Gibson – an only child – was just starting primary school. He went on to study foreign policy and law in Oregon and Washington, DC, although he never practised as a lawyer. He also spoke six languages, including Russian and French.

According to the best profile of Gibson I came across,† he worked for a few years in the office of Ray Moore, a Democrat senator for Washington State, before joining the US State Department in the late 1980s. According to the same article, his brief spell with the US government came to a stop when the call of

---

* 'Phil Gibson dies; Ex-Coast Justice', Associated Press, 29 April 1984.

† Matthew Halverson, 'Some Call Blaine Alan Gibson's Search for Malaysia Airlines Flight 370 an Obsession', *Seattle Met*, August 2016.

The missing Boeing 777-200ER, MSN 28420 (Line number 404),
delivered to Malaysia Airlines in May 2002.

The captain, Zaharie Ahmad Shah.

The first officer (co-pilot),
Fariq Abdul Hamid.

The author on assignment in the Philippines for *Le Monde* in 2013.

The daily press conference hosted by the Malaysian authorities at the
Sama-Sama Hotel at Kuala Lumpur International Airport.

Hishammuddin Hussein, the Malaysian Transport and Defence Minister, with Malaysian Airlines CEO Ahmad Jauhari Yahya and Inspector-General of Police Khalid Abu Bakar.

Interviewing former Deputy Prime Minister and Finance Minister Anwar Ibrahim while he was on bail in March 2014, in the office of the Parti Keadilan Rakyat (People's Justice Party), a few days after his acquittal was overturned.

Meeting retired First Admiral and former MP (Lumut), now Senator, Mohamad Imran Abdul Ahmid, in 2018. Imran has been one of the few prominent voices in Malaysia relentlessly asking for the public release of radar images and data.

With MP (Subang) Wong Chen and wife Yu Leng, in front of the iconic Petronas Twin Towers in Kuala Lumpur.

US President Barack Obama and Malaysian Prime Minister Najib Razak both smile as they participate in a joint news conference in Putrajaya, Malaysia, in April 2014.

Ghyslain Wattrelos talks to the press during a silent march towards the Elysée Palace in Paris to deliver a petition signed by 18,000 people, on the first anniversary of the disappearance of Flight MH370.

Former Prime Minister Mahathir Mohamad (1981–2003 and 2018–20) in his office in 2018. After having implied that the CIA would know what happened, 'Dr M' completely changed his suspicious stance regarding the fate of MH370 after he regained power in 2018.

Meeting with some of the Chinese families, including Ying Lei (fourth from right) and Jiang Hui (fourth from left), in Beijing in December 2018.

Remembrance ceremony held in Publika (Petaling Jaya) on 4 March 2017 on the third anniversary of the loss of the plane. Among others on the stage: Jacquita Gonzales (holding the mike), Grace Subathirai Nathan and Jiang Hui (behind the birdcage) , KS Narendran and his daughter (centre), Danica Weeks and her two sons, and Ghyslain Wattrelos.

In January 2016, Zakaria Muhammad and his daughter found a piece resembling a plane part on the east coast of Malaysia (Besut) that was immediately dismissed as 'not MH370' by Malaysian authorities, who never further identified the debris.

US amateur investigator Blaine Gibson speaks to the media after a meeting with the Australian Transport Safety Bureau and the Joint Agency Coordination Centre in Canberra in September 2016. He handed possible debris from missing Flight MH370 to Australian officials, saying several pieces had been blackened by flames, raising the idea of a flash fire on board.

French police inspect a large piece of plane debris that was found on the beach in Saint-André, on the French Indian Ocean island of La Réunion on 29 July 2015, before it is sent to France for further inspection. The technical investigation into the flaperon was shrouded in mystery, and very little information was ever shared with the families or the public about this important piece of debris.

Arriving in Kuda Huvadhoo by the weekly night ferry from Malé in May 2015. My very helpful guide Hussain Shakir (on his motorbike), with two of the witnesses – Zuhuriyya Ali and Humaam Dhonmonik – who saw a plane flying low in the early morning of 8 March 2014.

Lao Gong (former Chinese People's Liberation Army specialist in radio transmission) with his daughter, in Shenzen in March 2019. Mr Gong wrote a book entitled *MH370 Airlines Should Be Here* under the pseudonym of Long Wen

'This shows what I believe to possibly be MH370's cockpit/nose-cone debris. Its location would be in the South China Sea as of 16 March 2014, according to the satellite scans confirmed by the Image Hunter program,' says 'nodder-in-chief' Cyndi Hendry.

the wild and the unknown sent him exploring the collapsing USSR. This kept him busy, although it's not clear exactly how, for the following ten years. During this period – according to his own account – he would visit Afghanistan 'for vacations' and befriend rebels, proudly posing with their AK-47s. Around 2005, he started doing business in Laos, a landlocked nation in the heart of South East Asia, unfortunately very highly placed among the region's poorest and most corrupt countries.

He told the BBC that he sold the family house in Carmel, California, in 2014, to continue financing his lifestyle of travel, adventure and mystery-solving. His true goal, since he was little, had always been to visit every country in the world. When MH370 entered his life – or when he entered the MH370 saga – he had already ticked two-thirds of the list of roughly 200 countries, with Mozambique giving him his 177th bagged country. With no family, no day job and only a hefty inheritance to worry about, Blaine Gibson could have just lived the high life, but he was notoriously parsimonious, travelling, eating and staying anywhere on the cheap. His signature worn-out hat aside, he dressed rather poorly too.

Although he had an absolute passion for Lawrence of Arabia while he was a student (to the point of watching the David Lean film wearing a djellabah and a keffieh, according to his roommate during his years at Oregon University), his taste had somehow evolved to the point where he was now delighted to be called 'the real Indiana Jones', as the media were sometimes wont to do. In an interview on the French TV channel France 2,* he went so far as to say that Indiana Jones was 'his favourite character' and 'his favourite movie too'.

For friends who studied with him in Washington, DC, and stayed in contact, Blaine Gibson was always one of a kind, with slightly odd interests and a peculiar way of life. Not quite a misfit, but an enigma for sure.

* France 2, 27 July 2017.

When his dual passion of touring the world and finding MH370 took him to Australia, he had a meeting with the Australian Deputy Prime Minister Warren Truss, which surprised some observers. Why would a minister meet a full-time tourist, even if he did have a thing for MH370? When Gibson reached Perth, the Aircrash Support Group Australia, a group that, according to its website, supports 'victims and families of victims of aviation tragedies', facilitated a meeting between him and oceanographer Charitha Pattiaratchi, the only scientist I know of who predicted that MH370 debris could wash ashore in that part of the world before it apparently did. He suggested to Gibson that he should 'go and check Mozambique'.

Gibson did precisely this, in February 2016, and once set, it only took him a day to find his first debris. 'I asked local people: where do things tend to wash ashore, where do local people go to salvage things?' he recalled. The locals mentioned a particular sandbank that faced the Mozambique Channel. Gibson then hired a speedboat from Dolphin Dhow safaris, a day-tour company in Vilanculos on the Mozambique coast, and went to have a look, with Captain Bento and the owner of Dolphin Dhow, Sulaiman Junior. Although the tide meant that the three men only had a short time at the site, after only a few minutes from starting their combing operation Sulaiman picked up a large, grey, triangular piece of metal and screamed: 'Blaine, look at this!'

'I saw "No Step" written on it and I thought, whoa, this is from a plane and it could be from *the* plane.' Gibson told the BBC. He sent a photo to the ATSB, who replied very quickly and seemed 'extremely interested'. The Associated Press news agency broke the story a few days later. It quoted an 'anonymous US official' (I wonder, in passing, how many 'anonymous US officials' have been of service to the media in this story), who conveniently said that the piece 'could be from a Boeing 777'. The Transport Minister of Malaysia Liow Tiong Lai added that it was 'highly likely' that the piece was from MH370. And in no time, the world knew that, in broad terms at least, another piece of MH370 had been found.

The coastline of Mozambique is about 2,500 kilometres long. The Sulaiman–Gibson discovery, just a few minutes after they both alighted on the sand, and just a few days before the second anniversary of the disappearance, seemed to me to be somewhere between extremely lucky and miraculous. But from there on, Gibson seemed so gifted at finding plane debris on any beach he set foot on that miracles started repeating themselves. The media around the world loved it all the more, because it was so amazing and so incredible. Yet was it incredible – or simply not credible at all?

The only qualified person who had actually seen the first piece at the time was not that confident: João de Abreu, Director of Mozambique's National Civil Aviation Institute, told AIM, the Mozambique news agency, that any claim that the debris belonged to the missing Flight MH370 was 'premature' and 'speculative'. In his view, the object was too clean to have been in the ocean for the past two years.

But now the world knew that there might be other potential new debris following Gibson's discovery, and this prompted a South African teenager, Liam Lotter, to suggest that the large and rather immaculate piece of white panel with a thick layer of honeycomb-textured composite material inside that he had found on a beach to the south of Mozambique several months earlier could also be from MH370. No one even tried to explain how such a pristine piece could have travelled 6,000 kilometres in one of the planet's roughest oceans and arrived in Africa in so spotless a state, some 700 days later. There was simply no viable scenario in which this could have been possible. But many others caught the wreckage bug, and the harvesting season for plane debris reopened with a frenzied rush, similar to that on Réunion nine months earlier.

When these two first items arrived in Australia on 21 March 2016, Darren Chester, the Minister for Infrastructure and Transport, said that they would be examined in Canberra by investigators from Australia and Malaysia, as well as specialists from

Boeing, Geoscience Australia and the Australian National University. 'Because of the rigorous analysis to be performed, it is not possible to speculate on how long it might take to reach any conclusions,' Mr Chester said. But it took only three days to confirm that the debris was 'highly likely' to be from MH370. One month later, the ATSB Technical Examination Report on these two items stated:

> Stencilling on both parts of debris provided investigators with evidence of the link. The font and colour of a number stencilled on the first part conforms to that developed and used by Malaysian Airlines. The second part contained the words 'No Step' with stencilling consistent with that used by Malaysian Airlines and a fastener attached to the part provided evidence linking the part to the aircraft's production line.

But neither of these arguments should have been accepted. There were only so many aircraft stencilling types, and most airlines, as well as most military forces, used one or sometimes several of these. As for the fastener that was found attached to the part, it carried an identifying number that was consistent with, though not exclusive to, a Boeing 777, according to Jeff Wise's post of 17 March 2016. No further evidence was produced to establish the 'highly likely' MH370 provenance of this piece of plane debris.

Boeing, which was part of the 'rigorous analysis', did not say a word, and nor did Malaysia Airlines produce a photo showing the same 'No Step' stencil on any other of its many Boeing 777-200ERs that would have proven beyond doubt that the piece found was genuine. As with everything in this story, it was kept vague.

Actually, just like the case of the flaperon, some of the hardcore MHists turned to MH17, as it was useful for research and comparison that the plane shot down over Ukraine four months later was exactly the same type of plane and from the same batch order as MH370. They took the trouble to look through the thousands of sometimes harrowing pictures of MH17 debris, in search of the equivalent piece to the one found in Mozambique with the inscription 'No Step' on it. And these pictures were found. But this time, instead of the researchers suspecting that it was actually a piece of MH17, the comparison served to show several notable differences between the two wing stabilisers of MH17 and the item picked up on the sandbank during Gibson's expedition.*

Later in March 2016, so-called 'Part Number 3', an engine cowling with traces of the Rolls-Royce logo on it, was discovered in South Africa. Like the other parts found, it was also without barnacles, which many commentators found problematic until a picture of the same piece, taken several months before and this time covered with both sand and barnacles, surfaced in the South African press. The whole episode seemed bizarre. A 'Part Number 4', found in Mauritius in April, was later identified as an interior panel from the main cabin. In May, four more bits and pieces that looked like aircraft parts were collected in Mauritius and Mozambique. One of them was immediately dismissed, but the other three parts were considered by the investigators, both in Australia and in Malaysia, as 'almost certain' or 'highly likely' to be from MH370.

In early June 2016, Blaine Gibson went to Madagascar, where he teamed up with a French TV journalist and crew on Sainte-Marie Island. Once again, he struck unbelievable luck. Right in front of the camera he found two new pieces of potential debris. The find was accompanied by his live, on-site, professional commentary about the newly found debris, including cautious optimism as to its provenance. By now, Gibson had become an expert in his own right, almost a brand. On this occasion, which was even flukier than usual, the French journalist himself identified

---

* The stencil was not positioned in the same way in relation to the bolt holes, the skin of the Mozambique debris seemed be made of a different material and the letters on the Mozambique debris were smaller than those on MH17.

something that seemed to match pretty closely a TV screen from a Malaysia Airlines economy seat. In no time he tweeted a picture of his find, along with a fairly convincing image of the TV screen of an MAS Boeing 777. Despite the apparently very successful harvesting campaign, the Malaysian investigation team seemed in no hurry to take custody of these items. Many weeks later, five potential pieces of MH370 debris were still awaiting official attention in a hangar in Madagascar.

A key feature of bottles thrown into the sea at any one given point is their fast dispersal away from one another. Even a compact debris field only holds together for a certain time, as previous examples of plane crashes have shown. For this reason alone, it was almost impossible, statistically, to imagine that two items – let alone dozens – from the same faraway source would end up on the same beach a few metres apart, after spending 800 days at sea and travelling thousands of miles.

Defying all common sense and most of the basic laws of physics, Gibson started to compile a catalogue of 'Photographs of potential MH370 personal effects found on Riake Beach, Madagascar' so that families could check to see if they recognised a piece of hat, a plastic sandal or a backpack that had once belonged to their loved ones. He even managed to 'match' some items found on the beach to accessories identified on the surveillance video of the boarding at the airport. If any coherent logic or science were applied to this search for debris, much more caution should have been expressed about the validity of every new find. But as with the pings saga, the opposite happened: infatuation, excitement and no forensic follow-up.

By June 2016, several media outlets had upgraded their assessments from 'highly likely' and 'almost certain' to 'confirmed debris', without any thought being given to the nuances of each piece. The media passed on the good news without asking the most obvious question: how do we really know that the pieces found are from

MH370? Well, we didn't. If the Australian authorities were sure, would they not say 'for sure'? To me, 'almost certain' actually meant 'not certain'.

Perhaps it was because I had been more exposed to the sea than most people and also had a keen interest in the issue of ocean pollution, but this latest debris saga seemed to me just as chaotic and even less credible than any other episode I had so far come across concerning the loss of MH370. In the same way that 'very likely' had become the favourite expression for the deep-sea search (finding the plane was still deemed 'very likely' by the Australian authorities until March 2016), 'highly likely' and 'almost certain' were very soon the buzz-phrases used to qualify any kind of debris collected in the south-western part of the Indian Ocean that bore even the remotest possibility of having come from MH370.

In September 2016, with Gibson back in Madagascar a local fisherman handed him two fragments of what could well have been burnt debris. The fact that the fragments were burnt made them all the more interesting, as it invited new speculation regarding the fate of the plane. More headlines. More airtime. But as Gibson himself pointed out, they could easily have just been thrown into a fire after fetching up in the sand. Burning debris on the beach is a common practice in many parts of the world. The *Guardian* reported that Gibson flew – again – to Australia himself to hand over his latest findings to the authorities,* but in the end, according to the ATSB, these pieces were not MH370 debris. In fact, they were not even burnt.†

Among this avalanche of debris that had everyone confused and disorientated about what, where, when and how, by the end of

---

* www.theguardian.com/world/2016/sep/14/scorched-debris-missing-mh370-plane-fire.

† An ATSB statement from 22 September 2016 stated: 'At this stage it is not possible to determine whether the debris is from MH370 or indeed even a Boeing 777. What is known is that contrary to speculation there is no evidence the item was exposed to heat or fire.'

November 2016 two pieces of debris were finally conclusively linked to MH370. On 15 September, the ATSB confirmed that the wing flap found in June on Pemba Island, just off the coast of Tanzania, 'was confirmed as originating from the aircraft registered 9M-MRO and operating as MH370'. It identified the component as 'the inboard section of a Boeing 777 right, outboard flap'. Then, on 7 October, another wing part found in May 2016 on the island of Mauritius was 'conclusively determined as coming from missing Malaysia Airlines Flight MH370'. According to the ATSB, 'examination revealed the presence of a unique identifying number relating to the part's construction which allowed it to be determined as definitely coming from missing Malaysia Airlines Flight MH370'. But why didn't they provide the unique identifying number and show the documents that linked the piece to the Boeing number 28420?

As for the many other pieces that created such a feast of speculation, there was a much simpler explanation for their presence on these beaches. They could well be nothing more than the remnants of any of the planes that had crashed over the years into the southern Indian Ocean near this coastline. It is a fact that a very high number of fatal plane crashes have occurred in this area, at the top of the Mozambique Channel, in the Comoros, as well as further east. In 1996, a hijacked Boeing 767-200ER – Ethiopian Airlines Flight 961 – crashed near the Comoros, killing 125 of the 175 passengers and crew on board. It so happens that a Boeing 777 and 767 have a lot in common … In 2009, Yemenia Flight 626, an Airbus A310, stalled during its approach to Moroni in the Comoros. The plane crashed in the ocean between Madagascar and Mozambique. The well-known Mozambique current, a warm surface current that flows southwards along the African east coast through the Mozambique Channel, would have carried any floating debris from the Comoros along the coast of Mozambique and South Africa. In 1987, a Boeing 747 crashed to the east of Mauritius. Three distinct debris fields were identified. Some of this debris would surely have ended up on the east coast of Madagascar. Two smaller planes crashed in 2006, one off the coast of Réunion and one to the south-west of Madagascar. All of these crashes created tonnes of plane debris, some of which surely washed ashore on the neighbouring coasts. Once on the beaches, the debris may have been picked up and recycled for its scrap value – or just ignored. Unlike Réunion, most of these countries did not pay people to clean their coastline on a daily basis. Yet in all fairness, who needed debris for these well-documented crashes from the past, when the mysterious MH370 was so desperately in need of some of its own?

One important thing this 'new wave' debris achieved was to bolster the general impression that the plane undoubtedly crashed in the southern Indian Ocean, a message that all the countries involved – Australia more than any other – seemed very keen to get across, loud and clear. Just as happened when the flaperon turned up on Réunion, each time a piece of debris appeared somewhere, Australia's first comments were along the lines of: 'This reaffirms that the search area for MH370 is in the southern Indian Ocean,' as if anyone would be thinking otherwise. Gibson's quest and the media frenzy that he managed to create around himself were therefore of immense service to the authorities, reinforcing the idea that the plane crashed somewhere in the Indian Ocean.

The Malaysian government was so grateful to Gibson for all his good work that a representative formally offered him a present at a dinner organised by the next of kin in Kuala Lumpur on 3 March 2017, the third anniversary of the plane's disappearance. I thought it was quite daring for the government to so openly say, 'Thank you so much for what you are doing', given that the subtext was so clear: 'You have no idea how much your chasing debris around the African coast has helped our narrative.'

It all became even more surreal when the same Malaysian government representative presented a gift to a British woman called Yvonne Harrison, who as far as I could see had been acting as Gibson's personal assistant. When I tried to reach Gibson for an interview by leaving a casual message on one of the Facebook pages Harrison had set up relating to MH370, I received an email from her informing me that: 'Blaine [was] currently traveling so I am fielding press enquiries for him. Can you let me know what you need and I will pass on to him for consideration?' It sounded like surprisingly sophisticated secretarial assistance for a wild adventurer.

Although she had no connection whatsoever to the flight, Yvonne Harrison had been working very closely with Sarah Bajc – the girlfriend of Philip Wood, the only adult American on board MH370 – in the days following the plane's disappearance. She helped her with the Facebook pages, including one set up immediately after the plane's loss. In 2015, she started a new secret Facebook page, centred around Gibson's hunt and findings. And she seemed so dedicated to the cause that, just like Gibson, she flew all the way to Kuala Lumpur at her own cost for the third anniversary dinner – from London, in her case. None of the family members were able to figure out what her real job actually was. For the majority of them that I came to know, she constituted a complete enigma, albeit one that sent them surprisingly loving and caring messages. 'Even my best friend does not speak to me like that,' one of them told me, slightly at a loss as to this new character that had entered their lives without really being asked. Until that anniversary in March 2017, she had not met a single one of them, not even Gibson. Whoever this woman was – and whatever she did for a living – the Malaysian government thought it significant enough for her to be thanked with a bottle of French perfume. *Malaysia Boleh!*

This bounty of debris found on the African coast – whatever its origin – created a much-needed diversion to the complete lack of progress with the official investigation or the sea search. On the ships belonging to Fugro, the Dutch company leading the search, morale was low. And questions were being asked, including in the Australian senate. In mid-October 2015, Senator Alex Gallacher of the Australian Labor Party requested to see the tender process, the technical advice and the cost of the search operation.* He told Martin Dolan, head of the ATSB, 'There are people giving a lot of different senators – coalition, opposition and cross bench senators – a very different view of what you are actually doing there.' November 2015 was a particularly calamitous month: a case of appendicitis and another incident among the crew meant the *Fugro Discovery* lost almost two-thirds of its searching time as it had to return to port twice in quick succession.

But that did not prevent a fresh wave of optimism from washing across the media. On 11 November 2015, the website of the British *Daily Express* ran the headline: 'The MH370 crash site FOUND'. 'The wreckage will be found within a few weeks,' read another headline. 'Flightglobal's consulting editor David Learmount said that for those seeking a reason to be optimistic following a discouraging 20 months of searching the ocean without a result, there is definite cause for renewed hope this time,' wrote Geoffrey Thomas in *The West Australian*.† 'By 3 December [2015],' he continued, '*Fugro Discovery* expects to have completed the search of the area containing [...] the wreck of MH370.' By 3 December! Really? Unfortunately, by 3 December the search area that had been so strongly recommended by those few members of the Independent Group still obsessed with Inmarsat's calculations had not yet yielded the wreckage of MH370.

Yet during a 3 December press conference, Warren Truss, the Federal Minister for Infrastructure and Regional Development, revealed a newer and better 'hot' area of high probability. He also

* This request was put before the Rural and Regional Affairs and Transport Legislation Committee, 19 October 2015.

† See thewest.com.au/news/wa/captain-claims-to-have-pinpointed-mh370-crash-site-ng-ya-132065.

announced that the search operation was about to be boosted by the arrival of a fourth ship, one equipped with a T-SAS (towed synthetic aperture sonar) – the *nec plus ultra*. 'We remain hopeful and optimistic of locating the plane in the 44,000 square kilometres yet to be searched in this new priority area,' said Truss. He also added that China had offered to contribute A$20 million (£10.5 million) to the Australian search operation, a welcome gesture given that the total cost of the search had jumped to A$180 million (£94 million). Australia was to contribute A$60 million (£31.5 million), while Malaysia would cover the difference.

But more bad news kept on coming from the search front. On 24 January 2016, while conducting search operations in the southern Indian Ocean, the deep tow sonar vehicle being used by *Fugro Discovery* to search the ocean floor struck an undersea volcano and was separated from the vessel. In late May 2016, monster waves up to 18 metres high hit *Fugro Discovery*, forcing it further north and out of the search area. The outlook was then for more extreme weather, which would prolong the end of the search to August 2016. In late June 2016, Malaysia's Transport Minister Liow Tiong Lai announced during a two-day trip to Beijing that the search for MH370 might even have to be extended to October 2016, due to unfavourable weather conditions.

None of the complicated questions about the search ever reached the general public, with the Australian effort continuing to give the comforting impression that an answer to the mystery was still being sought. The Australian search teams supported the idea that MH370 was where they kept saying it was, implicitly making the official version appear credible and consistent, and helping to defer until later all other questions around the case.

On 22 July 2016, another trilateral meeting between Australian, Chinese and Malaysian ministers took place in Kuala Lumpur. It confirmed that the three nations had agreed to suspend the search in the absence of credible new leads following the exhaustion of the current priority search zone in the southern Indian Ocean. Fugro project director Paul Kennedy told Reuters, 'If it's not there, it means it's somewhere else.' That was pretty explicit, and the news agency summed up the message in a piece with the headline: 'We have been looking in the wrong place'. This buzzed around the world's newswires in no time, but Fugro must have been told off by the ATSB, as it quickly reacted with a new statement: 'Fugro wishes to make it very clear that we believe the search area to have been well defined based on all of the available scientific data. In short, we have been thoroughly looking in the most probable place – and that is the *right* place to search.'

In December 2016, to mark the 1,000th day of the plane's loss, a party of six next of kin decided to go to Madagascar to search for debris themselves. They wanted to alert the local population to keep an eye out for debris that looked like it might have come from the plane. 'Since the truth is being hidden from us, we might as well go and search by ourselves,' said 'the Frenchman', Ghyslain Wattrelos, who took a week off work to join the Madagascar trip. Despite Gibson's assistance, they did not find anything, although they succeeded in keeping the world's attention on their unhappy fate. The media was still refusing to forget this peculiar disappearance, as, quite apart from the more tantalising aspects of the mystery, most people sympathised with anyone who had lost close family members or good friends

The final piece of bad news for the families came in on 17 January 2017, when the ATSB announced that the search was over for good. It had gone on for 1,046 days at a cost of A$198 million (£103 million). 710,000 square kilometres of sea floor had been mapped, the largest single hydrographical survey ever mounted, including 120,000 square kilometres that had been scanned in high resolution. As large an area as it may sound, it was not even 0.2 per cent of the entire Indian Ocean. Although four shipwrecks were spotted in the process, not the slightest trace of MH370 had been found.

The group of Flight MH370 passengers' families united under the banner of 'Voice 370' was shocked and dismayed by the news that ATSB was calling it a day. They asked the government to 'suspend rather than stop' the search. Grace Subathirai Nathan, whose mother was on board and whom I met many times over the years, said to me at the time: 'Whether or not it is taking place in the right place, we just do not want the search to stop, because that will be de facto the closure of the file.'

Ten months later, the Australian Transport Safety Bureau published its official and final report on the search.* It started with a near apology: 'It is almost inconceivable and certainly societally unacceptable in the modern aviation era ... for a large commercial aircraft to be missing and for the world not to know with certainty what became of the aircraft and those on board.' The ATSB expressed its 'deepest sympathies to the families of passengers and crew on board MH370', adding, 'We deeply regret that we have not been able to locate the aircraft, nor those 239 souls on board that remain missing.'

The only salient piece of news provided by the report was that the plane had not turned out to be where they had so adamantly promised it would be. Yet the investigators had the nerve to assert that they now 'know better than ever before' where the plane was likely to be. So they searched for three years, yet stopped short of exploring a new area of less than 25,000 square kilometres', in which there was the 'highest probability' of locating the fuselage. That was obviously a clever way to keep hope on the menu – but was it either professional or morally acceptable?

The report also contained several oddities and red herrings, of which I will list but a few. For example, it referred to a last point of contact north of Sumatra that was only ever confirmed by one blurry and problematic slide that had been shown to some of the

* *The Operational Search for MH370*, 3 October 2017.

families gathered in Beijing's Lido Hotel on 21 March 2014. Although it was supposedly assessing the search undertaken in the southern Indian Ocean, the report also mentioned a route 'initially similar' to the one supposedly taken by MH370 that Captain Zaharie Ahmad Shah would have flown on his home flight simulator. As we'll discuss later, the document the report was referring to suffered from major issues and hence possessed no credibility whatsoever, so it was puzzling to see this dodgy and somewhat incriminating document quoted in the ATSB report.

As for its handling of the 'debris', the report was all over the place. On p. 106 it published a drawing of the aircraft sourced from the Malaysian Ministry of Transport that showed where exactly on the plane – wings, doors, engines, stabiliser panels, etc. – the 20 pieces of debris found in the western part of the Indian Ocean originated. Most of these had not been confirmed as being parts of MH370 and several were discovered in questionable circumstances. The most astonishing comment was that the 'ATSB and Geoscience Australia determined that no analysis by Boeing was necessary and retained the samples'. I'd have thought that a positive identification by Boeing of the pieces would have been essential, but the ATSB clearly chose to keep them out of the demanding spotlight of third-party verification.

Another oddity were the French satellite images dating all the way back to 23 March 2014, which made a bizarre comeback in the news in August 2017 and helped to establish the new search area mentioned above. If these images contained any interesting clues, 41 months seemed a long time to have elapsed before paying attention. If anything, producing these images looked like a desperate attempt to rekindle hope with very flimsy evidence.

As for recommendations, the report suggested better methods of automated satellite tracking. even though most pilots were adamant that long-haul planes were already triple-covered when it came to being tracked. In fact, if just one of the recommendations contained in the report on Flight AF447 had been implemented – that black boxes should detach on impact and float – the true story of MH370 would not still be a so-called mystery. In a sense, the 440-page ATSB report simply repeated the comments made in March 2014 by Ahmad Jauhari Yahya, CEO of Malaysia Airlines: 'We do not know how, we do not know why this tragedy took place.' After three years of searching, no one still had any idea how or any idea why this disaster happened.

In the end, when it came to the art of bungling a search operation and providing deliberate or accidental misinformation, Australia ran Malaysia pretty close. One might even say that Australia smashed Malaysia in this regard and taught them a lesson. The total fiasco surrounding the pings, the sudden and unexplained changes in search zones, the opportunistic switches to the official line, along with a string of totally unfounded declarations, were surely not what was initially expected from the 'real pros'. One thing, however, that the ATSB did do with steadiness and consistency during its three years coordinating the seabed search was spray the media, the public and the families with regular splashes of temporary good news. The official report seemed as botched and inconsistent as the search itself, bringing another unimpressive chapter in the lacklustre history of the ATSB to a close.

A year later, quite out of the blue, a British-American private company called Ocean Infinity, with an HQ in Houston, Texas, and London-based investors, announced that it would find MH370 within 90 days – the Malaysian authorities would pay them in the event of their successfully locating the plane in this time frame, otherwise they would foot the bill themselves. The hopes of the families were once again renewed. The initiative seemed providential, sparking a fresh bout of international enthusiasm for the tragic and baffling story of MH370.

'The whole world, starting with the families, is hopeful to find the plane so they can finally mourn,' Malaysian Civil Aviation

Chief Azharuddin Abdul Rahman said at the signing ceremony on 10 January 2018, speaking to the families of the passengers in a mall outside Kuala Lumpur's city centre. According to the contract, Ocean Infinity would receive between US$20 and $70 million if, and only if, it found the plane 'in less than 90 days'. The amount of compensation would be proportional to the time spent searching and the extent of the area explored. The campaign was to be completed by mid-April 2018.

The niche world of underwater exploration was caught by surprise. Until that announcement, Ocean Infinity were simply unheard of. Intrigued by their Good Samaritan attitude, I checked their website – www.oceaninfinity.com – and was first impressed, then puzzled, by their claim of '90 years of expertise'. Who on earth could have 90 years of expertise in deep-sea exploration? In the 1920s, Jacques Cousteau's first underwater adventures still lay far in the future ... As it turned out, the company had only been in existence for a few months, and MH370 was going to be their first operation. The '90 years of expertise' was just a marketing gimmick, based on the cumulative credentials of their respective employees in all professions, like the 20 years of consultancy experience of director Oliver Plunkett, a tax lawyer by trade.

Clearly the company had a nerve, but although they were newcomers on the scene, they also meant business, with both the equipment and the drive to fast become a force to be reckoned with. Chartering the *Seabed Constructor*, Norwegian company Swire Seabed's most recent ship, was already an indication of their serious commitment, even more so with a six-year lease. The imposing 115-metre vessel was well known for its powerful crane, which could hoist 250 tonnes from depths of up to 4,000 metres, and its two underwater intervention robots (ROVs). Fully furnished with a helicopter pad, Ocean Infinity had also equipped their ship with eight small autonomous submarines (autonomous underwater vessels or AUVs) of the latest model, the Hugin 6000, as well as eight automated escort boats (unmanned surface vessels or USVs) that followed their parent submarine from the surface and relayed the collected data to the main ship. In short, they had assembled a ship and associated systems of the highest imaginable calibre, with a complexity inconceivable only a few years ago, which could scan the equivalent of 140,000 football fields (1,000 square kilometres) in just 24 hours.

With these astonishing means, Ocean Infinity immediately placed themselves not just in the big league but right at the top of it. And thanks to the attention garnered by their involvement in the MH370 mission, the whole world had now heard of them.

Ocean Infinity's seemingly reckless approach nevertheless left many observers dumbfounded. 'I do not know of any company that can take on such a financial risk,' said veteran wreck searcher Paul-Henri Nargeolet. He estimated that mobilising such a ship would cost between $60,000 and $100,000 per day, while the AUVs alone cost about $5 million apiece. And then there was the question of costing the USVs, together with the specialist teams required to run operations and deal with the data. The investment required to undertake this search with these means was at least proportional to the size of the risk of failing: immense. 'Either they have information that no one else has and that gives them good reasons to believe in the new search area, or there is something totally incomprehensible about their approach,' Nargeolet told me at the time.

The international league of MHists were naturally intrigued by this latest and unexpected episode, and they followed it closely. From the time of its departure from Durban in early January, the *Seabed Constructor* was never alone on the high seas of the south. Round the clock, aficionados were glued to their computer screens, closely tracking this hi-tech vessel in real time. They checked its speed, its course, and, of course, speculated about its activities. The alarm was therefore quickly sounded within these specialised networks when, at the end of January, the ship simply turned off its transponder and went dark for 80 hours ... What on earth was happening? Had it found MH370?

Urged to explain this anomaly, Liow Tiong Lai, Malaysia's Minister of Transport, said on 6 February that the ship had 'spotted interesting geological formations'. He added that the research was 'progressing very fast' and that it was all 'very encouraging'. The explanation seemed feeble, especially given that by an unlikely coincidence (lost on neither the MHists nor the Australian press), this 'disappearance' took place very near two wreckages of old ships, pre-located by the initial Australian research (which, as we saw, had found four in total). Some newspaper then published the blurred images of a large trunk already shown in 2015 that belonged to one of the located wrecks. Was it full of sea water or full of gold? 'It's a classic [to turn off your transponder] in the craft. Especially when you're working [over a wreck],' Dave Gallo told me. This famous American oceanographer, former head of special projects for Woods Hole Oceanographic Institution (WHOI), had co-directed the search for Flight AF447.

Once all these clues were combined, a new hypothesis could be deduced. What if, under the guise of searching for MH370, Ocean Infinity was in fact making the best use of the extensive mapping produced by the initial Australian research to search for wrecks and treasure once thought lost? Around the same time, British television channel Sky News claimed that the main investor in Ocean Infinity was a wealthy businessman, Anthony Clake, a partner in a very large hedge fund in the City of London, Marshall Wace. 'Mr Clake, who oversees billions of pounds of clients' money at Marshall Wace, is understood to have invested in Ocean Infinity after being impressed by its advanced technology,' Sky reported. Anthony Clake happened to be quoted in a *Times* article from 2012 discussing 'celebrities and some of Britain's most senior business people who invested more than £110 million into marine treasure hunts, which allowed them to avoid millions of pounds in tax'. Having referred to Clake as a hedge fund tycoon, the story mentioned that he had personally invested £17 million in high-risk marine companies and had 'already found 11 wrecks and a haul of silver'.*

In brief, it looked like the people behind Ocean Infinity were super-wealthy financiers who were essentially avoiding taxes while mounting extraordinary operations on the high seas, which, if all went well, would make them even richer.

There was another clue that Ocean Infinity was looking for treasure at least as much as it was looking for MH370. This was the rumour that John Kingsford, the head of Deep Ocean Search (DOS),† might be on board *Seabed Constructor*. 'That's a sign that does not deceive,' another specialist in this sector told me. DOS made a big name – and an even bigger fortune – for itself in 2013 when it retrieved 100 tonnes of silver coins, at a record-breaking depth of 5,150 metres, from the British steamship *City of Cairo*, sunk in 1942 by a torpedo launched from a German U-boat.

Yet, officially, the *Seabed Constructor* was searching for the debris field of MH370, with those contacted on board during that time saying that they were under 'very strict confidentiality obligations'.

'There is a lot of commonality between looking for treasure and plane wrecks. It would make sense to do both things at the same time', said Nargeolet. Actually, Swire Seabed's ships had a reputation for treasure hunting – which some call 'plundering' – rather than submarine archaeology, according to another expert in the field. In the case of MH370, Dave Gallo insisted that the debris field, once located, should be treated as a crime scene. 'It's not because you have the best tools that you have the right method,' he

---

* See www.thetimes.co.uk/article/celebrities-saved-millions-using-tax-breaks-from-shipwreck-salvage-5z7thx8lhxz. See also www.telegraph.co.uk/finance/personalfinance/tax/9593444/Taxman-investigates-shipwreck-salvage-tax-break.html.

† DOS is a company based in Mauritius specialising in treasure recovery, which led the campaign to find and recover the fuselage of EgyptAir Flight 804 in 2016 in the Mediterranean.

warned. Before Ocean Infinity leased it, the *Seabed Constructor* found itself briefly in trouble with the Icelandic coastguard in April 2017, when its previous team were trying to recover four tonnes of Nazi gold from the German freighter SS *Minden*, which was transporting the bullion at the start of the Second World War. The *Minden* had been scuttled near Iceland to avoid surrendering its precious cargo to the British battleships that had intercepted it

As early as mid-March 2018, the sonars of the Ocean Infinity submarines had already scanned an immense surface, including the entirety of the 25,000 square kilometres designated by Australia as 'the highest probable zone' for locating MH370. But to no avail. By then, there was as little trace of MH370's hull on the seabed as there was hope on the horizon.

The search, nevertheless, continued beyond the set ninety-day deadline, and as had been agreed, Ocean Infinity did not get paid. But in addition to the access they gained to the newly produced Australian maps, this campaign also granted them the largest international media campaign on launch that they could ever have mounted. According to sources close to the company, they did indeed salvage some wrecks in the Indian Ocean. After that, in late 2018, they successfully located the Argentinian submarine ARA *San Juan*, which had been lost the previous year in the South Atlantic. And in July 2019, they found the French submarine *Minerve*, which had been missing, with its crew of 52 men, since 1968. 'They are incredibly efficient. They do in a few days what used to take months, and their AUVs now have up to 100 hours' autonomy,' commented Nargeolet, who now salutes these game-changers.

As it seems increasingly improbable that the plane will ever be found, it may be time to come to terms with another fallacy that has long been served up and that the ATSB reiterated in its final report when it stated that 'the reasons for the loss of MH370 cannot be established with certainty until the aircraft is found'. In fact, finding the hull may not solve the enigma of MH370. Even if the fuselage and the two black boxes were found one day at the bottom of some ocean, we won't learn much. The CVR, or cockpit voice recorder, only preserves the recent history – the last two hours – of cockpit noise, including the pilots' conversation, and it is not guaranteed at all that any revelations will come from the cockpit in that time period. As for the technical information recorded in the flight data recorder (FDR), all this will only tell us is the aircraft's altitude and exact flight path. Nothing more. Pretending that we needed the hull to understand or explain anything is simply a way to put off the moment when the two really difficult questions had to be faced: 'Why and how did this plane disappear?'

The only reason it remains crucial to find the hull is to provide closure to the families. In an interview she gave on the fifth anniversary of the disappearance, Grace Subathirai Nathan said: 'Of course, life goes on. But we never really moved on.' She said she counted out her years in plane years. The year she graduated in England was the year the plane – hence her mother – disappeared. 'And if you ask me what year I started working, I'd reply: the year after the plane disappeared. Because for a lot of us, time has stood still since that day.'

These comments reminded me of a conversation I'd had with Grace in Kuala Lumpur not long after the first anniversary. This bright young lawyer, who has been the very brave and dignified voice for all the Malaysian next of kin, was still completely devastated. She realised that she was underperforming at work, sometimes forgetting what she was going to say while in court. Her boss had made a slightly impatient comment along the lines of, 'It's been a year now, Grace', implying that it was time that she should get on with her life. She had been shocked to realise that other people had no idea that when there was no closure, the passage of time did not really heal anything. Or if it did, it took much, much longer.

The only positive outcome of the Indian Ocean search was that Australia and Malaysia now had extensive seabed maps of a totally unexplored part of the ocean, which were at the disposal of their oil and gas companies as well as their fisheries. These sectors would doubtless make great use of such detailed maps, just like the salvagers of Ocean Infinity had already done.

A few months after the end of the Ocean Infinity operation, the official investigation team produced its final report into the loss of MH370 in July 2018. This was supposed to close the file on the whole affair, which greatly distressed the families. But the lead investigator, Kok Soo Chon, former Civil Aviation Department director-general, was quick in clarifying at the very beginning of the press conference that, in fact, the report was 'not final' and that the search might continue. Over the years beyond the *Factual Information* report produced in March 2015, four interim statements had been published on the anniversaries of the loss. Only France was still pursuing a criminal investigation, although the regular change of judges to lead the process didn't augur much hope of success. But it is vital for the families that the process continues. 'The French investigation is very important for the Chinese families because, despite time going by, we still want and need to know the truth. Our life can't restart until we know,' Wang Yinlei told me when I met some of the families in Beijing in December 2018. He had lost his mother and father on the flight.

The *Safety Investigation Report* (undoubtedly of much higher standards than the ATSB report on the search) essentially admitted that the investigators 'did not know what happened to MH370', yet regretted 'a significant lack of evidence available to the team to determine with any certainty the reasons that the aircraft diverted from its filed flight plan route'. The lead investigator also hinted at some tensions within the investigation team. Interestingly, of the seven countries that had participated in the investigation,*

---

* The seven countries that had been invited to participate in the investigation were Australia (ATSB), the United Kingdom (AAIB), the United States (NTSB), France (BEA), China (CAAC), Indonesia (NTSC) and Singapore (TSIB).

Indonesia did not send comments after it had scrutinised the document, something that was interpreted by people close to the investigation as a clear repudiation of its findings.

The report ended by mentioning the possible intervention of an elliptical 'third party'. But when it was published, in the middle of the summer holidays in 2018, despite good live coverage by some international media including the *Guardian*, it was almost treated as a non-event. The tabloids couldn't really be bothered to check such a thick document and would rather resurrect, as they had done on a regular basis, the suspicions surrounding the captain.

11

Could the Captain Have Run Amok?

On board any flight the captain takes the lead. This is especially true during a major emergency.

In the other crashes I studied to try to find clues or similarities to what happened to MH370 (see Addendum), I discovered – to my initial bemusement – the propensity of the investigation teams to blame the pilots. The results of several famous crash investigations were at first presented to the public as being probable pilot suicide or pilot error, and were subsequently always known as such, even when years, sometimes decades later the real causes were identified and the pilots were cleared. The most recent saga of the 737 MAX disasters has sadly proved no exception. The trend is surprisingly blatant, but it has its logic. Blaming the pilot exonerates the plane and engine manufacturers from any wrongdoing, as well as the airline, whose business has got to continue uninterrupted. The insurers split the bill of the disaster and life goes on, albeit not without a sigh at yet another example of 'human error'. As for the dead pilot, he – most conveniently – will be unable to defend his name. It was therefore fascinating to observe that in the case of MH370 as well, from very early on, the captain became the target of a fierce and relentless smear campaign that has not ended to this day.

The scenario that regularly resurfaced was the idea that Zaharie Ahmad Shah was suicidal, that he was a mad mass murderer or a psychopath who had carefully planned this doomed flight on his simulator. The fact that the first investigation had found nothing suspicious about him did not stop dozens of media outlets (in particular, oddly, those from the UK, US, Australia and New Zealand) from continuously portraying the captain as the prime suspect in hundreds of media articles. His love life was said to be on the chaotic side. Politically, he had recently become a bit of a fanatic, with his feet firmly in the opposition camp. And as we saw earlier, Zaharie had also been accused of several strange pieces of behaviour – such as requesting more fuel than was needed – by some 'very highly placed sources' who talked to the private investigators hired by the families.

Then there were the leaks and the innuendo trickling down indirectly from the FBI or from the police about what he did with his simulator.* Even Rosmah Mansor, wife of Najib Razak, prime minister at the time, hinted at the captain's culpability.† Recently, a friend and colleague of mine from a major English-language newspaper who interviewed Najib himself, when he was facing dozens of judicial charges at the time, asked him candidly about MH370 at the end of their meeting. In the discreet tone of an insider sharing a confidence – and with a sorry face – the former prime minister told my friend he thought it was … the captain.

In mid-2019, a seemingly serious and lengthy analysis of the whole affair was published in the American magazine *The Atlantic*

---

* On 18 August 2016, *The Australian* published an article by former Emirates pilot Byron Bailey in which he wrote that he knew 'from a government source that the FBI had recovered from Zaharie's home computer deleted information showing flight plan waypoints … my source … left me with the impression that the FBI were of the opinion that Zaharie was responsible for the crash.' He also repeated the fallacy of the simulator flight to the Indian Ocean and wrongly attributed the story to the *New Yorker* rather than to the less respected *New York* magazine.

† On Australian Channel Nine's programme *60 Minutes* in August 2015, Danica Weeks, whose husband Paul Weeks was on board MH370, declared that the wife of the prime minister had told her that the pilots were responsible.

under the tantalising title, 'What Really Happened to Malaysia's Missing Airplane?' The story lined up a remarkable series of factual mistakes unworthy of even a novice MHist. The author also tried hard to popularise the idea that pilot suicides were a recurring thing. But of the four cases quoted, only two have been confirmed with no doubts. Pilot suicides do happen, but they remain extremely rare. It was troubling to see that a supposed 'specialist' would still portray EgyptAir Flight 990 and SilkAir Flight 185 as straightforward suicide cases when the investigations had showed the planes to have suffered major technical failures, not to mention the FBI admitting to have interfered by blaming the pilot in the case of EgyptAir (see Addendum, p. 384). But the biggest let-down in the *Atlantic* story about MH370 was its final 'revelation': Zaharie was 'clinically depressed', 'a troubled man' who had suddenly 'run amok'. In a nutshell, 'Zaharie was guilty', without even a proper trial. In February 2020, another low blow to the deceased pilot came from former Australian Prime Minister Tony Abbott, who declared in a Sky News documentary: 'My very clear understanding from the very top levels of the Malaysian government is that from very, very early on here they thought it was a murder-suicide by the pilot.' Although he declined to be specific about 'who said what to whom', Abbott said: 'I want to be absolutely crystal clear – it was understood at the highest levels that this was almost certainly murder-suicide by the pilot, mass murder-suicide by the pilot.' In other words, Malaysia knew it, but chose to protect him.

As squalid as one may find this far-right climate-change denier, who seems to be desperately missing the limelight after his short two years in power in Canberra (between 2013 and 2015), I am tempted to believe that, on this occasion, he was probably telling the truth, or rather, he was accurately reporting what he had been told in 2014, most likely by the then Prime Minister Najib. But there was simply nothing new in this. And he was just using his reputation as a former prime minister of Australia to add weight to unsubstantiated rumours and smears. We had already heard from many different sources that the 'highest level' of the Malaysian government had indeed been actively promoting the guilty pilot scenario, with no evidence whatsoever. It's hard not to notice that these accusatory articles and documentaries have been dispatched with an incredible, almost predictable, regularity. If a PR firm is currently in charge of making sure that, over the years, the suicidal pilot becomes the generally accepted thesis to the nonsensical disappearance of the B777, it is doing a shamelessly good job.

The expression to 'run amok' comes from a Malay word that has entered the English vernacular – spelt variously as 'amok', 'amuk' or 'amuck' – meaning 'to go wildly out of control'. But in Malaysia and Indonesia it refers to a recognised type of behaviour that is particularly well known. Stefan Zweig, Rudyard Kipling, Henri Fauconnier and Romain Gary are among the many authors who have been attracted to the region and have referred to the phenomenon. To 'run amok' describes a form of suicide accompanied by the release of lethal impulses in the sufferer, who is overwhelmed by a sudden impulse of murderous frenzy. It ends with the sufferer's death, but must be preceded by the killing of other people. In most cases, amok attacks are the work of mature men suffering from pent-up frustration, triggering a desire for revenge in them. To his detractors, the 'amok scenario' seemed to describe Captain Zaharie Ahmad Shah down to a T.

Ironically, the same people who accused the captain of having run amok simultaneously suspected him of having meticulously premeditated and executed the disappearance of the plane in cold blood, even though amok attacks and cold-blooded attacks are diametrical opposites. But no one seemed to have been paying attention to the inconsistency of the accusations directed at the captain.

Let's imagine for a moment the unnerving scenario in which Zaharie has indeed decided to end his life and the lives of all the people on board at the same time. And let's imagine that he wants to go out with the panache for which he is known. Not only will he die, he will also fool the authorities, outsmart the air traffic controllers, catch the Malaysian military out, embarrass Boeing and highlight the flaws in modern air communications technology. In short, he will do what no one else has ever managed to do: lose his plane and all those on board forever, without leaving the slightest trace.

Zaharie certainly chose the right moment to start executing his plan. After 40 minutes of flight, the plane has completed its ascent; it has left Malaysian airspace and has not yet announced its presence to the Vietnamese authorities. It is the captain who does the sign-off, meaning that the first officer is the pilot flying.* But there's no hurry. Everything is fine. The night is dark, as the moon had gone even before the flight took off.† The captain then asks his co-pilot to hand the controls back to him and go and chat with the first- or business-class passengers, as sometimes happens on Malaysia Airlines at this stage in the flight. Zaharie then locks himself in the cockpit.

Now alone at the helm, he sets his diabolical plan in motion: he turns to the left, flies over the Malaysia–Thailand border so as not to alert anyone, detours to the north to avoid Indonesia, then sets his course due south, where he will manage to do what no experienced pilot ever thought possible: a sufficiently soft landing on the high seas that the plane sinks in a single piece and buries itself, its human cargo and the mystery of its fate under 20,000 feet of water.

This story is easy to tell, easy to understand and easy to repeat. It's a pretty good story. Who, then, wants to be told that such a scenario is actually unrealistic in most of its details, starting with the lack of motive for a mass killing and ending with the improbability of a kiss landing in the middle of the southern Indian Ocean?

---

* In commercial aviation, when the flight crew is made of two pilots, one is called pilot flying (PF) and one is called pilot monitoring or pilot not flying (PM or PNF). It is for the captain, formally called the pilot in command (PIC) to decide who does what.

† At waypoint IGARI, where the plane officially came off the screens at 17:22 UTC on 7 March 2014, moonset had taken place at 16:37 UTC.

In any case, I became convinced early on in my investigation that the personality of the captain surely contained part, if not all, of the solution to the riddle I was trying to solve. Beyond the aviation enthusiast and the highly skilled pilot, who really was Zaharie Ahmad Shah? What kind of colleague, friend, father, husband and human being was he? What did he have in mind when he set off that night in March 2014 for this routine flight that he was quite familiar with? If he was in fact guilty of the crime, *what* was so wrong with this man or his life and *why* would he have committed such an evil act? And how valid are the clues his detractors have used to try to make him the great mastermind of this impossible 'mystery', the greatest aviation mastermind of all time?

The woman with a friendly smile who met me in the lobby of the New World Hotel in Kuala Lumpur's go-to suburb Petaling Jaya was the captain's eldest sister, Sakinab Shah. She was a serene and lively grandmother, recently widowed, who inspired both respect and affection at first sight. Like all Malays, she placed her hand on her heart after having shaken mine, a simple and common gesture in Malaysia that I always found beautiful. More than a year and a half after the plane had disappeared, Sakinab was still deeply affected, not just because she had lost her dear brother but also because of all the unpleasant things that had been said and written about him since. She was the eldest of nine siblings. Zaharie, or Ari to his friends, was the eighth child; he was 17 years her junior. It was plain to see that he was her favourite little brother. She knew 'pretty much everything about him' – that's how close they were.

The early years were not easy for this large family living in Penang in the 1950s.* The father, Mustafa bin Omar Khan, was a policeman. The mother, Fatimah binti Mohamed Noor, was

* Penang is an island off Malaysia's north-west coast.

uneducated. They lived in the poor quarters of the township; the children clearly understood the importance of doing well at school, and they did just that, not only at school, but also later on in life. Sakinab mentioned one sister who was a psychiatrist in Ireland, another who was a professor of sociology in Malaysia. She herself married a non-Muslim man. Quite a remarkable level of open-mindedness that you do not often find in the average Malaysian family, I thought to myself. 'Later, we used to tease Ari because he ended up being the only one out of the nine children not to have gone to university,' she told me with a cheeky wink.

A young neighbour called Dr Ghouse, now a successful businessman, remembered Ari, his elder by a couple of years, as being smart. When we met over a *teh tarik*,* Dr Ghouse told me a few stories from their youth. They were more or less part of the same band of students at Penang Free School. With its motto *Fortis atque fidelis* (Strong and faithful), it is the oldest school in Malaysia and numbers many sultans and ministers among its old boys. If Ari saw Ghouse having trouble with his homework, he'd drop his bicycle and go and help him, having fun at the same time.

Although he had not seen Ari since they were boys, it was Dr Ghouse, the distant childhood friend, who created the 'Friends of Captain Zaharie MH370' Facebook page. As a result of this Facebook page, intended to defend the pilot, Dr Ghouse was contacted by several of Ari's friends, colleagues and neighbours. 'Not one person who spoke to me about Ari ever said anything troubling about his behaviour. He was anything but mentally unstable.' But his initiative also earned him an unwanted visit from the Special Branch, Malaysia's internal intelligence service, as if honouring his lost friend was in some way suspicious. 'I told them that it was their job to make sure only the truth was told. If there hadn't been so many rumours floating around to tarnish Ari's name, I wouldn't have had to do what I did.'

* *Teh tarik* is a Malaysian speciality made of black tea and condensed milk.

From an early age, Zaharie was passionate about flying, Sakinab remembers. He enrolled in his first pilot training course in the Philippines, then immediately joined Malaysia Airlines. According to the employment letter enclosed in the Malaysian police file about him that I got access to, he started with MAS on 15 June 1981. Over the course of his career, he rose to one of the highest possible positions in the company for a pilot, combining the roles of Boeing 777 pilot, instructor and inspector. When he was not working for MAS, he'd be giving flying lessons, flying his remote-controlled model planes, playing with his simulator or making videos that he posted online. The videos are a testament to his cheerful and enthusiastic personality. Flying was his profession, his hobby and his passion.

'He was on a good salary and, being a pilot, had a lot of spare time that he spent making things. He could turn his hand to almost anything. His last invention was a remote control to raise and lower a chandelier in his house. When he cooked something new, he'd always bring it to us to taste. One day he tried to convince my husband that he had made the steamed dumplings he'd added to a broth. But my husband, who was Chinese, was not fooled,' recalled Sakinab, torn between laughter and tears.

'Everyone liked him. When he came to the surgery, he was nice to everyone and always had a story to tell,' recalled Dr Resha Malik, his dentist, when we met near the surgery where she worked. Zaharie took good care of his health. I joked with this charming woman about her Iraqi name; if certain British tabloids had known that the captain's dentist had been an Iraqi, some would have been tempted to add that to the list of suspicious facts. Dr Malik told me that several days before 8 March, she had called her patient to tell him that his crown was ready. He was in Dubai at the time, so his crown stayed on the shelf. This anecdotal piece of information at least served to quash another disturbing and widespread rumour – that the captain had no appointments, 'an empty diary', after 8 March. Well, he had at least one important appointment, with his dentist.

I asked Sakinab about the widely reported departure of the captain's wife, Faizah, who was supposed to have left the conjugal home on the night of the flight. This contributed to another widespread rumour, already mentioned, that his wife had just left him. But Faizah's departure on the night of the flight had a completely straightforward explanation. 'That was their routine,' Sakinab explained to me. The couple had two homes, the old one in Subang Jaya, and a larger and more recent one in Shah Alam. 'Given his excellent position, Ari had long wanted to buy a larger home than the first, which was really very modest. Of all the siblings' homes, his was the smallest. But his wife Faizah had never wanted to move or decorate the new house.' So, when he was there, they all lived in the new house where the kitchen and everything was better, and as soon as the captain left on a shift, his wife returned to their first home. The information that had given rise to so much speculation was technically true – his wife had indeed left the family home – but not in the way that everyone had understood. The reality was quite devoid of any of the imagined emotional implications. In fact, the couple, who had been married for more than 30 years, were rather nicely holding steady. There may have been crises and lapses – 'Ari was no saint,' his caring sister would simply comment – but it seemed that Zaharie was committed to his marriage.

The analysis of the captain's mobile phone calls by the Royal Malaysia Police actually showed that his wife's was the number he called most often (46 calls since January 2014) and the one that he called last before taking off on Flight MH370 on the night of 7–8 March.

As to the photo of Zaharie with an unidentified pretty young veiled woman and small children seated on a sofa, published without any caption when all attention was focused on the pilots, Sakinab explained to me that the woman was one of their nieces and that the photo had been taken on a Hari Raya day.* Sakinab

* Hari Raya marks the end of Ramadan.

phoned her then and there to ask her for more details for me. The young woman, then in the US, had posted the photo herself on her Facebook page, as a souvenir of her uncle, without it ever crossing her mind that it would contribute to the campaign to blacken her uncle's name. Eventually the niece sued the magazine that first published the slanderous article, and won.

There had also been talk of the pilot's despair and desire for political revenge after the new sentence, pending an appeal, to five years in prison for Anwar Ibrahim, the leader of the opposition in Malaysia. As mentioned earlier, the decision had been handed down on the afternoon of the flight. I met the man who first introduced Zaharie to politics. Peter Chong, an opposition politician, had met Zaharie by chance two years earlier, when he noticed 'this man who stayed behind to help stack the chairs' at the end of a meeting. He managed to convince the pilot to join the Parti Keadilan Rakyat (PKR), the People's Justice Party, led by Anwar. But according to Chong, who had seen the captain the week before the flight, Zaharie's interest in politics had waned in recent months, and he preferred to talk about his latest inventions and his flight simulator.

I also wanted to meet the captain's wife Faizah, but Sakinab told me that she was not well. Her children were worried about her. 'The family is going through hell,' said Sakinab, and time was only making the wound worse for her dear brother's family. It was during such times, when I met these honest people living their simple lives, ravaged not only by the initial shock of the plane accident but eaten away by the gangrene of mystery, aggravated in their case by the smear campaign targeting their much-loved Ari, that I became even more resolved in my determination to pursue the investigation. Sakinab herself regularly went through very difficult patches. When we met that first time, she had just discovered, thanks to a friend who warned her, that her name was being used for an active Twitter account that she knew nothing about. The account was clearly created to mislead, since all the people followed by the fake Sakinab Shah – @sakinabs -- were in fact dyed-in-the-wool MHists ...

The Malaysian police were equally interested in finding out as much as possible about the captain, interviewing dozens of people who knew him from all walks of life.* Although I did not manage to talk or meet Faizah Khanum binti Mustafa,† Zaharie's wife, she was the first witness to be interrogated about her husband.‡ Her statement started with some personal information – they married in 1982, had three children, age 31 years old (M), 27 years old (F) and 26 years old (M), and so on. She described his attitude as 'dedicated to his work, happy-go-lucky, a loving husband and a firm father'. Asked about his hobbies, she mentioned 'aviation, DIY, cycling and buying electronic gadgets to upgrade his PC simulator'. Confirming his new interest in politics, she told police that he was 'thinking of joining the People's Justice Party', the opposition party led by Anwar Ibrahim. Faizah revealed that her husband did not have any life insurance cover, and she also mentioned his view that their daughter should stay in Australia as he thought its quality of life was better for her.

Actually, the statements of everyone in the immediate family circle were pretty consistent about the family relationships. Ahmad Idris bin Zaharie, 31, the elder son, was married and had a five-year-old child. Nur Aishah binti Zaharie, 27, the only daughter, who had been studying architecture in Melbourne, mentioned the 'close family relationship'. The younger son, Ahmad Seth bin Zaharie, 26, denied rumours that his parents were divorced. The

* In the documents I got access to, more than 60 people gave testimony about Zaharie Ahmad Shah.

† 'Bin' for a man or 'binti' for a woman means 'child of' and is followed by the name of the father.

‡ The interviews took place on 15 March 2014 at 10 pm (the night when the prime minister announced a 'deliberate act'), then again on the afternoon of 10 April 2014 and 16 May 2014.

domestic helper who was interviewed said that there were no tensions between the couple, and a neighbour in this well-off community, an established businessman and a 'dato' at that, said that he never saw or heard any problem within the captain's family. He confirmed the 'hands-on' attitude of the captain; when at home, he would see Zaharie 'doing house chores such as sweeping the floor, painting and gardening'.

A pilot who flew with Zaharie to Amsterdam a few weeks before the fatal flight said they had a long and personal conversation about family issues, but he did not pick up on anything problematic or abnormal in the captain's attitude or comments.

Another childhood friend told the police of a random encounter with Zaharie in a cemetery on the day of the last Aidilfitri.* Zaharie, who was with his wife, told him jokingly that they were struggling to find his mother's grave. The very day before the flight, Zaharie must have been in his joker mood again, when he sent a picture of a man supposedly taking a bath but covered in mud because of a water shortage to a retired freelance photographer with whom he used to chat on WhatsApp.

Zaharie was a regular-to-heavy user of social media, mostly Facebook (239 friends on a 2012 account and 36 friends on a less used 2009 private account), as well as WeChat (47 contacts) and YouTube. On his videos posted on YouTube, he mostly explained how to use flight simulators and fix things, including air conditioners. He was not very active on Twitter, where, despite being followed by 3,717 users, he only followed 14 accounts. With more than 70 per cent of its entire population registered and active on Facebook,† use of the site had reached epidemic proportions in

---

* Aidilfitri (Eid al-Fitr) is a religious holiday for Muslims that marks the end of Ramadan.

† This rate was even higher than in the US (68 per cent), despite the less developed communications infrastructure. Interestingly, the majority of users were men (56 per cent).

Malaysia. The Head of the Department of Network Surveillance at the Malaysian Communications and Multimedia Commission (MCMC), who scrutinised all of Zaharie's phone communications and internet surfing, said he found 'nothing suspicious'.

Apart from the overwhelmingly positive comments, there was at least one air steward who found Zaharie 'not too friendly' because, he said, the captain 'chooses who to greet and whom he likes to talk to about his hobbies'. But realistically, that only went to confirm how normal a human being Zaharie was.

Just as I was starting to find the picture almost too perfect, I came across some not so flattering testimonies. A former technician with a phone company who was now in the car rental sector, to whom Zaharie 'doesn't talk much', mentioned a woman friend of his called Fatimah N. (not her real name), a kindergarten teacher, who was also involved in opposition politics as a volunteer. He told the police that Zaharie had had an affair with her recently. Fatimah had confided to him about the relationship with Zaharie. She even wanted a divorce from her husband. A few days before the tragic night, she told the technician in tears over the phone that she had quarrelled with Zaharie, even saying that she had prayed that his plane would crash.

The police had already interviewed Fatimah. According to the dates and times given in the report, she was interviewed a second time after her friend's testimony but there were no indications whatsoever of her special relationship with the captain in her own statement. She only mentioned that Zaharie was 'kind hearted, responsible and knowledgeable' and said she knew nothing about his family.

Another woman, who first met Zaharie in 2000, said she went out with him 'for dining' for about a year in around 2010, but she stopped the relationship once she learnt that his wife had found out about it. She retained a soft spot for him, and was definitely shaken by the news of the missing plane, as she sent nine emails to him between 9 March and 2 June, hoping he would just reply and confirm that he was still alive.

Sakinab had mentioned that Ari was no saint. Now it seemed that he was in fact a bit of a Casanova, although for most of the people with whom I discussed these incidents, including some men of his age, they just proved – if anything – that he was living life to the full.

Healthwise, the police report documented a generally fit and robust man. His pharmacist said that Zaharie would come about once every three months to stock up on items such as a 'toothbrush, Panadol (paracetamol), Vitamin C, medication for flu (Telfast) and medication for gastric trouble (Maalox Plus)'. It was mentioned elsewhere that he was also using inhalers and sometimes Celebrex, a standard nonsteroidal anti-inflammatory. Zaharie had suffered from mild asthma since his youth and suffered a serious paragliding accident in January 2007 that required an operation on his spine. A year later, he was still complaining of pain in the knee and in the neck, so he started using painkillers for occasional relief. The paragliding accident left him with a slight limp and a hump in his gait. He was a casual smoker, with a preference for Domingo rolling tobacco, and he occasionally drank socially. The same was said about the first officer in the much less extensive folder dedicated to Fariq. I knew from my time in Malaysia that drinking did take place, even within the Malay community.* While it was frowned upon to drink in public, it was tolerated among the more permissive Muslims as long as it took place in private.

Across these numerous and often repetitive testimonies, the words most frequently used to describe Zaharie were 'jolly', 'friendly', 'fun', 'cheerful' and 'kind-hearted'. On the professional side, people described him as 'soft-spoken', 'patient', 'calm', 'humble', 'polite', 'knowledgeable', 'disciplined', 'never angry' and

---

* Seventy per cent of Malaysian citizens are Malays (sometimes also called the Bumiputras, or 'sons of the land'), who are Muslims. The rest of the Malaysian population is made of Chinese (23 per cent) and Indians (7 per cent). The official state religion is Islam.

showing 'no sign of stress'. A fellow Boeing 777 pilot who flew several times with him over the years also mentioned that not once did he see Zaharie lose his temper.

His last hours before the flight seem as normal as can be. Faizah visited a female cousin, who also lived nearby in Shah Alam, from late morning. When she got home around 6.30 pm that Friday evening, Zaharie was sleeping. The taxi to the airport was only coming to pick him up later.* At 9.40 pm, Zaharie walked out of the house, escorted by a maid who was carrying his luggage, while another maid stood outside the front door.

MAS organised pool taxis for its staff, so Zaharie joined a colleague of his, a chief air stewardess, for the ride. She asked him where he was flying to that night and enquired why he was sitting up so straight. He mentioned that his leg felt numb on account of his back pain. But she told the police that he nonetheless looked fine, 'normal, cheerful and smiling'. According to the taxi driver, Zaharie did not make or receive any phone calls during the drive, nor did he smoke. But once he reached the airport, he called Faizah, 'just to say that he had reached the airport'. It was 10.31 pm. She wished him a 'safe flight and take care', as usual. Faizah was on her way to the smaller of their two houses, where she was staying with their younger son. All in all, a typical and mundane departure protocol.

There was one chance encounter before Zaharie boarded MH370. At around 11 pm, he bumped into an old acquaintance – a retired MAS employee – in the departure hall. They made the standard polite enquiries about each other and asked where they were heading to that night. To this man too, Zaharie looked entirely his normal self. Zaharie checked his Hotmail account from his phone at 11.13 pm and shortly thereafter boarded the plane.

* MAS uses a specific taxi company to ferry cabin crew in and out of KLIA, sometimes in pools according to where they live.

Given everything that had been said and written to blacken the captain's name, I was very surprised to discover that he was actually a man remarkably at ease with his job, with himself and with life in general. The more I found out about him, the more convinced I became that, whatever his shortcomings, there was simply no reason at all to imagine that he was planning anything sinister.

Then came the simulator story. In July 2016, *New York* magazine published a damning article with the sensational title: 'Exclusive: MH370 Pilot Flew a Suicide Route on His Home Simulator Closely Matching Final Flight'. The article stated: 'The revelation, which Malaysia withheld from a lengthy police report on the investigation, is the strongest evidence yet that Zaharie made off with the plane in a premeditated act of mass murder-suicide.' The story did not specify anything about the 'lengthy police report' that was supposed to have contained the two pages the 'scoop' was based upon – no name, no date, no context. The magazine claimed to have obtained the documents from the Malaysian investigation. But the story explicitly accused the captain of having planned a route on his simulator ending in the southern Indian Ocean that was incredibly similar to the one suggested by the officially accepted interpretation of the Inmarsat pings.

Dozens of prominent media outlets picked up the story without questioning the document's source nor its validity as evidence in the case. It provided an easy explanation to a complicated story, and what more could you ask for? The story also proposed two conclusions for the price of one: the fact that the captain had planned a route with no return that ended in the southern Indian Ocean not only incriminated him beyond all doubt, it also implicitly confirmed that the southern Indian Ocean was indeed the fatal destination of MH370.

Zaharie's reputation, already shaken by relentless negative media reports, was now shattered by this supposedly 'hard evidence'.

I was all the more shocked and appalled by the story that it was me, against my own will, who was responsible for this fake scoop that received so much international attention. Let me explain. When I first gained access to the confidential police report, I had indeed come across several slightly confusing documents relating to the captain's flight simulator. Folder 1 (entitled 'Pilot') dealt in great detail with the simulator: its features, its usage, its crashes, the recovered hard drives and so on. But at the very end of this folder there was a rather obscure graph that showed seven coordinates that had apparently been recovered from erased files from the captain's simulator. Yet the summary of the Royal Malaysia Police's inspection of Zaharie's flight simulator explicitly stated: 'From the forensic examination as of the report date, it is found that there was no activity captured [...] that conclusively indicates any kind of premeditated act pertaining to the incident MH370.'*

But the incriminating revelation on which the *New York* scoop was based, showing the suspicious flight path to the southern Indian Ocean on a graph, had actually been inserted, a bit out of the blue, as the last two pages of Folder 4, which was entitled 'SKMM Analysis'.† This folder dealt at great length with the communications and phone calls of the pilot and the co-pilot, and to a lesser extent, of the crew. It contained no detailed information about the simulator since everything had already been covered in Folder 1, the 'Pilot' folder. I was therefore somewhat puzzled to read in the summary of Folder 4: 'From the flight simulation data, which was recovered and examined by MCMC Digital Forensics

---

* According to the secret police report, the system crashed twice, once in December 2013 and three times in a row on 23 January 23 2014. According to the Malaysian police investigation, the pilot searched for solutions to the problem in December but not after the three consecutive system crashes in January. 'The log data shows that the Flight Simulator X was played four (4) times on 1 February 2014 from 2.:45 pm until 3.02 pm.'

† SKMM are the initials in Malay for the Malaysian Communications and Multimedia Commission (also given as MCMC).

Department, we found a flight path that leads to the Southern Indian Ocean. However, it is to be noted that the flight path to the Southern Indian Ocean is one of many flight paths that were recovered from the flight simulation data.' This comment in itself was highly problematic.

I then came across the graph where the coordinates had been joined up and placed on the background of a Google Earth image so that this reconstructed flight path looked incredibly similar to that of the official Inmarsat version.

The issue was that these 'points' were not supposed to be related to each other. They were fragments of files. Their technical parameters (altitude, fuel reserve, heading and so on) were grossly inconsistent with one another and nothing indicated that they ever belonged to the same flights. So joining them up was roughly equivalent to reconstructing a meaningful sentence with words selectively collected out of hundreds of documents thrown in a dustbin … an extremely far-fetched attempt to re-create a suspicious route.

I asked a Malaysian forensic lawyer for his view on these secret and confidential documents. After a few days of silence, his blunt reply came back. To him, the flight towards the southern Indian Ocean could only be a fabrication. He believed this was planted evidence, with the intention of arousing new suspicions against the captain once they were leaked. Which, sadly, was exactly what happened a few weeks later. The lawyer highlighted some blatant inconsistencies. For example, the summary of Folder 1 on page 3 read: 'The analysis is focused on the reconstruction of the flight simulator and analysing on the 6 hard-disks images for flight coordinates, flight planner and internet history analysis as to look for clues in finding the missing flight of MH370. The investigation shows that there is no conclusive information on explaining the missing of the Flight MH370.'

Besides, if the pilot had ever planned such a doomed route, why was this information not passed to the Australian search team? The last position (29.2°S, 98.8°E) was 1,300 kilometres away from where the subsea search was centred (37.5°S, 88.9°E). And again, if valid, why would the official report published in March 2015 make no mention of it at all?

Before I came to fully understand that this clumsy and incomplete document proved nothing other than possible foul play within the investigation team, I shared it with Victor Iannello, a member of the Independent Group. He urged me to pass it on to the American blogger Jeff Wise, as well as to Sabine Luchtenfeld, a German forensic psychologist he trusted, for the sake of discussing its contents confidentially in a working group. I yielded. Sadly, the moment Jeff Wise saw these two pages he could not resist the lure of a cheap scoop. He reneged on his categorical assurance to me that the matter would remain confidential and instead had his byline under the sensational *New York* 'Exclusive'.

In fact, the FBI initially said that the simulator contained 'nothing incriminating'. Several people quoted in the local media had actually said that the simulator was not working at the time it was taken away from Zaharie's home. In the first documentary, Zaharie's wife also told the police that her husband had been playing the simulator far less since June or July 2013 'because he failed to repair it for system crash when he moved the simulator to second floor's room [*sic*]'. The police report itself mentioned that most of Zaharie's last online activity was to explore the reason for the crash of his simulator system so he could try to fix it. Some people familiar with the same simulator program expressed doubt about the whole idea of a 'flight to nowhere', because in order to plan any flight you wanted to train on, the first thing you had to do was to input a destination, typically the code of an airport. The middle of the ocean would clearly not have been an option. Besides, if this were ever his plan, there would have strictly been no point for him to rehearse it on a simulator, as there was nothing technical to gain or learn from such a session. In other words, this whole simulator saga seemed shaky and poorly fabricated. But the real question, it seemed to me, was why and how this impossible route clearly incriminating Zaharie appeared in the police file about MH370.

As misleading as it was, the *New York* piece was nevertheless another massive blow for the family of the pilot who seemed by then to have given up on the fight to clear his name. Soon after Jeff Wise used the loose two pages to publish his damning story in *New York* magazine, *60 Minutes* in Australia scrambled to put together another 'exclusive' programme based on the same unfortunate evidence, this time reinforced by the claims of another so-called expert, Larry Vance.* Vance stated:

> This confidential analysis of the captain's home flight simulator reveals evidence that the captain tried to hide by wiping his hard drive. A month before the doomed flight, Zaharie plotted an almost identical route deep into the southern Indian Ocean, a simulation that clearly contemplated the jet running out of fuel over the open sea.

Because this fake information came on top of hundreds of articles and at least two books that had already claimed – or at least hinted – that the pilot had planned it all and was the sole person responsible for the loss of the jetliner and all those on board, even the belated regrets of Jeff Wise himself about his erroneous accusations against Zaharie did nothing to redress the general negative impression that had been built up about the pilot. Ironically, despite the formal refutation of the validity of this 'hard evidence' by its author, the article was quoted again and again. To date, *New York* magazine has not removed it from its website nor offered apologies to its readers for this major piece of fake news.

---

* Larry Vance is a Canadian air crash investigator whose book *MH370: Mystery Solved*, published in 2018, explicitly blamed Captain Zaharie for the disappearance.

Ill-portrayed and falsely accused, I am now convinced that Zaharie never had the slightest of deadly intentions. On the contrary, I recall what his friend Peter Chong once told me: 'If something were to happen when I was flying, it's Captain Zaharie I'd like to see in the cockpit. If anyone could save a plane in the most difficult circumstances, it would be him. He spent his time preparing for that.'

Having understood the scope of his skills and the depth of his passion for flying, I was driven to try to fathom a situation so unusual and extraordinary that even Captain Zaharie Ahmad Shah was unable to cope. Something major had evidently happened when the plane came off the radar screens despite the presence in the cockpit of a perfectly sane and happy pilot, operating at the top of his game. But, in fact, it has become almost irrelevant to defend the honour or the sanity of the captain because what he is being accused of having done is simply impossible, whether he was the best or the worst of men.

12

Not Everyone Is Buying
the Official Narrative

Despite the relentless campaign against Captain Zaharie and the steady flow of hopeful announcements that the hull was soon going to be found somewhere at the bottom of the Indian Ocean, there were nevertheless, scattered across the planet, a few no-nonsense and highly motivated MHists eager to denounce the fallacy of the southern Indian Ocean route. Some worked alone, some formed groups around a common conviction or task. Among the millions of people who volunteered to scrutinise countless satellite images over the Tomnod* online search, a small group of 'nodders', as the Tomnod searchers called themselves, grew very confident that they had seen the plane in the South China Sea. Except that they believed that they had seen it in bits and pieces on satellite images.

'Lots of people were finding debris and parts that seemed to be from the plane, as well as possibly bodies,' recalled Jonny Spendler, 50, a German IT consultant temporarily turned full-time nodder, who was one of the most committed of the group. There was an option for users to convert Tomnod's internal coordinates to Google Maps coordinates, but they soon got the impression that Tomnod was somehow interfering with the precise location of the

---

* Tomnod is a crowdsourcing search of satellite images (see Chapter 2, p. 22). It was acquired by DigitalGlobe in April 2013.

images people were searching. People were therefore searching hundreds of thousands of small squares of ocean images without knowing precisely what part of the sea they were inspecting. But Spendler, who had learnt to recognise silhouettes of ships during his 15 years in the German navy, came across what he thought were such convincing images of aircraft debris located off the coast of Vietnam that he could not resist the call of going to look for himself in real life. He dipped into his savings and mounted a diving expedition to go and find the remnants of MH370 in the South China Sea. But what he did not realise was that as much as he knew *what* he was looking at, he did not know *where* he was looking. 'I established the location to be about 60 kilometres south of Vung Tau. I wrote to Tomnod on Twitter to confirm the location of certain images, but they never replied,' he told me. As this was in June 2014, the Australian search was meanwhile going full throttle thousands of miles away Down Under, but Spendler never believed for a minute that the plane had made the almost impossible U-turn and all the rest.

He thought that scanning the seabed in the shallow waters of the South China Sea was not going to be too difficult, but a few days before he flew out to Con Dao, a diving island south of Vietnam, with his undercover diving operation all planned and under control, Tomnod suddenly announced a change in the numbering of the images and their coordinates. On 2 May, the references of the maps switched completely, from a numeric number to an alphanumeric number that actually referred the same maps to new places. People who were so curious as to want to know where they were searching had to use some locator links where they could enter the coordinates of their map and find out. But many nodders noticed abnormalities in the system. Debris they had initially spotted in one place was now located hundreds of miles away with the new location attribution system. People even noticed that pictures of debris they had already spotted supposedly in the South China Sea were now said to be in the Indian Ocean.

This meant that the objects Spendler had been looking at might be in a different place altogether from the one that he had carefully worked out ... By now it was too late to stop, so he stuck to his original plan and on arrival found a rather spotless seafloor with hundreds of fishing boats on the surface. 'I also saw two fishing boats that were dragging a line between them, searching the ocean floor for wrecks or objects. Our captain said that that is not normal for a fishing boat. And they trailed us for a couple of days,' he recalls. Four years later, when he reflected on his brash move, he said he would love to reopen the case should he find some financial backing.

Tomnod was clearly using these benevolent millions of eyes, but it seemed that there was deliberate or accidental miscommunication about the precise location of what they were looking at. One nodder told me that when she converted the coordinates, she ended up in some jungle-covered mountains. From that experience she formed the view that the vast community of nodders had been unknowingly used and abused.

Another man also thought he had found the plane and paid a high personal price. Michael Hoebel is a former recreational pilot from a little town called Tonawonda in New York State. Late in April 2014, after browsing thousands of Tomnod images like a good nodder, he came across one that just seemed too good to be true. It was an almost perfect match in size and shape of a Boeing 777, supposedly located just to the east of the Thai city of Songkhla, nearly on the latitude of waypoints IGARI and BITOD. According to Hoebel's analysis of the image, the plane seemed broken in two about halfway down its fuselage but remained in one piece. He immediately contacted WIVB, his local TV channel, and a journalist called Ed Drantch met him and reported his findings on 24 April 2014.* Hoebel also sent his images to the NTSB and the FBI, but

---

* wivb.com/2014/04/24/tonawanda-man-believes-he-has-link-to-malaysia-mystery/. (unavailable to 'our European visitors').

never received a reply. Then, completely out of the blue, the news website *IBT* (*International Business Times*) accused him of being a 'fraud pilot', raising doubts about his credibility. Next, he was slandered and defamed on social media, which probably explains why his discovery, extraordinary by any standard, was overwhelmingly ignored.

It might be worth noting that in mid-April 2014 the pings hunt in Australia had reached its peak. The media couldn't exactly make its audience hold its breath with stories that black box pings were being received from the murky deep of the southern Indian Ocean while reporting a few days later on a potential sighting of the hull in the very shallow waters of the Gulf of Thailand, could they? A certain degree of consistency is required to be credible. Apart from Hoebel's local TV station, some British tabloids reported his finding, but it was mixed with other stories of the plane possibly having been being found elsewhere. Interestingly, Michael Hoebel sued *IBT* for defamation – and won. In the testimony he wrote on the website of the successful legal firm he used, Clare Locke LLP in Alexandria, Virginia, he thanked his lawyers for having 'obtained a complete retraction of a defamatory article published in the *International Business Times* attacking the integrity of my analysis of satellite images in the search for missing Malaysia Airlines Flight MH370. With the false articles removed from the internet, the credibility of my work on this important project remains intact.'

Although I did not pursue this lead further, I had no reason to think that he was a fraud, a crackpot who had fabricated an image to attract attention to himself. On the contrary, he seemed an honest man who had possibly spotted the hull of MH370 – or something of significant size – very close to the last point of contact ... unless, of course, because of the muddling of the Tomnod coordinates, the location was very different from the one he had hoped for. If genuine, his discovery would have proven beyond all doubt that the plane neither crossed back over Malaysia nor ended up in the southern Indian Ocean – in other words, that the official narrative was a pure fabrication. Although Hoebel won his defamation case, his argument had been lost on the world stage and he was never given the chance to be taken seriously. I had a brief and essentially useless conversation with Ed Drantch, the journalist who had interviewed him in April 2014. All Drantch could remember was that Hoebel was a nice man. He had no way of helping me reach the man, even though – or so I thought – this was exactly what local TV stations were good at.

I eventually traced and contacted Hoebel, but we did not manage to talk. In the PS of one of the email messages he sent me, he kindly said, 'I'll be here if I can help you, and I don't mind sharing the satellite images if they will help you in your quest.'

After my book containing details of my initial investigation was published in French in March 2016, I was contacted by Carlotta Tatti, who introduced herself as a self-taught programmer based in Rome at the time, although 'young genius of cyberspace' might be a better description (she subsequently moved to work on a crypto-currency program in Lisbon). She was obsessed with this story, and would go without sleep for nights while doing remarkable and extremely comprehensive research on the internet relating to MH370. She had built up a treasure trove of documents, which she shared with me. She told me that she had reviewed the Tomnod search and its results: 'I noticed that the density and the quality of reports coming from the South China Sea were higher and better than from anywhere else. Reports coming from there actually resembled high-reflective – metallic – pieces floating on water instead of [what were obviously] waves or boats.' She was puzzled by this, but rather than travelling to South East Asia like Jonny Spendler, she tried to acquire higher-resolution images, which were normally available through DigitalGlobe. She was shocked to learn that the DigitalGlobe catalogue did not offer a single image for sale from the South China Sea between 8 and 15 March 2014. For there to be no pictures available for a specific area at a specific time like this was incredibly odd. Once again, was there something that people shouldn't see in that particular region during that period?

Nevertheless, she was able to buy an image that DigitalGlobe's WorldView-1 satellite had taken on 16 March, covering an area of about 60 square kilometres to the north-west of the Spratly Islands. According to Tatti:

When I opened this very large file for the first time I understood immediately I was seeing something unusual. Thousands of high-reflective pieces floating on the water were visible in the image, some as large as 30 metres and most of clearly man-made origin. The most striking one was a big triangular piece that resembled an aircraft tail with some sort of logo visible on it. To exclude any possible doubt, I analysed weather data for that day and place. The sea was just a bit breezy, so the wind could not have caused waves that may have resembled such big floating pieces. Clearly these were not waves, but man-made objects.

Very excited about what she was seeing, Tatti then decided to buy another image, this time from GeoEye-1, a DigitalGlobe satellite that captured full colour images at an even higher resolution than the WorldView-1 ones she had already bought. But to her great dismay, the DigitalGlobe reseller told her – without providing any more information – that the image was 'not available for purchase', despite the fact that it was in the catalogue. The whole episode confused her. Why was it not possible to purchase satellite images of that region for the days following the disappearance of the plane?

Among all the nodders, one stood out from the crowd, a sort of nodders' nodder, if you will. Former banker and amateur photographer Cyndi Hendry was a 'fifth generation South Floridian', who, like numerous other volunteers, had no formal training in the interpretation of satellite images when she started searching the Tomnod database. She quickly established a reputation for herself as a master at the game among the online community, which at the time was rebelling against the southern Indian Ocean narrative.

'I am self-taught in this satellite images business, but as a photographer I have an eye,' she told me when we talked over the phone. She scanned thousands of images and spotted hundreds that contained 'obvious pieces of plane debris, and not just B777 parts'. For her, the images were so telling that she needed no further proof. But not everyone had her talent. I must admit that I could barely see the shapes or objects she pointed out on the satellite images she sent by email while we were talking, to help explain her findings. To make her discoveries clearer to the average person, she did precise cuttings and overlays of parts of MH370, including the hull, the logo and the painted writing. One of her images shows 'very clearly' the 's' of Malaysia Airlines. On another, she was almost 100 per cent sure that she could see the nose of the plane with its distinct lines of colours below the windscreen. And she had hundreds of similar images.

But every time she flagged these images to Tomnod, Tomnod seemed to ignore them as irrelevant. Her skill at spotting debris and identifying what she had spotted by evaluating sizes and shapes very precisely with tools that took her months to develop did not escape the attention of other nodders. They were dismayed that her fantastic work seemed to be being wasted, and after a while, many of them wondered what their eyes and skills were really being used for. 'It felt like they [Tomnod] wanted us to flag debris to them but without ever admitting to us that we had spotted the plane or anything related to a very serious situation there and then,' Hendry said. She confirmed that Tomnod was never transparent about the location of the images: 'Sometimes you can see they openly deleted the coordinates of the images they ask you to look at. You can see this on your computer.' She also mentioned that some images offi-cially tagged by Tomnod as being from the Indian Ocean were in fact from the South China Sea. How could she tell? By matching the shape of the cloud cover that she sourced from other satellite databases. That's how far she would sometimes go to locate an image.

Hendry gave a good two years of her life to the search, and once she wrapped it all up, she published her impressive work on a dedicated Facebook page so that anyone could access it and use it, in the spirit of crowdsourcing. But when she returned to it one day, the folder containing the most telling pictures had been deleted and tagged as 'spam' by Facebook. 'It was mostly military planes-related pictures,' she said, as she believed she had spotted the tail of a DC-10 in the sea to the south of Vietnam. From what she saw on the satellite images, 'multiple aircraft were involved'. According to the screenshots and emails I was shown, Facebook did not inform her when they removed her folder and never replied to her enquiries as to why they had done so.

But her findings were not only noticed by Facebook, because she clearly recalled seeing her household rubbish being collected by what were self-evidently 'not garbage men'. 'When I saw this, I called my daughter. It made me more cautious [...] I think we [the US] have a hand in it, whether we hit the plane by accident or something else. I don't know. But we owe it to the families to come clean and let the truth come out,' she told me, regretfully suspecting some kind of American involvement. At one point, because she had become the go-to person among MHists looking at the South China Sea scenario, a fisherman from the region contacted her and told her he had found a plane part. He mentioned high tensions between China and Vietnam on the sea, and described some unusual incidents he had witnessed.

As for Carlotta Tatti, she brought to my attention odd changes and inexplicable mistakes that had started to appear about two years after the loss of the plane in the archives of the major flight data websites – Flightradar24.com, Flightaware.com and Planefinder.net – which she regularly monitored and recorded. The Boeing number attributed to the 8 March MH370 flight had now become 9M-MRQ instead of 9M-MRO. One of the sites continued to mention MH370 flights as late as July 2014, months after the last flight called MH370 took off. And then a search for 9M-MRO returned 'no result'. Incorrect dates and wrong planes were attributed to past flights … It looked as if the archives related to MH370 had been hacked and seriously tampered with. Now that most archived documents were digital and online, it was extremely disturbing to witness such obvious attempts at erasing or scrambling traces of what had happened surrounding the disappearance of MH370. Like many MHists, she also noticed that on these flight-monitoring websites were some ultrafast flights crossing the sky on that night, travelling at the speed of fighter jets or missiles, heading towards the route of MH370.

Tatti's search for any document related to MH370 on the NTSB (the US National Transport Safety Bureau) website proved very challenging too. After many attempts over a considerable period to find proof that even a single document about MH370 actually existed in the NTSB database, one day she received an unexpected answer. The NTSB suggested that she contact General Microfilms, the company in charge of their archives, and even provided her with an address. I was in touch with Tatti at the time, and this got us excited. But once the details were entered into Google Maps, it located a rather unassuming house, deep in the countryside of Northern Virginia. The NTSB also provided a phone number, which she then called.

According to the man who answered the phone, the file relating to MH370 was 'very thin'. He also mentioned 'a note that was unusual', and read a brief synopsis of the accident. The time of the crash was marked as 2.40 am (once again), though at a place called Pulau Perak. Pulau Perak is a tiny island, or a big rock, located on the western side of Malaysia near Butterworth Air Base and not too far from what the authorities claimed was the last glimpse of MH370 on the so-called Thai radar, shown to the families at the Lido Hotel. As we saw earlier, this radar image has since been largely dismissed. And in any case, the plane was seen here at 2.22

and not 2.40 ... The person on the phone also suggested there would be no further information relating to this case. The file was closed. This seemed an extremely sub-par investigation for the biggest mystery in civil aviation, involving the most important plane in Boeing's fleet, as well as three US citizens. Unless, of course, the real file is somewhere else.

Before and after Tatti, several people – American citizens and others – made enquiries to the CIA, the NTSB, the FBI, the NGA* and the NSA under FOIA (Freedom of Information Act) to get access to information relating to MH370. None have succeeded in any satisfactory way. The first to initiate such a process was celebrity attorney Orly Taitz on 24 March 2014. She made an FOIA request to the NSA for any and all documents relating to MH370. The response she received seemed to indicate that the NSA was in possession of documents but that they were classified.†

As early as May 2014, Timothy Akers, a British treasure hunter with a background as a marine archaeologist, was also crying foul to the Southern Indian Ocean story. Unlike the self-taught newbies 'nodders', Akers, then in his mid-50s, had been refining his own software, combining different layers of the light spectrum to scan imagery of land and seas, for decades. Initially using imagery from the low earth orbit satellite Landsat 5, his company Merlin Burrows already had a few famous finds to its credit, 'Viking long-boats, Chinese junks, sunken Bugatti ...'. But when he claimed to

---

* National Geospatial Intelligence Agency.

† 'We have determined that the fact of the existence or non-existence of the materials you request is a currently and properly classified matter in accordance with the Executive Order 13526, as set forth in Sub-paragraph (c) of Section 1.4. Thus your request is denied pursuant to the first exemption of the FOIA which provides that the FOIA does not apply to matters that are specifically authorized under criteria established by an Executive Order to be kept order in the interest of national defense or foreign relations and are, in fact properly classified pursuant to such Executive Order.'

have spotted numerous plane debris and even bodies in the South China Sea following the loss of MH370, he was essentially ignored. Just Yahoo News and some of the tabloids mentioned it. The media are not expected to tell two opposite stories at the same time, are they? And the mainstream media were already fully committed to the super exciting 'pings party' that was going on down under ...

Online, some of his images were dismissed as fakes. Just like Hoebel's, Akers' claims were swiftly pushed into oblivion. It's only when everything else in my investigation was bringing me back to the South China Sea that I contacted Tim Akers directly. He explained that he had been coordinating 19 satellites data utilising both military and civilian systems throughout the crash.

'We tracked and recorded [in the South China Sea] for nearly a year after the event and tried repeatedly to send them to search the sea around the North East coast of Vietnam but they refused point blank to go there. The evidence is shocking. Survivors were left to their fate,' he wrote to me in an initial email. I followed up with a long Skype interview that I recorded. He then told me that, among the hundreds of images which, according to him, show very discernible parts of plane, he spotted 'two ships recovering debris and one day we spotted a large ship with debris at the back'. As we Skyped, he showed me on his screen a debris with what he said was a Y with the exact squarish shape of the Malaysian writing on the hull of the plane. He then brought up the picture of a very swollen body washed ashore that he thought was coming from MH370. Akers also mentioned that some images taken over the South China Sea had been falsely reallocated to the Southern Indian Ocean: 'We were told real porkies' ...

I did not realise at the time how much his findings, based on his own analysis of his own satellite images were similar and consistent with those of Cyndi Hendry in Florida, of Jonny Spendler in Germany, of Carlotta Tatti in Italy ... In a way, the images he was describing were also very consistent with the scene that another witness I met later swore he saw on Vietnamese television. Timothy Akers died in January 2020 after a year-long struggle with pancreatic cancer. His long-term associate Bruce Blackburn confirmed to me in late 2020 that they still had a trove of evidence related to MH370 that they were just sitting on. He even mentioned emails between Vietnam and Malaysia discussing how to dispose of the debris. 'But we have not found the right partner yet and until then we must protect our inventory,' he added, reminding me that they were a commercial enterprise and that most of their projects were underfunded. But let's get back for a moment to the early days of the crisis.

Browsing some discussions on forums like Reddit, I had noticed the name of an MHist whose comments were much better-informed and sharper than average. He had been working on this case relentlessly, from day one and for the following two and a half years, and ended up putting together a very precise and well-crafted scenario that started with a major technical failure and ended with a crash in the South China Sea. More than two years after first coming across him, I managed to contact this 'Alan Tan' (not his real name). It took me a while, in part because his name was far from unique, so I came across several Alan Tans across the world in the process. Finally, I called an office in a provincial town in Malaysia, and after some hesitation over saying anything at all on the phone, Tan hinted that he had 'figured out everything regarding MH370's disappearance' and said he would share it all with me on condition that we met in person.

A few weeks later, I organised a one-night stay in his town, which luckily had direct flights from Hong Kong. I had explained to the international desk chief at *Le Monde* that this would be more of a 'deep background' trip (which meant that it would probably not translate into an immediate story), so I was very grateful when he agreed to send me over nonetheless.

Tan and I met in the lobby of the hotel in the early afternoon. It was very warm outside, and a thick and heavy curtain of rain was

creating the perfect background noise while obscuring the café to
the point that turning the lights on would have been welcome. We
sat and ordered some mixed juices. I could see that Tan was clearly
nervous. By way of introduction, he said:

> When this happened, I was flabbergasted. Like everyone in
> Malaysia, I was following every minute of this event. But
> suddenly I saw my government say, 'Go to the southern Indian
> Ocean,' just because the Americans said so. Probably because
> of my experience with the US, having studied and worked there,
> I smelled a rat. They clearly completed the initial search too
> quickly. It always takes time, at least several days, to find the
> first debris, especially when we are not sure of the exact crash
> point. And in any case, why are we not searching near the last
> point of contact of the last radar dot? That started my
> interest.

I was quickly confirmed in the impression I had formed over the
phone. In his early 50s, this man was educated, serious, dedicated
and knowledgeable – he seemed entirely credible. He was
definitely slightly paranoid too. About halfway through our
discussion, which went on uninterrupted for six hours, he excused
himself for a few minutes. He said that he could now go and tell
his driver to take the car home as he was reassured that the
meeting with me was not a trap to have him arrested by some
country's secret services. I laughed. As far as I was concerned, I
initially thought that I had wasted a day, a plane ticket and a few
hours of sleep when he started explaining to me that MH370 had
suffered a total electrical failure due to an isolated bolt of
lightning at or shortly after it had passed waypoint IGARI around
1.20 am, while cruising at 35,000 feet. In my view, the total
electrical failure scenario had been put to rest by this point,
having been thoroughly studied and subsequently dismissed. But
to be honest, I had probably not paid sufficient attention to these

technical failure scenarios. Somehow my brain was not primed for what seemed like such a boring cause for such an extraordinary event.

But in the many well-documented cases that I studied during the course of this investigation (see Addendum, p. 404), I learnt that a technical failure is one of the two most common causes that triggers a cover-up. The other is a military operation, whether an act of war or a blunder. The idea of a cover-up for a plane accident is not that outrageous, after all. It has happened before, indeed more often than is realised by the general public, whose attention span is usually short and shallow. In cases of technical failure, the strategy is always to address the problem as quickly and quietly as possible, but, circumstances permitting, without admitting it (or its extent) to a wider audience. The air safety investigators' absolute priorities are always to identify and fix the problem, and to ensure that it does not happen again; this much we can be sure about. But in the process – for strategic, economic, commercial, even occasionally diplomatic reasons – it might be deemed appropriate to buy time and tell a quite different story.

So, with this in mind, I forced myself to pay close attention to Tan's tightly knit scenario. As he was talking, I realised that perhaps the more interesting part of his research was not so much the cause of the accident he was adamant he had identified, but the incredibly precise and accurate observation of all the available data he had collected in the process. After 30 months of obsessive work, his office had become filled with thousands of MH370 files, to the point where his whole staff thought he had gone berserk and that his wife wanted a divorce.

He was by now absolutely certain that MH370 had been hit by lightning and that its Faraday cage effect had not worked. With the plane left without electrical power, its two engines shut off at 35,000 feet right in the middle of the night, halfway between the coastlines of Malaysia and Vietnam. Of course, a Boeing 777 fresh off the assembly line was fully protected against lightning strikes.

But MH370's structure had been somehow fissured by the repair it had undergone two years earlier, leaving its Faraday cage effect compromised and the plane vulnerable.* Although no active thunderstorms had been reported in the region, Tan found that another pilot flying that night in the same area had reported seeing 'limited scattered lightning'. So MH370 may well have flown across a storm cloud. 'A lightning strike, if not promptly discharged from the surface of a fly-by-wire aircraft, can penetrate into the aircraft and cause either a total electrical failure or the plane's brain to go haywire,' he said.

The strange way the plane's signal disappeared from the screens of the Vietnamese ATC in two stages, more than 30 seconds apart, instead of in a single go, hinted at a progressive disconnection of the systems. But another key piece of evidence he used to back up his scenario was the time the plane took to fly between the last two waypoints: IGARI and BITOD. These two waypoints were 37 miles (70 kilometres) apart and, according to the Ho Chi Minh ATC record, the plane took about 10 minutes to fly this distance. With a headwind of 15 or 20 knots, Tan worked out that it showed a plane flying at 220 knots, which happened to be significantly slower than its speed before IGARI (470 knots), but precisely the speed of a B777 that was gliding without engine power. 'From these 10 minutes of data alone, from 1.20 am to 1.30 am, if you are a bona fide investigator, you should work out that this plane has lost power,' he asserted. He further explained the fact that the plane came off the radar shortly after BITOD because of the angle of its glide. According to Tan, the plane went from 35,000 feet to about 20,000 feet around BITOD, and at that altitude and at that distance from the radars, the ATC from both Vietnam and Malaysia could no longer detect the plane. BITOD was located almost exactly halfway between the radars of both countries. It was there-

---

* The end part of the original wing had sheared off in a ground collision with another plane at Shanghai Pudong Airport in August 2012.

fore logical to assume that they both lost its track when it passed below the 20,000 feet ceiling.

When a Boeing 777 lost all of its power, it could still be steered thanks to three individual parts: two of its spoilers (numbers 4 and 11) and the vertical stabiliser. At 1.30 am, one of the pilots answered a call on the emergency frequency from Flight MH88, using the only VHF that had a backup stand-alone battery. Of the three VHFs located left, centre and right of the cockpit, this was the left-hand one. The plane then glided unpowered for about 20 minutes before hitting the sea. The rule that all pilots live by is 'aviate, navigate, communicate'. Communication comes last, all the more so in emergency situations.

At 1.43 am, the flight crew issued a distress call using the same left-hand VHF radio, saying they had to ditch. Tan believed the Mayday call that we mentioned before, which announced cabin disintegration and emergency landing, was picked up by the US Seventh Fleet, most likely USS *Pinckney*, which was nearby, and then relayed to U-Tapao military base, located too far away to receive the call directly. He believed that the time mentioned in the message was quoted in the time zone for PaCom (US Pacific Command, headquartered in Japan), which was standard practice. If so, the 2.43 am PaCom time would have indeed corresponded to 1.43 am local time.* It all added up nicely.

Tan was adamant that only the first pings reported by Inmarsat were genuine. The following ones were fabricated. He told me that among other flaws regarding the pings, some IG members had long identified mistakes in the period of the famous pings (which should be of 1 hour and 256 seconds). To his dismay, they agreed to work with this erroneous data all the same, instead of crying foul.

---

* Times quoted in American military communications are generally followed by a letter of the phonetic alphabet (Alpha, Bravo, Charlie) to indicate the time zone. 'Zulu' or Z after a time indicates that it is given in GMT or UTC time and L indicates Local. Malaysia and China times are GMT−8, whereas Vietnam and Thailand times are GMT+7.

'Whoever made up the data was not very good,' Tan commented. 'The time of cessation of the pings was chosen to coincide with the estimated time of fuel exhaustion, to sell the narrative of a plane flying until fuel exhaustion. But the pings had ceased earlier,' he said, further questioning the rationale of assuming that the plane was flying because it was sending pings. Although I had decided to dismiss the Inmarsat pings for the reasons explained earlier, I was delighted to hear from someone who had studied them closely, and thought that not only were they fabricated, but they were poorly fabricated.

In this scenario, since the plane broke up on impact after a partially controlled ditching, it created a limited field of debris that could be contained if it had to be. Tan even calculated the most likely place where MH370 would have ditched: about 60 miles (111 kilometres) after BITOD. Just like Jonny Spendler, Tan was tempted to go and check for himself. Assuming that the pilot was indeed trying his best to control the plane with no engines and no electrical assistance, Tan just could not make up his mind about the pilot's hypothetical preferred course of action after having passed BITOD. Would Captain Zaharie have kept to his planned route for the sake of being found more easily? Or would he have chosen to head closer to land to facilitate rescue operations following the extremely challenging sea landing? The two pilots to whom he'd been able to put the question both agreed that if your plane is falling and you have no time to reach a nearby runway, you aim to get as close to land, as fast as possible. According to Tan, as skilled and experienced as the captain was, his friends and colleagues mentioned that the only situation that might overwhelm him would be a total electrical failure.

There was one last point that continued to perplex Tan – how would the hull and its 239 bodies have been disposed of? Because the South China Sea is pretty shallow, would the plane have perhaps been covered by a camouflage net, like in the 1965 James Bond movie *Thunderball*, or buried under sand and possibly concrete to make it undetectable by sonar? Tan could not envisage a situation in which the remains of the hull would have been blown up underwater to destroy evidence.

Tan studied many other complicated crashes and noticed a higher rate of fatal accidents in planes that had been through some kind of structural repair in the past. If it was ever discovered that planes that have been structurally repaired are no longer 'lightning proof', a worldwide panic could ensue, and big commercial airline companies like Boeing would have some serious questions to answer. A small but significant part of the world fleet would be grounded *sine die* and the whole industry would be faced with a major crisis. This, according to Tan, was the real reason for the massive cover-up at play. So not such a boring scenario after all.

Despite all the facts and documented research Tan said he had gathered to back every step of his scenario, I still felt the need to submit it to the scrutiny of pilots, two of whom agreed to make themselves available for the exercise. Kim Stuart was one; the other was Tom, a Kiwi B777 pilot. This time, Tan travelled to Hong Kong. We all met on the top floor of the Aberdeen Boat Club, the ABC, in the meeting room that overlooks the iconic Jumbo Kingdom floating restaurant, with the screen of skyscrapers of the very densely populated island of Ap Lei Chau in the background. For Tan, this was the moment of truth he had long been waiting for. He explained his scenario in a much more detailed manner than I can relate here. Both pilots nodded in approval and seemed generally impressed with the scope of his knowledge and understanding, and the force of his logic. But once he had explained everything in detail, a crucial point arose. The pilots did not believe that a total electrical failure would shut down both engines … Tom seemed to doubt Tan's hypothesis, but said he would discuss it further with colleagues and try to test the scenario during his next training session on the simulator. Kim was adamant that when an engine fails (let alone two), the

APU* will automatically start off. Basically, the two pilots did not endorse this single key aspect of Tan's scenario.

Obviously, Tan was very disappointed. Shortly after his visit to Hong Kong, he messaged me, announcing that he was calling it quits. He had given enough time and energy to the whole affair. He was confident he had it figured out and was in no mood to adjust his reasoning following the pilots' input. His MH370 time was now over. He was going to try to save his marriage and address the massive work backlog at his firm. I never heard from Tan again but I remain convinced to this day that his work contains several important clues, key to solving the MH370 enigma.

The flawed logic of the official narrative and the abnormal lack of corroborating evidence did not escape a former senior military officer from the Chinese People's Liberation Army either. 'Mister Gong thinks like you, you must meet him!' the Chinese families had told me emphatically when we had a small gathering in Beijing in late 2018. As suggested, I contacted him and we met in Shenzhen soon after. Despite Mr Gong's limited English and the meagre leftovers of my Mandarin acquired in Taiwan, we managed to understand each other quite well, mostly thanks to our common knowledge of the case.

During his years in the army, Mr Gong's expertise had been in radio transmission. He therefore focused his study of the plane's fate on that aspect, and after a rather simple radio transmissions triangulation he reached the conclusion that it had met its end in the South China Sea. He also spotted many inaccuracies in the Inmarsat pings, which to him were related to a mixed bag of other flights. He was so sure of his findings that he too was willing to mount a search expedition to the exact place where he believed the

---

* The APU is an auxiliary power unit whose primary purpose is to provide power to start the main engines. APUs are also used to run accessories when the plane is landed with its engines shut down.

plane had nosedived and buried itself in the soft and muddy seafloor. But because of his staunch loyalty to Beijing's government and to the Chinese Communist Party, he was incapable of even contemplating any foul play on the part of the authorities. So despite his technical knowledge, he had to convince himself that the plane just encountered a dramatic failure and crashed without exploding on impact, hence leaving no trace.

As he spoke, over a dim sum lunch in a Laurel restaurant,* I discerned in him the same devouring passion – an obsession, in his own words – that I had seen in Alan Tan and some other MHists. 'People think I am related to 370 and some people who do not know my name simply call me "370",' he admitted with a laugh. But then the case has become seriously addictive to quite a few people. This retired senior military man from China, aka 370, had definitely fallen under the MH370 spell, just like all the hundreds of other scientists, amateurs, pilots and sincere MHists, as well as no small number of licensed crackpots around the world. After a number of years observing various specimens of this unique species first-hand, I realised that for those who got trapped in the dark recesses of the labyrinth, the only way out, eventually, was to create your own exit.

Before leaving, Mr Gong gave me two hard copies of his book in Chinese and a USB stick with the English version that was soon to be published under the pseudonym of Long Wen.† On the last page he explains his motivation:

I am writing a book, of more than two hundred thousand words, not because I am whimsical or delirious or fishing for fame. It is based on my 26 years of military career, 20 years of police practice, 6 years of the accumulation of assessment work and the

---

* Laurel is a popular chain serving traditional Chinese dishes across China.

† Long Wen, *MH370 Airlines Should Be Here: Analyses of Malaysian Airlines' Missing Plane's Whereabouts*, translated by Peng Lingyang and Yang Bo.

unswerving pursuit of Mao Zedong's correct thinking, as well as my good vision [*sic*] to find the missing aircraft and its crew as soon as possible.

We met again a few months later, this time in the meeting room of his daughter's real-estate business offices, located on the upper floors of a newly erected building. He had prepared a fully fledged presentation and wanted to test his theory against my own research. One assistant had seemingly been assigned the single task of constantly refilling my paper cup with tea, while Mr Gong commented on the slides that had been translated by a good friend of 'Mister Gong', who was also in attendance. This man was much younger than Mr Gong, and it was only after lunch, when he kindly gave me a ride back to the Hong Kong border at Luo Wu in his chauffeured car, that I discovered his lofty position in the Law and Order Department of the city of Shenzhen. I was astounded to be discussing the case of MH370, which I thought was classified in China, with these influential Chinese men, both members of the Communist Party. I was surprised and glad to see that, for their own logical reasons, they also vehemently dismissed the official narrative.

13

The Official Version Is Looking Shaky

At the risk of stating the obvious, a Boeing 777 doesn't just disappear. Such a plane might be hijacked, it might be the target of a terrorist attack, it might explode if a bomb goes off on board, it might be the victim of the pilot or co-pilot's murderous madness, it might experience a serious fault that the pilots are unable to fix, or it might be shot down accidentally or on purpose in an act of war.

But how is it possible to convince both the media and public opinion in the 21st century that a flying object the size of two blue whales put end to end, made in the USA, stuffed with electronic gadgetry and with hundreds of locatable mobile phones on board, has 'mysteriously disappeared'? The 'disappearance' scenario is less acceptable than ever in this era of drones and hyper-surveillance from all quarters, especially since stealth intelligence technology in space, such as the US Lacrosse system among others, has made such phenomenal progress since the days of Sputnik and Explorer 1 back in the late 1950s. While the most technologically advanced countries in the world are spending billions to try to build a completely stealthy plane, we are asked to believe that a massive Boeing 777 itself became stealthy in the middle of the night above the Gulf of Thailand.

Among the millions of people who are intrigued, like me, by this mystery, a few, the likes of the Spendler, Hendry, Tatti, Tan, or '370', worked very hard at finding the truth; yet many have simply latched on to a particular scenario and have given up making any serious effort to make it correspond to reality. At the end of 2015, a colleague in Hong Kong gave me what he considered to be a simple and definitive explanation. Following some sort of serious damage to the plane, the pilot in charge made a U-turn and set off for the nearest airport. But instead of typing in from memory the ICAO* code for Malaysia's Langkawi Airport, where he now intended to head, he mistakenly entered the code for an airport in the Antarctic. 'There are only two letters difference,' he tells me. In just a few minutes, both the pilot and co-pilot find themselves in a state of hypoxia through depressurisation of the cabin, while the plane continues heading towards the Antarctic. A typing error coupled with hypoxia due to unnoticed decompression, as has occurred in other cases (see Addendum, p. 405) – the hypothesis is as simple as it is believable. However, upon checking the ICAO codes myself, I noticed that Langkawi's is WMKL, and that the airport at the Australian base on Antarctica's Budd Coast is YWKS. In fact, only one letter is in the right place in the potential combinations. Statistically, with such a margin of error, the plane could have been set off in the direction of virtually any airport on the planet … So not a very plausible scenario after all.

A former RAF pilot who was familiar with the Nimrod crash, a controlled ditch that took place in Scotland in 1995, put another ingenious scenario to me. Recalling a scene from the movie *Thunderball* that had already inspired Alan Tan, he was convinced that MH370 was successfully ditched – at very slow speed and in a stalled attitude (nose up) – in some flat and shallow waters before slowly sinking. An underwater military operation could have easily taken place afterwards to retrieve whatever was in this plane that was not supposed to arrive in Beijing. The hull would then have been covered with some kind of camouflage, or even buried in sand and concrete, to become undetectable. Again, as attractive as

---

* International Civil Aviation Organization.

certain scenarios are – much more so, indeed, than the official version – they would be infinitely more convincing if they could be linked to a solid string of clues and defended with sound evidence.

At this stage of the investigation, many false leads had been eliminated and we believed that an outstanding and dedicated pilot was at the helm. Before looking at the few real clues that remained, let's take another closer look at the official version. It can be described in three phases. First, the 'deliberate act' of turning off the transponder and the ACARS system. Second, the turn left-and-back, and the ensuing flight over Malaysia and up the Strait of Malacca. Third, the flight towards nowhere that ended in the southern Indian Ocean.

When, on 15 March 2014, the Malaysian Prime Minister Najib Razak referred to a 'deliberate act', he was clearly putting the blame on *someone* on board the plane. His main argument was based on the fact that this guilty party had turned off the ACARS system, followed by the transponder, before radically altering the plane's route and ultimately ditching it in the middle of the Indian Ocean.

We have already established that there were no circumstances whatsoever that could justify switching off the ACARS system, which was why pilots were not even taught how to do it. But how did we know that the ACARS system was indeed deliberately switched off? I consulted several experts about this issue and discovered there was in fact no trace or proof that the ACARS system was actively switched off or otherwise. This system, which sends automated information messages about the plane's performance, does not send any message when it is turned off, period. The 8 March 2015 provisional official report gave absolutely no explanation about it and did not repeat the version of the events in which 'the ACARS system is switched off'. As far as the proven facts are concerned, we only know that the last ACARS bulletin was emitted at 01:07. We then know that the 01:37 bulletin was not received by Inmarsat, who were then supposed to have forwarded the bulletin, in this instance, to Malaysia Airlines and, possibly, to Boeing and Rolls-Royce as well. And that's it. This detail, the most crucial and the most pregnant with symbolic and emotional meaning of any in the official version, was in fact groundless. The claim that the ACARS system was deliberately switched off was pure conjecture on the part of Prime Minister Najib. Have we actually come to grips with the enormity of this deception? One would imagine that a head of state explicitly asserting false information about a commercial airliner's disappearance would be fiercely scrutinised by both the public and the press ... But that's only part of it.

As far as the transponder was concerned, Malaysian, Vietnamese and Thai radars agreed that the signal of A2157 (the call sign used for MH370) was lost around 01:21 after the plane passed over waypoint IGARI,* although it was still seen on primary radar after waypoint BITOD. The exchange between the ATCs of Kuala Lumpur and Ho Chi Minh City left no doubt about the fact that MH370 was still seen at BITOD. A primary radar can see a 'target' (plane, ship, etc.) from the echo it receives from it, but, unlike a secondary radar, it does not receive any information from it. But the sequence of events, as detailed in the official report one year later, was not consistent with this part of the narrative either. Indeed, if someone had deliberately turned off the transponder, the signal of the plane on the screens of the air traffic controllers who were monitoring the plane would have gone off in one go, altogether. This is not what happened.

The official report was very clear:

Radar recording showed that MH370 passed through waypoint IGARI at 01:20:31. The Mode S symbol of MH370 dropped off from radar display at 01:20:36, and the last secondary radar

---

* In its very first report, MAS actually indicated that 'Flight MH370 [...] lost contact with Subang Air Traffic Control at 2:40'. This one-hour discrepancy has remained unexplained.

position symbol of MH370 was recorded at 01:21:13. The disappearance of the radar position symbol of MH370 was captured by the Malaysian ATCC radar at 01:21:13. Military radar and radar sources from two other countries, namely Vietnam and Thailand, also captured the disappearance of the radar position symbol of MH370 at about the same time.

In other words, the plane's signal disappeared in two stages: first, the Mode S came off the screens of the ATCs at 01:20:36, five seconds after the plane passed IGARI. The Mode S of the transponder is the most complete, as it indicates speed, altitude and other flight data, as well as the squawk sign (or call sign). So all information related to Mode S went off first but the squawk sign (Mode C) stayed on. This was very odd. Then, 37 seconds later, the squawk sign of MH370 (A2157) also came off. This sequence of events in itself should have been sufficient to dismiss the 'someone turned off the transponder' part of the official narrative. The numerous Boeing 777 pilots I consulted regarding such a sequence of events were all equally puzzled. In broad strokes, they all seemed to concur: 'If you turn off your transponder, I don't see how the call sign can still appear.' According to the statements recorded by the Malaysian police (and that I could see), one of the air traffic controllers who was on duty on the night said that the 'plane label were [sic] diminishing from radar 5 miles after IGARI'; another one mentioned that he saw 'MH370 pass IGARI at 1.21' and that the signal was diminishing after that. This is not consistent with a transponder being turned off.

So, contrary to what was asserted by the Malaysian prime minister, there is no proof that either the ACARS system or the transponder was actually turned off. There was therefore virtually no evidence that any kind of 'deliberate act' took place. This constituted the first major flaw of the official version.

Years after I had established this, I was fascinated to read in the very official final report:

The investigation was unable to identify any plausible aircraft or systems failure mode that would lead to the observed systems deactivation, diversion from the filed flight plan route and the subsequent flight path taken by the aircraft. However, the same lack of evidence precluded the investigation from definitely eliminating that possibility.*

In short, the investigation team had no idea how the systems deactivation took place, nor did it corroborate in any way the imposed narrative that these instruments were turned off from the cockpit.

In any case, even if an aircraft switched off its transponder and disappeared from secondary (so-called 'civilian') radar screens, it would still be visible (though not identifiable) on primary (so-called 'military') radar screens. To complicate matters, in many countries, including Malaysia, civil aviation companies also possess primary radars, but they are generally less sophisticated and powerful than the military ones.

The trace left by MH370 on the primary radars in the region was therefore fundamental for confirming (or dismissing) the rerouted flight path taken by the plane after it abandoned its original route towards Beijing. Some details of 'which radar saw what' were released in the *Safety Investigation for MH370* report a year after the loss. Few people paid attention to it. In fairness, I also initially overlooked it.

Immediately after the disappearance of MH370, the one and only known radar image was the one that was shown to the Chinese families in Beijing's Lido Hotel on 21 March 2014, bearing the title 'Military Radar Plot from Pulau Perak to Last Plot at 02:22'. The reality of MH370 having actually been spotted there at that time by Thai military radar had been questioned and doubted from the early hours, including by Imran, the former admiral and Malaysian MP whom I'd met in March 2014 just as

---

* *Safety Investigation Report MH370*, July 2018.

Malaysia was coming to terms with the situation. People had initially noticed that the radar target shown on that so-called Lido image was more likely to be that of SQ68, a Singapore Airlines flight on the P268 route. But then another MHist, tweeting as @ KeyserSquishy, had suggested on 1 April 2014 that the location and time fitted even more precisely Emirates Flight 343 on route N571. It so happened that Flight UAE343 actually landed at 00:19, exactly the time of the last partial handshake, considered to be the time when MH370 crashed for good in the southern Indian Ocean. Some MHists deduced from this double coincidence that the Inmarsat data of that plane could have been partly used to provide data to cover MH370.

In any case, over time, the many defects of the 'Lido image' meant that it eventually lost all credibility. 'All the annotations added by Malaysia on the radar image shown that day were false, and as the projector was poorly adjusted, part of the image was not even visible,' British astrophysicist Duncan Steel, a member of the Independent Group (IG), told me in late 2014. Simon Gunson, the New Zealand MHist, who compared this image with the feedback from civilian radar, concluded that it was undoubtedly a clumsy mock-up produced by the public relations company that had been hired to deal with the families during the crisis. When it was released, this photo was the first and only proof that the plane had set a new westward course, but in the end it was a very weak sort of proof.

As early as August 2014, based on the initial work by another member of the IG, Don Thompson, Duncan Steel had re-created a map of all the military radars likely to have seen the Malaysia Airlines Boeing, of which he found 13 in all. According to him, once it had passed out of the range of Malaysia's French (Thales) and British (Marconi) radars, MH370 was still within range of at least two Indonesian radars and one Thai radar. South of Java, Australia had radars on the Cocos (Keeling) Islands and on Christmas Island. And what about the much-discussed Australian radar known as JORN (Jindalee Operational Radar Network), an over-the-horizon radar network that could monitor air and sea movements across 37,000 square kilometres? Its technical description said that it was designed primarily for air detection. The Jindalee radar at Longreach (Queensland), Alice Springs (Northern Territory) and Laverton (Western Australia) enabled Australian military commanders to observe all air and sea activity north of Australia to distances of at least 3,000 kilometres. This took in all of Java, Irian Jaya, Papua New Guinea and the Solomon Islands, and extended halfway across the Indian Ocean. According to official and public documents, it could even pick up stealth planes as early as 2000. But in the early hours of 8 March 2014, we were expected to believe that JORN was simply not watching in the right direction.* The US ships in the region, specifically present for the Cope Tiger military exercise† at the time, have not shared anything either.

In summer 2015, Victor Iannello, the American scientist I mentioned before, re-examined the radar data‡ described in the official Malaysian and Australian reports but without any supporting images. He went back over a certain number of earlier pieces of work on the subject. As a result, he was able to highlight several inconsistencies and errors, not least of which was the much-quoted 'left half-turn' made by the plane, as described in those official documents that had been made public. According to this nuclear science engineer, such a turn was quite simply beyond the technical capability of a Boeing 777. His explanation was that two radar

---

* According to *The Australian* on 18 March 2014, 'The system was not tasked to look westward towards the Indian Ocean on the morning of the MH370 flight because there was no reason to do so.'

† The annual trilateral air defence exercises involving the United States, Thailand and Singapore, discussed in Chapter 5.

‡ Victor Iannello, 'Some Observations on the Radar Data for MH370', 18 August 2015. See www.duncansteel.com/archives/1969.

images had been superimposed, those of MH370 and another aircraft that had more or less cut across its path. 'Fundamentally, I have come to the conclusion that it is possible no radar picked up any trace of MH370,' he told me over the phone when discussing his study. He sent a series of questions to the official investigation team, who promised him that the relevant answers and data would be included in the next investigation report in March 2016. When the report was published six months later, it did not include even the remotest hint of an answer to Iannello's precise and well-informed questions about the radar issue.

Yet another American IG member told me that Malaysia had shared very little information from its radars, 'even with the Australian team [...] The ATSB cannot understand why Malaysia doesn't share more information.' A large French delegation, including the three judges appointed to the case, led by anti-terrorist judge Alain Gaudino, together with several agents of the French Intelligence Services, went to Malaysia in December 2015. It seemed obvious that one of the key pieces of information the French team should try to get access to from their Malaysian counterparts should be the raw radar images: civil and military images, anything that could support the narrative of MH370 turning left and then flying over Malaysia. But as far as I know, no raw radar images were shared with the French judicial investigation.

In the end, only the Indonesian Air Force confirmed having seen Flight MH370 on its radars at the beginning of its forward flight towards Beijing as far as waypoint IGARI, but it had no echo on its radar when MH370 crossed back – according to the official version – over the Malay Peninsula. The excuse often heard was that Indonesia didn't share this type of information for strategic defence reasons. But was that really a valid argument when the aim was to locate a jetliner with 239 civilians on board, including seven Indonesians?

Might it not rather have been that these countries did not share their radar images of MH370 quite simply because they didn't have any? And if they didn't have any, was this because all the region's radars were out of action or switched off at that moment – or, more simply, because MH370 never flew back along the flight path given in the official version?

We do know one thing at this stage: no country and no ship in the region shared any radar image whatsoever showing MH370's flying its peculiar route. That made me think again of Duncan Steel saying, 'the absence of evidence is no evidence of absence'. But still, this absence of radar evidence – of radar images – should not have been allowed to go unquestioned.

More than two years after the plane's disappearance, I finally got a chance to talk to a radar expert in Malaysia. He told me two important things. First, he confirmed that the Malaysian civil aviation had no way to be sure that the primary radar images it detected, showing a plane crossing over Malaysia in the early hours of 8 March 2014, were in any way related to MH370. All they could assume was that it was a reasonably big plane by the strength of the return. He added that not everything in these images was consistent with the normal return of a Boeing 777. The second point was that the Malaysian Royal Air Force refused to share their own radar images of the same plane with the Malaysian civil aviation. 'Their primary radars are much superior to ours [civil aviation]. They surely know more about this plane.' I asked him if he thought the attitude of the Malaysian Royal Air Force was in anyway suspicious or unusual. 'Very,' he replied.

That prompted me to reopen the official report from March 2015 once again, this time on page 2, under the subtitle 'Diversion from Filed Flight Plan Route', where one could find some details of which radar saw what.

The report mentioned five primary radar sources from the region, but as we have seen, the only radars that spotted a plane flying over Malaysia from east to west were the Malaysian primary radars. The other radars of the region (Indonesia, Thailand and Vietnam) saw MH370 on its way to the IGARI waypoint, but not afterwards. This in itself should have been questioned and eventually explained by the investigation team.

The official report described the following sequence. At 1.21 am local time, the primary radar saw MH370 turning slightly right. That is perfectly consistent with the new alignment it was supposed to take to reach the next waypoint, BITOD. But almost immediately afterwards, according to the official narrative, it made a constant left turn in a south-westerly direction. At 1.30 am, the plane was heading west (231 degrees) at a ground speed of 496 knots and a height of 35,700 feet. Six minutes later, at 1.36 am, the speed of the plane changed from 494 knots to 525 knots and its altitude fluctuated between 31,100 feet and 33,000 feet. At 1.39 am, the heading was still generally west-south-west but the ground speed increased to 529 knots, although the plane was flying at 32,800 feet. The last radar return took place at 1.52 am, when the plane was to the south of Penang Island. For no obvious reason, the report did not indicate heading, altitude or speed for this last point.

After that, the plane was still tracked while it flew towards Pulau Perak, a tiny island over the Strait of Malacca, which it reached at 2.03 am. Finally, the plane abruptly disappeared at 2.22 am, 10 miles after waypoint MEKAR.

The second radar return that the official report mentioned came from the civilian radar in Kota Bharu. It described a plane that appeared and disappeared four times between 1.30 and 1.52.* It had a different code that looked like a call sign for every appearance: P3362, P3401, P3415 and P3526. But once again, no speed, altitude or heading were provided.

There were indeed many issues with these radar data and the way they were presented. For one thing, the plane described was

---

* Between 01:30:37 to 01:37:22 an aircraft coded as P3362. Between 01:38:56 to 01:44:52 an aircraft coded as P3401. Four minutes later, at 01:47:02 an aircraft coded as P3415 appeared again, then disappeared 01:48:39. At 01:51:45 an aircraft target, coded as P3426, appeared on the KL ATCC radar display but disappeared at 01:52:35.

referred to as 'MH370', even though there was no way to be sure it was indeed MH370, as the radar expert from Malaysia himself confirmed to me. A primary radar return does not indicate the identity of the emitting plane, a crucial difference between primary and secondary radars. As the radar expert said, 'We just know it is a big plane.' Once again, the authorities had simply assumed and then asserted that this plane was MH370.

There was another major consistency issue in the official report. Page 97 stated:

At 01:39:03am Ho Chi Minh ATCC first enquired about MH370 and informed KL ATCC that verbal contact was not established with MH370 and the radar target was last seen at BITOD. [...]

At 01:46:47am Ho Chi Minh ATCC queried about MH370 again, stating that radar contact was established over IGARI but there was no verbal contact. HCM ATCC advised that the observed radar blip disappeared at waypoint BITOD.

Actually, there were more than 20 mentions of MH370 being spotted at waypoint BITOD by the Ho Chi Minh Air Traffic Control Centre around 1.30 am. Yet, in the recap of the radar sightings, this was not mentioned at all. Why? Because, as true and as documented as they might have been, these sightings clearly stood in the way of the official narrative. Given that the two air traffic control centres responsible for tracking MH370 that night, namely the ATCs from Malaysia and from Vietnam, had both said or acknowledged that MH370 was still at BITOD at around 1.30 am, it could not have turned left to initiate its near U-turn just after IGARI ten minutes earlier. But most observers simply jettisoned the BITOD information, as important as it was, as if it had never existed. Truth is, if MH370 had been at BITOD as reported, none of the rest of the story could stand. The turn did not take place right after IGARI and it was simply impossible that the blip seen on the Thai radar at MEKAR at 2.22 am was MH370. So instead of keeping the last established presence of MH370 in the Vietnamese sky as the reference point in the search, the official narrative dismissed it in order to give the appearance of consistency to the new and seemingly fabricated narrative. Another typical example of not letting the truth get in the way of a good story.

Some other problematic aspects were more technical. Once again, I consulted the expertise of my Boeing 777 pilot friends. The flight caught by the Malaysian radar and described in the report was incredibly messy and erratic. Indeed, its altitude and its speed kept changing. The speeds registered were all above average cruise speed and even above the maximum speed possible for a B777.* But that in itself was not necessarily an issue, I was told. 'Ground speed does not mean much,' Jason explained. 'If you have a strong tail wind, your plane could achieve a much higher ground speed without actually flying faster in its own mass of air.' But of course! Much more significant and strange were the wild changes of altitude. The plane captured by the Malaysian radars was oscillating up and down from 31,100 to 35,700 feet in just a few minutes. This was unheard of for a B777. 'I see only two explanations for this radar return,' said Jason. 'Either the radar is not calibrated properly and these data are just erroneous, or the plane has encountered a very serious storm. You could lose altitude if you were enjoying strong tailwinds that suddenly stop. But even then, you would not lose 4,000 feet [1,200 metres] in a matter of minutes. No way!'

Well, there was no sign of any substantial storm, let alone a few clouds, on the satellite weather map of the region at the exact time of the plane crossing Malaysia from east to west. According

---

* The typical cruising speed of a Boeing 777 is Mach 0.84, which is 490 knots or 905 km/h at a cruising altitude of 35,000 feet. The maximum cruising speed at the same optimal altitude of 35,000 feet is Mach 0.89, or 512 knots.

to the report, the nearby airports did not mention 'any significant weather phenomena'.* Another detail was rather strange. Since MH370 had supposedly turned off its transponder, how could the plane picked by Kota Bahru have returned a code at every contact? 'You do not change your squawk unless ATC instructs you to do so and it is done manually in the flight deck,' commented Jason. Considering the oddities of these data, it was very tempting to conclude that whatever this plane was, its way of flying did not look consistent with that of a B777 and its emitting codes were incompatible with the fact that MH370 was supposed to have turned off its transponder by that time. In other words, all of this evidence pointed towards the same probability: that the plane described by these radar data was in most likelihood not MH370.

Someone I met in Indonesia almost three years after MH370 disappeared, and who had worked for several civil aviation authorities in Asia and Europe, told me that he saw the original Malaysian radar images, the ones that were never shared, not with the Australians and not with the French investigators. He was adamant that he saw the images of the mystery plane at 47,500 feet and then at 2,700 feet. This information never made it into the official report but had been reported by *The New York Times* one week after the loss.† IG members had questioned it. This fuelled the scenario of a super-expert pilot who would have taken his plane as high as possible to do away with all his passengers and then as low as possible to avoid radar detection. So here was I, sitting between a dusty fan and a small fishpond in a hippy café in Indonesia, hearing the same information that I had initially

---

* The Meteorological Aerodrome Report (METAR) issued at 16:00, 17:00 and 18:00 UTC from Kota Bharu Airport (WMKC), Kuala Terengganu Airport (WMKN), Penang International Airport (WMKP) and KLIA (WMKK) (Figure 1.7D below) did not report any significant weather phenomena.

† 'Radar Suggests Jet Shifted Path More Than Once', *The New York Times*, 15 March 2014.

dismissed, from another person who claimed to have seen these Malaysian radar images of a plane at a very high altitude. But the fact remains that a B777's supposed ceiling is 43,100 feet; and pilots seem to believe that the plane should never be taken near, let alone above, 45,000 feet. This was yet another clue that the plane seen at 47,500 feet on its flight back towards Malaysia could not have been a B777. As for the double blip on the radar images described to me, there was no way a plane, even less a B777, could be so high and so low in the blink of an eye. At that point in time, the radar must indeed have been looking at two different planes. This would be partly consistent with Victor Iannello's hypothesis that the supposed turn was just the crossing of another plane, and would also fit with what some people on the east coast of Malaysia had described: a big plane flying low in a completely unusual direction.

When the final investigation report was published in July 2018,* it seemed clear that the investigators themselves had issues with the radar data of the supposed sighting of MH370 by the Malaysian military radar. Here are a couple of passages from this official document: 'It became very apparent, however, that the recorded altitude and speed change "blip" to "blip" were well beyond the capability of the aircraft' (p. 3). 'Some of the speed and height variations were not achievable even after repeated simulator sessions' (p. 6). I am puzzled as to how the investigators could pretend to be relying on 'radar data' when they themselves explained that the given data was inconsistent with the capability of the aircraft ...

Shortly after the world heard that the plane was missing, Ghyslain Wattrelos was told by a reliable contact in Beijing that US Awacs planes had played a role in the MH370 operation. 'There were two US Awacs on site. Awacs planes registered in the US. The Americans

---

* *Safety Investigation Report MH370*, July 2018.

know what happened. That's all I can tell you,' his intelligence contact told him. He detailed the exchange in his book, which was published in 2018.*

A while ago, a contact from the Middle East told me that the plane seen crossing Malaysia was not MH370, as claimed by the authorities, but a Singaporean Awacs, an Israeli-made IAI EL/W-2085. From 2007 onwards, Singapore had acquired four modified Gulfstream G550s – their 'eyes in the sky' – that were used for airborne early warning and control. Two articles published by *The Malaysian Insider* that are no longer available online mentioned a 'Singaporean air traffic surveillance and control unit' that picked up a signal showing MH370 make a turn back before climbing 3,280 feet from its original altitude at 32,808 feet. Since the distance from IGARI to Singapore (330 miles) was too far for any land-based radars, it was a fair albeit educated guess to suggest that this surveillance unit was actually a 'flying radar'. One could assume that there were indeed many military planes in operation in that area in the days preceding and following the loss of MH370, because the tripartite Cope Tiger exercise (US, Singaporean and Thai forces) was about to start.

But I also obtained factual confirmation of the Singaporean 'eye in the sky' when I was given the files of the Pathumtani radar, located just north of Bangkok, for the days preceding and following the night of 7–8 March. These show more than 1,600 flights per 24-hour period, mostly commercial flights in and out of Bangkok but also some of the traffic in and out of Kuala Lumpur and Singapore. Several military vessels were mentioned and identified on this list, including as it so happened, at least one Singaporean Awacs plane with the hexcode 76E304. An Awacs can see air traffic within a radius of about 400 kilometres, so this plane alone knew exactly what happened on the night of 8 March 2014. Many more

---

* Ghyslain Wattrelos (with Gaëlle Legenne), *Une vie détournée*, Flammarion, 2018.

military planes were not explicitly identified and it took a bit of research to find out their identity, although some remained complete enigmas.

One US Air Force (USAF) plane was clearly identified as a C-17, with its hexcode shown on the list as AE0805. The C-17, commonly described as the workhorse of the USAF, is a big carrier. This one flew twice in the skies over Thailand, for two and a half to three and a half hours each time. When it left Pathumtani's radar screen on 7 March 2014, it was 23:35:35 Malaysian time. One hour later, MH370 took off from Kuala Lumpur. Among the USAF planes flying around Thailand on the day and night of the loss of MH370, there was also a C-146A. This plane is mainly used to 'provide U.S. Special Operations Command flexible, responsive and operational movement of small teams needed in support of Theatre Special Operations Commands (TSOC)'. In other words, it delivers teams of commandos as discreetly as possible wherever they were needed. Then there were mentions of a C-130 registered in Miramar, California, and of a C-5B Galaxy. The C-5 is among the largest military aircraft in the world, said to provide the USAF with a heavy intercontinental-range strategic airlift capability that could carry outsize and oversize loads.

The list of military planes in the region within 24 hours of the loss of MH370 also included KC-135 Stratotankers and numerous other military planes from the US, as well as from Thailand and Singapore. There were so many, I have not even checked them all … But what these data certainly indicated was that during the days and nights before and after MH370 went astray, there was a massive military presence in the sky and in the region.

Of course, if MH370 had been shadowed and blanketed by one or rather two Awacs planes, that could explain why the signal of the plane's transponder came off the ATC's screens the way it did, diminishing steadily 5 miles after Igari, as the air traffic controllers said in their statements to the police, and why the 01:37 ACARS bulletin was never received – it might have been sent normally from the plane, then just been intercepted and blocked by the Awacs's screen.

It might be worth emphasising again here that it was actually on the other side of Malaysia, the west side, that, according to the official version, MH370 was seen for the last time by Thai radar. The Strait of Malacca is one of the world's busiest and most strategically important sea corridors. All the oil from the Middle East heading for China and Japan passes through there, as do a huge proportion of China's exports on the reverse route towards Europe and Africa. I studied the area closely for a documentary on sea piracy that was shown on the Arte network in 2006.* The Indonesian, Malaysian and Singaporean navies keep a very close watch over the region, and US Navy vessels are never far away. In addition to the prodigious US Seventh Fleet (50–70 ships and submarines, 150 aircraft, 20,000 sailors according to its own website), which covers much of the Pacific as well as most of the Indian Ocean, the US also has a permanent naval and air force presence in Singapore. Since 9/11, Singapore has become even more important in its role as the Asian base for the CIA and MI6.

What appeared to be an exceptionally lax response, even by Malaysian standards, was all the less credible given that since 1971 Malaysia had been a member of the Five Power Defence Agreement (FPDA) that included the UK, Australia, New Zealand and Singapore. In the event of a breach of air space, precise protocols required fighter jets to scramble within a few minutes. Since 9/11, the Petronas Twin Towers† had been deemed an ideal target for terrorist attacks, prompting a thorough revision of these procedures. Yet on the night of 7 to 8 March, a massive unidentified

* *Malacca, le détroit de tous les dangers* (*Malacca: the strait of all dangers*), Arte, 2006, 52 minutes.

† Opened in 1998, the Petronas Twin Towers were the highest skyscrapers in the world until 2004.

plane would have flown over Malaysian airspace for 40 minutes without triggering any reaction?

Even more surprising was the fact that, according to the official version of events, MH370 flew right over the Royal Malaysian Air Force Butterworth Base in Penang, which was the headquarters for the FPDA's integrated air defence system, controlled by an Australian air vice-marshal.

Malaysia was severely criticised for its laxity and lack of professionalism. But wasn't it precisely to respond to this type of situation (that is, an unidentified aircraft flying over a region that the multipartite integrated air defence system, led by the 'real pros' – as the Australians were described in reference to the underwater search operation – was created? If so, why didn't this textbook case trigger any reaction at the Butterworth Air Base under Australian command? Was it because, like in the case of Malaysia's radars, everyone was asleep? Or was it simply because the plane did not pass right over the 'Five Powers' air defence base? To give an indication of the vitality of this little-known military agreement, less than three months after the loss of the plane, Australia met with its regional security partners (New Zealand, Malaysia, Singapore and the United Kingdom) between 22 May and 4 June for the military exercise Bersama Shield 2014, described as 'one of South East Asia's most significant regional exercises'. On 1 June, the defence ministers of the same five countries met in Johor Baru, Malaysia, and visited the Butterworth Base in Penang.

Heavy military and civilian maritime and air presence, radars, drones, Awacs planes and satellites; objectively, the Strait of Malacca, just like the South China Sea, is probably the worst place in the world to try to pass incognito or quite simply disappear.

It was nevertheless in this context, we are told, that Malaysia let pass a Boeing 777 that was no longer communicating with air traffic control and flying over its country in the opposite direction to its intended flight path. When questioned on Australia's ABC network a few weeks after the loss of MH370,* the Malaysian Minister of Defence and Transport, Hishammuddin Hussein, defended his inaction: 'It was not hostile; it was commercial; it was from our airspace; we're not at war with anybody. Even if we sent them up, are you going to say that we're going to shoot it down?' Shortly after this very weird if not inappropriate comment from a minister of defence, the journalist Caro Meldrum-Hanna astutely followed-up: 'Why shoot it down, though, if it's not hostile?' To which Hishammuddin Hussein replied with one of the most intriguing lines of this whole enigma: 'Well, the Americans would.' Why bring the Americans into the picture when they have mostly been absent from this crisis? And on what basis could a Malaysian minister of defence assert publicly that 'the Americans' would shoot a civilian plane?

But setting this aside, the minister of transport and defence was implying that the plane had been identified and was not considered a threat. But if the transponder was switched off, how did they know that it was the unthreatening MH370? And if they did know it was MH370, totally off course, wouldn't that have been enough perhaps not to 'shoot it down' as the 'Americans probably would have', but at least to raise an alarm? Hishammuddin's explanation made no sense whatsoever. This TV interview was an amazing document – alongside the inconsistency of what he said, the minister really came across as terribly nervous and ill at ease.

Just as there was nothing upon which to base the theory of a 'deliberate act', there was nothing solid to prove that MH370 ever flew back over Malaysia. On the contrary, the plane said to be MH370 had much more in common with a military plane than with a Boeing 777. Not a single raw radar image, not even from Malaysia, was made public to confirm that the plane sighted over Malaysia was actually MH370. Even the large French judicial dele-

* *LOST: MH370, ABC's *Four Corners*, 19 May 2014.

gation that travelled to Malaysia in December 2015 failed to obtain a single radar image. And there was nothing to justify the integrated air defence system not being activated by the passage of a B777 right above the Five Powers' air defence system's coordination centre in Penang. Unless, of course, what flew over the base was a known military plane, flying according to its mission in full contact with Butterworth Air Base.

A few days after MH370 disappeared, news broke that the co-pilot's mobile phone had been detected as the plane flew over Penang. This sounded like a nice proof that the plane did actually fly over Malaysia. The information related to this connection was never well established or clearly confirmed, but it was widely reported all the same. On 12 April 2014, CNN quoted a 'US official' who confirmed the story. Of course, many people asked, if one phone connected, why not a few more among the hundreds of others devices carried on board? According to the confidential files of the Royal Malaysia Police on this topic, all attempts to re-enact the connection the way it was described in the press failed during a real-life flight-reconstruction exercise with several phones on board. These files were in the so-called 'SKMM Analysis' folder, the Folder 4 that we came across in the discussion of the question of the simulator and Captain Zaharie's flight path.

One of the files states:

On 8 March 2014 at 1:52:57 am, MH370 Co-Pilot's mobile phone was reported as detected in Celcom's mobile network in Penang by Sector 2 of BBFARLIM2 Base Station. A flight reconstruction exercise has been conducted in order to investigate the capabilities of Celcom's cellular base stations, in particular BBFARLIM2 base station, to detect mobile phones and while in flight. Upon completion of the flight reconstruction exercise, the recorded data showed the test mobile phones being detected by the different base stations along the flight path of the flight reconstruction at different flight levels. However, BBFARLIM2

Base Station was not one of the base stations detected during the flight reconstruction.

So despite being breaking news at the time, strongly in support of the idea of a U-turn and flight over Malaysia, this information was never proven to be true either. The official report, one year later, dropped this 'clue' altogether and made no mention of it at all. With the benefit of hindsight, together with the understanding that MH370 was never picked up by the Malaysian radars, this co-pilot's phone-connection anecdote seems to have all the hallmarks of a fake story, planted early enough in people's brains to try to put flesh on the bones of the flight over Malaysia scenario.

No proof of a deliberate act, no credible radar traces of a flight over Malaysia and no more phone's pings – that only left the Inmarsat pings to support the official version.

We have seen that Inmarsat enjoyed an excellent reputation in the industry: reliable, efficient and cutting-edge. So cutting-edge, in fact, that the company had the resources to track a plane that had cut all communications systems, something that far exceeded its contractual agreement.

Yet, right from the start, certain Inmarsat engineers expressed their doubts. One of them even imagined that 'this could just be one big hoax that someone had played on Inmarsat' and that 'the aircraft went down and someone at the same time pretended to be that aircraft'.* Yet among the people best positioned to trick Inmarsat, you can't rule out Inmarsat themselves. Doubt as to the authenticity and reliability of the pings on which the entire Indian Ocean crash theory rested had therefore been around right from the start, even within Inmarsat's own team.

A former Inmarsat employee, whom I met in Jakarta where I was reporting on the aftermath of the terrorist attacks of January

* *Where Is Flight MH370?*, BBC Two, op. cit.

2016,* told me that even several years ago, before he left the company, Inmarsat had the technology to locate the planes that carry its equipment at any given time, meaning there was no need to call on the handshake pings at all to know where a plane was, all the more with an active Satcom.† He also told me that the firm's clients were unaware of this technology.

I had got wind of these doubts from a family source. During a meal with a group of young people, one of the party casually mentioned that he was fascinated by the story of this lost plane apparently traced to the middle of the Indian Ocean by a few pings picked up by a satellite company. He was surprised to be interrupted by one of his friends who said, 'Forget about it. My dad works for Inmarsat and they know very well what happened. The plane is not at all where they are looking.' The person who recounted this anecdote to me was at the dinner in question and I had no reason to doubt what he said. The parent concerned, when asked later for more details, vehemently denied everything and was visibly panic-stricken: 'None of this was ever mentioned or heard, and it must absolutely never be discussed ever again,' he warned, a reaction more appropriate to a major blunder of terrible consequence than to an unfortunate misunderstanding between father and son.

Since Inmarsat could theoretically locate any plane that had its instruments on board the moment the plane was lost, Inmarsat would have immediately looked at its data and seen for itself where the plane was. It should have taken Inmarsat minutes or hours but not days to confirm the approximate position of a plane. Yet it took Inmarsat a long time to come up with its 'explanation'. The

---

* On 14 January 2016, at least eight people were killed and dozens wounded after several suicide bombings and gun attacks took place in downtown Jakarta. ISIL claimed responsibility.

† The satellite communication system was inexplicably not working between 1.21 am and 2.25 am, but initiated a log-on at 2.25 and was back on from that point onwards.

silence of the company for this many days might be seen as a nod of approval that the plane was being searched for in the right area. 'They said nothing initially because the first search in the South China Sea seemed consistent with what they knew. If the plane had really gone towards the southern Indian Ocean, they would have come out immediately,' observed an MHist who had developed his own explanation of the whole episode, which I will describe later.

Late in 2016, I saw a very troubling exchange of emails between a passenger's sister and Malaysia Airlines. On 13 March 2014, the sister sent a message to an MAS employee in France. In it, she described her agony and requested that MAS clarify a series of points that the media had raised and that the passengers' families were very confused about. She mentioned the possibility of a missile having been being fired in the vicinity of the South China Sea, the plane debris found on the east coast of Malaysia on 8 March, the oil slicks, the large debris field spotted by the Chinese satellites and the latest news that the plane had kept on flying for several hours after it was last spotted. The MAS employee replied with a sympathetic message that includes this extraordinary passage:

> Regarding the media reports: the information stating that there is some data showing that the plane flew for four hours after the last contact at 1.07 is false. This information has been denied by Boeing and Rolls-Royce.

It was truly baffling that just a few hours before the White House announced that MH370 did indeed fly for many hours after it disappeared from radar screens, confirming the earlier scoop by *The Wall Street Journal*, an MAS employee shared some inside information in order to reassure this next of kin. Of course, the story of the plane flying for hours, first denied by Boeing and Rolls-Royce, became 'true' and the backbone of the official narrative. Clearly Boeing and Rolls-Royce had not yet been briefed when they told MAS that their own information did not corroborate the extra hours of flight scenario. Possibly relying on the same intel from Boeing and Rolls-Royce, the Minister of Defence and Transports, Hishammuddin Hussein, also vehemently denied these reports during the ensuing press conferences, but 'Mr No-No' had lost so much credibility at that point that no one took his statements very seriously any more.

Unsurprisingly, neither Boeing nor Rolls-Royce ever commented on this. As we have seen, Boeing's silence in this affair is in itself a mystery, an anomaly that has bamboozled the entire aviation sector. But what *is* certain is that Inmarsat never wanted to share all of its much-quoted data with the independent scientists of the IG or the families who wanted to be able to commission an independent study (see Chapter 6).

It stood to reason that the company should want the whole world to know all about its exceptional contribution to solving this unbelievable enigma. All scientists publish their data, research methods and calculations to allow for peer review. Inmarsat took the opposite approach; it released nothing publicly and kept totally silent, claiming a responsibility to Malaysia. It steadfastly refused to give any interviews despite receiving 3,000 media requests in four days.* From then on, anyone making a request was simply referred by the company to the only two programmes it had agreed to take part in: one on the BBC, the other on CNN, with nothing for the Chinese or Malaysian media. In December 2014, Mark Dickinson, Vice President of Satellite Operations at Inmarsat, also gave an interview to the industry magazine *Satellite Today*. When I asked for an interview in the summer of 2015, the press office suggested that I direct my questions about Inmarsat to Malaysia or Australia. Inmarsat even ignored the official requests for information from the French judicial inquiry.

* interactive.satellitetoday.com/inmarsat-exec-talks-about-operators-role-in-search-for-mh370.

What did they fear? Would a critical eye be able to detect certain flaws?

Several observers actually detected major anomalies. The most obvious one was that the official narrative and Inmarsat's sophisticated calculations had the plane turning back at waypoint IGARI, although, as we just saw, the plane was still seen and heard about 10 minutes later and 37 miles further east at waypoint BITOD by the Ho Chi Minh air traffic control.

Furthermore, the time of the last confirmed radio communication with MH370 was just after 1.30 am. The pilot of MH88 said he managed to establish contact with MH370 just after 1.30 am and heard mumblings from someone who he thought was the co-pilot. This radio contact was confirmed in the sixth media statement released on 9 March at 2.28 am, in which it was stated: 'It has been more than 24 hours since we last heard from MH370 at 1.30 am.'

'Inmarsat made several mistakes when they came out with their data. And once it was out, the only way to make the data stand was to pretend MH370 did not reach BITOD … But it is recorded by the ATC of Ho Chi Minh,' a keen MHist told me. In other words, to accept the Inmarsat story you had to dismiss the official records of the Vietnamese ATC as reported in the official report. The Inmarsat story and the Ho Chi Minh records were clearly incompatible, as was the 2.22 am radar sighting. If the information reported by the Vietnamese ATC was true and accurate, as one would expect, then Inmarsat's premise for its entire demonstration was wrong. Wasn't this a major issue that deserved an explanation?

It was no secret that Inmarsat was far more sensitive a company than it first appeared. Its 'Inmarsat Government' branch included the world's largest armies among its clients. 'Dedicated to serve the U.S. Government' is how Inmarsat Government describes itself on the 'Who We Are' page of its own website. Precisely where Inmarsat Government's loyalty lay could hardly be made more explicit.

For several years – and until 2011 – one of Inmarsat's main shareholders (27 per cent) was Harbinger Group, the US company co-founded by George H. W. Bush and a former CIA agent, with a number of subsequent episodes confirming the ties between Harbinger and the US intelligence agency. Inmarsat's close relationship with the Pentagon was shown by the fact that on 20 March 2014, the company announced that General C. Robert Kehler, of the USAF, was joining its board of directors. Until the end of 2013, General Kehler headed the US Strategic Command, reporting directly to the president and the secretary of defense regarding all operations and all projects involving the American armed forces in the fields of strategic dissuasion, space and cyberspace.

During his official trip to the UK in October 2015, Chinese President Xi Jinping paid only one visit to a British company, which happened to be … Inmarsat.* This visit raised a few eyebrows in the industry. 'Everyone knows Inmarsat does a lot of work for the United States and the United Kingdom,' as one insider told me. The *Financial Times* reported that the Chinese government had signed a project worth several hundred million dollars during the visit.

Some MHists have wondered about the sudden death of an Inmarsat employee who was involved in analysing the MH370 flight data. This satellite controller, who was in his early 50s, died on 17 March 2014 just as the definitive version of the loss of MH370 – the Indian Ocean crash – was about to be announced. He was described by his boss as a 'key member of his operations team'.† Intrigued by this information, IG member Rand Mayer told me how he cunningly called Inmarsat after-hours and found out that the man who reportedly died of a heart attack was called Stuart James Fairbairn. His obituary said he had 'died suddenly but peacefully'.

---

* Xi Jinping visited Inmarsat's London head office on 22 October 2015.

† interactive.satellitetoday.com/inmarsat-exec-talks-about-operators-role-in-search-for-mh370/.

In summary, what is left of the official version and its three pillars? Namely, first, the 'deliberate act' of turning off all communication devices, second, the U-turn and the flight over Malaysia and up the Strait of Malacca, and, third, the south-bound flight, based on Inmarsat data. The 'deliberate act', a concept that had already been used to unjustly incriminate the co-pilot on EgyptAir Flight 990 in order to cover up a technical fault (see Addendum), is a piece of pure conjecture by Prime Minister Najib Razak. Not a single raw radar image has been shown to support the route taken by MH370 according to the official version, crossing Malaysia east to west and then flying between Sumatra and Thailand. As for the role played by Inmarsat in this sad saga, it could cautiously be described as opaque and uncooperative with the media and the families.

With the underwater search failing to find anything at all in the area considered a priority, even the IG's hardcore rationalists have started to lose faith in the Inmarsat data. Some still believe – because from here on it really is a question of faith – in the validity of the Inmarsat pings, but they are fewer in number and weaker in their influence.

Let's admit it, on the face of it the official version has every semblance of a decoy. Almost seven years after the loss of the plane, the authorities' version of what happened to MH370 is even less credible than when it first surfaced. The sub-sea search led by Australia in international waters conveniently kept media busy, families' hope alive and people's attention focused somewhere. Nothing more. As for the plane debris found on the east coast of Africa, although we have been assured that three pieces were confirmed parts of MH370, no satisfactory evidence has ever been produced. Most of what the media has been told – and what it in turn has repeated – is unproven, unreliable or fabricated. Have the claims supporting the official version been substantiated by documents? Not really. What truly happened to the plane must be deduced from what we know for sure.

With such a wobbly official narrative, it becomes logical and reasonable to believe that something completely different happened to MH370, possibly a fatal crash in the South China Sea near the Gulf of Thailand, most likely shortly after MH370 was last seen by Ho Chi Minh ATC around 1.30 am at waypoint BITOD. So it may be time to go back to square one, to where the plane was last actually spotted, to see whether clues pointing to a different scenario can be found.

14

The Simple Scenario:
A Crash in the South China Sea

'The only way a plane [...] can disappear from a radar screen is if it really vanishes: an in-flight explosion or a crash,' said the seasoned former admiral Mohamad Imran,* when we met in Kuala Lumpur's parliament building in March 2014 at the very beginning of this story. He added that having spent much of his professional life staring at radar screens, he was certain that the plane never made a U-turn. This always stayed with me.

Trying to discover the how and the why for the disappearance of MH370 reminded me of a concept I studied in a course on logic during my philosophy classes at university. According to the principle of Ockham's razor, when there are two explanations for an occurrence, the one that requires the fewest assumptions is usually correct. In other words, the more assumptions you have to make, the more unlikely the explanation. It is basically what the US armed forces call the 'KISS principle' – keep it simple, stupid – to explain situations. The simplest and most obvious scenario in the case of MH370 is that of a catastrophic event close to the spot where the plane disappeared from Vietnamese and Malaysian radars. The last radio contact with the Malaysian air traffic controllers (ATC), was at 1.19 am when the captain pronounced those well-known and

---

* In late 2017, Imran, who became a senator the following year, urged his government to release the Royal Malaysian Air Force radar videos.

now somewhat poignant last words: 'Good night Malaysian three seven zero.' The plane then passed waypoint IGARI at 1.22 am. Ho Chi Minh air traffic controllers did not establish radio contact with MH370 but they saw it reach the next waypoint, BITOD, 37 miles away, at around 1.30 am. That's when a brief garbled conversation took place between MH370 and another plane that has not been officially identified. Very shortly after BITOD, the Ho Chi Minh controllers lost all radar return. This was more or less the moment when the most incredible disappearance in civil aviation history took place.

As described at the start of Chapter 2, several villagers and fishermen along the north-eastern coast of Malaysia reported highly unusual sights and sounds – loud explosions, the fan of a jet engine, a low-flying plane with lights 'as big as coconuts', what sounded like an incoming tsunami – above the sea that night. The local press should be praised for its good work in recording these many witnesses' statements in the ensuing days, and there were doubtless many more witnesses whose stories were not recorded. Reports of similar night-time sightings also came from the neighbouring Songkhla province in Thailand.

In fact, according to a retired engineer originally from the east coast of Malaysia, who contacted me sometime in 2018, most people from the region associated the bizarre activity observed that night with the airport of Hat Yai, located in the middle of the jungle, 200 kilometres across the border with Thailand. 'In the region, everyone knows that this airport is a famous trafficking hub. It is the closest airport from the last point of radio contact IGARI where the runway is long enough for a B777 to land,' he told me. His preferred scenario had MH370 landing there and then taking off again under a new identity, that of a cargo plane. He suggested that I find a way to gain access to the ATC logbook of that airport and check the activity that night. In my opinion, the plane or planes spotted by the local people during the night, especially flying so low and with 'big lights', did not match a B777 at all, but I was grateful he brought Hat Yai airport to my attention and mentioned that local people saw planes flying towards the sea or heading north. In essence, none of these sightings matched the supposed route of MH370 after the supposed U-turn. And not only did they contradict the official narrative, they also highlighted something completely unusual taking place at the same time in the same region.

Initially, but not for long, the mid-air destruction of MH370 in precisely this part of the world was actually the favoured scenario of most experts consulted. The idea that the plane crashed here rather than thousands of kilometres away was also consistent with the aforementioned anecdote that the captain's friend, Peter Chong, had shared with me; that when he was flying over the Gulf of Thailand on the night of Monday 10 March, on a Bangkok–Kuala Lumpur MAS flight, the captain to whom he had sent his condolences for the tragedy, had sent him a note back saying 'Wreckage to your left'.

'The fact that we are unable to find any debris so far, appears to indicate that the aircraft is likely to have disintegrated at around 35,000 feet,' a senior source involved in the preliminary investigations in Malaysia told Reuters in the days immediately following the disappearance.* If the plane had plunged intact from close to its cruising altitude, breaking up only on impact with the water, search teams would have expected to find a fairly concentrated pattern of debris, explained the source, speaking on condition of anonymity because he was not authorised to discuss the investigation publicly. Truth is, it often takes three to five days before one or several fields of debris are spotted.

At the very beginning of the crisis, Reuters quoted two more experts who initially favoured an on-site catastrophe scenario. 'Such a sudden disappearance would suggest either that something is happening so quickly that there is no opportunity to put out a

---

* Quoted in the *South China Morning Post*, 10 March 2014.

Mayday, in which case a deliberate act is one possibility to consider, or that the crew is busy coping with whatever has taken place,' said Paul Hayes, Director of Safety and Insurance at FlightGlobal's Ascend aviation consultancy. He thought the 'lack of a distress call suggested that the plane either experienced an explosive decompression or was destroyed by an explosive device'. A former board member of the US National Transport Safety Board, John Goglia, added, 'It had to be quick because there was no communication.'

The scenario of a crash in the Gulf of Thailand was also initially supported first and foremost by the Vietnamese Ministry of Defence. The information it published in the very first hours after the loss of MH370 went as far as indicating very clearly the time and location of the crash on the morning of 8 March. When looking closely at the relevant Vietnamese websites, I was surprised to see that within the first 48 hours, at least in Vietnam the idea that MH370 crashed in its territorial waters was presented as a certainty. The first dispatch, published at 10.16 am on 8 March on the *Tuoi Tre News* website, quotes a Vietnamese Navy communiqué according to which, 'The plane crashed at 01:40, 153 miles [283 kilometres] off Tho Chu Island.' Major General Pham Hoai Giang, head of the Vietnamese Defence Ministry's Rescue and Salvage Department, stated that 'Vietnam's search and rescue forces would take part in the search for a crashed Malaysia Airlines plane when there is a request to do so by the Malaysian authorities.'

I found in the archives of *Vietnam Express*, another online source of information, that at 9.50 am on the morning of 8 March, the Vietnam Emergency Rescue Centre had picked up the signal of one of MH370's distress beacons 120 miles (222 kilometres) southwest of Cape Ca Mau. The *Aviation Herald* website also mentioned at the time that 'Vietnamese search personnel have detected an ELT signal about 120nm south of the coast of Ca Mau.' This information was absolutely crucial, as the signal emitted by the ELT (emergency locator transmitter) beacon was unique and identifiable; the so-called Cospas-Sarsat monitoring system used worldwide would know exactly which beacon belonged to which aircraft, as the signal picked up could not come from any other aircraft.

So if this information was true, it was all that would be needed to prove that MH370 did in fact come down at that precise location. This piece of information was picked up by China's CCTV and the Chinese news agency Xinhua, but it was generally overlooked by Western media, possibly because Cospas-Sarsat, an intergovernmental organisation based in Montreal, neither confirmed nor denied it. It has to be said, however, that ELTs had a very poor record of efficiency, their main documented flaw being that they did not always go off on impact or upon contact with water as they should. Nevertheless, if and once they were set off, there was simply no way they could send incorrect data.

It was also possible that this report of an ELT signal was itself a mistake. Vietnamese translation is a headache, I was told by people who thought I was following a false lead. They told me a sentence mentioning a mere signal in Vietnamese could have become 'an ELT signal' in English. But translation usually loses details; it rarely adds them. In any case, there was no further trace of this information to be found on the internet, bar some screenshots taken by MHists when it was first published. And Cospas-Sarsat never replied to my enquiries.

On 8 March 2014, the Vietnamese authorities seemed to react in textbook fashion and asked all ships in the immediate vicinity of the last point of contact to be on the lookout for the plane. At 04:03 UTC (11.03 am local time in Vietnam) that day, the Haiphong Land Earth Station (LES)* sent a general Mayday call,

---

* The Haiphong LES was one of 29 similar ground stations that Inmarsat ran around the world. The region where contact with MH370 was lost was actually covered by an overlap of two Inmarsat satellites: the Pacific Ocean Region and the Indian Ocean Region satellites.

through an EGC message.* I saw a photo of a telex that a sailor took with his own phone. It read:

```
PRIORITY: DISTRESS
MAYDAY
THIS IS HAI PHONG LES
ALL STATIONS
FOLLOWING RECEIVED FROM VUNGTAU MRCC
AT 1720 (UTC)
07 MARCH 2014, AIRCRAFT NAMED MAS 370, MALAYSIA
   FLAG, LOST CONTACT AND CAPABLE [POSSIBLE]
   AIRCRAFT CRASHED
LAST CONTACT IN POSITION 06—56'N, 103—25'E,
   PASSENGERS 239.
VESSELS IN VICINITY REQUESTED TO KEEP A SHARP
   LOOK-OUT AND ASSIST IMMEDIATELY. PLEASE
   REPORT DIRECTLY ANY RELATED INFORMATION TO
   VUNGTAU MRCC
```

The message must have been received by all ships in the area. The Vung Tau Maritime Rescue Coordination Centre was located in nearby Ho Chi Minh City, at the southern tip of Vietnam. Separately, and corroborating the general Mayday call, a Malaysian sailor took a screenshot of the NAVTEXT† on his own ship when the news came up at 12.18 pm. It showed exactly the same message.

---

* EGC messages come from Inmarsat C EGC Safety NET service. They were used for broadcasting maritime safety information (MSI), such as weather forecasts, navigational and meteorological warnings, shore-to-ship distress alerts, SAR coordination information and other safety-related information to all vessels at sea in fixed geographical or pre-determined and coastal areas.

† NAVTEX is an international automated medium-frequency (518 kHz) direct-printing service used for delivery of navigational and meteorological warnings and forecasts, as well as urgent marine safety information to ships.

As early as 8 o'clock on the morning of 8 March, some Chinese and Vietnamese media channels were also reporting an SOS message sent by the plane, seemingly indicating that it did not make a U-turn and instead met its fate within about 90 minutes after the loss of contact. As we saw in Chapter 2 (p. 18), according to information published that morning by *China Times* (a Taiwanese online newspaper with pro-Chinese leanings) and almost simultaneously on China.com (a Chinese news website), the MH370 pilots requested to make an emergency landing. Several versions of this extraordinary piece of information circulated widely on the internet. At the time, Taijing Wu, a Taiwanese friend of mine who had worked for several years at the *China Times*, gave me his translation of these few lines of intriguing text:

> The United States Embassy in China stated that a US Army unit based at U-Tapao in Thailand had picked up a distress signal (SOS) from Flight MH370 at 2.43 am. The pilot was requesting an emergency landing, saying that the plane was about to disintegrate. The US Army forwarded this information to the Malaysian authorities.

But the Taiwanese journalist at the *China Times* to whom the article was attributed refused to indicate the source of his information: a communiqué from the US embassy, a press agency dispatch, a leak from a direct source or something else altogether. He repeatedly told Taijing that it was 'not convenient' to talk about this article; and then, finally, that he 'can't remember anything about it'. His evasive attitude merely reinforced the uncertainty surrounding this piece of news, which could otherwise have been crucial.

For a while, posters to several online forums as well as on Twitter continued to mention the fact that John Kerry, then US Secretary of State, had retweeted this information from his own account. But that tweet, if it ever existed, was quickly deleted. I only found posts and tweets mentioning it, but no retweets or screenshots of the original. I later asked another Chinese colleague, from Xinhua News Agency, to check whether Xinhua had ever dispatched this information. His answer was negative. The news had not been accredited to Xinhua in the first place, and although he had covered the MH370 story for them at the time, first from Vietnam and then from Australia, he could not recall anything about t.

In mid-2016, this same Xinhua journalist got back in contact with me to say that, according to his own research, the message was actually from a fake Weibo (micro-blogging) account under the name of the 'Embassy of United States of America in Beijing'. He had noticed that despite the American flag and the name, it was not from the genuine account of the American embassy as the Chinese characters used for the name were different – 'Embassy of the United States of America' rather than 'American embassy'. I was puzzled. The riddle seemed to have acquired an extra layer of mystery. But I was not convinced by his explanation. There might, after all, have been a slight difference between how the US embassy in China presented its name on its Weibo account and its Twitter account. Furthermore, it was unlikely that a journalist would have made up information like this, with such precise details as the name of a relatively obscure airbase in Thailand, U-Tapao in this instance, and an exact time, 2.43 am. And why would anyone pretend to be the US embassy to leak information related to this disappeared flight, especially in the very early hours of the crisis? Then again, secret services do this sort of thing all the time – sending people up blind alleys with false leads – and my Xinhua colleague himself might possibly have been on a covert mission to discourage me from looking any further into the message. But once again, it might be wise not to dismiss the simpler option. So, just for the sake of the investigation, let's classify this message as genuine and consider for a moment its content and consequences.

Interestingly, it referred to another military base used by the US in the region. Located in southern Thailand, U-Tapao is a Thai air base that was used on an ad hoc basis by the US Army. I must confess that, just like Diego Garcia, I had barely even heard of it until then, despite the fact that it had been at the heart of US operations during the Vietnam War, and was again used by US forces during the Afghanistan and Iraq wars (Thailand's official neutral status notwithstanding). It was also allegedly one of the CIA's 'dark sites', with a runway extending for three kilometres, sufficient for a Boeing 777 to land. If the 2.43 am actually referred to 2.43 local time, it meant that the plane continued to fly for an hour and 24 minutes after its last radio contact with Kuala Lumpur ATC (at 1.19 am). Since we have essentially dismissed the supposed U-turn (based on the lack of convincing radar images and the later results of the less-than-conclusive tests published in the final report), the plane's most logical course would have been to continue more or less in its planned direction.

The message stated that MH370 was 'about to disintegrate' at 2.43 am, with the pilots desperately trying to inform the ATC of an imminent crash landing to hasten the rescue mission. It must have been sent by VHF, and the report that it had been picked up by a 'US Army unit based at U-Tapao' meant that the signal was probably caught by an American military plane stationed in U-Tapao that would have been in the air at the time. The US staffer who posted the news in the first place, on behalf of the embassy, was probably confident that he or she was doing the right thing, following his or her job description. But it was then speedily withdrawn and erased because of its irrevocable consequences. If this message existed and had indeed been sent at 2.43 by MH370, then the die was cast.

For years, I found the possibility that this distress signal actually took place – with the pilot requesting an emergency landing saying that the plane was about to disintegrate – to be quite haunting. Eventually, some proof that MH370 did actually send this message came my way.

It was only in late 2019 that Patricia Thomas, a hardcore and incredibly resourceful MHist with whom I had long established a trusted relationship, sent me a new clue that she had forgotten about but that lent considerable credibility to the 'SOS message'. A pilot from Vietnam Airlines, who was flying in the region of Thua Thien Hue in the northern part of central Vietnam, had actually reported having heard the SOS distress call on the emergency frequency, somewhere to the north of Phu Bai International Airport. His statement was repeated both in a Vietnamese newspaper, the *Southern Daily*, and on Vietnamese TV, but no international news agencies picked it up. In the extracts of this pilot's message that I saw, no time was provided, but it was nevertheless the first tangible proof that MH370 might indeed have sent an emergency message just before crashing.* If this was further proved to be accurate, it would locate the crash in a completely unexplored and uncovered part of the South China Sea.

The Vietnam Airlines pilot's report prompted me to read once again the transcript of the triangular exchanges that took place during the night between the MAS operations centre and the air traffic control centres at Ho Chi Minh City (HCM ATC) and Kuala Lumpur (KL ATC). I could imagine the anxiety and confusion of these air traffic controllers, facing the most grotesque and tragic situation of their life, all chasing a lost Boeing 777 that had suddenly gone dark, with few other means of establishing where it had gone than staring nervously at their screens and calling each other for updates. Their recorded conversations were published in the Appendix of the first interim report.†

To a reader unused to ATC dialogue, their exchanges might seem on the verge of gobbledygook, because of all the grammatical mistakes, the repetitions, the many 'aaa's and equally many 'eer's,

---

* The range of a VHF signal from an aircraft can be calculated with this simple formula: Range in miles = 1.23x square root of the aircraft altitude. So if MH370 was still at 35000 ft its VHF range would be approximately 230 nm.

† *Factual Information: Safety Investigation for MH370*, Annex 13, 8 March 2015.

as well as the '*lah*'s at the end of sentences. Everything was included. One could in fact reasonably wonder whether the transcript had been drawn up to deliberately ridicule the Malaysian and Vietnamese staff involved, and, in doing so, diminish the credibility of these extremely important conversations. But for people familiar with Manglish, and I have had a few years of training in it, the dialogue is very easy to understand.

The situation was nevertheless undoubtedly confusing. Shortly after the loss of radar contact after waypoint BITOD at 1.30 am, the operations centre informed the air traffic controllers in KL: 'reference to the company Malaysian Airlines the aircraft is still flying, is over somewhere over Cambodia [*sic*]'.

So the air traffic controllers on the Malaysian side must have been somewhat reassured to know that their plane, which Vietnam couldn't spot, was nevertheless still flying. They might possibly have been puzzled, however, as to why the plane did not show up on the screens of either the Vietnamese or Cambodian ATCs; but in a way, it was for their counterparts on the other side of the Gulf of Thailand to find out, since the plane was well beyond their reach by this stage. So at 2.04 am, the Malaysian air traffic controllers passed the information on to Ho Chi Minh ATC and suggested they chase it up with the Cambodian ATC.

Thirty minutes later, at 2.33 am, the Malaysian air traffic controller got back to his interlocutor from Malaysia Airlines on duty at the MAS operations centre to let him know that the ATC in Vietnam still had 'negative contact' and 'no radar target' with MH370. He then added: 'But earlier we checked with [you] MAS, I think your side somebody said that the aircraft still flying and you already send signal to the aircraft?' 'Ya,' replied the MAS operation centre, who then confirmed to the KL ATC: 'Aircraft still sending the movement message […] positioning message.' And it provided a location for the plane: N14.90000, E109 15500. This placed MH370 along the coast of Vietnam, close to the seaside city of Da Nang. Therefore, according to these official recordings, the plane was still flying, and if not on its exact flight path, at least in the right direction. But the really shocking revelation came very shortly after.

Once the conversation with MAS operations centre was over, the KL ATC called his counterpart at Ho Chi Minh ATC in Vietnam. It was now precisely 02:37:50. Then, with no warning, as if it were happening in front of his eyes, the air traffic controller in Ho Chi Minh, who had been chasing MH370 for the last hour or so, suddenly told KL ATC: 'The aircraft is landing at xxxx [unintelligible].'* Two seconds later, and as could be expected, KL ATC replies: 'Say again.' Then one second after: 'Say again, say again for Malaysian three seven zero.' And another few seconds later, the KL controller shared the news he had just learnt from the MAS operations centre with Ho Chi Minh: 'Affirm Malaysian Three Seven Zero still flying aircraft keep sending position report to the airline okay to the company okay it last at time one eight three three at time one eight three three aircraft passed position one eer [sic] one four nine zero zero zero zero.' Unfortunately the transcript of that unbelievable conversation stops there.

It was puzzling, to say the least, to find this dialogue in the interim report. It so blatantly countered the official narrative that one wonders how it ended up being left there. According to the official narrative, at that time, the plane was supposed to have been on the western side of Malaysia and about to make its final turn towards nowhere – certainly not on the eastern side of Vietnam, just a few miles from entering Chinese airspace. And this incredible three-way exchange was actually printed in the official interim report! I read these bursts of conversation, again and again, and for a long time I just could not make sense of them. They suddenly seemed not only plausible, but also consistent with the emergency message request for landing that was timed at 2.43 am. Actually,

---

* This exchange is recorded in Appendix 1.18F in the Interim Report issued on 8 March 2015.

the five initial statements from Malaysia Airlines stated very clearly that contact had been lost with the plane at 2.40 am. The last contact time was changed, from 2.40 am to 1.30 am, from the sixth MAS statement onwards.

Could it have been by mistake? In fact, this fascinating information was supposedly denied one hour later. According to the same official report, at 3.30 am, 'MAS Operations Centre called in and spoke to Radar controller, admitting that the information from the "flight tracker21" was based on projection and could not be relied for actual positioning or search (Watch Supervisor logbook entry).' But there were certainly issues with this new information from Malaysia Airlines. First, you couldn't receive a positioning message from a flight tracking system. It made no sense. Also, technically, this supposed conversation (that essentially discredits the previous crucial dialogue between the two ATCs) was said to come from the 'Watch Supervisor logbook', although there was no voice recording. So there was basically no trace of this call. And other entries in the same logbook were not provided either. Why would this key conversation have not been recorded like all the other ones and why were such important supervisor logbook entries not included in the Appendix? So we end up with a stupefying dialogue, recorded and reported in the official report, where a Vietnamese ATC is saying, 'live' to his Malaysian counterpart, that 'the plane is landing'. Yet that record is being dismissed by a later conversation that was not recorded and only referred to in a 'Watch supervisor logbook', which was never produced … Isn't this extraordinarily fishy?

When questions were asked about the fact that MAS operations centre had indicated at some point that the plane was continuing to fly over Cambodia, the world was told that the signal identified and passed on was that of the tracker not that of the plane. Yet that did not make any sense, as there was no way that the MAS Operations centre would receive a positioning signal from MH370 that would require downloading if they were only looking at a tracker set on an automatic mode. Besides, if they were simply looking at an automated signal from a pre-entered route, it would have followed the normal flight plan and not decided to venture into unknown territory. But it seems no one has ever considered this simple scenario of the plane crashing in the northern part of Vietnam, off Da Nang, and close to China.

By the middle of the afternoon of Saturday, 8 March, Vietnam had begun search operations hundreds of miles south of Da Nang. The *CSB 2001* coastguard boat and the *SAR 413* search and rescue boat were called into action, while an An-26 plane took off from Ho Chi Minh City's Tan Son Nhat International Airport. 'They are moving south toward the area where the plane crashed at 1.40 am local time (18:40 GMT Friday),' *Tuoi Tre News* reported in a mid-afternoon bulletin. An additional An-26, six helicopters and a further nine Vietnamese ships were placed on standby. The Vietnamese authorities announced on Saturday that several ships would spend the night 'in the crash area'.

Many media outlets, both local and international, also reported that Vietnamese military planes had spotted oil slicks off the country's coast that could be a sign of the missing Malaysia Airlines passenger jet. 'Two of our aircraft sighted two oil slicks around 15 to 20 kilometres long, running parallel, around 500 metres apart from each other,' Deputy Chief of Staff Lieutenant General Vo Van Tuan told state-run VTV. 'We have sent vessels to the site of the suspected oil spills and they are expected to reach the site tonight. It's very likely that this is the sign of the missing plane.' Vice-Admiral Ngo Van Phat, who was helping to direct the search mission, told AFP later that day: 'I think the two oil slicks are very likely linked to the missing plane. However, we have to check carefully once our rescue boats get access to the area.' He said that the boats were around an hour from the site of the slicks and were expected to search a wide expanse of sea in darkness. On Saturday night, the Singapore-based *Straits Times* tweeted: '#Vietnam spot a column of smoke, oil slicks off its coastline.'

MH370 still had around 40 tonnes of fuel on board when it passed over Vietnamese waters. If the oil slicks were related to the loss of the plane, they would indicate a crash on the sea; if it had exploded mid-flight, the fuel would have evaporated. The next day, *The New York Times* quoted Lai Xuan Thanh, the head of Vietnam's Civil Aviation Administration, as saying that the discovery of the slicks could be the first hint of the plane's location. But air search operations were halted at nightfall due to lack of visibility, although the ships continued with their efforts.

On the morning of Sunday, 9 March, a *Tuoi Tre News* photographer boarded a Vietnamese Air Force An-26 and took a photo of a huge oil slick, which the plane's pilot, Senior Lieutenant Colonel Hoang Van Phong had spotted around 80 kilometres from the supposed crash site. The pilot added that 'the colour of the oil slick has faded and it could disappear in the next couple of days under the influence of the wind.' The Chinese satellite images of the objects that were spotted within a distance of 20 kilometres of each other also dated from the morning of 9 March, but, oddly, the images were only released three days later. They showed three very large objects within 11 miles of each other, sized 13 × 18, 14 × 19 and 24 × 22 metres, 121 miles east-south-east of IGARI. Because China shared the news a relatively long time after the debris was spotted, the two Vietnamese aircraft that were dispatched to the position identified by China and that scanned the area for a few hours saw nothing. This episode was reported on the *Aviation Herald* website, which kept a good chronology of the events: 'China's head of government ordered Chinese ships to the position to "try harder" to find the debris identified by the satellite images.' The head of China's Civil Aviation Authority (CAAC) stated that the Chinese satellite images showed smoke and floating objects, but 'at this time the CAAC cannot confirm these objects are related to MH-370'.

Another clue that pointed to a potential catastrophic event occurring in the South China Sea came from the University of

Science and Technology of China in Hefei, the capital of Anhui province, which announced a possible location for the crash site based on two unusual seismic recordings. These suggested a potential crash close to the last point of contact,* with the time of the event reported by the Chinese as being at 2.55 am on 8 March 2014, just 12 minutes after the mysterious message announcing the disintegration of the cabin. Very oddly, this information from Hefei was promptly discounted by US Geological Survey analysts at the National Earthquake Information Center, who reviewed it and came to a very different conclusion.† The counter-analysis by the American scientists completely dismissed the conclusions drawn from the two unusual recordings,‡ and placed the seismic events not in the Gulf of Thailand but on the west coast of Sumatra.§ One would naturally be forgiven for wondering how often an American scientific institution bothered to 'set the record straight' about the mistaken location of a couple of seismic events. With the help of a Chinese colleague, we asked the university in Hefei whether their American counterparts often commented on their findings. The answer was no, never. Given this response, one really has to wonder why the Americans would take the trouble of trying to discredit this finding of 'two unusual recordings' located close to the last point of contact.

This massive shock that took place so close to the place of MH370 going missing, yet too long (more than an hour) after the actual passage of MH370 near that location, kept my imagination

* http://seis.ustc.edu.cn/News/201403/t20140314_191123.html.

† The National Earthquake Information Center, part of the USGS, is located on the campus of the Colorado School of Mines in Golden, Colorado.

‡ earthquake.usgs.gov/earthquakes/eventpage/usc000nb9b#general.

§ The American report stated: 'The location coincides with a region of regularly occurring seismicity along the Sunda-Java trench. The character of the seismic waveforms also indicates that this event is consistent with a tectonic earthquake of magnitude 2.7.'

ticking over, until I came across a very similar 'unusual seismic event' that was in fact an underwater man-made explosion. In July 2016, the US Geological Survey recorded a 3.7 'rare seismic event' off the coast of Florida, a region just as quiet, tectonically speaking, as the Gulf of Thailand. A few days after the event, it was officially listed as a 'naval test explosion'. According to the website DefenseNews. com, the US Navy conducted the test in order to measure the resilience of a combat ship posted nearby. It is therefore plausible that the two unexplained seismic events that were detected and mentioned by the Chinese scientists were also explosions. Explosions of what, one might reasonably wonder. And in what type of circumstances would something explode at the bottom of the sea?

Well, the standard practice in most armed forces requires that a sunken ship or a crashed aircraft be blown up in order to destroy its unexploded ordnance (UXO) (not to mention ensuring that the enemy doesn't have the opportunity to enjoy the fruits of your technology). An old manual published by the Department of the Army* states explicitly: 'an incident involving crashed aircraft presents an EOD [explosive ordnance disposal] problem of considerable magnitude', so 'the quickest and simplest method for disposal of unexploded ordnance is to destroy it in its original position by demolition; this is the preferred method in all cases where other considerations permit'.

So could a mid-air collision have taken place between two military planes that very night, close to IGARI and BITOD? One plane might have managed to land back in Hat Yai airport (possibly the plane observed flying low and heading north above Kota Bahru), while the other might have crashed nearby ... If the crash had taken place that night near to IGARI, it could also explain the oil slicks spotted in the Gulf of Thailand, as well as the loud noises and the debris on fire falling from the sky, witnessed that night by

* U.S. Department of the Army, *Surface explosive ordnance disposal*, 1961, chapters 7 and 8.

several Malaysian people on the east coast. The explosion, 90 minutes after the crash of a fighter, would have got rid of the hull and potential UXO. This accident could have been collateral damage during the preparation for the Cope Tiger exercises, which were just about to start. But if such a controlled explosion took place, just a few miles away from the last radar contact of MH370 and less than two hours after the plane passed IGARI and BITOD, I find it hard to discount it as a pure coincidence.

Besides, if a plane had indeed crashed and was later destroyed by explosion where the Chinese university observed the explosion at 2.55, it would explain the assertiveness of the Vietnamese Navy when it declared in the morning of 8 March that 'the plane crashed at 01:40, 153 miles [283 kilometres] off Tho Chu Island'. They may just have been talking about *a* plane, not MH370. My next question for the military is therefore: can a disposal operation be planned and executed in one hour and fifteen minutes?

The potential scenario of a military plane crash in the Gulf of Thailand reminded me that Cyndi Hendry (the American MHist who worked relentlessly on the Tomnod images) was pretty adamant she had spotted the tail of a DC-10 to the south of Vietnam ... So many coincidences, yet even more loose ends.

On the afternoon of Sunday 9 March, events came thick and fast. At 2.40 pm, a Singaporean plane, which for the moment was the only plane other than the Vietnamese An-26 that was flying over the area, informed the Vietnamese authorities that it had spotted suspicious debris 100 kilometres south-east of Tho Chu island, and therefore still within the initial suspected crash area.

At 4.30 pm, Vietnam sent one of its coastguard's DHC-6 Twin Otter aircraft to investigate around position N8.792 E103.374, about 31 miles (57 kilometres) south-south-west of Tho Chu. Other press reports stated that late on Sunday afternoon, a Vietnamese DHC-6 seaplane with reporters on board had detected a piece of the plane's tail, as well as a rectangular piece of composite material with a rectangular opening with rounded corners in its centre.* From the photos they took, it looked like an aircraft door, but they couldn't be certain. Vietnam's Ministry of Information and Communication said in a post on its website that the fragments were believed to be a composite inner door and a piece of the tail. But it was getting dark. A ship registered as *KN 774* was sent to investigate on site.

The next day, Monday, 10 March, a commercial Cathay Pacific airliner on its way to Hong Kong reported a 'large amount of metal debris' to the south-east of the Vietnamese coast. This is how *Aviation Herald* website reported it:

Hong Kong's Air Traffic Control Centre reported on Mar 10th 2014 around 17:30L (09:30Z) that an airliner en route on airway L642 reported via HF radio that they saw a large field of debris at position N9.72 E107.42 about 80nm southeast of Ho Chi Minh city, about 50nm off the south-eastern coast of Vietnam in the South China Sea and about 281nm northeast of the last known radar position. A Thai cargo ship in the area was asked for assistance and has set course to the area but did not find anything unusual so far. A second vessel requested for assistance did find some debris but no details were provided. Following this finding Vietnam's Maritime Search and Rescue Services (MRCC) dispatched a ship to the debris field.

The Bloomberg news agency also reported that 'a vessel in the area confirmed material was floating in the ocean about 92 kilometres off the southeast coast of Vietnam in the South China Sea'.

Interestingly, while in the press room in Kuala Lumpur we heard talk of a multinational and tightly packed flotilla of dozens of ships and aircraft scouring the Gulf of Thailand, encouraging the world's media to describe a massive search, although a closer look at the

* 'Vietnam Searchers Report Spotting Plane Debris', *The Wall Street Journal*, 9 March 2014.

operation portrayed a rather lean intervention. A Vietnamese press report stated, 'At the request of China and the United States, Vietnam has authorised three Chinese ships and one US ship to enter its territorial waters to help with the search effort', but it did not say where in Vietnam, which meant that no one really knew where the effort was being made, as Vietnam has close to 3,500 kilometres of coastline. Yet this seemed to indicate that at least some of the search may have been taking place close to the shore of Vietnam or of a Vietnamese island, otherwise such permission would not have been necessary.*

Did this mean that all the other naval ships requisitioned to assist with the initial search effort in the South China Sea were kept at bay by the Vietnamese authorities, with plenty of ships ready on standby, but only a few permitted to go into the identified crash site area? Could this be the reason for the considerable frustration that was so apparent in the crisis operations centre in Kuala Lumpur? It would certainly go some way towards explaining the complaints about the lack of coordination in that initial search operation.

On the issue of 'which ship, where?', I noticed on some forums immediately after the disappearance that while the Malaysian authorities were talking about the deployment of a large number of ships in the South China Sea, some observers were wondering why the usual ship-tracking devices were showing an almost empty sea in the targeted area. On Reddit, one watcher wrote: 'Why those Maritime Traffic sites [like marinetraffic.com or vessefinder.com] do not show any ships there?' Would this indicate that ships were actually not at sea searching for MH370 as assumed or that the monitoring devices (VHF, radar, etc.) that these sites used were being jammed in such a way that the ships in the area were not showing?

---

* Vietnam claims 12 miles (22 kilometres) as the limit of its territorial waters, as well as an additional 12 miles as a contiguous customs and security zone. Vietnamese waters may therefore be counted as 24 miles from shore.

I also tried to check which American forces were in the vicinity of the potential crash area. Because of the recent as well as the forthcoming military exercises (Cobra Gold and Cope Tiger), because the plane was lost after a Singaporean waypoint (IGARI), because of the massive presence of the Seventh Fleet in the region, and simply because the US watch and listen to everything, it seemed relevant to know which US ship was located where, doing what, on 8 March.

Surprisingly, on the official website of the US Pacific Command (PaCom), generally not known for holding back, not a single statement had been left between 10 February and 7 April 2014 – that is, for a month on either side of MH370's disappearance, anything that could offer up a clue as to 'which ship, where?' had been erased. By comparison, in March 2015, PaCom issued 121 media releases in just one month. There had never previously been such a blank in the PaCom archives, as far back as I could check, nor since. What happened to justify such a blackout related to the activity of the Seventh Fleet before, during and after the loss of MH370? Was it undesirable for some US ships to be traceable during that time?

Some US ships were just randomly mentioned here or there in various articles: the USS *Pinckney* (DDG91), the USS *Kidd* (DDG-100), the USS *Denver* and the USS *Fort Worth*. Both the USS *Pinckney* and USS *Kidd* were *Arleigh Burke*-class Aegis guided-missile destroyers. Aegis is a sophisticated combat system that combines state of the art computer and radar technology to track and guide weapons to destroy enemy targets. When she was launched in 2004, USS *Pinckney* was described by the officiating Rear Admiral Charles Hamilton II as 'the 41st ship in the long, proud line of the *Arleigh Burke* class, and the most technologically advanced warship ever put to sea'. She must have been in the vicinity, as she joined the search in a matter of hours. At 9.30 pm on 8 March, the US Seventh Fleet (@US7thFleet) tweeted: 'USS Pinckney should be within helo [helicopter] range to launch its first search in about 2 hours.'* Considering the range of the Seahawk helicopters (450 miles, including time on site and return) and the maximum speed of the ship (around 30 knots), this would place the USS *Pinckney* about 200 miles (370 kilometres) from the Gulf of Thailand.

One of the four original statements relating to US Navy involvement in the MH370 search is titled 'US P-3 and USS Pinckney helicopter over Malaysian airlines search site' and comments:

A Navy P-3C Orion and an MH-60R helicopter launched from USS Pinckney (DDG 91) are searching over the last known communication and radar positions of Malaysia Airlines MH370, March 9, 2014. There has been no report of debris sighted at this time. The P-3 took off from Okinawa and arrived on station early afternoon March 9, with approximately three hours of fuel remaining for searching the site. Pinckney was diverted from a training mission in the South China Sea to search for signs of the missing aircraft. Its MH-60R Seahawk helicopters are designed for search and rescue, as well as anti-submarine warfare, anti-surface warfare, surveillance, communications relay, naval gunfire support and logistics support. USNS John Ericsson (T-AO-194) is en route to the scene to provide underway fuel and logistics replenishment, ensuring Pinckney and its helicopters can maximize their time on station.†

The fact that the Seventh Fleet sent a plane from Japan to contribute to the search was probably a good soundbite. But as we have seen from the Thailand radar data, the USAF already had a very wide range of planes available in the area. Why call up a P-3 Orion from Japan when you have, already deployed on site, dozens of planes to choose from, including several DC-10s and C-17s, at

* twitter.com/US7thFleet/status/442532969329082368.

† www.public.navy.mil/surfor/ddg91/Pages/USP3andUSSPinckneyhelicopter overMalaysianAirlinessearchsite.aspx.

least one C-130 (Hercules), as well as a C-146A, a refuelling aircraft in the region and many more military aircraft? Was the US reluctant to say publicly they were already there, and in force?

Among the many thousands of threads on the various military and aviation forums and blogs about MH370, a man whose online name is 'Ron Black' commented on his blog about the 'strange behaviour' of USS *Pinckney* and the apparent communication lockdown imposed on those on board the ship. Why would the *Pinckney*'s crew be prohibited from talking to their families or friends back home during that crucial time? I got in contact with the man behind 'Ron Black', a former Israeli soldier who worked in very hi-tech programmes both in his country and abroad. On 9 March, the commanding officer of USS *Pinckney* posted this message on the Facebook account of the ship:

Dear USS Pinckney Families and Friends,

By now many of you will be aware of USS Pinckney's assignment to contribute to the Malaysian Airlines Flight 370 search and rescue operations. For operational reasons we have minimized communications to support PINCKNEY's tasking. As you have come to expect, your PINCKNEY Sailors are focused and performing the tasks in which they have prepared for many years. While the outcomes are unknown at this stage, official Defense media will provide updates as more information becomes known. It is with a heavy heart that we respond to such an event. We thank you for your ongoing support.

Yours sincerely
Frank E. Okata
Commander, USN
Commanding Officer
USS Pinckney (DDG-91)
'Proud to Serve'

The next day, the same officer posted:

Dear USS Pinckney Families and Friends,

First, thank-you for the sincere messages of support; they are heart warming and well received by all personnel onboard. USS Pinckney's contribution to the multi-national search and rescue effort to locate Malaysian Airlines Flight 370 continues. Under the direction of Commander Seventh Fleet and Commander Destroyer Squadron Fifteen, USS Pinckney is searching an area within the Gulf of Thailand in the vicinity of where the aircraft was last located.

The entire crew of Pinckney is *working as an extremely tight team* focused on assisting Malaysian authorities piece together *this tragedy*. I *am incredibly proud* of the performance and commitment of everybody onboard Pinckney and I know from the messages we are receiving, that you are too [all italics mine].

On behalf of the crew I would like you all to know that our family and friends are constantly in our thoughts.[...]

Yours sincerely
Frank E. Okata
Commander, USN
Commanding Officer
USS Pinckney (DDG-91)

I did not really understand why the 'performance and commitment of everybody onboard' could make him so 'incredibly proud'. I would have thought that a commanding officer would feel proud about his men when they had been working really hard on a very difficult or demanding mission. At that point, the ship was supposed to be cruising around the Gulf of Thailand, not doing much more than trying to spot a field of debris. The use of the word 'tragedy' also seemed to indicate that Commander Okata already knew the fate of the plane while the rest of the world was still essentially hoping.

In a subsequent message, the following strongly worded reminder that all talk about the activities and the whereabouts of the USS Pinckney must stop was posted:

VERY IMPORTANT message to our PINCKNEY family and friends:

OPERATIONAL SECURITY (OPSEC) is imperative, as it ensures the safety of our operations and our personnel. Disclosing sensitive information could jeopardize the crew's safety.

When it comes to conversations with friends or posts on social media, please refrain from discussing information that could be detrimental to our mission.

Some of you may be aware of our schedule, location, and even what your PINCKNEY sailor does onboard, but information regarding these topics should NOT be shared. So please keep information such as deployment count-downs, port visits, and travel plans off of social media.

OPSEC is just as important among all of you as it is among the crew and we need your help to enforce it. Thank you for your continued support. We look forward to seeing you all!

Chief Edmands
USS PINCKNEY (DDG-91)
OPSEC Representative

Once again, one might well wonder what the location and the activity of the USS *Pinckney* sailors could well be that it should 'NOT [*sic*] be shared'.

* * *

With hindsight, several journalists who covered the search efforts out of Phu Quoc Island admitted that their role was 'more for optics than anything else'. They didn't have much to do there, with very limited access to any sources and little or no information to share on a daily basis. Only a 'happy few' were taken out on one of the Vietnamese search missions. In her report filed from a Vietnamese helicopter, BBC journalist Alice Budisatrijo mentioned at the time how ill-equipped the Vietnamese army were. Their eyes and a pair of binoculars were basically it. There were almost no pictures of the supposed international flotilla criss-crossing the sea in the vicinity of the last contact. 'The military exercise [around the last point of contact] has been grossly overstated by the media,' said Larry Bernier, a long-time American resident in Vietnam. This man, who ran a very successful diving centre for many years on an island off the southern tip of the country, told me, 'People think you are alone out there. But you should see what the sea looks like some nights. It is better lit than a city!'

In my attempt to find witnesses of this supposed widescale search operation, I went back to South Vietnam in 2018. I wanted to check with fishermen if they remembered that night in March 2014 and the massive search that followed. Along the Giang Thanh river on the west coast of South Vietnam on the Gulf of Thailand side, the colourful hulls of large fishing boats were tightly lined up along the bank, while massive ice blocks were being loaded into their holds before the ships cast off for trips that would last months. I found fishermen Dong Le and Bui Dinh Bac sitting on their idling motorbikes, chatting with friends. They recalled that morning quite well. They were at sea between the islands of Phu Quoc and Tho Chu when the call came through on the radio that all fishing vessels in the vicinity should be on the lookout for a crashed plane. They did not change their fishing routine and just hoped to come across something, because, strange as it might sound, it was considered a good omen to find corpses at sea. But none of them saw anything in their fishing patch. And apart from that initial radio call, they never came across anything relating to a search: no military ships, no planes or helicopters combing the area, nothing. I found all of this very odd and did not know what to make of it. Of course, the sea is huge, I told myself, and on the water you may not see another boat just a few miles away …

So, the only way to reconcile all of this was to conclude that either there was no such thing as an international large-scale search, or the real search that included those heroic US sailors as well as the Chinese ships was taking place elsewhere, and no members of the media witnessed it.

It was all the more puzzling that in the hours following the loss of MH370, what looked like a lot of potential debris – or at least a flurry of leads suggesting that there might be extensive debris fields – was very rapidly rejected by the US embassy in Vietnam, as well as both the Malaysian and the Vietnamese authorities. At 6 pm on Sunday, the US search and rescue forces, who had been completely silent up to that point about their involvement in the search, declared that the floating object spotted by the Singaporean plane was 'in no way related to MH370'. Major Thang 'Jacky' Ly, Chief of the Office of Defense Cooperation at the US embassy, stated categorically that this object was 'insignificant'. The case was closed before ever being opened.

The suspected life raft bobbing around in the Gulf of Thailand had become the lid of a large box; according to other media reports, 'an object that resembled a grey life raft, found 140 kilometres southwest of Vietnam's Tho Chu island, turned out to be a moss-covered cable, according to the aviation search and rescue coordination centre in Hanoi'. What had initially been described as an aircraft tail floating in the Gulf of Thailand ended up being 'logs tied together'. I struggled to understand how logs tied together could bear any resemblance to a piece of white fuselage, but that's what a Malaysian official said, and his account was confidently repeated by the media covering the story. And the Chinese satellite images of large debris? As we have seen, they had been released 'by mistake', according to Minister Hishammuddin Hussein. In any case, this slick soon became, according to certain articles, a coral reef – a coral reef floating along with the current. And if it was not a reef, it was marine fuel, according to other information.* In either case, any notion that it was fuel from MH370 was quickly dispelled. As for the key information that the signal from MH370's ELT distress beacon had been picked up at the same spot, it disappeared and is no longer available online. Last, the visual sightings reported by the local press on the Malaysian east coast have by and large been ignored.

I briefly mentioned in Chapter 2 the eyewitness account of Michael J. McKay, the 57-year-old New Zealand oil rigger who claimed categorically to have seen a plane on fire in the sky due west of his location when he went outside in the middle of the night 'and wandered around to an area at the back [of the oil rig] as usual for a cigarette and a coffee'. I never once doubted that this capable New Zealander with his considerable experience on oil rigs saw precisely what he described, as his profile and background made him a credible witness. When I started studying the South China Sea scenario, I had a second look at the very detailed and professionally drafted message he wrote at the time. The original message had been shown during an interview that a Vietnamese official gave in the ATC room of Phu Quoc Airport. A colleague took a picture of it and later shared it with me. It read:

Gentlemen, I believe I saw the Malaysian Airlines plane come down. The timing is right. [...] I am on the oil rig Songa Mercur, off Vung Tau† [he gave the exact coordinates of his 'surface location']. I observed (the plane?) [sic] burning at high altitude and on a compass bearing of 265 to 275 from our surface

---

* According to the spokesman for the Chemicals Department of the Malaysian Maritime Enforcement Agency (MMEA).

† Vung Tau is a city at the southern tip of Vietnam.

location. While I observed the burning (plane), it appeared to be in ONE piece [*sic*]. [...] From when I saw the burning (plane) until the flames went out (still at high altitude) was 10–15 seconds. There was no lateral movement, so it was either coming toward our location, stationary (falling) or going away from our location. [...] The general position of the observation was perpendicular/southwest of the normal flight paths (we see the con-trails everyday) and at a lower altitude than the normal flight paths. Or on the compass bearing 265–275 intersecting the normal flight paths and at normal altitude but further away.

He signed off with 'Good luck', his full name Michael Jerome McKay, and his passport number. The only missing detail in McKay's message was a precise time; he only said, 'The timing is right.'

His testimony was, however, dismissed by an MHist who calculated that from where McKay was on the oil rig, he could not possibly have seen MH370 at IGARI or BITOD. It's a strong point, suggesting that whatever Mike McKay saw on fire that night, whether it was MH370 or something else, it was closer to his oil rig than IGARI.

Whether or not what this man saw was indeed related to MH370, his report seemed to have enormous implications for what happened on that night in that area; whatever he saw required an explanation and should have been thoroughly investigated at the time. If what McKay described was actually MH370 or MH370-related, then the whole notion of a quiet and incognito U-turn westbound becomes untenable. But instead of being further interviewed by both the authorities and the media, this man was fired from his job and sent back to New Zealand *sine die*, as if his statement were of the utmost embarrassment. Why was the voice of this no-nonsense man hushed up with such indecent haste?

A year later, in the only interview he gave,* McKay repeated what he saw: 'a sudden glow of fire above the horizon, which caught my immediate attention'. It was much lower in the sky and outside the usual route of the planes that he saw every day. He told the journalist who met him in his home in Auckland that he first informed the Vietnamese and Malaysian authorities of the strange thing he had seen, then his employers. Soon after, he was fired for 'personal use of a professional computer'.

At the time of the event, the BBC had located the head office of McKay's company in Ho Chi Minh City and sent a reporter to talk to his colleagues. 'We are under strict instructions not to talk about this incident,' she was told. By a remarkable stroke of luck, another colleague bumped into Mike McKay himself at the airport in Ho Chi Minh City. He was actually leaving Vietnam and seemed abnormally stressed out. So much so, that when she – a petite and very friendly woman – just went up to him to say hello, hoping for a casual chat, he called security in a rather frantic manner. 'It was bizarre,' the reporter recalled. But she did not insist, and thought little of the incident at the time. 'Najib Razak had just announced that the plane had done a U-turn and continued to fly. The story in the South China Sea was over. Everyone was going home,' she told me.

In March 2019, I had another go at finding Mike McKay while I was on assignment in New Zealand for *Le Monde* to cover the Christchurch mosque shootings. I asked my old friend and colleague from my years in Auckland, New Zealander Mike Field, a former AFP bureau chief and Fairfax reporter, if he could help me out. 'The only registration you can't escape in New Zealand are the electoral rolls,' he told me. 'And the only way to check them out is by going in person to a public library and asking for the books.'

---

* www.dailymail.co.uk/news/article-2951991/Search-MH370-taking-place-thousands-miles-away-wrong-direction-insists-oil-rig-worker-notoriously-fired-reporting-believed-saw-jet-fire.html#ixzz3woqWyACu.

Sure enough, when Mike went to the library he found the name and the address of Michael Jerome McKay in a seaside neighbourhood called Red Beach, north of Auckland. We had briefly discussed how he should approach the man should he actually meet him. But as it turned out, there was no time for even the most basic plan to be put into action.

Mike found no one at home the first time, but on his second visit to Red Beach, in late 2019, there was 'a red ute' (an antipodean term for a coupé utility) parked in front of the garage at the top of the short but steep driveway leading to the house. Mike parked in the street and started to walk towards the house. 'The mail box was stuffed full and had not been cleared,' he noticed. Before he could reach the front door, he was met halfway up the driveway by someone who asked him what was he looking for. The two men were roughly the same medium build. 'His clothing style is about as average as mine. He must dress at Wal-Mart like me,' Mike told me wryly, when he described the very brief encounter between the two Mikes. The moment my friend Mike mentioned that he was looking for Mike McKay, he was told to 'please leave' in the most un-Kiwi manner my friend had ever encountered in decades of reporting in New Zealand. Surprised, to say the least, Mike had no choice but to go back to his car. While sitting at the wheel, slightly unnerved by what had just happened, he started reviewing the few pictures he had taken before this peculiar meeting. Just then, a nondescript white car drove past him to the dead end at the bottom of the street, made a U-turn and parked right behind him. The car's driver stayed inside, just watching Mike. When Mike eventually decided to leave, the white car escorted him back, all the way to the main road. 'The whole thing was rather spooky,' Mike told me on the phone shortly after.

The bottom line was that more than five years after Michael J. McKay wrote his email about MH370, was fired from his job and left Vietnam under enormous stress, it was still impossible to talk to him. It really looked as if this man was either under surveillance or under protection – or both. Another thing seemed clear. He had to stay well clear of reporters. Actually, over the years prior to this episode, he never replied to any of my messages, but in a very short email sent to a colleague, he implied he might just have been mistaken on that night in March 2014. If the fire in the sky that had been seen and described by the 57-year-old New Zealander working on an oil rig right at the time of the loss of contact was not MH370, then what was it? The South China Sea is not known for fiery UFOs crossing its night sky.

Another important voice that had gone oddly quiet was that of the highly respected Sir Tim Clark, the President of Emirates Airline. Emirates runs the largest fleet of Boeing 777s in the world,* and its chief was clearly not impressed with the 'disappearance' narrative. He had initially declared that 'he would not be silenced' on the matter.† 'We seem to have allowed MH370 to go into this black hole of "it could be one of aviation's great mysteries". It can't be left like that, never. I'm totally dissatisfied with what has been coming out of all of this. I will continue to ask the questions and will make a nuisance of myself, when others would like to bury it. We have an obligation not to brush this under the carpet,' he added.

I submitted three requests to meet Clark to follow up on his vigorous initial statements. I even offered to travel to Dubai, or to meet him wherever he might be in order to overcome any logistical issues. But in December 2015, a major codeshare deal was agreed between Emirates and MAS,‡ and his communications adviser let

---

* In 2020, Emirates's fleet includes 155 Boeing-777s, plus another 126 pending delivery.

† In October 2014, Clark lashed out in a long interview with German journalist Andreas Spaeth later published on 22 November 2014 in the *Sydney Morning Herald*: www.smh.com.au/world/full-transcript-emirates-chief-sir-tim-clark-on-mh17-and-mh370-20141121-11rc70.html.

‡ According to the deal, all MAS flights in and out of Europe except London are managed by Emirates.

it be known that Clark 'had nothing to add to what he previously said on that matter'. Yet, Clark has never said that he was now satisfied with this or that explanation, and he seemed so sincere right at the start of the whole affair. For a long time I pondered whether he had been somehow convinced that it was in the best general interest that the truth not be revealed, or whether he had even been forcefully silenced. According to an Australian diplomatic source in the Middle East, it was actually the ATSB, using – or rather, abusing – its leverage as regulator for one of Emirates' major destinations, who asked him to stop commenting about MH370. Apparently, Clark had no choice other than to comply, but he was so put out that he insisted on registering his annoyance with the Australian ambassador in Abu Dhabi.

Christian Courcelles is a Canadian citizen in his mid-50s who worked for many years in the aviation industry, initially as an electrical technician with Bombardier and then with the Royal Canadian Air Force. He contacted me very early on with his story, but at first I did not give him much time. At the beginning of the investigation, as we've seen, the plane was everywhere: in the Maldives, Pakistan, Diego Garcia, the Indian Ocean, even Kazakhstan and Somalia. As I progressed with my research and became increasingly drawn to the South China Sea option, I had a second look at his forceful and rather ground-breaking statement. We managed to meet in Bangkok in 2018, in the bungalow of my friend and colleague Bruno Philip, the South East Asia correspondent for *Le Monde*. The story he told us then was exactly the same as he had told me during a recorded Skype conversation three years earlier.

On the night of 8 March 2014, the day of the loss of the plane, Courcelles was double-screening in his flat in Bangkok, watching TV at the same time as chatting about the MH370 mystery on the Voyage Forum, a travellers' website based in Canada of which he had long been a member. He was zapping through the channels when he stumbled across photos on a Vietnamese channel that have haunted him ever since. The short report featured about five images that he was adamant were of MH370 debris, then some film of a search and rescue plane taking off. According to Courcelles:

> The first thing I saw was the front undercarriage. It was half submerged, just lying on the beach. I have enough experience to know exactly what I was looking at. Then I saw the vertical stabiliser with the Malaysia Airlines logo on it being pulled up from the surface. I also saw two people stepping onshore holding one of the black boxes that was in some kind of a see-through casing full of water.

Both Bruno and I thought the description of a black box being carried in a plastic container full of water was a bit dodgy, so we challenged him on this. 'I can only tell you exactly what I saw. It's not for me to explain it,' he replied.

I asked veteran wreck hunter Paul-Henri Nargeolet about this detail a few weeks later. To my great surprise, he told me that there was nothing in the slightest bit odd about it. 'It's exactly how we collect the black boxes from the sea. They have to be kept in water. It's standard procedure,' he said. The box is called an 'aquarium' in the pros' jargon and is supposed to be sealed once it contains the black box of a recovered plane. According to Courcelles's description, as well as the black box, debris was also being unloaded from a large fishing boat, not a military ship, and there was more debris just floating around. One apparently high-ranking Vietnamese army official was watching the operation. The water was crystal clear and you could see rays of sunlight shining through it. 'I was so stunned when I saw these images that before posting about it, I checked online if another MAS flight had ever crashed in the ocean. I then assumed it could only be MH370.'

But after he posted the words 'They found it' on the travelers' forum, he became the laughing stock of this small online community. 'I kept watching, hoping they would show these images again,' he said. But they never did. He then tried to find any information pointing to a ditching in the South China Sea. He found solace in some pieces of information that to him were consistent with a ditching scenario. 'What other explanation is there to the two parallel oil slicks that were initially spotted? Getting rid of your fuel is what you do when you have to do an emergency ditching.' He also mentioned what Michael McKay had seen from his oil rig. He said he would happily submit to a lie detector test if this would help anyone believe him, but for now he could only swear on the life of his children that he had seen what he saw.

When we met for a second time, in late May 2018 in Bangkok, he was as defiant as ever. He insisted that in my reporting I use his real name, as he was prepared to be confronted and challenged. 'I know for sure what I saw. What has happened is criminal. Truth will come out one day. It can't be otherwise,' he added, 'for me but mostly for the families.' Endlessly dwelling on the fleeting images he saw, he remained convinced that there was a massive clean-up operation after the ditching and that the Malaysian authorities covered up the whole mess with the complicity of Vietnam. I tried to get access to the archives of the two Vietnamese channels that are aired in Thailand, but Vietnam was about as forthcoming as a lost black box when it came to sharing information and I did not get anywhere with that attempt. Even if the channel showed this report only once, and even if the pictures and film showing large pieces of debris from MH370 have been destroyed, Christian Courcelles can't be the only one to have seen the images.

Needless to say, if accurate, his testimony is crucial. It means that the plane crashed in Vietnamese waters, close to shore. And that a clean-up operation started on the spot.

After our meetings in Bangkok, he was disappointed that I did not immediately file a story about the whole affair. I told him that, as much as I believed he was sincere, without further supporting evidence, he risked being ignored, at best, and being ridiculed by the MHist community, at worst. I reminded him how quickly –

very quickly, indeed – anything pointing towards a crash in the South China Sea had been discounted, dismissed, refuted and buried by the most influential groups of MHists online and, more importantly, by all governments affected by the crisis, however (apparently) marginally. I promised I would try to find more evidence that would lend credibility to his testimony. Which I believe we have done by now.

Most pieces of evidences suggesting a crash in the South China Sea have been ignored, dismissed, denied or just erased.

In the light of so many hints and clues to support some kind of simple South China Sea scenario, the lack of any obvious corroborative evidence to sustain the official narrative (either because it is being withheld or because there is none) is all the more striking. Compare the cluster of intriguing, telling and highly problematic and unexplained facts and observations that we have just explored relating to an accident of sorts in the South China Sea, with the fact that more than 5,000 kilometres away in the Indian Ocean, where they had been officially looking for the plane until January 2017, no one saw anything whatsoever. Between daybreak – around 6 am that day – and the time the plane crashed, c.19 am according to the Inmarsat pings, no sailor, fisherman or crew member, on a rig, a cargo vessel or any other ship saw a plane flying strangely towards the Antarctic or falling into the ocean after a spectacular nosedive or controlled ditching. For almost two and a half hours of daylight, not a single witness saw this rogue plane flying in a completely unusual direction and eventually crashing into the sea. And then, once MH370 supposedly crashed there, the largest ever search operation undertake at sea – one that lasted for weeks – failed to find a shred of evidence, despite deploying more than a hundred ships and dozens of aircraft from 24 countries – all manned by thousands of the best professionals. And after the official underwater search failed to locate the slightest trace of MH370 in that part of the globe, the new campaign, with the dramatically augmented means of Ocean Infinity, also returned empty-handed. Is this *incredible*, as we have heard ad nauseam, or is it simply *not credible*?

Will global public opinion rouse itself at some point and realise it is entitled to demand a plausible explanation of what happened to Flight MH370? Or, distracted by other mysteries and hypnotised by other new catastrophes, will it prefer to slip into its default comfort zone and forget: forget 239 people from 14 different countries who innocently boarded a jetliner on the night of 7 to 8 March 2014; forget their friends and family who are still waiting for answers; forget the inconsistencies in the official version that was never based on anything provable; forget the insult that this episode represents not just to the victims' families, but to all who board a plane confident that they will land at some stage, to us all if we continue to pretend to believe that this plane 'disappeared mysteriously' despite no tangible evidence to support the official version imposed on us. If public opinion does not wake up, and if no one who knows has the courage to say what really happened on the night of 7 to 8 March 2014, this is how I imagine the event will be described in the civil aviation history books of the future:

Flight MH370: Kuala Lumpur–Beijing, 8 March 2014

> **Description:** Deliberate act to hijack an aircraft and change its course towards the southern Indian Ocean
> **Figures:** 239 civilians, 1 Boeing 777-200ER and 10 tonnes of cargo declared missing
> **Motive:** Unknown
> **Precise circumstances:** Unknown
> **Crash site:** Unknown
> **Person(s) responsible:** Unknown
> **Claims of responsibility:** None
> **Witnesses:** None
> **Proof to date:** None

Debris: None for 16 months. Right flaperon found in
Réunion in July 2015. Two other parts later found in
Mauritius and Pemba Island (Tanzania)

Search for proof: 100,000 square kilometres of seabed in the
southern Indian Ocean

Search cost: A\$200 million

Search results: None

Comment(s): Generally considered the 'greatest mystery in
the history of civil aviation'

Epilogue

The disappearing act

One night, with my fatigue and frustration ever increasing from this seemingly never-ending endeavour, I did a silly internet search about the craft of making things disappear. From the *Manual for the Beginner Magician* to *The Secrets of David Copperfield*, all methods had one tactic in common: at the time of the disappearance you need to distract the audience's attention with a noise, a hand movement, a spotlight – something. The key to a successful disappearance is diversion: grab the audience's attention and make them look elsewhere while you execute your sleight of hand. If MH370's 'disappearance' is indeed a sleight of hand on a massive scale, there has been a fantastic simultaneous effort of diversion, and seemingly more than one.

The world's media has been complicit in the affair, mostly passively, by not questioning enough, and occasionally actively, by spreading unchecked, erroneous or false information. Public opinion is not, and is not supposed to be, that gullible. Everyone knows the MH370 story does not add up. Everyone knows a Boeing 777, possibly the safest plane in the history of civil aviation, does not disappear without a trace in one of the most politically sensitive regions of the planet. So rather than being incredible, the official narrative is simply not credible. Yet the idea that we are being blatantly cheated by the governments we are supposed to trust is so uncomfortable and so problematic that, for the sake of our mental comfort, we choose to look elsewhere and welcome *any* alternative explanation, including one that makes no sense and falsely accuses a decent man of being a mass murderer.

Disinformation is an old game, probably as old as humankind. Over the ages, methods have multiplied in number, diversified in type and improved in quality. In the case of MH370, many different means were deployed at the same time. The advance of truth has been crippled from day one.

First of all, the *simplest* scenario in which the plane crashed shortly after it was last seen on radars by the regional ATCs was quashed and tampered with in record time, despite a cluster of clues and a wealth of corroborating evidence. If, as we just found out, the real last point of radar contact was neither BITOD (at 1.30) nor IGARI (at 1.22) but instead along the north-eastern coast of Vietnam at around 2.40, even the basic scenario of a fatal accident near the so-called last point of radar contact (BITOD or IGARI) was already a diversion of sorts.

According to the first statements by Malaysia Airlines, contact was lost at 2.40 am. It looks like, during the first few hours, Malaysia Airlines had not yet been instructed to adjust its narrative, so the airline company only said what it knew at that moment: that its operations centre was in contact with the plane up until 2.40. This fits sadly but perfectly with the incredible comment by the HCM air traffic controller who, at 2:37:50, said that 'the plane is landing', although the essential transcript of the conversation stops less than a minute after this crucial comment. And it is also consistent with the SOS message, timed at 2.43, indicating that the plane was disintegrating and requesting emergency landing facilities, a message that was heard by a Vietnam Airlines pilot who was flying nearby ... But all of this, and probably much more, was distorted, buried and denied. The initial deception was therefore to say that the plane had been lost from radar at IGARI, when in fact it continued to fly not just beyond BITOD, but possibly for another 80 to 90 minutes. After a few days, the bigger deception – the

Inmarsat pings narrative – was introduced when it became obvious that with currents in the South China Sea pushing debris south anyway, too many observers in this part of the world would complicate the task of a quiet clean-up.

Second, an abundance of alternative scenarios appeared and were widely disseminated: the bad co-pilot, the mad captain, the stolen passports of the young Iranian men, the suspicious cargo of mangosteens, the attempted attack on Diego Garcia, the Freescale pattern, the E/E Bay, the remote-control hijacking, the lithium batteries, a fire in the hold, the organ-harvesting scandal ... Even if any of these many scenarios had been the real one, how could anyone pull it apart amid so much conflicting information?

On top of all this, doubt was abundantly served by an army of experts filling airtime on all the major TV channels with conflicting analysis of unproven conjectures ...

While the White House and the official investigation team asserted that the plane was resting on the floor of the southern Indian Ocean, a retired US general claimed that it was 'in Pakistan', quoting 'reliable sources' on a major television channel, Fox News. At the same time, leaks from the FBI referring to the captain's flight simulator seemed to point the finger towards the Diego Garcia military base where he had supposedly practised landing.

To the south, the north and the west ... The only direction that no one was mentioning any more was the most obvious one, the east and the South China Sea.

Down Under, the big deception was taking place. The Australian authorities tried very hard to keep a small flame of hope alive for as long as possible, under the dubious authority of the Inmarsat pings. Remember the complete absence of credible debris on the ocean surface, the large fuel slick treated as a serious clue by a very senior Australian officer, even though the plane was supposed to have crashed following fuel exhaustion, the sonars being launched completely randomly, then the pings beeping everywhere and CNN breaking its audience records, until the search finally was wrapped up, ending as a bitter failure. To whoever inspected it closely, Australia's search operation struggled to deliver any sense of consistency or credibility from the outset. Of course, all its noise and renewed promises served the message that the plane was some-where 'down there'. It somehow rekindled itself each time a tiny piece of unregistered potential plane debris appeared somewhere on a beach on the east coast of Africa, often thanks to the free services of the eccentric, jobless and polyglot American globetrot-ter self-assigned to the task. It even got a momentary second or third life, with the Ocean Infinity operation in 2018.

In a way, the search led by Australia only ended as a complete failure if one considers that its mission was really to locate the hull of MH370. But if, as we understand it now, its real task was simply to create a diversionary spectacle, it should, on the contrary, be considered a resounding success. And it even provided very useful mapping of the ocean floor to the oil and gas sector, as well as to the fisheries. Once the horde of global media had shifted its atten-tion to the southern hemisphere, Australia managed to keep the show going for more than three years, very far away indeed from the real crash site, where whoever was in charge of cleaning up the traces of the real disaster had all the diversion they needed to execute a smooth disappearing act.

In other words, Australia actually fulfilled its diversion mission with flying colours. I wonder how long it will take before we hear from politicians who are in the know. A senior officer from the Australian Navy explicitly told me that, at his level, no one was fooled by the real purpose of the 'pings operation'.

In a way, Tomnod also played a significant role in confusing and misdirecting some very dedicated people, all eager to help locate the plane or its debris. Eventually, in the middle of the summer of 2019, after nine years of activity, Tomnod announced with a tweet that it had 'retired'. This is how the MH370 operation was wrapped up on Maxar's blog:

More than 1 million square kilometres of satellite images were loaded into Tomnod and volunteers were asked to tag oil slicks, wreckage, rafts and other objects of interest. More than 10 million people contributed, which at the time was more web traffic than Instagram users. More than 14 million tags were placed during 775 million map views, giving first responders key clues on where the plane might be found.*

And then, the key sentence: 'The mystery of MH370's location endures today.'

After my book was published in French in March 2016, I was invited to talk in certain bookshops. One evening after my talk at Parenthèses, the go-to French bookshop in Hong Kong, one man commented:

It's funny. At the time, my best friend, who works with the secret services in the Middle East, called me in Beijing and told me bluntly: 'The Americans are in deep trouble. They have shot down a civilian plane. I wonder how they will extricate themselves from this mess.' So I waited for that news to come out sooner or later. Instead, a few days after the loss of the plane, I heard this extravagant story of the plane lost in the southern Indian Ocean. I was flabbergasted …

His comment was made in front of everyone, including Eric Berti, the French consul general, who shared the audience's stupefaction. Unsurprisingly, I never received any further comments when I tried to follow up on his lead.

In all truth, it was not the first time I'd been the recipient of anecdotal remarks along these lines. Many Italians were convinced

---

* Maxar is the new name for DigitalGlobe, the company that had acquired Tomnod in 2013. See blog.maxar.com/news-events/2019/in-the-blink-of-an-eye-looking-back-on-nine-years-with-tomnod?utm_source=twitter&utm_medium=social.

from day one that MH370 was simply shot down, because they remembered their own tragic case, the 'Ustica massacre' of 1980, when a civilian plane was seemingly downed by an unidentified missile, most probably French, above the Mediterranean (see p. 400). People also recall Korean Airlines Flight 007, mistaken for a US military plane and shot down by a Soviet fighter jet in 1983. More recently, in January 2020, a Ukrainian plane in Tehran crashed two minutes after take-off, when it was hit by two Iranian missiles in a case of mistaken identity. To be fair, a messed-up military operation was first hinted at by Malaysian Transport and Defence Minister Hishammuddin Hussein himself, who, when grilled on Australian TV about Malaysia's inaction, basically implied that in similar circumstances (i.e. a rogue aircraft entering their airspace), 'the Americans' might have shot down the plane. If nothing else, his body language during this key interview was a tell-tale sign of enormous embarrassment. Actually, a nephew of the Captain had shared with me a telling anecdote along the same lines. When I met him in 2018, he had recently attended a wedding where he had randomly caught up with a former class mate who was now quite high ranking in the Ministry of Defense. He asked her candidly if she knew anything about the plane. 'All I can tell you is that they are collateral damage. I am very sorry for your uncle,' was her reply before walking away. This now sounds to me like a blatant admission of a military operation, though she would not specify whose collateral.

Besides, the abnormal vagueness of the cargo manifest, like the 2.5 tonnes of very poorly documented Motorola electronics equipment, coupled with the presence on board of at least four spook-like men, including two seated in business class and two seated right below the Satcom antenna, forces us to be open to the possibility that there might have been 'something or someone' in or on the plane that some other country – let's say the US, just for convenience – did not want to see reach China. This would also echo what a Malaysian source who was trying, early on, to sell me information relating to the fate of the plane had written in an email: 'The explanation to everything that has happened is INSIDE the plane.' 'Inside the plane' to me means either passengers or cargo – or both.

But a Chinese high-flyer, someone familiar with jetting around the world, including between Kuala Lumpur and Beijing, pointed out to me that if the sensitive thing 'inside' the plane had been a person, it would have made much more sense to put him or her on a private jet. In 2014, private aviation was already booming, he said, and customs formalities were exceedingly lax for private passengers in both KLIA and Beijing Capital, the airport in the Chinese capital where the private jet terminal is located. However, if the task was to move a bulky and sensitive cargo, using a standard commercial flight made more sense.

Most military people I talked to over the years of this investigation tended to go for some kind of military explanation, followed by a large-scale cover-up, to explain this mysterious disappearance. But every one of them agreed on one thing: that shooting down a civilian plane could seldom be a Plan A. Though it has happened on some documented cases (including KAL007 and MH17), it is hard to fathom any military force's motives for planning a cold-blooded shooting down of a plane carrying more than two hundred civilians from a wide range of countries. So if MH370 was destroyed in a military action of sort, it was more likely a blunder, a messed-up Plan B or, to quote another colourful US military acronym, a situation that went 'SNAFU' – 'Situation Normal All Fucked Up'. Reflecting on all this, I concluded that what had probably happened was the improvised, and most likely unwanted, consequences of a Plan A that went terribly wrong.

It is risky indeed, if not downright dangerous, for a journalist's credibility to venture into the sketching out of hypothetical scenarios, even based on a cluster of solid clues. Yet ever since I started investigating this case, very much with the next of kin in mind – the few I know, and just as much the thousands of others I don't know – I was constantly asked: 'So, what do you think has happened?' I always preferred to highlight what I thought had not happened.

But having gathered so many bits and pieces, over the years and across the continents, let me for a moment enjoy the freedom granted by the writing of a book, as opposed to an article in a serious newspaper, to now try to create a purely fictional scenario. The most elaborate and far-fetched military narrative I could put together, gathering the many clues and leads collected, points towards a secret service mission that indeed did go SNAFU. All countries involved agreed to cover it up for a variety of reasons, not least the bargaining power that harbouring such a secret would grant them.

Let's say, based on educated hearsay, that there was a spying device, most likely US made and of very high technological value, in the cargo hold of MH370. Something that the Chinese really wanted to get their hands on. It is public knowledge that China, sometimes with the complicity of Russia, has long been trying to acquire highly sensitive US military materials relating to stealth and drone technology, to cloaking planes and things in general. It is possible that whatever its exact provenance and nature, a special cargo in that category arrived in Kuala Lumpur and made its way to KLIA to embark onboard MH370. Early in 2014, US forces were being withdrawn in volume from Afghanistan, with tonnes of equipment being shipped and flown out. Once in Malaysia's capital under Chinese patronage, the safest way to send the 'stuff' to Beijing was to place it covertly not only on board a civilian plane, but on Malaysia Airlines, the national carrier. MH370 was ideal for such a mission: a direct night flight that was already used on a daily basis for trafficking tonnes of illicit goods under the romantic tag of year-round 'fresh mangosteens', which in all likelihood refers to anything but.

When the US grasped that their precious cargo had been stolen and would sooner or later be on its way to Beijing, astutely protected under the shield of a civilian plane, they saw red. They were unable to launch a discreet operation in Kuala Lumpur, so had no other alternative than to mount an airborne cargo confiscation. Plan A was developed: intercept the plane, make it land in a prepared airport nearby, promptly confiscate the problematic cargo with the support of ground teams and swiftly send the plane back on its route to Beijing.

With all the military presence in the region that had been dispatched to participate in the Cope Tiger tripartite air defence operation, Plan A could have been a perfect real-life war game. The precise location in the sky at which the operation was planned to commence makes perfect sense. Waypoint IGARI is controlled by Singapore (a loyal military partner to the US) and ideally located where the Malaysian air traffic controllers do their handover to their Vietnamese counterparts and vice versa. Had Plan A gone well, MH370 would have arrived in Beijing with a one- to two-hour delay. Any technical or medical excuse, like a business-class passenger's heart attack, would have easily covered the unplanned stopover in the darkest hours of the night when most passengers would be asleep, or trying hard to find some sleep during this red-eye flight. Furthermore, plane delays in China are a daily occurrence. Plan A would therefore have been a non-event. China would have been taught a stern lesson not to steal technology that was not theirs, and the secret mission would have been accomplished with a happy and well-executed ending for the orchestrators.

But Plan A did not go as planned.

The first step was to divert the plane as it changed air zones and blank its communications. So as soon as MH370 passed IGARI, two Awacs planes sandwiched MH370 and completely blocked its magnetic field and all its communications, effectively cloaking it and rendering it invisible. While the Awacs planes were shadowing MH370, most likely from above and below, the interception and diversion operation took place.

Ghyslain Wattrelos, the French senior executive with Lafarge in Beijing, whose wife was on board with two of their children, had written in his book that US Awacs played a role in the MH370 operation. 'There were two U.S. Awacs on site. The Americans know what happened,' his intelligence contact had told him. Separately, a military contact told me, as an aside in a conversation, 'Awacs have phenomenal jamming capabilities.' That's how I got to my sandwich scenario: there were Awacs on site, Awacs can jam anything better than you think, so these two Awacs just cloaked MH370. It seemed pretty straightforward. Incidentally, the Awacs intervention could nicely explain the progressive loss of the transponder signal (which took more than 30 seconds to fade from the ATC screens, instead of disappearing instantly), as it may have taken a little while for the planes to move into position. It could also explain the garbled conversation that the pilot from another flight tried to have with MH370 (see p. 302). And it could further explain the oddities observed by some MHists who were watching the air traffic at the time on a loop on FlightRadar24 in that patch of the sky. Not only was a very fast point visible, strangely identified as KAL672, crossing the sky much faster than all the other planes, but it was also noticed that when MH370 disappeared from the screen, several other flights that were nearby simultaneously disappeared as well. The only difference was that, unlike MH370, the other flights reappeared a little while later.

Among the air bases in the region with landing strips long enough for a Boeing 777, the military base of U-Tapao would seem the ideal one. As we saw (pp. 313–314), this had long been used as a secret base for the US Air Force (USAF) in the region. But Hat Yai Airport in southern Thailand, renowned for its flourishing regional trafficking business, may have also been made ready for the transfer. 'When a mission of that calibre is mounted, we do what we call "layering", meaning we need options. In a scenario like this one, it's very likely that at least two landing locations had been prepared,' I was told by someone familiar with the type of operation I envisaged.

The flurry of unusual activity that was noticed by villagers on the east coast of Malaysia and Thailand that night fits in well. On the Pathumtani radar data I was given, I noticed a C-17, a big carrier that was still in the sky an hour before MH370 took off from Kuala Lumpur. There was also a C-146A, which, as we saw in Chapter 13, is used for the swift and discreet delivery of special ops forces. There was also mention in the Pathumtani data of the presence of a C5-B Galaxy, among the largest military aircraft in the world, one that provides the USAF with a heavy intercontinental-range strategic airlift capability that could carry outsize and oversize loads.

But then came the hitch. Daring yet theoretically feasible, Plan A did not take into account the strong personality of Captain Zaharie. This was a man who fully understood his mission, who had a high sense of responsibility towards his company and, more importantly, towards his passengers. He knew his plane inside out. He was in charge. Over the years, he had imagined the worst challenges that he might ever encounter in the cockpit, including at night and above the sea. But in his wildest simulations, he may not have foreseen suddenly receiving an order from a foreign military command to change course. According to people who knew him well, he was the type who would have instinctively challenged this kind of instruction.

Keeping his cool and maintaining his course, he could have said something along the lines of: 'I am en route with my passengers to Beijing. Unable to comply with military orders. I will take orders from MAS. I'll remain with my original flight plan route. Over.' Understanding the trap they had fallen into, the pilots may have had time to activate the Tango code, a secret transmission that is supposed to inform MAS that they were being hijacked, immediately before all their communications got jammed. The seemingly odd news published on 13 March by the Malaysian newspaper *Sinar Harian* (*Daily Sun*) that the Tango code had been activated was confirmed by two MAS pilots during their interviews with the police. In the transcript I saw, one of them said that at about 04:00, as he was flying to Istanbul, he saw the code 'Tango' appear on the ACARS screen. The message stated: 'Kod Tango declared for all MH flight [*sic*]'. It is not clear to me whether Zaharie managed to alert MAS that his plane was being hijacked, like the senior pilot told *Sina Harian*, or whether it was just MAS who informed all the other planes that one of their planes, MH370, was missing by sending this Tango code around, although both might also have happened consecutively. In any case, despite both its confirmation by MAS and the transcripts of the interviews recorded by the police saying that the code had been emitted, any mention of the Tango code was completely absent from all official reports.

So either because the pilot refused to comply with orders that were inconsistent with his planned route and mission, or for a range of other possible reasons, Plan A failed. Despite being shadowed and threatened, Captain Zaharie continued to fly his plane as best he could and as close as possible to his filed planned route. MH370 had gone dark and silent, but it was still flying – and still heading towards Beijing. There may then have been some intimidating warning shots. Based on the multiple debris fields spotted by the nodders, it's also possible that in the process of targeting MH370, another plane that was part of the operation got hit. Once again, this has happened before (see the Ustica tragedy described on p. 400). Mike McKay, the New Zealand engineer on his oil rig, saw something burning. And the villagers on the east coast of Malaysia heard an explosion and other loud and unusual noises, as well as witnessing large objects falling from the sky on fire more or less at the time of the interception. On several flight-monitoring websites (like FlightRadar24), MHists spotted very fast unidentified objects flying towards MH370's route that night. Were they fighters? Were they missiles?

From what we assume to be the interception time, around 1.20 am at IGARI, until 2.33 am, where according to the positioning message received by MAS Operations Centre, MH370 was located at N14.90000, E109.15500, the plane would have travelled either 580 miles (1,074 kilometres), if it flew straight from one point to another, or around 650 miles (1,203 kilometres) if it flew along the coast, closer to its initial filed planned route. This gives an average speed of 477 knots for the straight route (580 miles/73 minutes × 60), which is consistent with the speed of the plane before IGARI (470 knots). To travel the coastal route, it would have had to have reached a much higher speed, 534 knots (650 miles/73 minutes × 60), which is beyond the official maximum speed of 513 knots (950 km/h) for a Boeing 777-200ER. It therefore seems more likely that the captain chose to take the shortest possible route. This is also consistent with MH370 being initially located above Cambodia by the MAS Operations Centre. Feeling threatened, he might have thought that reaching Chinese airspace as quickly as possible was his best bet. It so happens that at 2.25 am, as the plane started approaching Chinese airspace, its Satcom* started working again, as if the Awacs planes had decided to disperse rather than be caught on Chinese radar. So the mission aborted when MH370 was nearing an extremely militarised area, with the key Chinese nuclear submarine base called Yulin Naval Base, located south of Hainan Island, 150 miles north from Da Nang, and the much disputed (and de facto occupied by China) Paracel Islands.

Yet the incredibly daring escape attempt by the pilots of MH370 did not succeed. According to the same Middle Eastern source that mentioned the Awacs, the plane was eventually targeted and hit with 'laser weapons systems' (LaWS); these were officially being tested by the US military during this very period, as mentioned earlier (p. 107). The shooting down could have been a blunder, but

---

* 'Satcom' is a generic term for all satellite communications. It operates by using satellites to relay radio signals between the sender and receiver, and covers very long distance and wide areas. On MH370, the Satcom system provided functions for audio and text communication, ACARS data and in-flight entertainment. (Source: *Safety Investigation Report*, 2018.)

it could also have been a last resort to stop the plane and its special cargo from falling into China's hands.

Having constructed this hypothetical scenario, based on hundreds of clues, I have no reasons to completely eliminate the possibility that it was in fact China, seeing this imposing deployment of several planes arriving unannounced right into its airspace, and in this highly sensitive region, that just shot at MH370, with no time to establish that a civilian plane was unwittingly part of the threateningly tight formation. Remember the Chinese ambassador telling the families that the whole affair was 'very complicated'?

One way or another, the two world superpowers were both probably involved in the loss of MH370, most likely up to their necks. Hence they would have had no choice but to somehow agree that it was in their best common interest to erase all possible traces. But as we saw, even erasing traces leaves traces.

In the case of an in-flight explosion, pieces can still fall over a very large area. Debris spotted by nodders was plentiful in the region, but never properly located – or acknowledged – by Tomnod. According to other sources, the plane was only partially damaged, enabling it to ditch, for better or for worse. To facilitate the rescue operation in case there were survivors, the pilot might still have aimed at ditching not too far from the coast or from an island. An in-flight explosion would explain the 2.43 am SOS message reporting that the cabin was disintegrating and requesting an emergency landing.* And the fact that a Vietnam Airlines pilot heard the message and reported it confirms beyond all doubt that this SOS emergency call was genuine and took place.

Since the impact location was precisely known, seemingly inside Vietnamese waters, a clean-up operation could have been relatively

---

* In the case of the Tehran disaster (Flight 752) 'up to 19 seconds' of conversation had been captured in the cockpit after the first missile struck the plane, proving that the 2.43 distress message could have been sent by the MH370 pilots even after a missile would have hit the plane. (Press conference August 2020 by the Civil Aviation Organisation of Iran (CAOI).)

well organised, providing that all the local and international media were held at bay and fed with reams of entertaining nonsense, keeping them busy and distracted for as long as possible. According to the testimony of former Bombardier employee Christian Courcelles, bits and pieces of debris were being collected as early as the same day. He was adamant that he even saw one of the black boxes being carried ashore. We also know that Vietnam allowed Chinese and American ships into its territorial waters. From there on, the cleaning-up operation was possibly going full speed ahead. It is even possible that the USS *Pinckney* got involved. Its commander said how 'incredibly proud' he was of the bravery of his sailors and mentioned a 'tragedy' when the rest of the world was still waiting to know where MH370 had gone.

Although this jarring scenario aligns with many of the facts we have established, it still has some loose ends. How, for example, do we know that it was China that had this cargo under its control in Kuala Lumpur? We saw that 'fresh mangosteens' is more than likely simply a codename for a wide range of illicit goods that transit, possibly daily, via KLIA (Kuala Lumpur International Airport), one of the world's main hubs for black-market traffic, in particular the trade between Africa and China. And the private investigation report commissioned by Sarah Bajc (see Chapter 6) stated that a Chinese person escorted some cargo, that had supposedly arrived a few days earlier from Pakistan to be loaded on MH370. The MAS cargo staff mentioned to the private investigator that they all paid attention because this was most unusual.

While I highlighted the poor quality overall of this private report and dismissed many of its findings, I was nevertheless intrigued by the fact that Sarah Bajc, the self-appointed spokesperson of the next of kin, not only didn't want it released; she didn't even want it shared with the other families. I came to wonder whether the report did in fact contain some embarrassing bits and pieces of the truth. The problem is that this cargo, supposedly from Pakistan and hand-delivered, was nowhere to be found on the consignment of the plane. If it were so significant as to trigger such a large-scale operation, it couldn't have been tiny, otherwise someone would have hand-carried it.

I therefore had another look at the cargo documents. In the final report I noticed that the enormous Motorola shipment, the second heaviest (at 2,650 kg) on board MH370 that night, had not been subject to a security screening.* It seemed unbelievable that this hadn't been widely challenged at the time it was made public. No one seemed to have realised how problematic it was that this massive load of electronic equipment had never been passed through an X-ray before being loaded onto MH370; neither in Penang, where it originated, because 'there were no available X-ray machines large enough to screen the consignments', nor in KLIA, despite the obvious availability of large machines there. The report simply states: 'The cargo arrived [in KLIA] on the evening of 7 March and was loaded onto MH370 without going through additional security screening.' Apparently, there was only an external visual inspection of the shipment in Penang, which 'did not involve the breaking down of the cargo'. In other words, this massive shipment was merely given a glancing look in Penang, before the consignment was loaded on a truck that was then sealed by MAS security and customs, then sent off to KLIA.

'Unscreened cargo is most unusual. If the plane was going to the US it would be an absolute no-no. But even on one to Beijing ... I am baffled,' the head of cargo of one of the largest cargo airlines told me. He mentioned a rare instance, in London, where he had to deal with loading aircraft engines onto a plane; because there were no scanners large enough to do the job, they had to bring in special sniffer dogs. Perplexed, to say the least, by this finding, I was further mystified to read in the official investigation report that the sealed truck that delivered the shipment from Penang to

* Ibid., p. 424.

KLIA, about 400 kilometres away, was 'under security escort'. A 'security escort' for a load of 'radio accessories and chargers'? In Malaysia? Not only is this unheard of in the context of Malaysia, but it simply makes no sense. 'The only places I may have heard of trucks being escorted was in Russia a long time ago, and in Mexico when some new Apple products were being launched,' said the same cargo professional.

At the beginning of my investigation, I had browsed through the documents available about the cargo and found the description of the Motorola consignment to be surprisingly insubstantial. Discovering years later that this very cargo had not been X-rayed, yet had been transported under escort, was both unsettling and slightly spooky. Exploring this highly unusual cargo a little further, and keeping in mind the idea that the plane might have been diverted in order to retrieve some cargo before it reached Beijing, I checked exactly where it had been located in the hold. It so happens that it was perfectly placed to be the first thing to be swiftly offloaded, using the front cargo door. The fact that this shipment did not go through X-ray, in blatant disregard of international security procedures, was very vaguely described in the airway bill; that it was special enough to require an escort made it, if not a smoking gun, at least another highly problematic feature in the case.

In this tweaked version of a similar hypothetical scenario, the 'precious cargo' would more likely be sent to China by the US, to be used for their own – that is, American – benefit. China could have got wind of this operation and so was eagerly waiting for the special cargo to be delivered in Beijing, where it would just grab it. But whether the cargo was meant for China or for some American organisations in Beijing, one thing looks certain: whatever was planned on that night went awfully SNAFU.

I also wonder, from the profile I formed of Captain Zaharie – a great pilot, strong-headed and dedicated to MAS – if it is really plausible to assume that he would challenge an order from a foreign military command telling him to change course. His friends say so, because he was principled. Facing a catastrophic scenario involving a hostile military intervention in the air, he could have sensibly yielded to orders, yet he chose to do what he thought was the right thing. If this is what truly happened, he obviously chose a very wrong 'right option'.

On the military side, because the time frame for action was exceedingly tight – an hour or two – there may have been excessive haste and some bad decisions that induced a very messy outcome.

The US demonstrated uncharacteristic discretion throughout this crisis. Four months prior to the loss of MH370, I witnessed at the front line their remarkable humanitarian operation after the devastating passage of Typhoon Haiyan through the Philippines.* In this apocalyptic environment, the extraordinary might and efficiency of the US Navy was simply staggering. In Asia, as elsewhere around the globe, the American empire has seldom been known for being either shy or slow in coming forward. But after the loss of MH370, we saw and heard very little from the US, despite the explicit commitments they have to the region.

Surprisingly too, the US has never issued the slightest reproach to the Malaysian authorities for such a disaster, which, after all, involved a Boeing and three US nationals. Their absolute supremacy in surveillance is no secret, and their satellite coverage of the region has been modestly described as 'thorough' by high-ranking US sources. Yet not a single satellite image from the countless satellites, civil and military, that the US positions above the South China Sea, nor the slightest radar echo from the many ships and planes that were in the region, has been forthcoming from the Americans to help locate the plane wreck in any of the crash zones considered. The US opted, at least at first sight, for this most unusual hands-off approach and contributed very little, where it would have been so easy for them to have done so much more. The White House did

---

* Haiyan was one of the most violent super-typhoons ever recorded. It struck the Philippines on 8 November 2013, killing well over 6,000 people.

not even send its condolences for MH370, as it does for most major plane crashes.

Revisiting this odd, reserved attitude of the Americans, I remembered a comment made by a Malaysian friend who was very close to the inner circle of the Malaysian power structure. He mentioned that the White House had been on the phone 'every day' during the first days of the disappearance. This shocked me at the time. While the Americans were suspiciously absent in the public eye throughout the entire crisis, the office of the President of the United States was following the affair directly from behind the scenes to the point of making daily calls to the office of Minister for Transport and Defence Hishammuddin Hussein, aka Mr No-No ... What sorts of situation in the world would warrant such close monitoring, not by the secretary of state, not by the Pentagon, but by the White House itself?

A former foreign correspondent in Washington gave me the answer: 'When the White House calls in such a manner, it is obviously not to get information, as one can assume they have all the information they need through their own methods. It is more to make suggestions as to what to do or to say next, and to keep the situation under their control.'

In what should have been another tell-tale sign of something highly unusual, the FBI immediately sent its people on the ground not only to the MAS offices in Kuala Lumpur, as a person close to the investigation had told me in March 2014 (see p. 16), but also to several other strategic places and companies, as I later found out. To their dismay, several key personnel working in sectors related to sky surveillance and space communications in the region, including in Singapore, have had to sign affidavits and commit to not share anything they saw or remember of that night.

On 8 March 2014, President Barack Obama was on a weekend family vacation in Key Largo, Florida. That's where he was 'briefed' about the situation, according to Josh Earnest, a White House spokesman quoted by Bloomberg. On Sunday evening in Florida, Monday morning in Beijing, a phone call was arranged between

Chinese President Xi Jinping and Obama.* The Chinese government has a knack for picking annoying times to place calls as a way of expressing to their counterpart that the matter is of utmost importance.

The leaders of the two most powerful nations in the world don't just pick up the phone to discuss the current state of world affairs, let alone a just-gone-missing plane, do they? This peculiar phone call seems slightly more in line with some kind of major bilateral crisis. According to several Chinese media sources, the situation in Ukraine was discussed during this call, but Xi Jinping also told his American counterpart that he was 'deeply concerned about the safety of the people on board the aircraft, including Chinese and American passengers, and [that] China will continue to maintain close ties with the United States'.

Knowing that the Chinese censors meticulously redact the transcripts of these phone calls, I can't help but find this exchange a bit odd. Why would the Chinese president express his 'deep concern' to his American counterpart about this missing plane? And then why state, immediately afterwards, that China will continue to maintain close ties with the United States? Could this be the diplomatic translation of 'we know what you have done but we are happy to negotiate'? Barack Obama for his part plainly expressed his condolences over the lost plane and stated that the US was willing to fully cooperate with China in the search and rescue effort. Considering the voracious appetite the media had for the MH370 story at the time, I was surprised to note that the few Western media outlets that did report the Xi–Obama phone call made no mention of the MH370 part of the conversation.† But the

---

* As reported by China's state broadcaster CCTV and the *People's Daily*, the Chinese Communist Party mouthpiece.

† According to the Associated Press (AP), the main purpose of the Obama initiated call was 'to court China's support for efforts to isolate Russia over its military intervention in Ukraine'.

explanation for this is simple: it is nowhere to be found in the White House official readout of the call.* The president's office decided to completely omit the discussion related to MH370. Why? Another case of erasing traces?

It looks like the Chinese side may have been a bit annoyed by the American 'oversight'. Two weeks later, when the same two presidents were in The Hague on the occasion of the third Nuclear Security Summit, they briefed the press ahead of a bilateral meeting that was to take place in the privacy of the US ambassador's residence. The US president, who was the first to speak, seemed to mention everything he could think of, from climate change and nuclear security to the situation in Crimea, as well as his wife and daughters currently sightseeing and playing ping-pong in China. But he did not say a word about MH370, which was still at the top of the world news agenda. When President Xi's turn to speak came, in a clear attempt to set the record straight, the first item the Chinese leader brought to the world's media attention was the fact that President Obama called him recently 'to express sympathy over the missing Malaysian Airlines flight'. Xi Jinping also thanked Obama for 'instructing relevant American agencies to join the search for the missing plane and to share information with the Chinese side'. This time, there was no way the White House could omit or deny the fact that MH370 was the topic of the Xi–Obama phone call that had taken place two weeks earlier. Xi then also mentioned a follow-up letter sent to him by Obama that offered, among other things, 'to address common challenges through practical cooperation'. A very smart way from the Chinese president to subtly let his American counterpart know that he is not off the hook for MH370 yet. But at the time no one noticed what now looks to me like a very clear subtext.

Yet, as we saw in the field, the Americans were mostly proactive

* Readout of the President's call with President Xi of China, Office of the Press Secretary, The White House, 10 March 2014.

in turning attention away from the South China Sea,* where they had several ships in the immediate area. Thanks to tip-offs from US sources, some of the most authoritative media outlets were key in shaping the story that soon became the 'official narrative'. On 13 March 2014, *The Wall Street Journal* was the first to claim that the plane had continued to fly for several hours after the last radar contact. This was the real turning point, and the start of the new storyline regarding the fate of MH370. According to an email that I mentioned earlier, both Boeing and Rolls-Royce informed Malaysia Airlines that this information was 'false' when it was first published. And according to a top source at Rolls-Royce, the firm never received any information related to the flight after the batch sent at the end of the rise to cruising altitude. In other words, the source who told *The Wall Street Journal* that Rolls-Royce had this engine data must have made it up, because Rolls-Royce never even received it.† At the time, CNN also quoted 'a senior aviation source with detailed knowledge of the matter who told [star presenter] Richard Quest on Thursday that there was no technical data suggesting the airplane continued flying for four hours and said specifically that *The Wall Street Journal* account was wrong.' But the White House confirmed *The Wall Street Journal* story shortly after, and that's how the false information – false, according to the two companies who should know best about the location of their plane and their engines – became true. Malaysian officials, to their credit, denied and resisted this announcement for several days. With hindsight, I wish CNN had the courage to maintain the

---

* On 9 March 2014, the US embassy in Hanoi wasted no time in loudly declaring that the debris found in the South China Sea had 'nothing to do with MH370'. Several days later, the US indicated that it had 'no element to confirm the debris seen by the Chinese satellites'.

† According to my source, the engine data on B-777 at the time was transmitted via VHF, before take off, and at the end of the initial rise to cruising altitude. During the flight the data would be collected regularly but only transmitted once the plane started its descent.

version of its own trusted 'senior aviation source' and had challenged the new narrative that was taking shape during these crucial moments. Instead it quickly fell in line and even took the lead in the wild-goose chase that was going to unfold down under.

On 15 March 2014, *The New York Times* added a further layer to the new official narrative by claiming that, after its U-turn (something that was by now treated as a *fait accompli* worldwide), MH370 had climbed very high to lose its passengers, prior to flying very low to avoid radar detection. This piece of information, which should have been questioned before being published and which was more likely to be related to another plane, also played its part in reinforcing the idea that something sinister and deliberate was taking place within the cockpit, as did the next piece of 'evidence' added to the official narrative, this time brought to air by CNN.

On 12 April 2014, CNN quoted an unnamed 'US official', who confirmed that Flight MH370's co-pilot's mobile phone had been detected as the plane flew over Penang. Once again, this story was never officially confirmed, and it has since been studied and dismissed by the Malaysian police. The idea of a phone connecting to a local tower was nevertheless highly effective in reinforcing the idea that the plane did fly over Malaysia. During the first weeks of the event, when confusion prevailed, these leads carried considerable weight, particularly because they came from well-regarded media sources. They were essential in diverting attention away from the simple scenario of a crash in the South China Sea.

When, seven weeks after the loss of MH370, Barack Obama visited Malaysia, he finally, albeit very briefly, presented the condolences of the US to the victims' families. And that was about the only mention of MH370 during his entire visit. It was as if the case were closed. The safest aircraft manufactured by Boeing had mysteriously disappeared with 239 people on board. So be it.

If the tragedy of MH370 can be credited with providing some kind of positive outcome, it is surely the astonishing rapprochement that subsequently took place between the US and Malaysia. The two countries that had so little in common for decades became friends overnight, despite the gigantic scandal known as 1MDB that Prime Minister Najib Razak was involved in, so vast that even the US Justice Department was investigating it. But that did not stop President Obama from inviting Najib to play golf on Christmas Day in Hawaii in 2015, nor President Trump from welcoming him to the White House in September 2017.

China's attitude is no less strange. With 60 per cent of the passengers being Chinese nationals (134 out of 227), China paid the highest price by far in this catastrophe. Beijing therefore had good reason to assume the lead in the crisis. And, initially, China did take things to the next level (see Chapter 2). It sent several ships to join in the early search operation in the South China Sea, it was the first country to share satellite images of large pieces of potential debris, and it even let the victims' families protest loud and clear, including publicly in front of the Malaysian embassy in Beijing. But overall, it laid low.

China also only reluctantly cooperated with the Australian-led underwater search. Beijing failed to attend the trilateral meetings it was supposed to have with Malaysia and Australia in Canberra on several instances, clear signs of its lack of enthusiasm, which could also be interpreted as a diplomatic rebuff towards the Australian exercise. When China finally agreed to contribute financially to the Australian operation, it provided only 10 per cent of the total budget. If China knew exactly where the plane had crashed because it had been part of the clearing-up operation, why would it contribute millions to the exercise in sheer diversion that Australia was proudly leading?

If one reflects on the words of the Chinese ambassador when he addressed the families in the first few days after the flight's disappearance – 'This is very complicated. You cannot understand' – it is tempting to believe that China too has long known more than it has ever said. But China always turns a crisis into an opportunity, and if it had just witnessed a major US fiasco, it was surely in a position to bargain something big in exchange for its silence. Could it be that the US would turn a blind eye to the steady and seemingly unstoppable construction of massive military installations on several of the disputed islands in the South China Sea? If such an arrangement was ever obtained, basically a green light from Washington given to Beijing to do whatever it wanted in the South China Sea within a certain timeframe, China wasted no time in putting it to good use. On 2 May, China moved its giant, $1 billion oil rig, Haiyang Shiyou 981 (HD 981) near the Paracel islands in waters claimed by Vietnam. That very bold move triggered a wave of anti-China protests in Vietnam and a string of serious incidents at sea. But Washington did not lift a finger. In early June, China sent another four oil rigs (three deepwater platforms and one jackup rig used for shallow waters) into the South China Sea, sending a clear sign that it was stepping up its presence in the disputed region. Reuters news agency reported: 'State oil behemoth China National Offshore Oil Company (CNOOC) has long said that in a bid to boost production it wanted to explore in deeper waters off China. It announced new projects in the western and eastern South China Sea in the second half of 2014. CNOOC has said it would increase by up to a third its annual capital spending for 2014, to almost $20 billion.' *The Global Times*, English language mouthpiece of the Chinese Communist Party called the deployment of the rigs a 'strategic move'. This time, US President Obama made a vapid comment: 'It is important for us to be able to resolve maritime disputes in accordance with international law, and encourage all parties concerned to maintain a legal framework for resolving issues, as opposed to possible escalation that could have an impact on navigation and commerce.' And that was it. China then launched further land reclamation activities both in the Spratly and Paracel Islands: drilling, piling, filling atolls with mountains of sand and concrete, building military harbours and airstrips at breakneck speed. In a few months, Fiery Cross reef alone was transformed into a 274 ha (677 acres) Chinese military base, boasting a 3,125 metre runway.

Isn't it ironic that while Australia was attracting the world news headlines, with its claim to be overseeing the largest (bogus) search operation in the history of mankind, China was quietly performing an incomparably more ambitious, more costly and more consequential operation?

I was really puzzled at the apparent stoicism of the Americans in this regard, as they must have discreetly choked at every Chinese barge of sand they saw on their satellite images, steadily crossing from the continent to the disputed islands. It did not seem consistent with US regional policy to let these mammoth military installations be built by China in broad daylight. But again, if it was all part of a deal to make sure no one knows what happened to MH370, then …

Vietnam is obviously also in the know, perhaps more than anyone else, but this former communist state is a black hole from which it is very hard to report. Yet no one can deny the dramatic rapprochement between the US and Vietnam seen during Obama's second term of office (2013–17), when a flurry of bilateral visits between America and Vietnam took place at the highest level. It may also be a coincidence, but six months after MH370, the US arms embargo that Vietnam had long wished to be lifted was eased. It was fully lifted in May 2016. Meanwhile, bilateral trade between Vietnam and the US picked up dramatically. By 2016, Vietnam had become America's fastest-growing export market; in 2018, the trade deficit reached the staggering figure of $55.8 billion, in favour of Vietnam. There may have been other sweeteners too. Blunders can be costly, and silence comes at a bitter price.

I am not sure where to place the French government in this affair. I was told, early on in my research, that one of France's 'big ears' intelligence installations located on some remote islands had heard the interception operation. I never saw any direct evidence of this, but two years later I came across another person whose job was to transcribe these recordings and who alluded to their content in a similar way. One way or another, France may have known from day one. Then, in July 2015, came the flaperon episode. Up until to that point, France may have chosen to remain silent, just watching from the sidelines to see how this disaster in waiting was going to be handled. But the flaperon episode forced France to commit. Either France was willingly complicit in the flaperon deceit operation from its very conception, or the surprise landfall in Réunion caught the French authorities off guard and made them reveal their hand.

It should have been very straightforward for the experts to dismiss or at least question the authenticity of the debris based on the simple fact that it was missing its identification plate. But as we saw, despite the initial reluctance from the French experts to confirm the debris as a part of MH370, as well as Boeing and NTSB experts not being 'fully satisfied' after they saw the flaperon, that it was from MH370 (as reported by the *New York Times*), France suddenly joined the chorus of nations who were hammering the narrative of the plane crashing in the southern Indian Ocean. After all, France was not going to compromise its relationship with all of these allied nations over a broken piece of plane wing. Yes, it had – and still has – a formal investigation going on, but the judges leading it were being transferred to different offices, in other regions, on a regular basis, a rather safe way to make sure the investigation did not make any substantial headway. The first-ever French presidential visit to Australia took place in November 2014, followed, in April 2016, by France winning and signing off on a massive A$50 billion (£27 billion) submarine deal with the country. François Hollande also made the first-ever French presidential visit to Malaysia in 2017, where other juicy military equipment contracts were signed and others, like the Rafale fighter aircraft, simply discussed.

Malaysia has borne the brunt of the criticism throughout this whole affair. Its exceptional incompetence was splashed across the world's media, with the Malaysian administration being incessantly mocked and ridiculed for its shortcomings.

But if Malaysia stood out as the real guilty party in this tragedy, who would have wished to protect it by covering this event with such an elaborate web of mystery? If Malaysia alone were responsible for this catastrophe, its culpability would in all likelihood have been exposed and Malaysia would have been crucified all on its own. Therefore, is it not more plausible to imagine that its role was rather that of the 'useful idiot', the patsy, the forced accomplice in an affair that is far more complex than it might at first appear? Under the cover of its unprecedented and quite outstanding ineptitude, Malaysia shouldered full responsibility for this tragedy. It is quite possible that when, at the highest level, the decision was taken to go for the cover-up rather than facing up to the ugly truth, the fact that Malaysia was part of the equation may have been a decisive, albeit risky factor. Malaysia would have just been instructed to continue to play the candid and naive part: 'I know nothing, I understand nothing, I am trying my best *lah*!'

Those who met with the Malaysian government in the first hours and days following the loss of Flight MH370 described the prime minister as having been deeply distressed. As corrupt and shrewd as he may be, Najib Razak is no actor. It is worth noting that in all the key moments when Najib spoke to serve the new Inmarsat narrative, he referred to what he had been told by, mostly, the UK. The words he chose on the definitive 24 March announcement are crystal clear. Najib said, 'Inmarsat and the AAIB have concluded that Flight MH370 flew along the southern corridor and that its last position was in the middle of the Indian Ocean.' Most people remember what the prime minister of Malaysia said, but few paid attention to the fact that, according to his own words, he was just repeating what he had been told by the UK Air Accidents Investigation Branch (AAIB). Actually, by interpreting the Inmarsat data and then convincing the Malaysian government that the data was reliable, the UK also played a major role in imposing the Inmarsat narrative. In Najib's own words, it was the AAIB that had established the final crash site of MH370. Malaysia was just repeating this. So, is Malaysia the guilty party, 'the useful idiot' or the victim in this affair? I'd go for the 'useful idiot' who was very useful but potentially not that idiotic, as it would surely have negotiated a very hefty price for the prolonged humiliation it endured.

But the MH curse might not have ended there.

Let's now imagine the even more outrageous ensuing acts to this initial hypothetical disaster.

After the special delivery to Beijing failed miserably because of some third-party interference (most likely by the US, with the support of its usual partners in crime or through the services of proxies), Putin makes an offer to his Chinese counterpart Xi, who is still a bit of a novice in office. When the MH370 episode happens, President Xi is a week away from celebrating his first year as the head of China, during which short period he and Putin wasted no time in growing remarkably close. When MH370 happened, they had met five times already, and by September of the same year, there will be a further four meetings.

So, after the hypothetical downing of MH370 by the US, a civilian jet that carried mostly Chinese citizens, Putin tells Xi: 'What happened is not acceptable. Leave it to me.' It is payback time. And it takes place four months and ten days later. A twin plane to MH370 – same make, same model, same engines, same airlines, almost same name (9M-MRD versus 9M-MRO) – carrying almost sixty more people (298 against 239), this time mainly Westerners (Dutch, Australians, British …) gets shot down above Ukraine in pure Mafia style, where you hit back at the niece or the brother so that the boss gets the message. And the message, from one group of secret services to the other, could not be clearer: 'You mess with us, we'll mess with you.' And possibly, 'How long do you want to play this silly game?'

If Xi and Putin had to agree on this diabolical tit-for-tat scenario before the go-ahead was given, the timing was perfect. The two leaders were together just a few hours before MH17 was shot down, on 17 July. In one picture from the BRICS summit that closed on 16 July in Brazil (UTC-5), the two leaders may be seen shaking hands warmly, and their reciprocal smiles can only be described as ... beaming.

The explanation for this extraordinary enigma is never going to be straightforward, and several layers of deception can be anticipated. I can't rule out the possibility that the hypothetical scenario I have come up with is still too simple – or even wide of the mark. Having stood up for the captain, who in my opinion has been unfairly accused, I certainly do not mean to imply, in my scenario, that any individual or company knowingly took part in this deception. When I submitted its basic outline to someone familiar with these sorts of undercover operations, I received two comments. First, the more outrageous the scenario, the more likely it is to actually be the truth. Second, because traceability is the major concern in these situations, most governments would use proxies. They would ask nation friends or hire professional groups to do a job on their behalf, to keep the game muddy. And when the time for dishing out blame comes around, the game may get even more muddy as the party that is wrongly blamed may choose, for its own reasons, to take responsibility for something it knows it did not do and that its accusers also know it did not do. The 1988 Lockerbie disaster is a case in point.* According to several books and documentaries revisiting the event,†

---

* On 21 December 1988, Pan Am Flight 103 was destroyed by a bomb, crashing onto the town of Lockerbie in Scotland, killing all 259 people on board and 11 people on the ground.

† The BBC 2016 documentary *HyperNormalisation* shows fascinating archives evidencing how the Lockerbie investigation was twisted and bent in order to make Libya the guilty party. The same thesis had been exposed in *African Manipulations* by Pierre Péan in 2001.

investigators in Europe knew for certain that it was a Syrian attack, but the US decided that the Libyan leader Colonel Gaddafi should be blamed for it. Years later, the US actually asked Gaddafi to admit responsibility for the attack and pay compensation in exchange for the lifting of sanctions. And Libya did just this, although not without crying foul. The result is that almost everyone today believes that Lockerbie was indeed a Libyan attack. How Machiavellian is this? Most governments would argue it is just realpolitik. As I have discovered (see Addendum, p. 379), every plane accident is complex for its own reasons. But the case of MH370 is so exceptionally Byzantine that the guilty party failed to produce even a mildly credible cover-up story.

Beyond being unsubstantiated and morally questionable, the relentless accusations levelled at the pilot are ludicrous for the simple fact that accusing him of mass murder does not solve in any way the riddle of the disappearance of a massive commercial airliner carrying 239 people. If the pilot wanted to commit mass murder–suicide, why would he bother making his plane and his passengers disappear? And if, for whatever obscure reason, he had wanted to make his plane disappear, why then did he take a completely absurd zigzag route, rather than simply continue to fly towards the Pacific, which is an even bigger and even deeper ocean than the southern Indian Ocean? More importantly, to gain any credibility whatsoever, the accusers of the pilot would also need to explain how MH370 managed to fly stealthily for several hours and for as many thousands of miles, a feat never previously achieved even by the most sophisticated military plane, despite billions of dollars of research over several decades. Each and every one of the 12 million passengers (notwithstanding Covid) who board a plane every day must hope that their plane won't be up to the same mind-boggling trick. Disappointingly, however, it seems that as long as public opinion can vaguely associate this impossible case with some form of explanation, in this particular instance putting the blood on the pilot's hands, the world will continue to pretend to be satisfied, and ultimately will give up. I believe it is time to completely reject and challenge not just the pathetic accusations about the pilot but, more widely, the entire official narrative. It seems inescapably clear at the end of this investigation that something completely different to what the media were told happened. I have established that MH370 did not U-turn, did not fly over Malaysia and, to cut a long story short, never crashed in the Southern Indian Ocean. Many more clues point to a covert interception attempt that went terribly wrong, with a fatal accident happening around 2.40 am between Vietnam and China. If what we suspect here is close to what truly happened to MH370 and its 239 passengers, I can't find better words that those chosen by US President Barack Obama about MH17: 'an outrage of unspeakable proportion.'

Over the course of this investigation I have met a fascinating cross-section of humanity. People are captivated by mystery, even more than by power, money or genius. Mystery attracts madmen, mystics and the plainly curious, just as much as scientists and those who thirst for truth. Scientists reject and fight mystery because it runs counter to all that they stand for. At one stage of this investigation, my meetings with the cream of the crop of MHists, serious and brilliant women and men of good faith, could be counted as one of the most exciting aspects of my research. Yet the relentlessness of the members of the Independent Group to get the Inmarsat data to talk has not been rewarded. Some of them became so embroiled in this challenge that they were no longer able to entertain the notion that the data might not only be wrong but was provided with the explicit intention of misleading the search. Later, I discovered and met – online and in real life – equally committed MHists with no concerns other than finding the truth for the well-being of all the friends and families of the 239 people on board. Their passionate work has greatly helped my own research. More than once, I came across sources who were initially very willing to help and promised to deliver more information. Alas, in several cases, there was little if nothing that followed the initial information. Some sources simply broke off contact, while others multiplied excuses to the point that it became useless for me to persist. There were also a few other fascinating leads that I chose not to mention here to protect the people involved.

I continue to receive and seek out information, not just about the where, when and how, but also about the why of this tragedy. By now, I know of several people who are privy to the whole truth. Families need the truth. People who know must find the courage and strength to speak out. I salute those who have already shared with me their portion of relevant information, helping me to put this as yet incomplete jigsaw together.

If my years in Malaysia have taught me anything, it is to take my time. There is an old Malay proverb that runs, 'The fish are hanging, the cat is waiting.' I didn't get it initially. But I now feel like that cat, who is sitting under rows of fish that you see hung to dry on washing lines in the warm wind on the east coast of Malaysia. Waiting and watching. Just like the drying fish, the complete truth is out there. It will fall in due time.

Addendum

A few (very) instructive examples
of airline crashes

Every time a plane crashes, all one hears and reads is that flying is still the safest way to travel. Nevertheless, 2014 and 2015 seem to stand out as exceptionally black years, especially in Asia. In 2014, after the disappearance of MH370 in March, Flight MH17 was shot down in Ukraine on 17 July. Taiwan's TransAsia Airways Flight 222 crashed while attempting to land on the island of Penghu on 23 July. Air Algérie Flight 5017 crashed in Mali on 24 July, and Indonesia AirAsia Flight 8501 crashed in Indonesia in December. In February 2015, another Taiwanese plane, TransAsia Airways Flight 235, crashed into the Keelung River. In March, Germanwings Flight 9525 hurtled into a mountain in France. In June and August, two planes – an Indonesian Air Force KC-130B Hercules and Trigana Air Service Flight 267 – crashed in Indonesia On 31 October 2015, Metrojet Flight 9268 crashed in the Sinai. And these were only some of the bigger air accidents. Yet, by annual statistics, it was no more or no less than average.

In each case, was human failure or technical failure to blame? Was it the pilot or was it the plane? An air accident is usually caused by one or the other, sometimes a mix of both. Crashes can also be caused by external factors: a missile in the case of MH17, a titanium alloy strip that had fallen from another plane onto the runway in the case of the AF4590 Concorde, a flock of Canada geese getting sucked into the engines in the case of US Airways

Flight 1549 – which made an emergency landing in the Hudson River – or a fire in the cargo hold, as in the case of UPS Airlines Flight 6 that crashed in Dubai. It would seem that no two air accidents are alike.*

Out of curiosity and to see how they might be similar or comparable to MH370, I selected a few well-known crashes – hoping to discover some insights that would help me to better understand or imagine what could have happened to the flight that is the subject of my investigation. I had no idea what I was going to come across and therefore decided to share this part of my research as an addendum to this book.

Pilot suicide: the investigators' favourite explanation

When an aircraft experiences a technical problem, the passengers' survival is in the hands of the pilots. If the plane crashes, the captain and the co-pilot are logically the first suspects.

If a pilot wants to kill himself, bringing his plane and his passengers down with him, there currently exists no sure-fire way of preventing him from doing so – apart from the other pilot, the crew or the passengers physically stopping him. However, once he is alone in the cockpit behind the armoured security door, the fate of the aircraft is sealed.

Germanwings Flight 9525: a mentally ill pilot

The most recent and memorable case of pilot suicide was that of Flight 9525 of the Lufthansa subsidiary Germanwings. On 24 March 2015, an Airbus A320 flying from Barcelona to Düsseldorf crashed at full speed into the side of a mountain in the southern

* Various documentaries and counter-investigations have suggested other reasons for the Concorde crash, including a fire in one of the engines.

French Alps. The aircraft exploded on impact and the 150 people on board perished instantly. Apart from the engines, wheels and a few pieces of the airframe, the great majority of the debris recovered measured less than 30 centimetres. The first officer had locked the cockpit door from inside and disabled the digital code panel. The captain pounded on the door and demanded, via the address system, to be let in. The first officer refused. Alone in the cockpit, he 'intentionally set the automatic pilot instructions for the plane to descend until it collided with the terrain'.*

Though I have not looked deeply into this case, the conclusion seems beyond dispute: the first officer, who suffered from serious mental health issues, was responsible for the crash. This crash nevertheless raises the issue of the airline's responsibility to monitor the health of the pilots it employs. It also highlights the dilemma presented by having a totally secured cockpit door; security measures in place since 9/11 mean that cockpit doors are impenetrable, but in this case these security measures prevented the captain from saving the plane and its passengers.

Aviation authorities had already been alerted to similar incidents. Less than a year earlier, the captain of an Air New Zealand flight,† furious about a delayed take-off after his first officer was subjected to a random alcohol test, locked the first officer out of the cockpit, causing panic among the crew. The incident, which had no serious consequences, was a reminder of the potential risks of secured cockpit doors. Both men were disciplined, and required to undergo psychological counselling and additional training.

Mozambique Airlines Flight 470: another recent case of pilot suicide

In a similar case, on 29 November 2013, the pilot-in-command of Mozambique Airlines Flight 470, carrying 33 people from Maputo

---

* BEA preliminary report on Germanwings Flight 9525, May 2015.

† Air New Zealand Flight 176 from Perth to Auckland, 21 May 2014.

in Mozambique to Luanda in Angola, locked his co-pilot out of the cockpit before crashing the Embraer 190 into Namibia's Bwabwata National Park. As in the case of Germanwings, the pilot ignored shouting and banging on the door.

Until the nightmare of the Germanwings flight, the two best-known cases in recent aviation history of pilot suicide on large passenger airliners were the 1997 crash of SilkAir Flight 185 in Indonesia in which 104 people died, and the 1990 crash of EgyptAir Flight 990 off the coast of New York, which killed 217 people. The facts about both of these cases are much murkier than one might assume from what is generally said about them.

SilkAir Flight 185: an almost perfect suicide

At 15:37 on Friday, 19 December 1997, SilkAir Flight 185 – a Boeing 737 – left Jakarta's Soekarno-Hatta International Airport. It was scheduled to arrive in Singapore two and a half hours later. At 16:10:18, Jakarta air traffic control instructed the pilots to maintain their cruising altitude and to contact Singapore air traffic control upon reaching waypoint PARDI. The Boeing's pilots acknowledged the message. This was the last communication with Flight MI185. Thirty-five seconds later, the plane plunged into the Musi River in southern Sumatra. The aircraft, which lost its tail before crashing, was completely destroyed by the impact and its black boxes could provide no usable data. There were no survivors among the 104 people on board. According to the investigation report, the plane, flying in clear weather, had sent no distress signal before crashing.*

Because the aircraft was made by Boeing, the US was asked to take part in the investigation. As it happened, the conclusions

---

* National Transportation Safety Committee, *Investigation of Aircraft Accident SilkAir Flight MI 185 Boeing B737-300, 9V-TRF Musi River, Palembang, Indonesia, 19 December 1997, Final Report*, Jakarta, 14 December 2000.

reached by the American National Transport Safety Board (NTSB) differed radically from those of the Indonesian investigators. In a letter to the Indonesian investigators dated 11 December 2000, the NTSB concluded that 'the accident can be explained by intentional pilot action', as the Boeing 737 presented no 'mechanical malfunctions or failures'. The US investigators promoted the theory that the captain, Tsu Way Ming, had committed suicide. He had been subjected to disciplinary measures and run up considerable debts, they said. Indonesia's National Transportation Safety Committee, in charge of the official investigation, refuted this theory, on the absence of any proof to back it up. The final report of the investigation thus emphasised the impossibility of establishing the cause of the accident due to lack of information and lack of proof – especially given the extent of the destruction of the aircraft.

Seven years later, the case took a dramatic turn with the decision of the Los Angeles Superior Court in a legal action brought by the families of the passengers. Based on new expert analyses, the court found that the crash had been caused by a malfunction of a servo valve in the plane's rudder. When there is such a malfunction, the servo valve can cause the rudder to jam or even to do the reverse of what pilot input commands it to do, rendering the aircraft totally uncontrollable. A similar defect may have actually caused a number of Boeing 737 crashes: United Airlines Flight 585 in 1991, USAir Flight 427 in 1994 and Eastwind Airlines Flight 517 in 1996.

The first time rudder failure occurred – in 1991 on Flight UA585 – the NTSB failed to identify it. The investigation report concluded that the loss of the aircraft could not be explained. It was only when a similar accident occurred three and a half years later with another Boeing 737 (USAir Flight 427), and then a third time in 1996,* that the case of Flight UA585 was reopened.

Is it plausible that in 1997 it had not occurred to the US investigators of the SilkAir crash that this fourth sudden and bizarre

---

* Eastwind Airlines Flight 517, 6 June 1996.

dive by a Boeing 737 in six years might have had similar causes to those of the three previous accidents?

Yet despite the aircraft model's damning record, the US investigation focused on the Singaporean pilot's personal problems in order to support the suicide theory, meaning that it was not until seven years later that the technical cause of the SilkAir crash was recognised. If it was a technical failure, then it was not a suicide. Parker Hannifin Corporation, the manufacturer of the faulty servo valve, was ordered to pay damages of US$43.6 million to the three families who were the plaintiffs in the case. Neither Boeing nor SilkAir, however, was found liable.

This case is a glaring illustration of the reluctance of the NTSB, an eminent authority on civil aviation safety, to consider aircraft technical failure as a cause, preferring instead to lay the blame on a human being – and a dead human being at that.

In any case, the crash of SilkAir Flight 185 is still generally labelled 'pilot suicide' in the world's collective memory, as well as in most lists and blogs on the subject.

EgyptAir Flight 990: another 'almost perfect suicide'

Another famous case of 'pilot suicide' goes back to 31 October 1999 and had a major impact at the time – especially in the United States. EgyptAir Flight 990, a Boeing 767 flying from Los Angeles to Cairo, had taken off in the middle of the night from its scheduled stop in New York. Half an hour later, with 217 people on board, the plane suddenly lost and then regained altitude, before dropping again and crashing into the Atlantic Ocean 100 kilometres off the coast of Massachusetts. There were two full flight crews – two captains and two first officers – who were to share flying duties during the more than 10-hour flight. The first two-man team was to work from take-off through the first four hours of the flight, after which it would hand over to the second team, before taking over again one or two hours before landing in Cairo. Again, there are several versions of the story. Let us begin with the best-known version.

Twenty minutes after take-off, Gameel Al-Batouti, the first officer of the relief flight crew, entered the cockpit, saying he wanted to replace the co-pilot who was at the controls. Although Al-Batouti was one of EgyptAir's longest-serving co-pilots, he had never been promoted to captain. One of his children was seriously ill. The insistent exchange between the two first officers is on the cockpit voice recordings. The co-pilot at the controls was determined to remain there, as he was assigned to do, but his older colleague finally prevailed. This left the captain of the first flight crew alongside Al-Batouti, the relief co-pilot who was to gain tragic fame, flying the plane.

Shortly after the switch, with the flight proceeding smoothly, captain number one left the cockpit to go to the toilet, leaving Al-Batouti alone at the controls. It was then, according to prominent US media outlets, that Al-Batouti said loudly, 'I have made up my mind.' This statement seems to have been followed by a series of events that sent the aircraft into a sudden, uncontrolled dive. Despite the plane's nose-down pitch, the captain was able to get back to the cockpit, where he found Al-Batouti. The captain pulled forcefully on the lever to try to recover the plane and ordered the co-pilot to do the same: 'Pull with me!' But the plane had lost 4,500 metres in 36 seconds, was now exceeding its maximum operating speed and its fuselage was breaking up. On the recordings, Al-Batouti is heard at several points to shout, *'Tawakkaltu ala-Al-lah!'* ('I rely on God!'). Despite several attempts to halt the plane's descent, and although it briefly regained altitude, the plane was pulverised upon impact with the ocean's surface. Very little debris was found: one body, a few life jackets, some seats and the inflatable evacuation slides.

Adding everything up – Al-Batouti's insistence on taking over the controls before it was his turn to do so, his seriously ill child, his career-related frustrations and his horrifying declaration of intent ('I have made up my mind') – a convincing case could be made for the plane having been brought down by relief co-pilot Gameel Al-Batouti. This was the version of events given to the media; it appealed to people's emotions, it made sense given the context of instability in the Middle East, and it designated a culprit who was dead and therefore unable to defend himself.

The investigators lost no time in wrapping things up. Even before the black boxes were recovered, the NTSB was talking about a 'deliberate act'. I came across this expression while reading a counter-inquiry by French journalist Jean-Paul Mari.* It struck me because it was precisely the expression used by Malaysian Prime Minister Najib Razak at the press conference he gave on 15 March 2014. However, the official version of the 1999 disaster began to fall apart when it was learned that Al-Batouti's declaration, 'I have made up my mind' – communicated by the FBI to the Associated Press news agency and very widely repeated thereafter – was fake. Pure invention! The cockpit voice recorder (CVR) never recorded this statement and the co-pilot never pronounced it. Associated Press never published a formal correction, only a terse dispatch indicating that the co-pilot had not said these words. By that time, the media had moved on to other things.

Although the co-pilot did in fact say *'Tawakkaltu ala-Allah!'* several times, this was acknowledged in the end to be a common Arabic expression that is no more a sign of fanaticism than is an exclamation of 'Gosh!' or 'Oh, my God!'. Claims that the co-pilot was suffering from frustrations in both his career and his personal life were also difficult to prove. In his counter-inquiry, Mari wrote: 'Gameel earned a lot of money from his travel bonuses [...] He had never wanted to sit the exam to become a captain. [...] He loved shopping and had called his son to tell him to come to Cairo

---

* Jean-Paul Mari, 'Contre-enquête sur une catastrophe aérienne, EgyptAir: le suicide était presque parfait' ('Counter-inquiry into an air catastrophe: The suicide was almost perfect'), 9 December 1999. www.grands-reporters.com.

Airport to help him carry two tyres that he had bought in the United States.' However, because of the shocking nature of the invented statement, the idea of suicide remained stuck in people's minds despite evidence to the contrary. At this point, the public no longer knew how they knew or why they knew. They only knew that they knew. The suicide of Al-Batouti had become a *fact*.

'The investigators jumped on the suicide theory because this suited everybody!', commented Byron Acohido, a security journalist with an excellent reputation in aviation circles.* The NTSB's March 2002 report on Flight MS990 differed from its report on the SilkAir accident in that it mentioned 'anomalies in the control levers of 767s', but it nevertheless concluded that the cause of the crash was a suicidal act by Al-Batouti.

Cairo did not fall for this. In its own report, the Egyptian Civil Aviation Authority explicitly accused the US investigators of having done everything possible to stifle reports of a possible technical failure. The Egyptian Civil Aviation Authority's conclusion was scathing: 'Nowhere in the 1,665 pages of the NTSB's docket [...] is there any evidence to support the so-called "deliberate act theory".' It did, however, mention 'the accumulation of evidence showing anomalies in the elevator system of the accident plane [that] makes a mechanical defect a plausible and likely cause of the accident'.

The Egyptian report cited four other accidents caused by elevator malfunction, including a 2000 Aeroméxico flight and a 2001 Gulf Air flight. The report also added: 'Both the FAA† and Boeing agree that the shearing of elevator bellcrank rivets – an issue that the ECAA has urged to be explored in greater detail – can cause an uncommanded dive.'

The FAA ordered checks and the replacement of elevator rivet fasteners on all Boeing 767s, clearly convinced that this type of

* Ibid.

† The FAA is the American Federal Aviation Administration, the regulator of civil aviation in the US.

failure could result in loss of control of the plane. The case has been amply documented since,* and there is no longer any doubt that the fatal accident of Flight MS990, like several others, was at least partly caused by technical failure. Nevertheless, like the SilkAir disaster, Flight MS990 is still classified as 'pilot suicide' in the collective memory.

These serious technical issues have since been resolved. They belong to the past, and revealing them today has less impact. At the time, however, such revelations would have had a devastating effect on Boeing's orders, which were already insufficient to keep even half of the company's production lines busy. Had it been officially acknowledged that all of the accidents described above were related to manufacturing defects attributable to the world's largest aircraft builder, what would have become of Boeing and its 165,000 employees?

Human error: the investigators' second-favourite explanation

Just as cases of pilot suicide do occur occasionally, there have also been genuine instances of human error. Such errors, nevertheless, almost always occur in association with what pilots refer to as other 'parameters', such as a technical glitch that is then wrongly handled. Nor are they always as clear-cut as investigation reports would have us think.

---

* 'Mayday-S03E08-Death and Denial (Egyptair 990)' Air Crash Investigation, *National Geographic*, 2 November 2005.

TransAsia Airways Flight 235: a gross and deadly error

The Taiwanese carrier TransAsia Airways Flight 235 provides a particularly explicit example. On 4 February 2015, two minutes after take-off, the pilot announced that one of the ATR 72's engines had stopped and he sent out a distress call: 'Mayday! Mayday! Engine flame-out.' The plane's altitude at this point was still only 1,500 feet. A pilot familiar with this model of plane built by the Franco-Italian company ATR commented on this scenario:

> When there's an engine failure on an ATR, the engine that's still working automatically compensates. The pilot at the controls normally just has to manage the plane's trajectory. In a case like this one, it would mean correcting the direction and keeping the plane from stalling until a safe altitude was reached. During this time the co-pilot makes the flamed-out engine safe, which means switching it off completely.

However, instead of following this routine procedure, one of the pilots inadvertently switched off the only engine that was still running. He could be heard exclaiming: 'Wow, pulled back the wrong side throttle,' according to the official investigation report.* It was impossible to restart the engine, but there was just enough time to steer the aircraft towards the nearby Keelung River. Before the plane crashed, one of its wings struck a taxi travelling along the viaduct next to the river. Of the 58 people on board, only 15 survived. According to the provisional report on the investigation,† the pilot in command had failed a simulator training test a year before because he had been unable to deal with the issue of engine flame-out during take-off, although he re-sat the test a month later

---

* Taiwan Transportation Safety Board, *Final Report on TransAsia Flight GE235 Occurrence Investigation*, 30 June 2016.

† Ibid.

and passed it. Seven months earlier, another TransAsia Airways ATR 72 had made a failed landing; Flight GE222 crashed into a building, killing 48 of the 58 people on board.

Following these two accidents, Taiwan's civil aviation authority ordered additional training for all TransAsia pilots and the temporary suspension of 29 of them. Again, it appeared that there was nothing more to be said.

Paradoxically, several people who saw the crash came away with the impression that the pilots had acted heroically. 'Pilots of crashed TransAsia flight hailed as heroes' was the heading of an article in British newspaper *The Telegraph* published on the same day. At the time, the causes of the accident were not known. It was only observed that the pilots had managed to aim for a river in the middle of the city, thus considerably limiting the human and material damage – which is true. By the time the details of the accident became known, the world's attention had already turned to something else that had just happened.

Air France Flight 447: a combination of parameters

The BEA's final report on the crash of Air France Flight 447* highlighted a combination of technical and human failures – or rather a wrong human reaction to a technical failure. AF447 was an Air France A330 on an overnight flight from Rio de Janeiro to Charles de Gaulle Airport in Paris on 31 May–1 June 2009, with 228 passengers on board. The fatal sequence of events began at 02:10, four hours after take-off and a few minutes after the captain left the cockpit to take a rest. The plane entered an area of icing and the pitot tubes that indicate the aircraft's speed suddenly became blocked. Numerous other measurements then became incoherent.

---

* *Final Report on the accident on 1st June 2009 to the Airbus A330-203 registered F-GZCP operated by Air France Flight AF 447 Rio de Janeiro–Paris, July 2012* (available at www.bea.aero/docspa/2009/f-cp090601.en/pdf/f-cp090601.en.pdf).

The United States aviation authorities consider this a 'catastrophic' situation to be addressed immediately. This is not the view of the European authorities, who even today consider the loss of measurement of speed to be only a 'major' issue.

Laurent Lamy, who lost his brother in the crash, had been studying the case for the past six years when I contacted him in 2015. He had a fairly precise, second-by-second idea of what happened in the cockpit after the automatic pilot had disengaged and the succession of warnings came in:

> The plane is in level flight but the screen (falsely) tells the pilot that it has lost around 400 feet, or more than 100 metres. The pilot then goes into climb in order to reach cruising altitude. This seems all the more logical that the information on the Flight Director screens also indicates that the plane must be kept in climb. Lastly, the reverse starting and stopping of the stall warning, discovered after the crash, would have further aggravated the situation: when the pilot gave the order to climb, the stall alarm stopped, and when he gave the order to descend the alarm was triggered. You couldn't get more perverse than that!

The record only said that the two first officers at the controls (the captain was on a break) had 'climbed instead of descended'. In other words, they had not reacted to the stall. However, if one examines the details of the accident, it seems that they had no alternative but to do what they did. In the end, the aircraft was pretty much at level pitch when it hit the sea: there had been no obvious human failure. Shortly after the plane was located, in 2011, French Transport Minister Thierry Mariani stated that the pilots had been 95 per cent responsible for the accident and the aircraft 5 per cent responsible. And once again, in the collective memory, the accident is put down to human error.

Nevertheless, on 2 July 2009, *Le Figaro* published correspondence between Air France and Airbus in which Air France wrote: 'In late March 2009, two new incidents [involving pitot tubes] have been recorded, including a first such incident on an A330. This brings the total number of incidents to nine, of which eight concern the A340 and one concerns the A330.' And on 13 July 2009, another incident caused by Thales pitot tubes occurred on the AF1905 Paris–Rome flight. In other words, the issue that led to the loss of AF447 had already been seen at least nine times previously on Air France planes alone – and it happened again a month and a half later. In these 10 other cases, the pilots managed to control the situation and deal with the issue, in conditions that were probably less complex than those encountered by the AF447 pilots. It is reasonable to think that if it had not been for this issue, the plane and its 228 passengers would have arrived safely at their destination.

From August 2009, without waiting for another incident to occur, the European Aviation Safety Agency (EASA) had required airlines to remove all of their Thales AA type probes (pitot tubes). This may be another case of overlooking the true culprit; according to Laurent Lamy, this might not be the probes themselves but the probe heat computer (PHC) that controls automatic de-icing. Lamy says that it was after Airbus modified the PHCs in the summer of 2008, including on the model of pitot tube used on Flight AF447, that there was a series of incidents when the pitot tubes became 'iced up'. From 2001 to 2008, however, there had been no icing issues with these same probes.

The families of the victims of AF447 felt that it was time for Airbus to own up to its responsibility and for the public to realise that automation has been taken too far. They were demanding a fair trial. 'A new judge has been appointed and there will be a third round of expert investigations. We are very patient because we know that the legal authorities need a great deal of time to truly understand the reasons for this rather complex and particularly unusual accident,' Lamy told me at the time. 'But knowing everything we know now, it would be unacceptable for there not to be a criminal prosecution.'

Finally, ten years after the accident, in July 2019, the public prosecutor's office dismissed the case against Airbus but requested that Air France face trial for manslaughter and negligence in the training of its pilots. Then three months later, the investigating judges of the Paris court also dismissed the case against Air France. The main organisation of the next of kin, the Association entraide et solidarité vol AF447, called this judgment 'an insult to the memory of the victims' and said that they would appeal. As for Laurent Lamy, the nolle prosequi was so upsetting that he decided to distance himself from the case he had fought for relentlessly during the last 10 years …

One quickly realises that when it comes to deciding who is liable for a plane crash – the dead pilots on the one hand, or the aircraft with its reputation and that of its country of origin to think of, on which thousands of jobs and billions of dollars' worth of contracts may depend, on the other – the pilot's honour is not worth much.

And when the pilot emerges alive from the crash he is meant to have caused, things get more complicated still.

Air France Flight 296, or the 'Habsheim crash'

On 26 June 1988, an Airbus A320-111 performed a demonstration flyover at the Habsheim Air Show, having taken off from Basle–Mulhouse Airport. The pilot-in-command, 44-year-old Michel Asseline, had been with Air France for 20 years, had accumulated more than 10,000 flight hours and enjoyed a solid reputation. He had directed the flight tests of the A320 and had already tested the aircraft beyond its official limits. He was confident. His first officer was Pierre Mazières, who had comparable experience and had recently become a captain.

This was the beginning for the A320, a new model for which Airbus Industrie had great plans. The first model had been delivered three months earlier, and this was to be a very important demonstration. But during the flyover the plane dipped very low

– lower than planned – and failed to rise again, clipping the tree-tops of the nearby forest. Branches clogged the engines, and instead of climbing, the brand new A320 sank into the forest a few seconds later, from which an enormous cloud of black smoke and flames rose. The audience was shocked and terrified. Most of the 136 passengers were successfully evacuated, but a woman and two children perished in the fire.

On emerging from the plane, both pilots said that they did not understand what had happened – why the plane had failed to climb even though both of them had applied full power, pulling with all their might on the controls.

The final report following the BEA's investigation,* however, emphasised four pilot errors as the cause of the disaster. In March 1997, nearly nine years after the crash, the Colmar criminal court sentenced Asseline, the pilot in command, to 18 months in prison, with 12 months suspended, for 'major recklessness' and 'multiple cases of misconduct'. His pilot's licence was suspended for eight years. Co-pilot Pierre Mazières received a suspended 12-month prison sentence for 'personal misconduct', with suspended sentences being handed down to three others. Thus, the pilots, the airline and the air show's organisers were found liable for the accident. The BEA experts absolved the plane's manufacturer Airbus Industrie from blame, despite the pilots' statements, which remained consistent from the moment they left the aircraft.

The handling of this case, in which 'the crew was sanctioned without proof of any negligence in order to save a manufacturer's reputation', has been strongly condemned by many, including France's National Airline Pilots' Union (Syndicat National des Pilotes de Ligne, or SNPL).† The pilots' union also criticised the

* 'Commission d'enquête sur l'accident survenu le 26 juin 1988 à Mulhouse-Habsheim (68) à l'Airbus A320, immatriculé F-GFKC, 24 April 1990', p. 20.

† P. Gille and H. Gendre, 'Habsheim ou la Raison d'État', SNPL, available at www.crashdehabsheim.net/Dossier%20SNPL%20presentation.htm.

investigation's vagueness on certain points, its lack of rigour, its omissions and its anomalies: specifically, the fact that the two black boxes had been seized by the French civil aviation authorities (Direction Générale de l'Aviation Civile) on the evening of the crash and held for 10 days. There were suspicions that the data contained in them had been tampered with. Germain Sengelin, the Mulhouse judge assigned to conduct the judicial inquiry, told the TV channel France 3 that he had been subjected to pressure 'from the highest level'.*

Fellow Air France pilot Norbert Jacquet stood up for his colleagues on Flight AF296, openly contesting the official version of the Habsheim crash. He believed that the aircraft's computer system had overruled pilot input. When a certain low altitude was reached, the computer system forced the plane to land, despite the two pilots' best efforts to bring it back up. For Jacquet, there could be no doubt that the A320 provided 'excessive pilot assistance' and was therefore defective. In his book *Airbus, L'assassin habite à l'Élysée* (*Airbus: The Murderer Lives at the Élysée Palace*), he wrote:

> Michel Asseline pulled on the control to climb. He pulled quickly, all the way back. And what did the elevators do? They did the opposite of what they should have done! (i.e., they went into 'descent' mode). The logical consequence of this was that the plane failed to climb. At this moment, the engines were doing 91% of the maximum speed, faster than that day's 83% take-off speed! The aircraft accelerated towards the trees instead of climbing. It was catastrophic.†

* Ina, 'Suite crash Airbus Mulhouse', 2 June 1989, available at www.ina.fr/video/ CAC90001481.

† Norbert Jacquet, *Airbus, L'assassin habite à l'Élysée*, Éditions Premières Lignes, 1994, p. 75.

For leading this crusade, during which he condemned 'the State's lies', Jacquet was fired without compensation and his pilot's licence was revoked. Air France cited psychiatric reasons, even though none of the three psychiatrists consulted found the slightest thing wrong with the pilot, whose passion was air safety. Jacquet believed that defects related to the excessive automation of Airbus planes could explain the crashes of at least two other A320s: Indian Airlines Flight 605 on 14 February 1990 and Air Inter Flight 148 (the so-called 'Mont Sainte-Odile' flight) on 20 January 1992. Both planes crashed when landing. He also condemned certain Airbus models' inability to handle stalling. Needless to say, he now has few friends left in the aviation industry, let alone at Airbus.

In the autumn of 2015, when dining at an Italian restaurant in the Soho district of Hong Kong, I was by chance seated next to a former Air France pilot. He remembered the Habsheim crash very well, and told me a story he had heard directly from the girlfriend of the co-pilot on the Habsheim flight. Shortly after the crash, she had been the victim of an attack while alone in her home. Four masked men broke in, removed all of her clothes and partially shaved her, including her private parts. They left her with the following instructions: 'Tell your boyfriend to keep quiet or else we'll be back to finish the job.' Traumatised by the incident, she and her boyfriend filed a complaint. But when they went to the police station a few weeks later to ask how the inquiry was progressing, they were simply advised 'not to insist', but to 'be careful when crossing the street'. It was a chilling story, the sort of thing I associated with other places, other political systems, values other than those of France. Still, I had no reason to doubt the pilot's story. For a legitimate police investigation to be halted, the orders would have had to come from very high up. This incident – shameful for a country like France, where the rule of law prevails – happened in addition to the unjustifiable treatment of former pilot Norbert Jacquet. Today, Jacquet continues to be a whistle-blower on all civil aviation issues related to the ultra-automation of planes. To him, the 737 MAX double disasters are further cases in point.* Last time I talked to him, he said he would rather not reveal where he was based. He told me that his tenacious battle ended up ruining him and made him spend a total of 20 months locked up, including one month in emergency psychiatric detention. But what exactly was his crime?

The case of the Habsheim crash sharply illustrates the state's determination from that point on to protect the commercial interests of Airbus and reveals the extreme lengths to which it is prepared to go. Will the two pilots on the Habsheim flight ever be fully rehabilitated? Will Norbert Jacquet, whose greatest crime was wanting to alert his employer and public opinion to the risks of the new computer programs installed on board Airbus planes, ever receive an apology from France?

Although initial orders of the A320 were affected by the controversy, this model nevertheless became one of Airbus Industrie's greatest commercial successes.

As we have seen, there are relatively few cases where the pilot is genuinely at fault. But the aircraft manufacturer – be it Boeing or Airbus – appears never to be to blame. And if the manufacturer ever is at fault, this fault is only ever marginal. Unlike the pilot, it can count on being fully protected by the government of its home country.

---

* Lion Air Flight 610 crashed on 29 October 2018, killing 189 people. Five months later, on 10 March 2019, Ethiopian Airlines Flight 302 crashed, killing 157 people. It was quickly established that both accidents resulted from the malfunction of a new automated control called the Maneuvering Characteristics Augmentation System (MCAS). All 387 Boeing 737 MAXs used by 59 airlines across the world at the time were grounded.

Military blunders

As mistakes go, shooting down a civilian aircraft is a serious one. Such errors have nevertheless definitely been committed on several occasions. In other crashes – including MH370 – it remains just a hypothesis.

Ukraine International Airlines Flight 752: the wrong target of two consecutive missiles

On 8 January 2020, less than three minutes after take-off from Tehran Imam Khomeini International Airport, Ukraine International Airlines Flight 752 was hit by two surface-to-air missiles that were launched, 23 seconds apart, from an Iranian military site located eight miles from the airport. All 176 people on board the Boeing 737-800 died. The Iranian aviation authorities initially blamed human and technical errors, saying that the aircraft burst into flames after a fire started in one of its engines, causing the pilot to lose control and crash into the ground. The Ukrainian airline strongly refuted 'pilot error', saying that the pilots had exclusively been trained for the Tehran flights for years. After a few days of denial, the Islamic Revolutionary Guard Corps, a branch of the Iranian Army, admitted it was responsible for the catastrophe and attributed it to human error, as someone had mistaken the plane for a hostile target.

The accident took place at a time of extreme political and military tension, with Iran on its highest state of defensive alert a few hours after it had launched a missile attack on two US military bases in Iraq, as retaliation for the US assassination of Iranian Major General Qasem Soleimani in a targeted drone attack. Iranian President Hassan Rouhani eventually said that the shoot-down was 'an unforgivable mistake'. In accordance with Annex 13 of the Chicago Convention, the American NTSB, the French BEA, as well as Ukrainian, Swedish and Canadian investigation authorities, along with Boeing, were invited to join the investigation team.

Malaysia Airlines Flight 17: 298 dead after a Buk missile hit the plane

Four months after the disappearance of MH370, another Malaysia Airlines Boeing 777 (exactly the same model and delivered at the same time) crashed – Flight MH17 from Amsterdam to Kuala Lumpur, with 298 people on board. The incident happened at 4.20 pm in east Ukraine, and plane debris and bodies were found scattered over several square kilometres. The final report of the Dutch Safety Board* indicated that the crash had been caused 'by the detonation of a 9N314M-type warhead launched from the eastern part of Ukraine using a Buk missile system'.† The report did not specify who fired the missile, but assigned responsibility to Ukraine because of its failure to take precautions; the country should have closed its airspace to traffic because of the armed conflict that was going on at the time in that part of the country.‡

Iran Air 655: when the US Navy 'confused' an Airbus A300 with an F-14

On 3 July 1988, an Iran Air Airbus A300 was flying from Bandar Abbas in Iran to Dubai, on the other side of the Persian Gulf, on what should have been a 28-minute flight. The plane was carrying 290 passengers, mostly Iranian. It was nearing the end of the Iran–Iraq war (1980–88), and a year after the American frigate USS

---

* Dutch Safety Board, *Crash of Malaysia Airlines light MH17*, The Hague, October 2015.

† Press release, The Hague, 13 October 2015.

‡ Dutch Safety Board, *Crash of Malaysia Airlines flight MH17*, op. cit., p. 253.

Stark had been attacked by an Iraqi Mirage jet.* The atmosphere was tense. At 10.24 am, seven minutes after take-off, the Iran Air plane was struck down by two missiles. The plane's tail and one of its wings were destroyed. Control of the aircraft was lost and it crashed into the Gulf. The two missiles had been fired by the American missile cruiser USS *Vincennes*, which had reportedly 'confused' the Airbus with a hostile F-14 after several failed attempts to make radio contact with the plane (on the military and civilian emergency frequencies).† Speaking before the United Nations, George H. W. Bush, then vice president under Ronald Reagan, said that the USS *Vincennes* had acted 'appropriately'. In 1996, under a settlement reached at the International Court of Justice, the United States paid US$61.8 million to the families of the victims.

In the case of this crash, it was at least clear who was responsible for the destruction of the plane and the deaths of the 290 passengers on board. However, a crash that happened in Italy continues to haunt the victims' families more than 40 years later.

Itavia Flight 870, aka the 'Ustica tragedy': an inquiry that has lasted almost 40 years

Whenever I discuss the disappearance of MH370 with my Italian friends, there seems to be no doubt in their minds as to what happened: MH370 was struck down by a missile, just as Itavia Flight 870 – a DC-9 that was travelling from Bologna to Palermo with 81 people on board – was struck down to the north of Sicily on 27 June 1980.

---

* The 17 May 1987 attack on the USS *Stark* left 37 Americans dead.

† International Court of Justice, 'Aerial incident of 3 July 1988' (*Islamic Republic of Iran v. United States of America*), Volume II, The Hague, 2000, p. 22: 'The aircraft was perceived as a military aircraft with hostile intentions and was destroyed by two surface-to-air missiles.'

An explosion occurred 50 minutes into the flight and the DC-9 broke into several pieces, then disappeared from the radar screens. The accident had an immediate international impact. 'How could such a modern, safe airliner just suddenly vanish?' people asked. Thirty-five years later, exactly the same question was posed about the disappearance of MH370.

Two days after the Itavia 870 crash, the Italian investigative journalist Andrea Purgatori published an article in the newspaper *Corriere della Sera* suggesting that the DC-9 had been hit by a missile fired by a fighter jet – probably French – that was intended for the plane of Libyan leader Muammar Gaddafi. His source was an air traffic controller in Rome. Targeting the 'Guide of the Revolution' – considered public enemy number one by the West – and killing 81 civilians instead, was definitely what one would call a significant military blunder.

The scant debris was scattered over an area of 200 square kilometres, which corroborates the theory that the plane broke up mid-flight before striking the sea's surface. The three unidentified radar echoes to the west of the Itavia plane suggest a fighter jet arriving with the sun behind it, an air camouflage technique used by fighter pilots from the earliest days of aerial combat. 'In the days following the accident, I learned directly from people who were in the area recovering surface debris of the DC-9 that it included parts of an American-made missile, specifically the fins,' said Paul-Henri Nargeolet, who at the time was serving with the French Navy. He pointed out that 'just because it was an American missile doesn't mean it was fired by an American plane'.

But the official inquiry mentioned traces of explosive (TNT) among the debris – a discovery that would later be contested. In the context of the time (five weeks after the crash, a bomb exploded in Bologna's central railway station, killing 85 people), the theory that a bomb exploded inside the aircraft did seem very plausible. The first inquiry was inconclusive: was it an explosion inside the plane (a bomb) or outside the plane (a missile attack)?

Under pressure from the victims' families, a second inquiry was opened. The report of 17 March 1989 concluded that it had been an explosion caused by a missile fired from an unidentified aircraft. The door of the hold, which had been fished out of the water, had two holes whose edges pointed inwards, which was incompatible with an explosion from inside the aircraft. A year later, events took a dramatic turn when two of the Italian investigators retracted their statements, saying that there was insufficient proof after all to validate the missile theory.* Could the missile theory have made someone uncomfortable?

The third report came 14 years after the crash. The international experts called upon had insisted that, in order to be able to conduct a genuine inquiry and draw a conclusion on the case, the many missing pieces of the plane had to be found.

Nargeolet was involved in these underwater searches, and when pieces of the plane were brought up from a depth of 3,600 metres under the direction of Ifremer, a French oceanographic institution, he remembered what he had been told about missile debris in 1980:

On the outside of a piece of fuselage that we had brought up I discovered traces of metal that were 'external' to the plane. I photographed them, took samples and handed everything over to the person heading the investigation committee. The chairman of the investigation committee told me a few days later that what I had given to him, that is to say the photos and the metal samples, were 'of the highest importance'. A few months later, this same chairman said – I believe to an Italian Senate committee – that I never gave him anything.

* A. Frank Taylor, *A Case History Involving Wreckage Analysis: Lessons from the Ustica Investigations*, Cranfield University, 1998.

Nargeolet acutely sensed a case of very high-level *omertà*, and, not surprisingly, this third technical investigation invalidated the findings of the second investigation and concluded that the crash had been caused by a bomb exploding inside the aircraft. No one had fired a missile at the plane after all.

The Italian courts ignored the conclusions of the technical inquiries and continued their own investigation. In June 1997, *Corriere della Sera* published an article titled 'Suicides and strange incidents: 15 deaths since the [Ustica] tragedy'.* The article lists 15 witnesses in the Ustica case who had died in mysterious and sometimes bizarre circumstances. At the last count, 20 deaths appear to have been caused by 'the after-effects of the investigation'. Clearly, the truth must not be known. The Italian public nevertheless remains convinced that this civilian aircraft was struck down by a 'friendly' American or French missile fired in error.

On 25 June 2007, former Italian Prime Minister Francesco Cossiga accused France of causing the crash,† and in a book published in 2010, an Italian judge criticised France for thwarting the investigation.‡ In 2013, the Court of Cassation ruled in favour of the missile theory – but remained silent about who fired it – and ordered the Italian government to pay €100 million to the victims' families. In July 2014, Italian Prime Minister Matteo Renzi decided to make the archives of the case public. French monthly newspaper *Le Monde diplomatique* then published a fascinating article by the journalist Andrea Purgatori, who assigned responsibility as follows: Italy had allowed its airspace to be violated and then covered it up;

* Giuliano Gallo, 'Strani suicide o incidenti: 15 morti misteriose dopo la tragedia', *Corriere della Sera*, 18 June 1997.

† Cossiga's statement was made on public radio and on Sky TV: 'The French knew that Gaddafi's plane was going to pass by [this route]. [...] It was they who, with a naval aircraft, fired a missile [...].' Quoted by Andrea Purgatori, *Le Monde diplomatique*, July 2014.

‡ Giovanni Fasanella and Rosario Priore, *Intrigo internazionale*, Milan, Chiare Lettere, 2010.

the United States was, at the very least, a witness and may also have been complicit; and the DC-9 was probably shot down by France.

What is to be learned from this tragedy? That after three official inquiries drawing three different conclusions, after the deaths of 20 direct or indirect witnesses in the case, and after over 40 years of anger and indignation on the part of the victims' families – echoed by Italian public opinion – we still do not know the whole truth about this affair. We also see that each time the truth revealed itself, through a missile fin, pieces of a warped fuselage or traces of melted metal, it was either disparaged or ignored. The countries involved in this affair had already decided what the official truth was going to be.

Technical failures and emergency situations

Also deserving of mention are the many cases in which an emergency situation arises during a flight – which may be related to aircraft technical failures, to maintenance issues, or to the passengers or cargo being carried. In the vast majority of cases, the problem is identified and resolved by the pilots, the cabin crew or ground assistance without the passengers ever suspecting anything. As pilots put it: 'That's what we're here for!'

British Airways Flight 5390: happy ending to near disaster

One spectacular incident of this kind occurred on 10 June 1990 on Flight BA5390 from the English city of Birmingham to Malaga. Thirteen minutes after take-off, the left cockpit windscreen flew off, sucking the captain, who had just loosened his lap belt, halfway out of the aircraft. He held on, clinging to the flight controls with his legs, until the purser arrived. The purser latched his hands onto the captain's belt and was able to hold him down for the next

20 minutes, suffering a dislocated shoulder as a result. The first officer managed to make an emergency landing in Southampton as the cabin crew did their best to calm passengers who were panicking in the violent wind sweeping through the cabin. The plane touched down with all passengers safe and sound. The captain, whom the crew had believed to be dead, emerged almost unscathed, suffering only from shock, frostbite and a few fractures.

The maintenance crew had used the wrong size retention bolts to fix the new windscreen, but the crew on the flight were remarkable in their handling of the resulting emergency. Unfortunately things do not always turn out this way.

Helios Flight 522: oxygen-starved pilots

On 14 August 2005, the Boeing 737 on Helios Airways Flight 522 was flying from Larnaca in Cyprus to Prague, with a scheduled stop in Athens. Five minutes after take-off, the low-pressure alarm sounded but was misidentified by the pilots. Just before take-off, an inspection had been carried out on a door that had shown signs of pressurisation leakage on the previous flight.* The pressurisation system had been set to manual mode for a test that was carried out and had not been reset to automatic. The captain radioed the ground engineer to clarify the situation. Meanwhile, oxygen masks were released in the cabin but not in the cockpit, where this procedure is not automatic. The pilots thus continued their ascent, not realising that the plane was unpressurised. Hypoxia – lack of oxygen – produces effects similar to those of a very high level of blood alcohol (incoherence, inarticulateness, disorientation). The pilots' messages to air traffic control quickly became incomprehensible, then stopped altogether.

* Similar incidents had occurred on the same aircraft, including one less than a year earlier, when it had experienced rapid decompression due to a defect in the rear door. The pilots managed to bring the aircraft down to an altitude with sufficient oxygen and no one was injured.

By then the plane was over the Greek mainland, where the authorities on the ground suspected a hijacking or other terrorist act, so they scrambled two F-16s to intercept the plane. When these jets arrived on the scene, their pilots on either side of the Boeing could see no one at the controls: the captain lay sprawled on the floor and the co-pilot was slumped unconscious in his seat. On automatic pilot, the plane continued on its course. A valiant cabin attendant later entered the cockpit and tried in vain to make contact with air traffic control. Finally, the plane crashed 'all by itself' into a mountain, killing the 121 people on board. This crash has been compared to MH370 because of the brief, very confused exchange between an unidentified pilot on a different flight and the MH370 cockpit, at the request of Ho Chi Minh air traffic control. The poor quality of the exchange as reported by the pilot of the other flight suggested that the Malaysian pilots could also have been suffering from hypoxia.

UPS Airlines Flight 6 from Dubai: a fire in the hold started by lithium batteries

On 3 September 2010, UPS Airlines Flight 6, a Boeing 747 cargo aircraft, was flying from Dubai to Cologne. Twenty-two minutes into the flight, the pilots raised the alarm: there was a fire in the hold and it was spreading quickly, but they were experiencing radio failure. They tried to return to Dubai but missed their landing and crashed several kilometres from the airport. According to the final report,* the crash was caused by an uncontrollable fire in the hold started by flames from lithium batteries. As we have already seen, MH370 was also carrying lithium batteries – at least 221 kilograms of them, according to the cargo manifest.

* General Civil Aviation Authority of the United Arab Emirates, *Air Accident Investigation Report on Uncontained Cargo Fire Leading to Loss of Control Inflight and Uncontrolled Descent into Terrain Boeing 747-44AF N571UP*, 3 September 2010.

TWA 800: a fuel tank explosion, really?

Because entire books and documentaries have been dedicated to flight TWA 800, I had initially decided not to mention it here; that is until I received a first-hand account testimony that seemed some-what related to it.

The TWA Boeing 747 exploded 12 minutes after take-off from JFK international airport (New York) on 17 July 1996 at 8.30 pm and crashed into the Atlantic Ocean off New York's Long Island. It was Rome-bound via Paris, with 230 people on board. To this day, two main theories prevail to explain the catastrophe. The official one is that fuel vapours in one of the fuel tanks were ignited by a short-circuit. And that is what would have triggered the massive explosion that destroyed the B-747 almost instantly. But many people, including experts, found the fuel tank explosion scenario not acceptable, wondering how a limited quantity of fuel vapour could create a sudden explosion of a magnitude that would anni-hilate an entire 747 in a matter of seconds.

The other explanation is more simply that of a missile strike. It is based on a cluster of clues, including the fact that similar inci-dents never had such devastating impact, the statements by several witnesses, who saw very clear streaks of fire (missile-like) heading towards the sky at the time, and the findings of explosive residue on the debris, among other anecdotal pieces of evidence corrobo-rating this scenario.

In 2013, former NTSB investigator Henry Hughes, who had worked on the case, told Reuters he believed a bomb or a missile caused the Boeing 747 to crash. He, along with five other investi-gators, petitioned the agency to reconsider the conclusion of its investigation, saying the initial probe was flawed. 'The witness statements, the physical evidence and other facts clearly show there was an explosion external to the aircraft, not the center fuel tank,' Hughes said. He further accused the NTSB of having discounted witness statements, radar data, explosive traces and holes in the fuselage that pointed to an external explosion. But, after he had raised these concerns, rather than look into them, the NTSB simply reallocated Hugues from aviation to highway investigations, before he later retired.

Phil Bobet, a former Swissair captain, had read the original French edition of my book and offered to share some information with me. When we met in March 2019, in a café in Paris, I had hoped it would be related to MH370 and was somewhat disappointed when I realised it wasn't. But, regardless, his testimony was spine chilling and could shed new light on the TWA 800 disaster.

He was flying Swissair 127 on 9 August 1997, between Philadelphia and Zurich, and was on the first leg to Boston. His plane was nearing the area where TWA Flight 800 went down. Bobet had just mentioned Manhattan to his passengers when he interrupted his address to report a near miss by a round white object. 'We saw something white, very shiny and with no wings, coming straight towards us, at a very high speed much faster than a plane,' he told me. He immediately notified New York ATC and Swissair. I later found his original exchange with ATC, as recorded and reported in the NTSB report into the incident, obtained by The Canadian Press (CP) two years later: 'I don't know if it was a rocket or whatever, but incredibly fast, opposite direction,' said the pilot. 'In the opposite direction?' asked the controller. 'Yes, sir, and the time was 2107 (GMT). It was too fast to be an airplane. It passed over the cockpit, slightly right of centerline. If it had been any lower, it would have hit the aircraft. As the object passed by, there was no noise, no wake turbulence, and no disruption or anomalies with any of the flight or engine instruments.' The NTSB report also mentions that the first officer said he was bent over to adjust the volume on his headset when he looked up and saw the object pass overhead, so close that he ducked his head because he thought it would hit them. Everything happened so fast that they did not have time to take evasive action.

After the shock of this near-miss collision, Bobet was further surprised by what happened upon arrival in Boston. He and his colleagues were met by the FBI and the NTSB and they were interrogated separately. 'The FBI guy was so hostile and trying so hard to discredit my description of what had happened that I had to ask him to change tone or I would call my embassy,' Bobet remembered. When he returned home to Switzerland and discussed it with the airline, he thought he should get to the bottom of the story, as what had happened to his plane could potentially happen to other flights. Despite the American side suggesting at one point the pilots may have seen a weather balloon (which made no sense whatsoever), he later discovered that similar very close encounters with unidentified flying objects had also happened to at least two other flights (one from Pakistan and one from Venezuela).

Despite the enormous value as corroborating evidence in the TWA 800 case, Bobet was asked to drop the case. Eventually, only UFO believers ever took his statement seriously.

Possible lessons from these accidents and inquiries that could help in solving the case of MH370

Aviation authorities have learned lessons from most of these accidents. Since the crash of UPS Airlines Flight 6, the transport of lithium batteries is more strictly regulated. The laws have changed a great deal since this accident, especially after the July 2015 International Civil Aviation Organization conference, leading some observers to believe that the authorities might know more than they let on about what caused the disappearance of MH370. As we have seen in other cases, even if regulators pretend not to know the cause of an accident, they may still take measures to keep it from happening again.

Since the Air Inter Mont Sainte-Odile crash – mentioned only briefly above – all planes must be equipped with an emergency locator transmitter (ELT) that is automatically activated upon impact or in contact with water. Again, the regulations are evolving. Since 2005, these ELTs must transmit signals on two frequencies: one detectable by satellite (406 MHz), and the other on the emergency frequencies of all planes and ships that might be near the crash zone (121.5 MHz). MH370 had four ELTs, but in the case of AF447, none of them worked. Indeed, according to an ICAO report on 173 crashes of planes equipped with ELTs, the device was activated in only 39 cases.* The report on the AF447 inquiry called for improvements in this area.

However, in this area, as in so many others, the measures taken often seem 'too little, too late'. Many pilots are alarmed at how slow regulators are to impose new regulations or exploit new technological advances. The AF447 crash in the sea led to the identification of numerous possible improvements that would facilitate searches in similar cases – but five years later, when the situation was repeated with MH370, none of the measures suggested had been implemented. 'It's unacceptable,' protested Laurent Lamy. 'Seeing that what was learned at the cost of 228 lives with AF447 had not even been applied five years later just brings back our sadness.' By 1 January 2018, black box pingers were required to sound for 90 days (instead of 30) and to transmit over a greater distance. By 1 January 2020, black boxes had to be ejectable and able to float. If Malaysia Airlines had implemented these measures, locating the MH370 aircraft would no doubt have been easier – as long as it was in the area where the search was being conducted.

To conclude this fragmented analysis of a few air disasters, two common characteristics emerge, despite the diversity of the accidents.

Regardless of the number of victims or the human tragedy caused by plane crashes, the initial trauma suffered by victims' loved ones is often worsened or compounded by the lack of trans-

---

* *Factual Information: Safety Information for MH370*, op. cit., p. 33.

parency that characterises the inquiries into these accidents. Such inquiries are always lengthy, laborious and complicated, and are subject to enormous political, diplomatic and economic pressures.

The grief of the loved ones is disturbed, shaken and reawakened with each stage of the inquiry, with every doubt that emerges, with every new piece of genuine or false information. In the case of MH370, the families were deprived of their grief. The total absence of credible proof – even of the crash itself – made it impossible for them to grieve.

As for these inquiries' marked tendency to blame pilot error rather than machine error, I could not have imagined when I decided to do a comparative study of a few well-known plane crashes that I would be opening such a Pandora's box. I had not expected to uncover such hypocrisy on the part of aircraft manufacturers and governments, and had no idea of the extent of the means deployed in certain cases to stifle information about the real but unsayable cause of a plane crash.

Because the *obvious* cause of the accident is seldom the actual cause.

Because the *official* cause of the accident is seldom the actual cause either.

Because what is said at the start rarely matches what comes out in the end.

And because there is seldom a single cause, but usually a combination of factors.

In a word, in the unfortunate case of an air crash, truth is almost bound to be the first casualty.

Acknowledgements

For reasons of security and brevity, I have not named the amazing constellation of people who have helped me during this seven year endeavour. Piecing this jigsaw together would not have been possible without the hundreds of people – pilots, scientists, academics, diplomats, engineers, politicians, whistle-blowers, fellow journalists, hackers, mercenaries and military personnel – scattered around the globe, all of whom I have either met in person or online in Malaysia, Vietnam, Cambodia, Laos, Singapore, Thailand, Philippines, India, Indonesia, Australia, New Zealand, China, Hong Kong, Japan, Taiwan, USA, Canada, England, Scotland, France, Germany, Belgium, Holland, Switzerland, Italy, Portugal, Israel, United Arab Emirates, Maldives, Mozambique, Mauritius, Madagascar, Reunion … Some offered their expertise or analysis, others helped with stacks of documents and some with a decisive half-sentence. I wholeheartedly thank each and every one of you.

My heartfelt thanks also go to my publisher at HarperCollins, Jack Fogg, and his team, Holly Blood, Sarah Hammond, Alan Cracknell, Josie Turner, Julie MacBrayne and my copyeditor Mark Bolland, as well as to my agents, Jo Lusby and Marysia Juszczakiewicz who made this book happen; to my long-term employers, *Le Monde*, RFI and Radio France; to Les Arènes, who published the initial version of my investigation in French in 2016; and, obviously, to my precious family, starting with my husband Philippe, my sons Paul, Adrien and Cosmas, and my wonderful friends, who have endured with infinite patience and kindness my resolve in solving this enigma.

All along, my thoughts have been with the next of kin who have heroically stood tall and firm during this harrowing nightmare, requesting that they be told the whole truth which they are entitled to.

Index

Nargeolet, Paul-Henri, 72–3, 79, 228, 339, 401, 402
Nathan, Grace Subathirai, 140, 141, 166, 223–4, 232
Nazim, Mohamed, 152–3
NBC News, 126, 142
Negroni, Christine, 59, 60
The New Straits Times, 56
New York magazine, 250, 253, 254
The New York Times, 21, 177, 290, 320, 367, 371
Noble, Ronald, 24
'nodders', 256–8, 261–3, 356, 358
Note Printing Australia, 53
Nour Mohammad, Pouria (passenger), 23
NTSB, *see* US National Transport Safety Bureau
Nuclear Security Summit (The Hague), 365
numerology, 85

Obama, Barack, 47–8, 363–5, 367, 369, 376
Ocean Infinity operation, 226–8, 231; report, 233–4
Ocean Shield (ship), 69–70, 71
oil slicks, 18, 22, 71, 319–20, 322, 332–3, 347
organ-harvesting, 115, 347
Orion, P-3, 20, 67–8, 327–8
Ostrower, Jon, 198

Pakistan, 110, 113; cargo delivery from, 137–8, 359
Pantai Seberang Marang, 17
Paracel islands, 369
Paris Match, 150–1, 155, 167, 179–80
Parti Keadilan Rakyat (PKR), *see* People's Justice Party
passengers: American, 34; Australian, 3; Chinese, 2, 4, 5, 46, 87, 89, 139, 140, 368; embarkation, 1–3, 144–5; French, 3; Iranian, 23–5; Malaysian, 3, 46, 87, 89, 140; manifest 23, 90, 143–4; seating, 131, 350; Ukrainian 3–4, 84; *see also* families
passports, stolen, 23
Pathumtani radar, *see* radar data, Thai
Pattiaratchi, Charitha, 212
Pearce Air Base, Perth, 68
Pel-Air Westwing accident (2009), 59–60
Pemba Island debris, 217–18
Penang Island, 21, 131, 240–1, 287, 360, 367; *see also* Butterworth Air Base
People's Justice Party, 28, 44, 244, 245
Perth: Hishammuddin visit, 78; memorial, 196; *see also* Joint Agency Coordination Centre; Pearce Air Base

Philip, Bruno, 338, 339
Phu Quoc Island, 331, 333
Pike, John E., 102
pilot: errors, historical 388–97, 411; MH370, *see* Zaharie Ahmad Shah, Cpt.; suicide scenario, MH370, 235–6, 238–9, 250; suicides suspected historical, 380–8
pings: black box, 63, 70, 73, 324; fabricated, 123, 271–2, 274, 283, 376; frequency, 72–3; handshake, 9, 31, 32, 299; Inmarsat analysis, 31–4, 54–5, 58, 81–3, 86, 347, 372; locators (TPLs), 63–5, 69–70, 71; other sources, 75; period, 70, 271
Pinckney, USS, 271, 326–30, 359
pitot tubes, 390, 392
The Plane That Wasn't There (Wise), 84, 114
Planespotters.net, 108–9
Pléiades 1-A/1-B (satellites), 65
Poh Seng Kian Company, 92, 93–4
Pongsak Semachai, 197
probe heat computer (PHC), 392
Pulau Perak, 21, 264, 287
Purgatori, Andrea, 401, 403–4
Putin, Vladimir, 373–4

Le Quotidien de la Réunion, 170, 182

radar: Chinese, 224, 282–3, 254; Indonesian, 286–7; lack of data, 105–6, 113, 285–6, 297; Malaysian, 21, 54, 286–7, 288, 289–91; over-the-horizon, 106, 131, 284; primary/secondary, 280, 282, 283, 286–8; Thai, 11, 12, 264, 282, 283, 285–6, 292–3, 294, 327, 354; Vietnamese, 10, 286–7, 288
Rahman, Zaaim Redha Abdul, 188
Rasheed, Ibrahim, 153–4, 155
Reddit, 325
remote control scenario, 114–15, 116
Renzi, Matteo, 403
Réunion: debris, 169–79; search, 179–82
Reuters, 39, 222–3, 308, 369, 407
rocket debris, 198–9, 203–8
Rodrigues Island, 180, 209
Rolls-Royce, 8, 81, 300, 301, 366; Trent engine, 108, 207–8, 215, 366
Roos, Jonti, 25–6
Rouhani, President Hassan, 398
Royal Malaysian Air Force, 20–1, 45, 202; *see also* Butterworth Air Base

Royal Malaysia Police, 10, 29, 93–4, 103, 120, 242, 245, 251, 281, 297, 355, 367
Royal Thai Air Force, 197, 198
rudder failure, 383
Russia Today, 89, 110

Saeed, Adam, 164
Safety Investigation Report (Ocean Infinity, 2018), 233–4
Sainte-Marie Island debris, 215–16
Sama-Sama Hotel, KL 13, 22, 39
San Juan, ARA (wreck), 231
Sastind, 19, 299
Satcom antenna, 4, 350
satellite data: Chinese, 19–20, 65, 66, 320; DigitalGlobe, 260–1; French, 65–6, 67; Landsat 5, 265–6; Thai, 66; Tomnod, 22, 256–7, 258, 260, 261–3, 358; *see also* Inmarsat
Satellite Today, 300–1
Schuster-Bruce, Alan, 31–2, 33, 34
Seabed Constructor, 227, 228, 230
seabed mapping, 79, 229, 232, 348
Seahawk helicopters, 326–7
search, initial, 16, 19, 20, 22, 30, 37, 309, 318–9, 323–4, 325–6, 359, 368
search, southern corridor (first phase), 58, 59, 60–2, 65–78
search, southern corridor (second phase), 79–81, 84
search, underwater, 63–5, 69–76, 78, 79, 84, 304, 341, 368
search, 2018, *see* Ocean Infinity operation
seismic signals, 320–2
servo-valve, 333, 384
seventh arc 185
Seventh Fleet (US), 112, 273, 326
Shanghai, Pudong Airport accident (2012), 6
Shaariibuu, Altantuya, murder, 49–50
Shah, Cpt. Zaharie Ahmad, *see* Zaharie Ahmad Shah, Cpt.
Shah, Sakinab, 240, 241, 242, 243–5
Shakir, Hussain, 157, 159
shipwrecks, 229, 230
sightings, reported: Gulf of Thailand/Malaysia east coast, 16–17, 56–7, 208, 307–8, 322; Maldives, 102, 131, 149–51, 153, 154, 155, 156, 159, 160–2, 163–4, 165–6; South China Sea, 18, 333–15, 337, 340
Sina Harian (*Daily Sun*), 355
Singapore, military activity, 292, 293
Singapore Airlines, 41, 45
60 Minutes, 254
Sky News, 229, 237